Conflict in
Aristotle's Political Philosophy

SUNY series in Ancient Greek Philosophy
———————
Anthony Preus, editor

Conflict in
Aristotle's Political Philosophy

Steven Skultety

Cover art by Kelly Adkins.

Published by State University of New York Press, Albany

© 2019 State University of New York

All rights reserved

No part of this book may be used or reproduced in any manner whatsoever without written permission. No part of this book may be stored in a retrieval system or transmitted in any form or by any means including electronic, electrostatic, magnetic tape, mechanical, photocopying, recording, or otherwise without the prior permission in writing of the publisher.

For information, contact State University of New York Press, Albany, NY
www.sunypress.edu

Library of Congress Cataloging-in-Publication Data

Names: Skultety, Steven, author.
Title: Conflict in Aristotle's political philosophy / Steven Skultety.
Description: Albany : State University of New York, 2019. | Series: SUNY series in ancient Greek philosophy | Includes bibliographical references and index.
Identifiers: LCCN 2018054474 | ISBN 9781438476575 (hardcover : alk. paper) | ISBN 9781438476582 (pbk. : alk. paper) | ISBN 9781438476599 (ebook)
Subjects: LCSH: Aristotle—Political and social views. | Conflict of interests. | Common good. | Political science—Philosophy.
Classification: LCC JC71.A7 S58 2019 | DDC 320.01—dc23
LC record available at https://lccn.loc.gov/2018054474

10 9 8 7 6 5 4 3 2 1

Contents

Acknowledgments — vii

Introduction — ix

Part I: Conflict in Imperfect Cities

Prelude — 3

1. *Stasis* as Civil War — 5

2. The Unique Problem of Partisanship — 33

3. Managing Mistrust in Average Cities — 57

Part II: Conflict among Perfect Citizens

Prelude — 87

4. Dispute and Disagreement — 93

5. Contending for Civic Flourishing — 117

Part III: Aristotelian Conflict and Modern Political Thought

Prelude — 149

6. Conflict and Constitutionalism — 153

7. Conflict and Democratic Theory — 181

Conclusion	215
Notes	217
Bibliography	259
Index Locorum	267
General Index	277

Acknowledgments

Although revised, several chapters of this book are based on my previously published work. I am grateful for permission to make use of the following. Chapter 1 makes use of "Delimiting Aristotle's Conception of *Stasis* in the *Politics*," *Phronesis* 54 (2009) 346–70 (by permission of Brill). Chapter 2 is based on "Aristotle's Theory of Partisanship," *Polis* 25 no. 2 (2008) 208–32 (by permission of Imprint Academic). Chapter 4 makes use of "Disputes of the *Phronimoi*: Can Aristotle's Best Citizens Disagree?" *Ancient Philosophy* 32 (2012) 105–24 (by permission of Mathesis). Chapter 5 builds on "Competition in the Best of Cities: Agonism and Aristotle's *Politics*," *Political Theory* 37 no. 1 (2009) 44–68 (by permission of Sage).

In one form or another, I benefited from audience feedback at meetings of the Northeastern Political Science Association, the Mississippi Philosophical Association, the Society for Ancient Greek Philosophy, the Central Division meeting of the American Philosophical Association, the Southern Society of Philosophy and Psychology, and the MidSouth Philosophy Conference. I am very grateful for the suggestions of the following talented students who read and commented on this work: Aaron Graham, David Guinea, Kyra Kinnaman, and Christopher Rogers. My former student, Kelly Adkins, created the artwork for the cover—a beautiful gift for which I am deeply thankful. Along the way, I also profited from the advice of many distinguished scholars who, though they may disagree with my interpretations, were kind enough to encourage my explorations. I owe a special word of thanks to Christopher Bobonich, Tad Brennan, Bryan Garsten, David Konstan, Richard Kraut, Sara Monoson, Josh Ober, Tim Roche, Peter Simpson, Steven B. Smith, the anonymous reviewers for SUNY Press, as well as to my colleagues in the Department of Philosophy and Religion, the Department of Classics, and the Law School.

Finally, I would like to acknowledge the support I received here at the University of Mississippi in the lovely city of Oxford. The Office of Special

Research and Projects generously made me a Research Fellow the first year I arrived; I have received several College of Liberal Arts Summer Grants; and I was also fortunate enough to be nominated for, and receive, a National Endowment for the Humanities Summer Stipend. Funding for research in the humanities at public institutions can never be taken for granted, and I feel very fortunate to be the recipient of this help.

Introduction

Many philosophers are willing to entertain the possibility that Aristotle's moral psychology and ethics have some contemporary relevance, but it is rarer to find those who think that Aristotle's ancient theories of governance and the organization of political power could inform our current condition in any meaningful way. After all, modern political communities are highly pluralistic, fractious, and incredibly complicated; Aristotle, by contrast, could only ponder constitutions appropriate for hopelessly small cities that were simple, homogeneous, and aspired to quasi-organic levels of organization. The difference between these two views is not merely that modern thinkers discuss conflict more than the ancients, or that modern thinkers understand political society as a response to a basic condition of chaos and lawlessness while Aristotle sees political society as a response to the human wish for friendship and higher activities of virtue. Rather, the claim is that only modern philosophers are willing to *accept* that there will always be splits and distinctions *within* the social and political orders of the community itself that need to be theorized:

> The peculiarly modern distinctions which began to emerge with Niccolò Machiavelli (1469–1527) and Thomas Hobbes (1588–1679) between state and society, specialized officials and citizens, 'the people' and government, are not part of the political philosophy of the Athenian city-state. For this city-state celebrated the notion of an active, involved citizenry in a process of self-government; the governors were to be the governed.[1]

On this reading, there is something "peculiarly modern" about recognizing the divisions among citizens that arise from intractable debates, zero-sum decisions requiring winners and losers, and the difficult question of who among them should rule and be ruled. Ancient political philosophers simply theorized different ways of governing for some ultimate goal, so they could only explore the contrast between governing for the sake of the common good (the correct end which would unify the city) and governing for the sake of self-interest (the incorrect end which would divide the city). Ancient philosophers did not have to *reconcile* themselves to ineliminable disunities built into the fabric of political life itself, for they could always interpret such conflicts as mere symptoms of bad governance. So it is that we find contemporary philosophers stating that "conflict, social and psychological, was the great evil for Plato and Aristotle"[2] and claiming that these ancient thinkers trace all conflict to imperfection:

> Both Plato and Aristotle treat conflict as an evil and Aristotle treats it as an eliminable evil. The virtues are all in harmony with each other and the harmony of individual character is reproduced in the harmony of the state. Civil war is the worst of evils. For Aristotle, as for Plato, the good life for man is itself single and unitary, compounded of a hierarchy of goods. It follows that conflict is simply the result either of flaws of character in individuals or of unintelligent political arrangements.[3]

The ancient world featured small, quasi-natural holistic communities that, when successful, could aspire to familylike levels of unity. Plato and Aristotle, wedded to notions of psychic and civic harmony, were unable to think their way beyond such norms of the ancient city life, so there was no way for them to conceptualize conflict as anything other than the "great evil" of political life.

The first motivation for writing this book was to raise the hue and cry against such interpretations that would rob ancient political philosophy, and *especially* Aristotle's political thought, of the subject of conflict. Setting aside the odd suggestion that ancient political lives were somehow simpler than the lives we are living now, as well as the highly problematic assumption that Aristotle's attitude toward conflict was similar to that of Plato, I hope to show in this book that it is deeply misleading to suggest that Aristotle embraced a political philosophy that uncritically aspired to civic holism or to suggest that he failed to appreciate that differences and conflicts among citizens might be caused by something other than bad governance. It is certainly true that Aristotle understands conflicts such as civil war, partisanship, and deep distrust of the constitution as being antithetical to the best sorts of political environments. It is also true that Aristotle made great efforts to develop proposals for how communities could eliminate, or at least manage, such disunity. But such regrettable problems, I shall argue, are not the only types of conflicts we find Aristotle attributing to political communities. He accepts and commends both disagreement and competition among the best sorts of citizens living in the best sorts of cities.

This brings me to my second motivation in writing this book. There have been other scholars who, like me, believe that Aristotle's conception of political conflict deserves attention. I hope to offer an interpretation that reframes and systematizes Aristotle's understanding of this subject in a way that has not before been attempted. Let me here briefly offer a summary of how my work fits into this broader scholarly context.

Nicholas White, in *Individual and Conflict in Greek Ethics*, does a fine job exposing the absurdity of interpretations that assimilate Aristotle's work to those political theories that portray an ideal community as a giant piece of clockwork or a group mind-meld. But most of White's attention is devoted to Aristotle's understanding of what White takes to be conflicting moral imperatives to lead the life of the politician and to lead the life of the philosopher. Even setting aside my own doubts that Aristotle recognizes what we call "moral imperatives," it seems to me that White focuses too much of his discussion on the deliberative conflict within each individual as he or she engages in decision making. Though the topic of deliberation bears upon the issue of political dispute, White never explores whether *intra*personal deliberative conflict might or might not promote *inter*personal political conflict. These two, I will argue, are not identical, and the latter demands separate treatment.

By contrast, Robert Mayhew's *Aristotle's Criticism of Plato's Republic* does offer an analysis of political, interpersonal conflict. However, though I am convinced by this excellent piece of scholarship, the approach taken in this work is almost exclusively a *via negativia*. Mayhew unpacks Aristotle's arguments for the claims that cities are not metaphysically unified in the way Plato believed, that Plato was wrong to promote intensely high levels of civic affection, and that Plato made a mistake to endorse any scheme that would collectivize property. In all these ways, we are shown why Aristotle does not support promoting Platonic unity. But one is then left wondering how Aristotle himself thinks of the possibility of conflict on its own terms. Does anti-Platonic disunity always have the same shape and form? What causes it? Is conflict one sort of event that happens for one sort of reason? Does Aristotle think of such conflict, even if inevitable, as still regrettable? Why or why not? These are the sorts of questions my project attempts to answer.

Another work that directly addresses communal conflict is Bernard Yack's intriguing *Problems of a Political Animal: Community, Justice, and Conflict in Aristotelian Political Thought*. This book does have a goal with which I am sympathetic: it aims to critique those who interpret Aristotle as embracing a conflict-free political ideal. Unfortunately, Yack relies on the worrisome argumentative strategy of explaining political conflict as the by-product of an absence of applicable philosophical theory. Chapter by chapter, his tactic is to show that substantive notions like nature, justice, and friendship do not undergird Aristotle's theories of political order as they have traditionally been understood to do. Yack adopts an antifoundational approach, believing that the only way to make room for political conflict in an Aristotelian city is by arguing that Aristotle denies the existence of extralegal stars by which rulers should guide the ship of state.

While Eugene Garver does not embrace an antifoundational reading, his *Aristotle's Politics: Living Well and Living Together* nevertheless offers something like a Yackian account of conflict's origins. On Garver's reading, there are many nonnatural constitutional forms (and associated principles of justice) by which average humans order their civic lives, but there is no clear way to pick the best among these forms since none directly embody the natural, normative *telos* of human flourishing. So, while Garver believes that there are, as it were, extralegal stars beyond the ship of state, he does not think that this fact solves the artificial problem of how the crew should be organized. This explanatory gap is *the* source of political difficulties, diversity, disputes, and contest.

In her work *A Democracy of Distinction* Jill Frank argues for an interesting variation on this theme. Like Yack and Garver, Frank thinks there is a role for conflict in Aristotelian political thought, and, like them, she believes that conflict cannot be suppressed by virtuous decision makers turning to fixed normative notions for guidance. What is different, however, is that Frank traces the origin of conflict back to unique differences among individual agents. On her reading, it is the fact of ineradicable individual diversity that, when handled poorly, leads to political conflict. It is also this fundamental fact that, when handled well, allows for genuine harmony—what Frank calls "a unity of the different." Such harmony is achieved by agents virtuously seeking a mutual advantage that, though it never erases primordial diversity (and the associated threat of conflict), nevertheless makes civic friendship possible. Thus, for Frank, while the inapplicability of "essentialist" substantive norms does not by itself condemn agents to endless struggle, it nevertheless keeps civic agents on perpetual notice: the conflict born of individual diversity is a haunting presence that can always erupt if the harmonizing work of politics ceases to be done.

Interestingly, the two most recent books that focus directly on the subject of Aristotelian political conflict tacitly accept this inapplicability theory of conflict's origins but argue that Aristotle *does* take substantive concepts of justice, friendship, and nature to apply to political life and virtuous decision making. As a result, both end up portraying Aristotle's ideal community as utterly conflict-free. Kostas Kalimtzis's *Aristotle on Political Enmity and Disease* and Ronald Weed's *Aristotle on Stasis: A Moral Psychology of Political Conflict* portray conflict as the absence of teleology—they portray conflict as that which falls beyond substantive notions captured by theoretical reason. It is then no surprise that both Kalimtzis and Weed cast political conflict in the role of a corrosive, anticommunal agent. For them, political conflict is analogous to disease, and they conclude that Aristotle's normative commitments are implacably opposed to conflict *tout court*.

In this book, I reject the view that political conflict is incompatible with traditional Aristotelian ethical notions because it avoids the assumption made by these scholars that political conflict is one sort of problem to be accounted for by one sort of *explanans*. Aristotle has quite different theories of, and divergent explanations for, civil war, partisanship, constitutional mistrust, legal and political dispute, and political competition. These do not represent different points on a continuous spectrum of "troubles" or "dissensus"; rather, they designate distinct activities. As a result, because conflict is not of one kind, and because different sorts of conflicts can happen for different sorts of reasons, it turns out there is also no need to think that Aristotle adopted one normative attitude toward conflict per se. On my reading, he believes that legal and political disputes should be taking place in the best sorts of cities; he celebrates political competition; and neither of these positive endorsements is at odds with his uncompromisingly critical assessment of partisanship, rebelliousness, and outright civil war. So we need not make any sort of concession to any version of antifoundationalism for we need not admit that conflict can only enter an Aristotelian city when there are no theoretical stars by which the ship of state can be guided. Nor do we need to concede that Aristotle could allow conflict into his political theory only by accepting some dark, pessimistic truth that there is an ineradicable degree of contagionlike civil war infecting every city. On the contrary, I hope to show that for Aristotle some types of conflict are part and parcel of how human beings undertake fully flourishing political lives, while others are different in kind and antithetical to the common good of the city.

Recognizing what we might therefore call the "multivocality of conflict" not only saves us from erroneously attributing to Aristotle either a conflict-free ideal or unstructured agonism, but also brings into view an interesting similarity between Aristotle's approach to politics and that of recent theorists.

Over the last half-century, Aristotle has featured in many familiar debates over which fundamental values should take priority in guiding the basic commitments of contemporary political institutions. Whether the value being championed is liberty, equality, or community (or some version or combination of these), Aristotle is often cited, by both admirers and critics, as someone whose thought can help us appreciate what such commitments would render, or fail to achieve, in any given society. For those who believe that Aristotle can serve some role in current thought, the debate about the priority of political value naturally leads to attempts to show that Aristotle can aid in our comprehension of liberalism, republicanism, egalitarianism, or communitarianism.

The third motivation I had for writing this book was to show that Aristotle has the potential to play a role in a very different kind of contemporary political debate: namely, that over the meaning and nature of democracy. Once we appreciate how Aristotle understands conflict in community, I believe a number of interesting parallels between his approach to political philosophy and that of twentieth-century "leadership" models of democracy come into focus.

Organizing Principles and Chapter Content

There are three goals on behalf of which this book is *not* organized. First, there are already several works that provide excellent overviews of Aristotle's political thought, and it is not my goal to add another. If the reader is looking to get a grasp of the totality of Aristotle's political philosophy, I recommend Richard Kraut's *Aristotle: Political Philosophy*; Fred Miller's *Nature, Justice, and Rights in Aristotle's Politics*; Richard Mulgan's *Aristotle's Political Theory*; and Peter Simpson's *Philosophical Commentary on the Politics of Aristotle*. The arguments I advance here deal with many overarching themes, but the reader should be warned that I make no attempt at being synoptic. This book is an analysis of the specific subject of conflict in Aristotle's ethical and political thought, followed by a brief discussion of the significance this subject has for his contemporary relevance. This book is not intended to be a general summary or running commentary.

Second, by titling this book *Conflict in Aristotle's Political Philosophy*, I do not mean to promise an analysis of one specific Greek word that could plausibly be translated as "conflict," along with a philological discussion of that word and how it shows up in Aristotle's political texts. As my first chapter will make clear, such an approach would not serve my purposes well since my overarching argument is in support of the conclusion that Aristotle never conceived of intracity conflicts as taking one form. To the extent that this argument has merit, there is no reason to assume that tracking any given word would successfully illuminate all the dimensions of civic conflict. Besides, even if Aristotle had used only one conflict word, his penchant for using the same word in stricter and looser ways would still necessitate the sort of investigation that I am here undertaking—there would still be a need to develop convincing interpretive arguments about which sort of event, exactly, Aristotle had in mind when using a conflict-related word in this or that particular passage.

In fact, there are many places in the texts where Aristotle describes civic struggle without even using conflict words. Consider the following statement: "This results in a city coming into being that is made up of slaves and masters, rather than free people: the one group full of envy and the other full of arrogance. Nothing is further removed from a friendship and a community that is political" (*Pol.* IV.11 1295b21–24).[4] Or consider this example: "[W]hen [a great-souled person] meets people with good fortune or a reputation for worth, he displays his greatness . . . since superiority over them is difficult and impressive . . . and there is nothing ignoble in trying to be impressive with them" (*NE* IV.3 1124b18–22). In the first passage, Aristotle is describing the incredibly dangerous condition of unmitigated partisan opposition, and in the second passage he portrays a kind of high-minded one-ups-manship. Both passages involve humans who are at odds with one another in some way, but neither passage deploys any obvious conflict-related word such as "war" [*polemos*], "to revolutionize" [*neoterizein*], "battle" [*machē*], "faction" [*stasis*], "dispute" [*amphisbētēsis*], "rivalry" [*hamilla*], or "contest" [*agōn*]. While sensitive to language, my project is one of political philosophy rather than philology, and for that end I have done my best to offer arguments about how best to interpret Aristotle wherever he describes how, or implies that, political animals are not unified in some way.

Finally, while it is true that this book concludes with a discussion of how the subject of conflict sheds light on some similarities between Aristotelian political thought and contemporary democratic theory, readers should not assume that I have organized this entire project around the single interpretive goal of ensuring Aristotle's relevance. This book does not begin by adopting the outlook of a particular contemporary political theory, and then test, chapter by chapter, the degree to which aspects of that modern view can be discovered in Aristotelian texts. On the contrary, in the first two parts of my book, I attempt to set out the geography of Aristotelian political conflict, independently of any given contemporary concern. Part I is an analysis of Aristotle's treatment of the unfortunate and regrettable conflicts that plague sub-standard cities, and part II offers an investigation of the conflict that Aristotle believes would take place in even the best imaginable political community. It is only in part III, after sketching portraits of a number of different constitutional and democratic theories, that I argue that Aristotle's multivocal understanding of conflict shows his political philosophy to be more similar to one of these than others.

As far as specific content is concerned, each of the three parts of my book is preceded by a short prelude that explains the motivation for, and offers an outline of, the topics to be discussed. However, for those readers who may be more interested in one specific topic rather than the book as a whole, or even one part of the book, a brief overview of each of the chapters follows.

In chapter 1, "*Stasis* as Civil War," I argue that Aristotle does not use the word "*stasis*" (variously translated as "civil war," "faction," "sedition," etc.) to refer to *all* sorts of conflict, encompassing everything from the competition of neighbors to the bloodiest of battles. On the contrary, *stasis* specifically means "civil war." Showing that Aristotle narrowly delimits the meaning of the term is important for my argument because it blocks any assumption we might make that his admonitions against *stasis* are signs of some general, negative attitude toward conflict per se.

Chapter 2, "The Unique Problem of Partisanship," explores Aristotle's unstinting criticism of democrats and oligarchs and the origin of his belief that these two groups will be implacably locked in hostile opposition toward one another. The key to understanding Aristotle's negative view, I argue, can be found by appreciating the extraordinary precision with which he constructs their partisan political identities. Democrats and oligarchs are defined by no fewer than the four distinct elements of (1) an incorrect theory of justice, (2) an emotional defect, and (3) a very specific intellectual fallacy—all of which are then reinforced by (4) a misguided theory of happiness. Recognizing who Aristotle takes these partisans to be and appreciating how narrowly he defines them allows us to understand why he essentially banishes them from the best possible city and why this banishment still leaves plenty of room for other sorts of disunity among model citizens.

Chapter 3, "Managing Mistrust in Average Cities," examines Aristotle's conception of the conflict produced by the long-term causes of civil war before any fighting actually takes place. This kind of conflict, which results from inhabitants becoming increasingly mistrustful of the constitutional order and the associated responses rulers take to manage it, has many different forms in different kinds of constitution. Nevertheless, Aristotle's portrait makes it quite clear that this sort of tension, though highly variegated, is an affliction of average cities that involves either rulers or ruled who lack virtue. Constitutional mistrust is not the sort of problem the best sort of city would have to bear or manage.

Chapter 4, "Dispute and Disagreement," turns away from the unfortunate conflicts of suboptimal political life and examines conflicts of which, I believe, Aristotle approves. Even people of perfect human virtue can have serious and intractable disagreements with one another. I argue that Aristotle anticipates such disputes occurring within political institutions of the best kind of city and that he in no way interprets such disagreement as a failure, shortcoming, or even limitation. Rather than any concession to a pessimistic "realism," Aristotle approves of debates as being the very fabric of joint deliberation among human beings, and he thinks of joining such a dispute as a rather noble undertaking that constitutes virtuous participation in the practical action of a community.

Chapter 5, "Contending for Civic Flourishing," takes up the subject of competition. Disagreeing with fellow citizens is something quite different from being competitive with them, and while some readers might admit that intractable epistemological challenges will persist in even the best cities, fewer may grant that political competition will remain as a city becomes better. Yet I argue that this is indeed how Aristotle thinks of civic life. I argue that in his "city of our prayers" there are four types of competition that actually *increase* as civic conditions improve: (1) traditional "competitive outlays" in which citizens strive to out-do one another with their civic contributions, (2) competitions among citizens for high offices, (3) competitions to see which proposal made in the deliberative assembly is best, and even (4) competitions among deliberators themselves to make the winning proposal that sets the *polis* on a path toward flourishing.

Chapter 6, "Conflict and Constitutionalism," offers an initial attempt to investigate whether Aristotle's understanding of conflict resembles that which is recognized in familiar modern political theories. Given that Aristotle develops such a detailed set of recommendations for how cities can best handle distrust to prevent open rebellion, it is reasonable to wonder whether Aristotle's philosophy anticipates the most famous modern political theory of conflict management: constitutionalism. Unlike those who believe Aristotle was too Pollyannaish to even be aware of such possibilities, I argue that Aristotle's theory of conflict shows that he actually entertained notions that are strikingly similar to the ideas that later became known as rule by law, limited government, balanced powers, and even separated powers. However, while he was aware of such possibilities and their appeal, I conclude that Aristotle was not convinced that such tactics could ultimately prevent civil war. Though he recognizes the sorts of conflict to which constitutionalism is a plausible response, Aristotle's conception of the causes of conflict leads him to embrace a political philosophy considerably different from that of constitutionalists.

In chapter 7, "Conflict and Democratic Theory," I argue that it is a strand of twentieth-century democratic theory that is most similar to Aristotle's approach. After a brief overview of major models used to theorize contemporary democracy—democracy as self-government of the people, deliberative democracy, agonism, and interest pluralism—I draw the conclusion that Aristotle's treatment of conflict is most similar to that portrayed in the democratic theory known as "plebiscitarianism" or "leadership democracy."

Part I

Conflict in Imperfect Cities

Prelude

A great deal of the conflict we meet with in life is regrettable. When we hear that "conflict has erupted" in a given country, or that "conflict has broken out" in a given city, we usually imagine human beings violently attacking each other, and we often wonder whether those involved are treating each other viciously. We picture riots and then appallingly brutal crackdowns, shootings, and indiscriminate retaliations, and we may even worry that some group is attempting to wipe out opponents in systematic fashion. We fear the onset of communal breakdown with participants who have dropped any pretension of following ethical norms.

Yet even when the conflict that grabs our attention is not atrocious, we still believe that something regrettable is taking place for all those who have joined the fight. Take, for example, the case of justified war. Though the participants may be doing their best to follow basic codes of conduct, and though they may be fighting for some reasonable purpose or cause, it is still the case that fighting in war is not the best way for these human beings to spend their time. Most would agree with Aristotle's assessment that "war [*polemon*] must be chosen for the sake of peace, work for the sake of leisure, necessary and useful things for the sake of noble ones" (*Pol.* VII.14 1333a35–36). Virtuous people may need to fight in war, but war is not their highest end—the end they would choose for its own sake. On the contrary, it is noble pursuits found in peace and leisure that serve as the ultimate goal of a life well lived.

This book is not a study of war—an examination of the scope, nature, and causes of violent conflict among cities—but rather an assessment of how Aristotle understands conflict among the inhabitants *within* one and the same political community. However, here in part I, we will see that Aristotle believes that much of the conflict that takes place within cities does indeed resemble war in several key respects.

First, Aristotle develops an extraordinarily sophisticated theory of *stasis* that is meant to explain how and why cities suffer the total communal breakdown of civil war (chapter 1). This type of conflict involves an attempt by factionalizers to change the constitution by force or fraud, and it is usually precipitated by inhabitants suffering from some sort of vice. There are times when even virtuous people may need to engage in *stasis* to correct a flawed city. But while this may occasionally be the best option for excellent agents living within deeply imperfect regimes, the internal war of *stasis*, like the violence of external war, is still regrettable for all those involved. No one would attribute such conflict to the best sort of political environment.

Aristotle's account of *stasis* also offers a theoretical framework for appreciating the danger posed by the antagonism between rich and poor (chapter 2). These two groups are not identified simply by their unequal economic statuses, but by a suite of psychological defects that leads them to engage in endlessly divisive partisanship—a type of conflict that exacerbates and intensifies the causal factors that push cities toward outright civil war.

Finally, in addition to the partisanship between these specific two groups, there is another, general type of simmering conflict that Aristotle imputes to flawed cities. Before reaching the dire stage of all-out civil war, the factors that cause *stasis* in the long term can, in the short term, inspire inhabitants to distrust the constitution governing their city (chapter 3). Such distrust takes many forms, and in each case is a function of the different inhabitants' characters as well as the structure and identity of the ruling class. This is why we find Aristotle offering so many different techniques for managing mistrust; just as the unfortunate problems faced by average communities are complex, so too are Aristotle's recommendations for how rulers might respond to them.

Chapter 1

Stasis as Civil War

To understand how Aristotle conceptualizes conflict, it is important first to clarify how he uses the word most often associated with conflict in ancient Greece: "*stasis*." This word was used by many in the ancient world to cover a broad swath of conflicts we find in shared political life: "[A]ll levels of intensity were embraced by the splendid Greek portmanteau-word *stasis*."[1] Without any clear conceptual boundaries, the word could apply to civil war, sedition, fighting, tension, troubles, disagreements, and, generally, any of the ways human beings could be at odds with one another in the city.

The main goal of this chapter, however, is to establish that Aristotle does not use the term in such a sweeping way, and to argue that he uses it with great precision. For Aristotle, *stasis* is catastrophic conflict that involves a radical alteration of the *polis*. *Stasis* is nothing less than civil war.

More than philological accuracy is at stake in interpreting Aristotle's use of this word. First, appreciating how Aristotle delimits the meaning of *stasis* brings into sharp focus the ways in which he adopts a self-consciously anti-Platonic approach to issues of civil war. Unlike Plato and other ancient thinkers who think of *stasis* as civic conflict per se, and who take it to be explained by the root cause of uncontrolled appetite, Aristotle thinks of *stasis* as a distinct sort of political event that can be caused in many different and distinct ways. Distancing himself from the Platonic theory, Aristotle endorses a view far closer to what we find in some of the multifaceted accounts offered by ancient historians.

Second, once we realize that Aristotle defines *stasis* with precision, we can better appreciate the scope of his advice to politicians to do everything they can to prevent *stasis* in their cities. Rather than being a clarion call to end all conflict, and thus a call for perfect coordination and holistic harmony, this is advice for addressing the causes of civil war. His counsel to suppress such a calamity should not be interpreted as a recommendation to quash all types of conflict whatsoever.

I. What Is *Stasis*?

The text of the *Politics* is littered with talk of *stasis*, *diastasis*, and those who *stasiazousi*, but it is only in *Pol.* V.1–4 that Aristotle attempts to explain what, exactly, he means by these terms. At the most general level, *stasis* is a prominent type of constitutional change [*metabolē*],[2] distinguished from other types of change caused by such things as electioneering (V.3 1303a14), carelessness (a16), or unnoticed, gradual alteration (a1). But when it comes to offering a positive account of what *stasis* is, Aristotle describes it as being a kind of action, identified by a certain sort of means being used for attaining a certain sort of end. Specifically, *stasis* is that species of political change in which participants use the instruments of force or deceit (V.4 1304b8) to change the form of the constitution (V.1 1301b6–10) or, though they leave the form unchanged, try to get the constitution "in their own hands"; to alter the "degree" of the constitution; or to change a specific part of the constitution (b10–26).[3]

Notice that, described thus, *stasis* does not exist in the way that a chair exists or a specific living substance exists; rather, it designates a type of social action altering the civic constitution.[4] Thus, when we read that a city is filled with *stasis*, *Politics* V.2 suggests that Aristotle would have us ask such questions as: *Who* are the people acting in this way? Have these actors *decided* to use force, or are they using fraud as their means? Do they *wish* to accomplish some goal that will leave the constitution of the city intact, or are they *planning* to alter the city's form? In other words, because *stasis* exists as social action, understanding it not only involves noticing changes in patterns of external political behavior, but also requires grasping the psychology of the agents engaged in such action. Documenting the beliefs and desires that cause people to change a constitution, therefore, is not a coincidental investigation, but a crucial component of understanding *stasis* itself.

While even a cursory reading makes it clear that these sorts of action-oriented causes are of most interest to Aristotle in *Pol.* V.1–4, it is no small task to make sense of his rather convoluted account. The broad outline, thankfully, is not too difficult to comprehend since he explicitly declares that the *archai* or *aitiai*[5] of *stasis* are "three in number" (for the sake of readable translations, I will use the generic "faction" and its cognates to translate "*stasis*" and its cognates):

[1] how those who factionalize hold themselves and [2] for the sake of which things, and [3], third, what are the origins

[*archai*] of political disturbances and factions among people. (V.2 1302a20–22)

We can see clearly enough that Aristotle would have us draw some sort of three-fold division among the causes of *stasis*; but getting clear about what, exactly, Aristotle means by each of these three is more difficult. My own interpretation of how Aristotle comprehends *stasis* and these causes rests on three main claims.

First, Aristotle thinks that there is a surprising degree of psychological similarity among all those who engage in faction.

Second, Aristotle is drawing a temporal distinction among these causes: he offers [1] the first and [2] second causes as a psychological portrait of those who actively engage in faction, and introduces [3] the third cause to identify factors that, at an earlier time, helped to create factionalizing mindsets.

Third, among the elements in a factionalizing psychology, Aristotle draws a distinction between the general motive of factionalizers, on the one hand, and the specific opportunities agents attempt to exploit when they decide to initiate faction. The [2] second cause depicts the decision that initiates or "triggers" active factionalizing, while [1] the first cause describes a general wish.

I.1. A Universal Profile of Factionalizers

Aristotle describes [1] the first cause of *stasis* as "how those who factionalize hold themselves [*pōs te echontes stasiazousi*]." I take it that he conjugates the verb and participle in the present tense because he takes himself to be depicting people who are performing a certain kind of action that is in progress. All of his descriptions of the first cause of *stasis* represent it this way. For example, when he spells out the details of the first cause, he again uses verbs and participles in the present tense:

> For faction is everywhere [*pantachou*] due to inequality, when unequals do not receive proportionately unequal things (for example, a permanent kingship is unequal if it exists among equals). For people generally [*holōs*] engage in faction pursuing equality [*to ison zētountes stasiazousi*]. (*Pol.* V.1 1301b26–29)[6]

In the next chapter, Aristotle elaborates:

> One must establish what, most of all, is generally the cause [*aitian katholou*] of people being in some way disposed to change—a cause which we already hit upon in earlier discussion. For those who desire equality factionalize [*isotētos ephiemenoi stasiazousi*] if they believe [*nomizōsin*] that they are getting less, even though they are the equals of those who are getting more; whereas those who desire inequality and superiority do so when they believe [*hupolambanōsin*] that, though they are unequal, they are not getting more but the same or less. (Sometimes these desires are just, sometimes unjust.) (V.2 1302a22–29)

Once again, this description reveals something about people who are *already* factionalizing.

What, exactly, is it that is revealed? Aristotle's expanded account here in *Pol.* V.2 portrays the first cause as this: not getting as much as one *believes* one deserves, coupled with a desire to rectify this *perceived* injustice. On this reading, Aristotle uses verbs of thinking and believing to emphasize that factionalizers may, or may not, have a correct, or even partially correct, conception of justice. When Aristotle here claims that "Sometimes these desires are just, sometimes unjust," he signals to readers that his foregoing discussion was focusing upon the factionalizers' *subjective* perception of justice, regardless of whether that perception is correct or not. In this way, Aristotle is able to identify a cause of faction that we might find in perfectly virtuous people, partially just oligarchs, partially just democrats, and even unjust tyrants (or extreme oligarchs and democrats acting tyrannically). For example, in a city where all inhabitants are similarly virtuous, but one person holds a permanent kingship, faction may start because the virtuous believe they are getting less power than they deserve. However, in a (genuine) aristocracy where a few virtuous people rule, this same belief might lead the poor to factionalize. And again, in a democratic city where everyone is treated as arithmetically equal, the virtuous may factionalize if they think they are not getting the superior appointments they believe they deserve. And yet this same desire for superior treatment might cause the rich to factionalize in a city where virtue is used as the standard for merit, and even cause the richest person of all to factionalize for despotic power. In all these cases, we have people motivated by a desire for equality, in either its arithmetic or proportional form.

It is by picking out a feature that might be shared by both virtuous and vicious agents alike that Aristotle can offer a universal account of this cause of *stasis*. That Aristotle hopes to identify such a universal is suggested by his claims that faction is everywhere [*pantachou*] explained by this first cause, that this cause is universal [*katholou*], and that it holds generally [*holōs*]. Of course, in the realm of human affairs, we would not expect any generalization to hold without exception, and we must also remember that Aristotle thinks there are types of constitutional change that are not caused by faction. But, all the same, Aristotle thinks that the first cause so regularly appears as an element in factionalizing that it can be described as a universal feature of *stasis*.[7]

However, though this first cause of faction may be universal, it is narrowly circumscribed and accounts only for what motivates factionalizers; it does not explain how this motivation translates into specific behaviors and decisions. So, while we know that the ultimate end of those who engage in faction is changing the constitution, the details of their choices on the way to achieving their long-term constitutional goals are not captured by the first cause alone.

The second cause of *stasis* helps to fill this gap. This is the cause of *stasis* that Aristotle identifies as [2] that "for the sake of which" agents factionalize. He offers the following expanded description:

> The things about which people factionalize [*stasiazousi*] are profit, honor, and the opposite of these. For because they also flee dishonor and penalty, either for themselves or for their friends, they factionalize [*stasiazousi*] in cities. (V.2 1302a31–34)

Out of all the possible near-term goals factionalizers might adopt, why does Aristotle think they aim at honor and profit? My interpretation of the first cause of *stasis* offers a ready explanation: the first cause is a wish to correct perceived distributive injustice, and Aristotle tells us elsewhere that such justice governs the "allocation of honor, wealth, or any of the other things that are to be divided among members of a constitution" (*NE* V.2 1130b31–32). In other words, since the motivation of factionalizers is getting more of what they believe they deserve, it is no surprise that they aim at the goods in terms of which desert is rendered.[8]

Note that the second cause, like the first, picks out an aspect of agents who are actively in the process of factionalizing: the verbs and participles are conjugated in the present tense. Moreover, once again Aristotle is attempting to offer a universal description of this second cause: profit and honor are the goals of factionalizers in cities . . . that is, in *all* cities.

In conclusion, Aristotle lays out a surprisingly sweeping and unitary account of factionalizing psychology.[9] Whenever and wherever we ask factionalizers, "What are you doing?" we might hear in response, "Fighting injustice," a description of the first cause. But we might also hear responses that describe the second cause: "I am trying to avoid the unjust fines that I've been asked to pay," "I intend to gain the honor of having high office that has been denied to me by the *dēmos*," or "I am attempting to help my friends gain the profit and honor that they deserve on the basis of their war efforts." When constitutional change is induced by faction, Aristotle believes that the agents involved will nearly always be motivated by the belief that they deserve more from the constitution than they currently receive, and they will be undertaking specific actions concerning money and honor.[10]

I.2. Causal Triggers versus Spectacles

Taken together, the first two causes provide a portrait of those engaged in faction, but because they only describe action in progress, they shed little light on why factionalizers have come to have the outlook that they do. These causes offer no background history that explains how agents have come to believe that they are not getting what they deserve.

This, I take it, is the reason that Aristotle identifies [3] a third cause of *stasis*—"the origins [*archai*] of political disturbances and factions among people" (*Pol.* V.2 1302a22)—and introduces it this way:

> The causes and origins [*aitiai kai archai*] of changes, from which people are disposed [*hothen autoi te diatithentai*] in the manner discussed and about the things mentioned, could be taken to be seven in number, or more. (1302a34–37)

There are several reasons to think that this third cause operates at an earlier time than the other two causes (which are here obliquely referred to as "the manner discussed" and "the things mentioned"). First, it is only when describing the third cause that Aristotle makes a point of using the word "*archai*," and this word, unlike "causes [*aitiai*]," has connotations of "origins" or "beginnings." Second, when Aristotle says that these are the origins "from which [*hothen*]" there are factionalizing mindsets, he implies that these causes existed before such psychological states. Finally, Aristotle's choice of verb—"are disposed [*diatithentai*]"—suggests that these factors helped to bring about a transformation in some alterable component of agents' psychology that can be disposed, managed, or oriented (these are all common meanings of "*diatithentai*") in one way at an earlier time, and then in a different way at a later time. If Aristotle had intended the third cause to describe some permanent feature of agents, we would have expected a different verb.[11]

According to this interpretation, Aristotle posits [3] the third cause to account for a turn toward a new and distinct *factionalizing* orientation in some inhabitants' psychology, but the third cause is not meant to explain, all by itself, the *entire* psychological profile of those who are altered. This theory of faction is not meant, for example, to explain why human beings possess different conceptions of *eudaimonia* or account for their diverse understandings of justice, merit, honor, money, or power. Similarly, the theory of faction is not aimed at explaining why and how different people develop different emotional repertoires during their upbringing. On the contrary, the third cause only narrowly identifies typical factors that turn people toward factionalizing, and it introduces these factors without presupposing that they always work in the same way, at the same rate, for every kind of agent. For example, while it may take repeated exposure to many different kinds of situations to turn a virtuous person into a virtuous factionalizer, it may take very little to flip an oligarch into a factionalizing oligarch. The very thing that strikes a would-be tyrant as innocuous may strike a democrat as irksome; what seems mildly worrisome to a virtuous citizen, may seem intolerable to a dynastic oligarch. Aristotle is attempting to set out a universal theory of the sorts of things that turn inhabitants, whoever they might be, toward faction; but he does not thereby claim that all factionalizers share a worldview.[12]

At any rate, as the passage quoted above indicates, this third cause of *stasis* is presented as a group of seven (or more) factors. But, despite this additional seven-fold complexity, the general account is simple: *before* agents decide to factionalize, there are seven causal factors that could be responsible for putting agents into that faction-prone frame of mind (usually, and in different ways, at different rates, etc.).

Yet as soon as we examine the list of seven causal factors that make up [3] the third cause, we run headlong into what I take to be the trickiest interpretative problem of *Pol.* V.1–4. When Aristotle generates his list, he cites profit, honor, arrogance, fear, superiority, contempt, and disproportional growth.[13] This list is puzzling: it begins with profit and honor, the very same items he already identified as constituting [2] the second cause of *stasis*. Moreover, the reader cannot simply set this aside as a bit of sloppiness on Aristotle's part: he himself flags the reduplication at V.2 1302a37–38, explaining that these two items are indeed the same as those used before, "but not in their manner of operation [*ouch hōsautōs*]." What does that mean? How could the "manner of operation" of profit and honor be so different that they act as two entirely separate causes of *stasis*?

In *Politics* V.3, Aristotle discusses and explains all seven factors of the third cause, and then he begins V.4 with the following sentence: "*Staseis*, therefore [*oun*], are not over small issues, though they arise from small matters; rather, they are carried on about great issues" (1303b17–19). Aristotle takes this to be the conclusion (note the "therefore" [*oun*]) readers are supposed to draw from the preceding chapter, which, on the face of it, might have struck them as merely a random assortment of "small things." The first sentence of V.4, I propose, is supposed to prevent that misreading: these "small matters" deserve a place in the theory of faction because they cause inhabitants to worry about the "great" issues of equality and justice.

This opening sentence of V.4 thus offers us a way to distinguish the respective causal roles that profit and honor play as Aristotle's second and third causes. On the one hand, in V.3 1302b5–14, Aristotle is describing how profit and honor help to set the stage for *stasis*: inhabitants witness allocations of profit and honor that strike them as ominous, and, seeing these, they begin to worry about big issues; by witnessing such things, they begin to worry that the basic principles of their city are unjust and begin to contemplate constitutional change. Now, as I said before, different agents may interpret specific allocations in different ways; the point here is that profit and honor are working in the same manner as all the other causal factors of the third type described in V.3: they operate as *spectacles* that, over time, can put inhabitants into a certain frame of mind, whether or not they and their friends are directly involved.[14]

By contrast, in their role as the second type of cause, profit and honor are meant to explain why agents have decided to factionalize *now*. In this role, profit and honor explain agents who are no longer worrying about their constitution but have decided to take matters into their own hands and act. While the third cause of faction consists of *spectacles* that put agents into a faction-prone frame of mind, the second cause of faction consists of *triggers* whereby faction commences. A specific opportunity to receive honor or profit (or avoid dishonor or loss, for oneself or for one's friends) acts as a last straw that agents believe must be addressed by initiating faction.[15]

Besides accounting for the reduplication of honor and profit, another benefit of this interpretation is that it explains Aristotle's motivation for following the V.3 discussion with V.4 1303b17–04a17. The basic theme that holds together this latter stretch of text is that politicians who want to prevent *stasis* had better be prepared to intervene earlier rather than later in the social dynamics of their cities: once the stage for *stasis* is set (which, on my interpretation, is a stage built by having one or more of the seven causes produce inhabitants who feel that they live under an unjust regime), the slightest perceived misallocation of honor or profit can trigger *stasis*.

Indeed, all six of the historical examples that Aristotle provides at this point in the text work in exactly this way: what might, in isolation and superficially, look like some extremely small (even petty) dispute about honor or profit affecting only a few elite groups or their friends ends up precipitating full-scale *stasis* that engulfs a constitution. A jilted lover in Syracuse dishonors his former companion; brothers in Hestia dispute over patrimony (i.e., profit); a fleeing bridegroom dishonors his bride's family in Delphi; a father in Mitylene is dishonored because his sons are rejected as mates; two men among the Phocians fight over a heiress (I take it that both profit and honor are involved here); and the father of a bride feels dishonored because he is fined by the groom's father, who has become a magistrate.[16] All these small slights trigger a deeper constitutional crisis.

II. What *Stasis* Is Not

In scholarship that addresses the issue of conflict in the ancient world, it is not unusual to find it asserted that the word "*stasis*" was used by philosophers, historians, dramatists, and politicians in a rather broad and all-encompassing manner.[17] Although Greeks consistently acknowledged a contrast between the inter*polis* conflict of war [*polemos*] and the intra*polis* conflict of *stasis*, it is suggested that they shied away from making fine-grained distinctions among the different ways in which inhabitants could be at odds with one another in normal city life. "*Stasis*" was thus meant to capture what is best left unclear, but always to be avoided.[18]

Now, this may or may not be a helpful way of characterizing a facet of ancient Greek thought; in fact, as I will make clear below, I do think it quite accurately characterizes Plato's conception in the *Republic*. But I fear we are making an interpretative mistake to claim anything like the following:

> *Stasis* is the Greek word that Aristotle, and the ancient Greeks in general, use to characterize the whole range of political conflict

and competition among individuals and groups. It is important to keep in mind that *stasis* refers for Aristotle to a broad range of phenomena from everyday competition between political factions to extraordinary violent events such as civil wars and other attempts to overthrown established governments.[19]

Setting aside the ancient Greeks in general, I do not believe Aristotle characterizes *stasis* in this way. His theory of *stasis* is meant to designate a very specific sort of political event, not a broad category encompassing all different kinds and intensities of conflict.

Here is my first argument against this "portmanteau interpretation" of *stasis* in Aristotle's thought: I simply cannot find any clear-cut examples in the *Politics* where the term is used to signify anything short of a major political crisis in which the regime is tearing itself apart; in each case, Aristotle has in mind the sort of *calamitous* clash that we associate with the term "civil war." If we go through and carefully consider each of the sixty-six occurrences of *stasis* or one of its cognates in the *Politics*,[20] searching for examples of humdrum *staseis* that the portmanteau conception promises we should find, we will come up empty-handed.

Out of all of these examples, there is only one short stretch of text in *Pol.* V.4 that might suggest that *stasis* can be used to describe innocuous, small-scale conflict. In quick succession, we find the following four statements: "Even the small ones [the *staseis*] grow strong whenever they occur among those in authority [*kuriois*]" (1303b19–20); "it is necessary . . . to break up the *staseis* of the leaders [*hēgemonōn*] and the powerful [*dunamenōn*]" (b27–28); "generally, the *staseis* of the notables [*gnōrimōn*] make the whole city join in" (b31–32); "In Mytilene, a *stasis* concerning a heiresses was the source of many misfortunes" (1304a4–5). These passages pose a threat to my delimited interpretation if they show that Aristotle thinks of even the innocuous, apolitical squabbles common among associates as examples of *stasis*.

But these examples from V.4 are anything but quotidian spats among apolitical inhabitants. First, the conflict Aristotle is attributing to these inhabitants seems to be nasty and violent: Aristotle is not here describing heated dinner conversations, but rather conflicts in which weapons are drawn and people are ready to harm one another. Second, notice that the situations Aristotle describes all involve people who are *politically* consequential (authorities, leaders, the powerful, and notables). The fights they are having with one another are not isolated events limited to the participants, and the broader fate of the city is tied up with their conflict. Indeed, remember the context of this entire passage: Aristotle is emphasizing that legislators need to take steps to prevent *stasis* from breaking out in the first place, because it is an illusion to think that, once it begins, it is containable. On the contrary, *stasis* makes the "whole city" suffer and leads to "many misfortunes" because the constitution itself is pulled into bitter struggle.

Thus, while some scholars have claimed that Aristotle uses "*stasis*" as a general word to cover all ranges of conflict, I maintain that the reader will be hard-pressed to find any compelling textual examples that will support this claim.

However, in addition to this purely text-based response, I think a conceptual argument can also be made against the portmanteau interpretation. If I have offered a correct interpretation of Aristotle's causal theory of *stasis* in *Pol.* V.1–4, then it is also clear that Aristotelian *stasis* could not refer to most types of conflict that were regular features of political life in ancient Greek cities.

Consider competition. Is it plausible to think that Aristotle conceived of competitions staged in the city as *staseis*? Surely not. We have seen that when agents actually engage in *stasis*, they are motivated by a sense of injustice. But inhabitants of a *polis* can engage in athletic, dramatic, liturgical, and political competitions without a sense of having been treated unfairly.[21] Indeed, if competitors feel a sense of injustice at all, it would be as a *result* of the way the competition was conducted, not as a condition that *caused* the outbreak of the competition as *Pol.* V.1–4 would require. Moreover, and perhaps more decisively, Aristotle says that agents who are engaged in *stasis* use force or deceit to accomplish their task; but this is not part of the modus operandi of legitimate competition, which always transpires within agreed-upon rules and norms.[22]

The fact that factionalizers use force and deceit also implies that Aristotle would never conceptualize legal disputes as *staseis*, even though such conflicts do often involve litigants who are motivated by a sense of injustice and who began their dispute because of a perceived misallocation of profit that they intend to recover. Court disputation is not carried out with force or deceit, but by judgment: "[A] judicial process [*dikē*] is a *judgment* [*krisis*] that distinguishes the just from the unjust" (*NE* V.6 1134a31–2). Moreover, in those passages of the *Politics* where Aristotle mentions both courts and *stasis*, it is clear that he distinguishes what goes on inside the courts from any sort of *stasis* that might erupt outside of or because of them. For example:

> But let us set aside these courts as well as the homicide and aliens' courts and talk about the political ones, about which, when not well managed, there are factions and constitutional changes [*kinēseis*]. (*Pol.* IV.16 1300b35–38)

Even though Aristotle does not explain to the reader which courts he has in mind when talking of the "political ones," this passage suggests that Aristotle conceives of the legal disputes of the courts as being causes of *stasis* and would not identify them as being *staseis* themselves. Similar, but even more dramatic, is the following passage:

> *Staseis* also arise over marriages and lawsuits when some members of an oligarchy are scorned by others and are driven to start a faction . . . Faction in Heraclea and Thebes arose over a decision in a law court, when Eurytion (in Heraclea) and Archias (in Thebes) were justly but factiously [*stasiastikōs*] punished for adultery by the courts. For motivated by rivalry [*ephiloneikēsan*], their enemies had them bound in the pillory in the marketplace. (*Pol.* V.6 1306a31–b2)

In the first part of the passage, it is quite clear that lawsuits are different from factions: rather than being identified with lawsuits, we are told that *staseis* arise *over* lawsuits. In the second part of the passage, Aristotle gives us examples of adulterers being "justly" but "factiously" punished by the courts. Though at first glance this description appears to blur the line between *stasis* and court disputes, I take it to do quite the opposite: while the courts are successfully performing their normal function of rendering justice in disputes (the wrong-doers receive punishment), here the courts are being used in such a way that they lead to something *beyond* their proper function. Aristotle is insisting that these adulterers are not being punished in a normal way, but rather abnormally—*factiously*.[23] Moreover, the fact that the courts are here operating "factiously" does not suggest that court disputes are themselves *staseis*; on the contrary, the courts are here operating in a way that will give rise to faction because an oligarch emerges from them highly aggrieved.

Finally, let us consider whether it would be appropriate to identify the partisan machinations of oligarchs and democrats as activities of *stasis*. As I will discuss at length in the next chapter, these two groups are constantly at odds with one another, and Aristotle says that both groups are particularly prone to engage in *stasis* when they find themselves in a constitution that does not embody their "assumption" [*hupolēpsis*] about justice (*Pol.* V.1 1301a37–39). But despite the inescapable problems with democrats and oligarchs, I do not think it is correct to conceive of their endemic antagonism as *stasis*.

First, partisan conflict in the *Politics* only takes place between groups with different conceptions of justice. This consideration, all by itself, implies that we cannot simply identify *stasis* as being the same thing as partisanship since Aristotle frequently describes *stasis* as an activity that can take place just as readily *within* like-minded groups as between them. Indeed, it is the very possibility for such intragroup *stasis* that leads Aristotle to maintain that "democracy is more stable and freer from *stasis* than oligarchy" (*Pol.* V.1 1302a8–9): poor democrats will engage in *stasis* with the rich, while rich oligarchs will engage in *stasis* with democrats *or against other oligarchs*.[24] Thus, if partisan antagonism is to be thought of as *stasis*, it could only be considered to be some specific species of *stasis*.

But there is reason to think that Aristotle would deny that partisanship is any sort of *stasis*. Consider his depiction of the so-called "middle-regime": "That the middle constitution is best is evident, since it alone is free from *stasis*. For least of all do factions and dissensions [*staseis kai diastaseis*] occur among the citizens where there are many in the middle" (*Pol.* IV.11 1296a7–9). The middle constitution, chock-full of middling citizens, is here praised because it is *stasis*-free. Yet in the very next chapter, Aristotle suggests that the rich oligarchs and poor democrats who are stranded within this middle constitution, now safely out-numbered, nevertheless retain an adversarial relationship with one another: he states that the legislator in a middle constitution need not worry that the two partisan groups would ever conspire together to overthrow the constitution "since neither will ever want to serve as slaves to the other" (*Pol.* IV.12 1297a2). This suggests that even within *stasis*-free middle-regimes, there is simmering partisan conflict between these two groups.

Third, if we were to take the sort of conflict that exists between oligarchs and democrats to be *stasis*, we would then be led to the unacceptable interpretation that nearly all cities are always in *stasis*. After all, typical cities inevitably feature rich and poor inhabitants (IV.3 1289b28–31) who wish to establish oligarchies and democracies (IV.11 1296a22–32); so if partisan antagonism is the same thing as *stasis*, then we will have to say that *every* city is already embroiled in *stasis*.[25] Yet this interpretive conclusion flies in the face of Aristotle's declaration that legislators "try above all to drive out *stasis*" (*NE* VIII.1 1155a25–26) from their cities and seems deeply at odds with the fact that Aristotle offers *Politics* V and VI as a roadmap for how cities can take proactive steps to avoid the destructive change of *stasis*. Rather than being a permanent attribute of typical cities, *stasis* is treated as a threat that constitutions can try to avoid for the sake of preservation.

In summary, *stasis* is not conflict per se, but is rather the major conflict of civil war. Aristotle always portrays this sort of conflict as an existential civic threat and gives us good reason to distinguish it from competitions among citizens, legal disputes and debates, as well as the typical partisan antagonism found between poor democrats and rich oligarchs in nearly all cities. While many other ancient thinkers may have used "*stasis*" in a broad sense, Aristotle breaks with this common use by developing his own carefully delimited, tricausal account.

But why would he break with this tradition? Some readers may worry that the sheer novelty of the position I am attributing to Aristotle renders my interpretation somewhat suspect. What, they may ask, would motivate Aristotle to put so much energy into developing an account that would have struck so many of his contemporaries as idiosyncratic?

In the next two sections, I will bolster my interpretation by offering an answer to this question. On the one hand, I believe Aristotle develops this distinctive account of *stasis* in order to launch a deep and thoroughgoing critique of Plato's portrayal of political change in the *Republic*. Moreover, and on the other hand, I believe Aristotle develops his theory of *stasis* to better suit historical narratives. As I will argue below, several ancient historians betray no expectation that there be any one "root cause" that is more or less necessary and sufficient for civil war; rather, they suggest that civil war can come about from a number of different combinations of long-term causes that, given certain near-term factors, make major conflict possible. By developing his delimited, tricausal theory of *stasis*, Aristotle is not engaging in egregious eccentricity, but he is attempting to cultivate the approach of what we might think of as a theoretically informed historian.

III. Stasis and Plato's Theory of Political History

Usually, when scholars consider the critique of the *Republic*'s account of constitutional transformation (aristocracy → timocracy → oligarchy → democracy → tyranny, *Rep.* 545c–575d), they quite reasonably gravitate to the criticisms Aristotle lays out in the latter part of *Pol.* V.12 where he attacks Plato by name.

The main thrust of Aristotle's charge at that point in the *Politics* seems to be that the patterns of constitutional change we find in the political histories of actual *poleis* are far more diverse than Plato's theoretical progression would allow: constitutions usually change into their opposite types, yet Plato seems to think that they undergo slight modifications to similar types; oligarchies frequently turn into tyrannies, but Plato thinks they turn into democracies; tyrannies frequently transform into all sorts of different types, but Plato's account seems to require that tyranny be either a sort of constitutional dead-end or, equally implausibly, that tyranny leads to the best constitution.

Of course, the most obvious way for any defender of Plato to respond to such attacks is simply to deny that the progression of *Rep*. VIII and IX was meant to be an immutable law of history. That way, regardless of how many discrepancies Aristotle would like to point out between actual history and Plato's theory, he will be missing the point. Plato, such a defender could maintain, was only trying to introduce a variety of constitutions for the purposes of his ethical argument that virtuous people are happier than the vicious; the story of a regime progression is little more than a literary device. Again, one could argue that Plato merely wants the reader to understand that each type of constitution has a unique congenital defect that makes some developments more likely than others. On this reading, Plato is laying out a series of probable or likely transformations but is in no way endorsing any notion of a necessary historical law.

If Aristotle's attacks were limited to the empirical criticisms of *Pol*. V.12, such responses would certainly dull the edge of his critique. But I do not believe that Aristotle's criticisms of Platonic regime progression are limited to V.12. Instead, the account of *stasis* given in V.1–4 can itself be understood as advancing a supplementary critique that is much more sophisticated and interesting than merely pointing out historical discrepancies.

First, regardless of Plato's explanation for why this or that particular regime transforms into some other specific regime in the *Republic*, it is impossible to deny that he unabashedly endorses a universal explanation of constitutional change:

> Come, then, I said, let us try to tell in what way a timocracy would arise out of an aristocracy. Or is it a simple principle that the cause of change in any constitution is *stasis* breaking out within the ruling group itself, but that if this group—however small it is—remains of one mind, the constitution cannot be changed? / Yes, that's right. (*Republic* 545c–d)

It is not clear why Plato endorses this extraordinary claim that constitutions change only if *stasis* occurs in the ruling class. But it is quite clear that Aristotle is going out of his way to demolish this thesis in the first few chapters of *Politics* V. As I have already mentioned, he makes a point of identifying three ways in which constitutions change without *any* sort of *stasis* whatsoever taking place—an obvious jab at Plato. Moreover, and just as importantly, Aristotle deliberately constructs an account of constitutional change that allows for *stasis* to arise out of the bad relations *between* rulers and ruled, in no way limiting constitution-changing *stasis* to the ruling class alone.[26] Indeed, the account developed in *Pol.* V.1–4 actually predicts that *stasis* will frequently be initiated by inhabitants who believe that they have been unjustly denied the honor of ruling altogether or who believe that those in the ruling class are behaving arrogantly, irresponsibly, or arbitrarily toward the ruled. Aristotle's acute worries about rich and poor partisans even suggest that this type of ruling-vs.-ruled *stasis* is the most frequent sort of constitutional change the political scientist will observe: as I have already mentioned, Aristotle warns that democrats and oligarchs will engage in *stasis* the moment they find themselves outside the ruling class, and it is clear that they will do this regardless of how much unity exists among rulers.

But beyond this critique of the claim that *stasis* in the ruling class is a necessary condition for regime change, another (and, I think, even more profound) criticism *Pol.* V.1–4 makes of Plato's theory of progression becomes clear once we recognize that, throughout the *Republic*, different types of conflict are habitually lumped together under the general heading of "disunity" or "trouble" and then treated as if they were all more or less the same sort of phenomenon. For example, when Plato famously declares that "until the philosophical class wins control, there will be no end of trouble for city or citizens" (501d), the reader is supposed to understand that "trouble" subsumes an exceptionally wide range of political phenomena; indeed, it apparently includes any and all intra*polis* activity that cannot be modeled after those "things of the eternal and unchanging order" (500c). Again, painting with a very broad brush, Plato asserts that politicians involved in the typical jockeying that takes place in "the majority of cities nowadays" (that is, the "people who fight over shadows and struggle against one another in order to rule") should be thought of as being engaged in "civil and domestic war" (520c–521a). Similarly, during the course of his notorious argument that the greatest good for a city could be attained if citizens were to use "mine" and "not-mine" about the same things (461e–465d), Plato, without any hesitation, runs together conflicts between rulers and ruled, masters and slaves, rivalries of different families, lawsuits and accusations, dissentions, and factions—implying that all of these present the political theorist with more or less the same sort of disunity.

Given the interpretation of *Pol.* V.1–4 that I have defended here—an interpretation according to which *stasis* is a precise type of political conflict to be carefully delimited and distinguished from others—it should come as no surprise that I take Aristotle's rejection of the portmanteau conception of *stasis* to be another aspect of his attack on Plato. The substance of this critique is not that Plato ignores empirical history, nor is it a mere reiteration of the *Pol.* II.2 attack in which Aristotle lambasts the notion that maximal unity is a legitimate *telos* for a *polis*. Rather, by offering an analysis that delimits the notion of *stasis* to a very precise political phenomenon, Aristotle has implicitly called into question the catch-all nature of Plato's claims about political disunity.

The attack, however, does not end there. As we have seen, Aristotle's carefully delimited conception of *stasis* is accompanied by a distinctive causal analysis of *stasis*. I believe that Aristotle not only rejects Plato's "portmanteau" conception of *stasis*, but that he also intends *Pol.* V.1–4 to critique Plato's view that *stasis* (and thus the constitutional changes it brings about) is explained by what we might call a "root cause." Seeking a common cause that will explain all the conflict-ridden activities he takes to be of one type, Plato suggests that conflict is everywhere and always to be explained in the following manner:

> We won't say yet whether the effects of war are good or bad but only that we've now found the origins of war. It comes from those same desires that are most of all responsible for the bad things that happen to cities and the individuals in them. (*Republic* 373e)[27]

Plato later develops the distinction already hinted at here between war (an inter*polis* phenomenon) and the intra*polis* problems of *stasis* (469b–471), but, significantly, this passage announces that *all* the types of conflict are to be explained by the exact "same desires." And which desires are these? The history of constitutional transformations in *Rep.* VIII makes it clear that all the "bad things" that happen in cities are based on the same root cause of irrational appetite: secret acquisitiveness destroys the aristocracy (547b); flagrant acquisitiveness transforms the timocracy (550d–51a); single-minded acquisitiveness destroys the oligarchy (555b); and lawless appetite brings down democracy (563d–e). Though the pistons and gears may differ, irrational desire of the body is the fuel that drives each stage of Platonic regime progression: remove this element from the story, and constitutional history stops in its tracks.

Aristotle's treatment of *stasis*, however, approaches the question of causality in a profoundly different way. *Stasis* is not everywhere and always a symptom of a single "root" cause, and it is most certainly not to be explained by appetites running amok.[28] On the contrary, though Aristotle's factionaries are set in motion by some specific opportunity regarding profit or honor (the second cause), this action is motivated by a sense of injustice (the first cause) that has been nursed by a large and diverse set of long-term causes (the third cause). The text gives us no reason to think that these three causal factors are efficacious only in vicious souls, and at no point in the narrative are irrational appetites cast in a leading role. On the contrary, if we had to pick just one element to play the leading role in the Aristotelian drama of *stasis*, it would surely be the content of the agents' rational beliefs concerning what is just, appropriate, and beneficial.[29] In particular, beliefs about equality explain why a given agent initially interprets the spectacles of the third cause as signs of injustice, characterize the content of the agent's desire for equality in the first cause, and show why the agent seized this or that opportunity for honor or profit in the second cause.

Indeed, the fact that Plato privileges out-of-control bodily appetites over rational beliefs in his explanation of *stasis* is precisely one of the aspects of *Rep.* VIII–IX that most exasperates Aristotle. Consider the following criticism of Plato's account of why timocracy changes into oligarchy:

> It is also absurd [*atopon*] to hold that a constitution changes into an oligarchy because the office holders are money lovers and acquirers of wealth, and not because those who are far superior in property holdings think it unjust for those who do not own anything to participate equally in the *polis* with those who do. (*Pol.* V.12 1316a39–b3)

Aristotle is quite clearly fed up with Plato. He begins the sentence with the word "*atopon*" to emphasize his frustration. But now notice what, exactly, bothers Aristotle so much. He is objecting to the *type of explanation* Plato has offered for a change of regime; he is objecting to a brand of political science that would have us believe that historical change can be adequately explained by merely citing this or that collection of perverse appetites.[30]

Aristotle thinks it "absurd" to explain constitutional transformation by citing irrational appetites, and I believe that he has purposely designed his own account of *stasis* in *Pol.* V.1–4 so that it avoids this mistake and thus throws Plato's entire approach into question. Remember, after all, that he has developed an account that is supposed to accommodate both vicious *and* virtuous actors. After describing the desire for equality that is always the first cause of *stasis*, he goes out of his way to say that "sometimes these desires are just, sometimes unjust" (1302a28–9). Again, while his theory can account for the motivations of vicious oligarchs and democrats who so frequently initiate civil war, he insists that the account is every bit as applicable to the most noble inhabitants of a *polis*: "the greatest factional division [*diastasis*] is probably between virtue and vice" (V.3 1303b15), and "those who would be most justified in starting *stasis* . . . [are] those who are outstandingly virtuous" (V.1 1301a39–40). At each of its three stages, the psychological elements that explain the action of *stasis* can be correct or mistaken, upstanding or deviant, well-grounded or reactionary.

In summary, *Pol.* V.1–4 attacks the Platonic conception of regime change at its core. There simply is no such thing as a single "root cause" of *stasis*, and Aristotle takes Plato's candidate for what that cause would be to be "absurd." Moreover, not only is Plato's causal analysis flawed, but his very conception of *stasis* is deeply misguided because it does not properly delimit *stasis* from other types of conflict. Finally, even if we were to overlook these dramatic mischaracterizations, Plato has wrongly made *stasis* among the rulers a necessary condition for constitutional transformation when it is no such thing.

IV. The Athenian Constitution, Thucydides, and Polybius

By breaking so decisively with Plato, and by theorizing *stasis* in a manner so at odds with other ancient Greeks, Aristotle opens up a new area of investigation about a topic that had been largely ignored by earlier philosophers. Nevertheless, though Aristotle's extended theoretical treatment of *stasis* is exceptional, it would be a mistake to think that his conception of *stasis* is entirely unique. On the contrary, the interpretation I have offered here helps us to appreciate some interesting, specific ways in which the Aristotelian approach to the topic of *stasis* resembles that deployed by other ancient historians.

First, consider the historical narrative offered in the *Athenian Constitution*. Whoever wrote this work[31] uses the word "*stasis*" in a specific way: it designates a violent uprising by some major status group that is attempting to upend the constitutional order without the approval of any other political body. For example, the Athenians ask Solon to act as arbitrator between rich and poor after the people rise up in long-enduring and "violent" [*ischuras*] *stasis*. Solon accepts this challenging assignment, offering an elegy as he does so that begins: "I mark, and sorrow fills my breast to see, Ionia's oldest land being done to death" (5.2).[32] Solon is not being asked to intervene as a technical expert in some small policy debate or to referee an everyday partisan disagreement: he is being asked to confront near-catastrophic conflict that is upsetting the basic norms of communal life. Similarly, Solon conceives of *stasis* as an abnormal condition when he passes the following law:

> Finally, seeing that when frequent factionalizing [*pollakis stasiazousan*] took place in the city, some citizens simply accepted any given outcome due to their laziness, Solon made a special law for such people, enacting that whoever did not take an active part [*mē thētai ta hopla*] on either side in a time of civic factionalizing [*stasiazousēs*] should be disfranchised [*atimon*] and have no share in the city. (8.5)[33]

Admittedly, this is a slightly different use of "*stasis*" than we find in the *Politics*. Instead of referring only to the onset of civil war, it is here associated with the acrimonious and menacing clashes that, at any time, could send the city spiraling into civil war.[34] But this somewhat broader use hardly challenges the basic point: it still signals an extraordinary crisis that Solon believes deserves an exceptional response. The kind of conflict that is the target of this special law is different in kind from the mere disputes [*amphisbētēseis*] that, for example, are said to arise over how to interpret Solon's laws because of their obscurity (9.2).

When recounting the period after Solon's departure, the author of the *Athenian Constitution* continues to reserve *stasis* to designate severe and violent conflict that threatens the basic fabric of the *polis*. We are told that four years of peace came to an end (13.1) when the coastal dwellers, people of the plains, and hillmen organized themselves into factions [*staseis*] (13.4) over the issue of which group would control the office of archon. The author cannot be suggesting that this *stasis* brought an end to a utopian four-year period in which Athenians never disagreed, disputed, or competed with each other; we are told the formation of the factions brought an end to "peace" [*hēsuchia*] in Athens, and it is reasonable to think that ending peace means beginning some condition that resembles war. Moreover, the conflict that ends these four years does not concern some trivial and obscure issue: the archon Damasias is driven from his archon office by force [*bia*], and the three factions then agree to a settlement whereby there will be ten archons (13.2)—much like warring cities would negotiate an end to hostilities. Reflecting on this constitutional transformation, the author draws the following lesson: "This shows that the Archon had very great power; for we find that they were always factionalizing about this office." So, *stasis* involves an end of peace, the use of violence, and a fundamental change in the constitution.

In the historical summary of the period of Athenian tyrants, *stasis* again designates a condition resembling civil war. When Peisistratus asks for a bodyguard from the people by claiming that he has been attacked by "opposing factions" [*antistasiōtōn*] (14.1), he is trying to convince them that he is under physical attack by an organized group. Outright assault among groups is again implied when Megacles tells an expelled Peisistratus that he is being "harried by faction" [*tē stasei*] (14.3), when both the factions [*staseis*] of Megacles and Lycurgus scare Peisistratus into fleeing (15.1), and when our author reflects that, after the rise of Cleisthenes, "almost the chief initiative in the expulsion of the tyrants was taken by the Alcmaeonids, and they accomplished most of it by faction [*stasiazontes*]" (20.4). None of this is typical aristocratic jockeying for accepted roles within a recognized order; these are violent conflicts among high-profile individuals for monocratic control.

Finally, we should note that the author of the *Athenian Constitution* believes that the word "*stasis*" is no longer appropriate for the conflicts that take place after the Cleisthenic reforms of 508 BC. These democratic alterations are described at the exact midpoint of the *Ath.Pol.*'s constitutional history (in chapter 21), and all fifteen mentions of "*stasis*" (or its cognates) occur in the first twenty chapters. The single exception is found in the last chapter, chapter 41, and here is it only used to describe conflict back in the days of Solon: "The third [constitution] was the one that followed the *stasis* in the time of Solon, from which democracy took its beginning" (41.2). This exclusively pre-Cleisthenic use is surprising because the later history of Athens clearly involves a great deal of agitation and contentious conflict. There is the downfall of the democracy, the end of the rule by four hundred, the takeover by Lysander's oligarchy of thirty, the rule by two groups of ten, and then the reinstallation of democracy—and this is not even to mention the political assassinations of Ephialtes, Theramenes, or the fifteen hundred political executions perpetrated by the thirty. The savagery and gravity of post-Cleisthenic conflict seems as severe as that before the democracy. So why is only major-league conflict of the first twenty chapters labeled "*stasis*"?

The answer, I believe, is that the author of the *Ath.Pol.* conceives of all constitutional conflict after 508 BC as being legitimated (or as being given the veneer of legitimacy) through a formal procedure recognized by the constitution. Though the conflict is contentious, these transformations do not take place through the purely apolitical mechanism of internal war that dispenses with any such approval. Consider the memorable overthrow of democracy in 413 BC:

> In the period of the war therefore, so long as fortunes were evenly balanced, they continued to preserve the democracy. But when after the occurrence of the disaster in Sicily the Lacedaemonian side became very strong owing to the alliance with the king of Persia, they were compelled to overthrow [*kinēsantes*] the democracy and set up the government of the Four Hundred, Melobius making the speech on behalf of the resolution but Pythodorus of the deme Anaphlystus having drafted the motion, and the acquiescence of the mass of citizens being chiefly due to the belief that the king would help them more in the war if these limited their constitution. (29.1)

The change takes place because of a resolution and the acquiescence of the people. Similarly, the transition from the four hundred to the five thousand is effected procedurally, "having passed by vote a resolution that no office should receive pay" (33.1), and even the change to oligarchy under the thirty takes place thus: "[W]hen Lysander sided with the oligarchical party, the people were cowed and were forced to vote for the oligarchy" (34.3). Of course, this is not to say that this assent is offered in anything like what we might call "ideal deliberative conditions." Nevertheless, there is a procedural imprimatur that frames the transition and thus clearly distinguishes it from a condition of internal war.

Like the author of the *Athenian Constitution*, Thucydides also reserves "*stasis*" for nothing less than major civic upheaval. No one can read his description of the savage conflict within Corcyra (III.69–85) without concluding that what "*stasis*" refers to in this stretch of text is civil war. Indeed, this famous passage gives an unparalleled account of the effects upon those who become active participants in a raging conflict where all restraints have been set aside. There are shocking changes in the perception of ethical norms, radical alterations of agents' goals, and even subtle modifications of language that distort the way participants describe their own behaviors.

Beyond reserving the term for civil war, Thucydides also makes the Aristotelian move of carefully distinguishing the long-term causes of civil war and the near-term causal "triggers" that set the *stasis* in motion. In III.70, Thucydides traces the long-term cause of this *stasis* back to agents of Corinth who were canvassing citizens and intriguing with the rich to turn Corcyra's government away from democratic Athens. The rich citizens of Corcyra develop into a group that has contempt and distrust of democracy, and this inspires them to make an unsuccessful attempt to bring the leader of the common people, Peithias, to trial. But this plot to change leadership through the courts only inspires commoners to organize themselves into a party that can push back against the machinations of the rich. It is in this fraught setting that Peithias decides to take some rich citizens to trial for sacrilege. When these wealthy citizens are convicted, and they conclude that there is no way for them to avoid paying a heavy fine, they decide that it is time to factionalize: they kill Peithias along with sixty of his followers, and this attack inaugurates the violence and fraud of *stasis* across the island.

This causal explanation is quite similar to the sort of analysis suggested by *Politics* V. The actual decision to initiate faction is precipitated by an event involving money (Aristotle's second cause). But this small trigger suffices for faction only because it takes place in an environment of great unease—an environment produced by the rich treating Peithias with contempt, the growing dissimilarity of the rich and the commoners, and the fear that the rich are not only advocating for a change in policy but also pushing for a more oligarchic constitution. These are all events Aristotle would classify as the third cause of faction.

It is interesting to note how Thucydides, in his history of the Peloponnesian War, makes use of similar distinctions between short and long-terms causes when he offers an account of why the Thirty Years Peace dissolves and war reignites between Spartans and Athenians:

> As for the reason they broke this treaty, I first cite the causes [*tas aitias*] and the grievances [*tas diaphoras*], so that no one will have to investigate that from which [*ex hotou*] such an extensive war arose among the Hellenes. For I believe, on the one hand, that the truest claim is that it was the Athenians becoming great and the fear gripping the Spartans that necessitated the war (though this never appeared in a speech), while, on the other hand, there

were those causes openly professed [*hai d' es to phaneron legomenai aitai*] by both sides on account of which they embarked on war when they dissolved the treaty. (*Historiae*, I.23.5–6)[35]

A distinction is here drawn between the causes that operate when conflict breaks out (the "grievances" and the "openly professed" causes of war) and the unannounced causes that operated at an earlier time and put people in a combative frame of mind (Athenian greatness and Spartan fear). Although Thucydides is here discussing war rather than civil war, the temporal distinction resembles that between the second and third causes of faction of *Pol*.V; indeed, recall that both fear and superiority are explicitly listed by Aristotle as versions of the third cause.

Moreover, in these descriptions of war and civil war, note that Thucydides, like Aristotle, has no interest in identifying a single "root cause" of violent conflict. The long-term causes of *stasis* in Corcyra are contempt, dissimilarity, and fear; the long-term causes of renewed war between Athens and Sparta are superiority and fear. While Thucydides nowhere pauses to justify these methodological commitments in the course of his history of the Peloponnesian War, it does seem that he, like Aristotle, wishes to avoid oversimplifying the causal nature of war and civil war, and that he wants readers to appreciate that there are many ways, by virtue of many different types of causes, that such violent outbreaks can take place.

The Greek historian Polybius actually makes a point of criticizing other historians who offer too simple an account of the causes of the war between Rome and Carthage:

Such claims come from those who do not grasp how the beginning [*archē*] differs from, and to some extent is set apart from, both the cause [*aitia*] and the pretext [*prophasis*]—for these are the first of all the events, while the beginning is last of all the events described. (*Histories*, III.6.6)[36]

Polybius is here describing war rather than civil war, but he is drawing distinctions that are strikingly similar to those I have found in Aristotle's account of *stasis*. Polybius goes on to explain that he puts the "beginning" last in the temporal sequence of conflict because it refers to "the first attempts to execute and act upon plans which have already been decided" (III.6.7). That is, it picks out the moves made after participants decide to engage in violent conflict at a particular time and place. In the Aristotelian account of *stasis*, it would thus correspond to the description of the force and fraud factionalizers use to change the constitution. Moreover, note how Polybius makes a point of sharply distinguishing cause and pretext. This resembles Aristotle's careful separation of the factors that initially make inhabitants of a *polis* feel that the constitution is unjust (the third cause) from the manner in which acting for profit or honor ignites *stasis* in a particular situation (the second cause).

When Polybius describes the long-term causes of war, he too refuses to conceptualize these in terms of some univocal "root cause." Instead, like Aristotle and Thucydides, he believes that a proper causal account of war must be able to accommodate a wide and diverse set of events. Polybius describes his use of the term "cause" in the following manner:

> [C]auses are the things that come before and lead to judgments and opinions: that is, our notions of things, our dispositions, our calculations about them, and all those things on account of which we arrive at our judgements and then set out. (*Histories*, III.6.7)

This sounds remarkably similar to Aristotle's conception of how the seven factors of the third cause lead to *stasis*: they operate as spectacles that put inhabitants into a certain frame of mind.[37]

In conclusion, I have offered these brief historical treatments of *stasis* and war to show that the theory that I am attributing to Aristotle—that *stasis* refers to the precise event of calamitous war within the city rather than all sorts of conflict, and that understanding the occurrence of such a momentous event requires distinguishing multiple causes rather than one "root" cause—is not some entirely eccentric view.

That said, I do not wish to minimize differences between the account of *stasis* we find in the *Politics* and that offered by these other thinkers. As we have seen, the author of the *Athenian Constitution* slightly extends *stasis* to include the menacing clashes that take place before there is a fight to change the constitutional order. Moreover, while Aristotle insists that the first cause of faction is everywhere a desire for equality, neither Polybius nor Thucydides gives belief about justice any such role. Perhaps this is one of the major differences between the inter*polis* conflicts of war and the intra*polis* faction. Civil war involves inhabitants who live together in the same community, so we might expect claims of justice to figure more prominently in the motivations of combatants.

In any case, such differences do not alter the overarching point. For Aristotle, *stasis* is an extraordinary type of conflict when it takes place in a city—a civic calamity. And when he develops his account of this sort of conflict, he adopts a decidedly anti-Platonic approach that, while more systematic and theoretical than his predecessors, resembles that used by historians when recounting the origins of violent conflict.

V. The Ideal of *Stasis*-Free Politics

There are many passages in Aristotle's corpus where he makes it clear that the best sorts of cities are *stasis*-free. A particularly important passage can be found in the *Nicomachean Ethics*:

> It also seems that friendship holds cities together and that legislators take it more seriously than justice. For concord [*homonoia*] seems to be similar to friendship, and they aim for it most, while *stasis*, being enmity, they most seek to drive out. (VIII.1 1155a22–26)

No one could read such a passage and then think that Aristotle was somehow generally pro*stasis*. Although virtuous people may sometimes wish to engage in *stasis* to make constitutions just (*Pol.* V.1 1301a38–40), and could even on rare occasions find themselves in situations where acting on such a wish would be prudent,[38] passages like this one make it clear that a life devoted to factionalizing would not be happy. This impression is strengthened when we also remember that Aristotle calls the middle regime best precisely because "it alone is free from *stasis*" (*Pol.* IV.11 1296a7), asserts that friendship is the greatest civic good "since in this condition people are least likely to engage in *stasis*" (II.4 1262b8–9), and constructs "the city of our prayers" of *Pol.* VII–VIII in such a way that it is completely devoid of *stasis*.[39]

Now, *if* we attribute to Aristotle a univocal, portmanteau conception of *stasis* that encompasses *all* varieties and degrees of conflict, then such passages cast Aristotle in a generally conflict-averse light. Even if he believed that conflict (of any stripe) was a necessary evil that sometimes had to be endured to achieve some sort of higher good, we could still say that Aristotle would prefer, in the best-case scenario, to have virtuous citizens living in cities from which all conflict had been removed, root and branch. With some justification we could say that, for Aristotle, political conflict and political perfection are always inversely related, just as we find in Plato's *Republic*.

However, in this chapter, I have tried to show that such an argument, which begins by saddling Aristotle with a portmanteau conception of *stasis*, is misguided. Anyone who notes his worries about *stasis* and then construes these as misgivings about competitions, political rivalries, lawsuits, and all other activities in which human beings are at odds with one another is running together types of activities that Aristotle may be treating separately. Like many other Greek thinkers, Aristotle does believe that the best cities are *stasis*-free. Indeed, there is a way in which cities in *stasis* cease to be cities:

> Their [the Spartans'] habit is to divide the people and their own friends, create anarchy, form factions [*stasiazein*], and fight one another. Yet how does this sort of thing differ from such a *polis* ceasing for a time to be a *polis*, and the political community dissolving? (*Pol.* II.10 1272b11–15)

But when he sets out his theoretical account of what *stasis* is in *Pol.* V.1–4, he delimits this notion so as to render it a precise political phenomenon with a carefully explicated, tripartite causality.

In the end, delimiting *stasis* makes possible an entirely new line of questioning that has been neglected in the literature on Aristotle. Setting the activity of *stasis* aside, which is exclusively directed toward altering constitutions by force or fraud, how exactly does Aristotle conceptualize the other types of conflict that typically take place within a city? For example, how does he conceptualize competition? Political rivalry? Legal disputes? What normative judgments does he make about these? And how, exactly, does he think about the clashes between democrats and oligarchs that are not *staseis*, but seem more worrisome than other kinds of pedestrian disagreements? Having put *stasis* in its properly defined place, we can turn to the corpus anew with a whole range of questions that have the potential to make Aristotle relevant for a modern world that remains stubbornly fractious.

Chapter 2

The Unique Problem of Partisanship

Given the argument of the last chapter, we can appreciate why Aristotle believes that *stasis* goes hand in hand with enmity and hatred. Such internal war is marked by indignant actors fighting to make major changes to the city using force or fraud. It is no stretch to say that for any city, *stasis* is a catastrophe.

When we read through Aristotle's ethical and political works, however, it becomes clear that *stasis* is not the only kind of conflict that involves problematic indignation and hatred: in particular, we repeatedly find Aristotle emphasizing that there is an incredible level of acrimony that exists between oligarchs and democrats whenever they must confront one another in civic life. Indeed, it is striking that when Aristotle begins his analysis of constitutional change and *stasis* in *Politics* V, he actually begins his analysis with a discussion of democrats and oligarchs. It is *their* assumptions, and *their* conceptions of justice, that he identifies as familiar causes of civil war: "[W]hen one or another of them [the democrats or oligarchs] does not participate in the constitution in accordance with their assumption [about distributive justice], they factionalize" (1301a37–39). Elsewhere, he refers to oligarchs and democrats as those "who are disputing over [*amphisbētountes*] constitutions" (III.9 1281a9). Throughout the *Politics*, whenever Aristotle describes the relation of these two groups, he describes them as engaged in some kind of struggle. How, exactly, does Aristotle conceive of this conflict that takes place between them?

While we cannot simply identify the antagonism between these groups as *stasis* (since, as I argued in the last chapter, they are deeply at odds with one another in the middle regime that Aristotle praises as *stasis*-free, and the universality of their antagonism would imply that every average city is already in *stasis*), we also cannot ignore the extreme danger that Aristotle believes their perpetual opposition poses for civic life. When Aristotle lays out his conception of the best sort of city in the *Politics*—a city that exists "according to our prayers" and is freed from many of the unnecessary shortcomings that hobble average cities—we find that the clashes between oligarchs and democrats are conspicuously absent. In fact, not only do we find their fighting removed, but we find that Aristotle has altogether banished both groups from this city.

It is clear, then, that oligarchs and democrats are especially prone to conflict with one another, and it is clear that Aristotle thinks that their clashes have no place in an optimal political order. What is not clear, however, is *why* Aristotle takes oligarchs and democrats to be so reliably hostile to one another or *why* he believes their conflicts are always so likely to engulf the city in civil war.

The goal of this chapter is to uncover the source of this malevolent opposition and to develop a clear picture of how Aristotle conceptualizes this conflict. Once we do this, I believe we find that Aristotle has taken great pains to craft two unique, theoretical, partisan political identities.

I. The Priority and Problem of Political Identity

One of the striking features of the *Politics* is the frequency with which Aristotle uses the procedure of first establishing (or assuming) specific social identities for those who inhabit the *polis* and then drawing substantive political conclusions based upon these. For example, in the opening book of the *Politics*, it is (notoriously) the fixed identity of slave, barbarian, woman, child, and Greek male upon which Aristotle builds his argument for the existence of multiple communities that differ in kind. When a (Greek) male and female live together, a certain household community results; when a natural slave and freeman live together, a different kind of master/slave community is produced; when a number of equal, free, Greek men live together, there is a distinctly political community. Similarly, in order to argue that there are multiple species within each of the six constitutional genera, Aristotle begins by setting out a robust list of potential constitutional actors: farmers, craftsmen, traders, hired laborers, warriors, judges of disputes, those who engage in competitive outlay, and office-holders (IV.4 1290b38–91b2). Only after these distinct social identities are introduced does he generate different species of democracy and oligarchy by imagining the sorts of constitutions that result from inserting different combinations of these characters into ruling positions.[1]

Ultimately, this prioritization of identity is likely a symptom of the analytical method Aristotle endorses in *Politics* I—the method of first understanding incomposite parts and then understanding the whole (1252a17–23). But, general methodology aside, it is clear that Aristotle prioritizes social identity in his political theory because of the way he conceptualizes constitution [*politeia*]. On his view, unlike the way we often use the term in contemporary discourse, the constitution of a city is not a written document that enumerates the powers and offices of government and that spells out what these powers are. Rather, an Aristotelian constitution is the way citizens are living with one another—as Aristotle puts it, "a constitution is a sort of life of a *polis*" (IV.11 1295a40–b1). There are two ways such a civic life can be described. First, political scientists can describe a constitution by identifying the order [*taxis*] of its specific and diverse offices (III.6 1278b8–10, IV.1 1289a15–16), thereby characterizing the *politeia* insofar as it functions as political system. But, even more fundamentally, Aristotle believes that a constitution is only fully characterized when we explain *why* rulers support a system's being arranged in a given manner, and this requires that political theorists identify who it is that—to put it bluntly—calls the shots in the city. Because this group establishes the basic orientation of the life that citizens are leading with one another, Aristotle declares, in *Politics* III.6, that this *politeuma is* the constitution (1278b11). Thus, if we want to understand the politics of a city as an Aristotelian, the question with which we must begin is not so much What constitution does this city have? but rather the sociological question of *Who* is the constitution here?[2] In particular, if we want to understand democracies and oligarchies, we must understand who the democrats and oligarchs are. After all, "the character peculiar to each constitution usually safeguards it as well as establishes it initially—for example, the democratic character, a democracy; and the oligarchic one, an oligarchy" (VIII.1 1337a14–17).

Though he does not say so explicitly, it seems reasonable to think that Aristotle would have us use this same method for understanding the political conflicts caused by oligarchs and democrats. After all, if grasping their character is crucial for understanding the respective constitutional *orders* that each tends to establish, it seems reasonable to think that understanding their respective characters will be every bit as important for appreciating the unique *disorders* that each group typically inaugurates. The conflicts of democrats and oligarchs, like their respective constitutions, must be addressed using Aristotle's general method of privileging political identity.

Yet here we run into an interpretive problem: as others have complained,[3] it seems that Aristotle is maddeningly confused in his portrayal of democrats and oligarchs and that he cannot make up his mind about who, exactly, they are. The problem is not that Aristotle further divides democrats into subgroups (farmers, craftsmen, businessmen, sailors, laborers, and metics) and distinguishes oligarchs who have only wealth from those who possess wealth, good birth, and education. Rather, the worry is that the fundamental traits he uses to characterize each group as a whole seem different at different points in his investigation; worse still, some of these attributions are putatively inconsistent. As a result, the lessons and conclusions that Aristotle would have the reader take away from his treatment of these deviant actors, and the particular nature of the threat they pose to politics, might also seem confused.

However, even though these are reasonable worries, I believe it is possible to develop an interpretation of democratic and oligarchic identity that clears Aristotle of the charge of inconsistency. By attributing divergent traits to these groups, Aristotle is not changing his mind or contradicting himself as some claim, but he is establishing a theory by which multiple, distinct traits jointly define who these political actors are. I hope to show that, rather than contradicting himself, Aristotle is carefully constructing complex social portraits of these groups in an attempt to describe a major threat to *poleis* of classical Greece: partisanship.

I.1. Three Familiar Traits

Let me begin by describing the relationship among three different traits of democrats and oligarchs that are nearly always mentioned in scholarly accounts of Aristotle's portraits: their numerical size, their economic status, and their respective beliefs about merit.

The first, and most obvious, aspect of democratic and oligarchic identity is numerical. Indeed, the term "oligarchy" is derived from the word "*oligos*," which means few, and the "*demos*," the people who have the *kratos* in a "democracy," are also referred to as the "*plēthoi*," the many or multitude. In *Politics* III.6, it is the numerical attribute of rulers—whether they are "one, few, or many"—that distinguishes different kinds of deviant and correct constitutions. Surely Aristotle uses this trait in his classificatory scheme because, in the world as we happen to find it, this sociological numerical attribute regularly does an adequate job of picking out democrats and oligarchs from other political actors (III.8 1279b34–80a6): walk into an average city and ask to speak to the "many," and you will be greeted by democrats; ask to meet with the "few," and you will probably end up speaking to oligarchs. Therefore, at a minimum, the numerical trait resembles what Aristotle calls a "distinctive property [*idion*]" (*Topics* I.5 102a18–31). In the average political world as we happen to find it, minority/majority status tends to be "reciprocally predicated" of oligarchs/democrats.

Soon after using this attribute in his classification, however, Aristotle makes it abundantly clear that the numerical trait, while usually distinctive, is not central to the social *identity* of these two groups: that is, it does not provide a *relevant* answer to the question Who are these people? He argues for this point in *Politics* III.8 by asking the reader to engage in a thought experiment in which one city is ruled by a rich majority, and another is ruled by a poor minority. The former city, he maintains, should still be called an oligarchy because of the economic status of the rulers: the rulers, though a majority, are best identified by the fact that they are rich; similarly, the latter constitution should be called a democracy because the rulers are poor. In short, when we ask, "Who is the constitution here?" Aristotle apparently believes that the answer "the rich" or "the poor" is more central, while "the few" or "the many" is more peripheral. Of course, *all* of these are still *distinctive* traits in the world as we happen to find it, but the economic status of the individuals seems to be more significant to their identity than their sheer number.

In addition to the numerical trait and the economic trait, Aristotle also says that oligarchs and democrats possess distinctive theories of distributive justice. For even though their conceptions of merit are instances of the universally held notion that a person's desert should be proportional to his worth, they nevertheless have different conceptions of worth. Democrats determine a person's worth based on his free citizenship,[4] and oligarchs measure it by wealth (*NE* V.3 1131a25–29; *Pol.* III.17 1288a19–24; V.1 1301b35–02a2).

Although wealth is more central than number to the identities of democrat and oligarch, I do not think that *either* of these traits reaches the level of being essential; rather, a careful reading of *Politics* III.8 shows that of the three traits discussed so far, only the merit component helps to define these political actors. For although Aristotle says, "What does distinguish democracy and oligarchy from one another is poverty and wealth"—which might sound like a clear endorsement of the centrality of the economic trait for identity—he goes on to finish his thought this way:

> [W]henever some, whether a minority or a majority, rule because of their wealth [*dia plouton*], the constitution is necessarily

[*anagkaion*] an oligarchy, and whenever the poor rule, it is necessarily a democracy. But it turns out, as we said, that the former are in fact few and the latter many. For only a few people are rich, but all share in freedom; and these are the reasons they both dispute [*di' has aitias amphisbētousin*] over the constitution. (1280a1–6)

The numerical trait is obviously being severely downgraded ("whether a minority or majority"). More importantly, we see that the belief about merit is sharply upgraded above that of wealth: notice that it is not the wealth of rulers per se that makes a city an oligarchy, but the fact that the city permits people to rule *because of* [*dia*] it. When citizens hold a belief that wealth *merits* rule, it is this fact about the *politeuma* that makes it necessary [*anagkaion*] to identify it as an oligarchy. Similarly, while it is distinctive of a democracy that it is controlled by the poor, it is the fact that these "all share in freedom" (the object of the democratic belief about merit) that is most central. Wealth and freedom, *not* wealth and poverty, are the "reasons they both dispute over the constitution."

In the last chapter, I quoted a passage that further supports this interpretation. Recall that Aristotle thinks it ridiculous to explain political history by citing uncontrolled acquisitiveness; now note that Aristotle is also ranking a belief about merit over the mere fact of possessing a quantity of goods:

> It is also absurd [*atopon*] to hold that a constitution changes into an oligarchy because the office holders are money lovers and acquirers of wealth, and not because those who are far superior in property holdings *think it unjust* for those who do not own anything to participate equally in the *polis* with those who do. (*Pol.* V.12 1316a39–b3)

Aristotle is stating that mere economic status is not helpful for giving an account of these people as political actors. The fact that they are "far superior in property holdings" will distinguish them in society. But though wealth is a distinctive property—and the fact that a person cannot be both rich and poor (IV.4 1291b7) helps to ensure that it is distinctive—it is not this trait that ultimately discloses the relevant political information about who they are.

Based on these reflections, we can concoct our own thought experiment inspired by *Pol.* III.8. Suppose Aristotle were confronted with a group of people who were poor, who made up the majority of inhabitants, and yet who also firmly believed that wealth entitled a person to rule. Aristotle, I believe, would insist that such people should be called oligarchs. Likewise, if he were presented with a very small group of rich people, who nevertheless insisted that free citizenship was the basis of rule, he would call them democrats. Of these three traits, the belief about merit is the most central aspect of their political identity.[5]

I.2. A Few Problems Solved

In the next section I will go on to argue that there are other, equally important traits besides the merit component that we must attribute to democrats and oligarchs to capture their identity fully. Before investigating these, however, let me pause to show how the central importance of the belief about merit to identity, and the peripheral importance of both wealth and numerical size, helps to clear Aristotle of some of the charges that are leveled against him.

First, Aristotle has been accused of adopting inconsistent descriptions of democrats and oligarchs in *Politics* III.8 and IV.4. It is claimed that in III.8 he makes economic status "essential" and the numerical trait "accidental" but that in IV.4 he turns around and claims that both traits are essential.[6] This charge is misplaced, however, on two counts. First, we have seen that in III.8 *neither* numerical *nor* economic status is essential (though both are distinctive). Second, I take Aristotle in IV.4 to be restating the position of III.8—that a belief about the *basis* of rule, a belief about the *reason* a group has authority to rule, is most crucial for correctly classifying a constitution. In IV.4, he points out that if you find a few well-born people running a city, you should not rush to call it a democracy when you notice that the rulers are also free (1290b7–14). Similarly, the mere fact that rulers are rich does not make the constitution an oligarchy: if they are ruling "*because* [*dia*] they are the multitude" then they are not really oligarchs (90b14–15). Thus, it is best to translate b17–20, where Aristotle draws his conclusion, this way:

> There is a democracy whenever the free have authority over ruling, though they may also be a poor majority, and an oligarchy whenever the rich have authority, though they may also be a well-born minority.[7]

In the world as we find it, the free citizens of a city, taken as a group, will usually be poor and constitute the majority; the rich, on the other hand, will usually be few and well-born. However, even though these "many parts" (90b8) can be found in the rulers of oligarchies and democracies, it is that *because of which* they are ruling—that which bestows *authority* on their rule—that is most relevant. In short, this passage in IV.4 advances the same position as III.8.[8]

But this apparent solution seems to raise another problem. If the conception of merit is an essential trait of their identity, and democrats are defined by the fact that they base merit on free status, how will their majority status not also end up being essential? "If, in accordance with the democratic principle of freedom, office and power are to be distributed equally to all of free birth, then democracies will necessarily involve majority rule. Therefore, if freedom is essential to democracy, there seems to be an essential connection between democracy and the many."[9]

I do not believe that this exposes any contradiction. It is true that Aristotle's democrats must necessarily embrace the notion of rule by the majority: anyone who believes that merit is based on freedom must then embrace "arithmetic" justice and conclude that the majority should rule.[10] But a person *believing* that the majority should rule on the basis of justice is something quite different from that same person *being in* the numerical majority himself, and it is this latter sociological fact that we have been calling the nonessential "numerical trait." So, while it is essential that democrats believe in majority rule, they are only accidentally in the majority.

II. Explaining Intractable Conflict

From these considerations, it should be clear that the interpretation I have offered supports a broadly non-Marxist reading of Aristotle's conception of partisans. Many other scholars have argued that Aristotle is not an economic determinist, and they have carefully documented the various ways in which the Marxist conception of class conflict as a universal explanation of political transformation does not fit well with Aristotle's own political theory.[11] I have argued that economic status is not even a defining trait of who these people are—not even appropriate for a proper description of political actors, let alone adequate for an analysis of how they interact with one another or instigate political change. Indeed, if any interpretation is suggested by what I have said so far, it is that Aristotle's description of everyday political life is best described as *pluralistic*. The distinct groups that inhabit the *poleis* differ from one another in their conceptions of justice.[12] Thus, instead of a

Marxist clash of economic classes, we might think that the conflict between Aristotle's democrats and oligarchs resembles an abstract, legalistic dispute about political frameworks, much like the polite debate that Herodotus describes taking place among Darius, Megabyzus, and Otanes about whether monarchy, oligarchy, or democracy is preferable.[13]

But the pluralistic interpretation of democratic and oligarchic social identity cannot be correct either. However misguided the Marxist interpretation of Aristotle is with respect to a purely economic explanation of political change, it is alive to an important feature of the *Politics* that the pluralistic account ignores. If we carefully attend to the description of conflict between democrats and oligarchs, we find Aristotle describing actions that go far beyond mere debate or even heated disagreement. The *Politics* is littered with a number of shocking descriptions that depict these two groups locked in bitter, unending, and apparently endemic conflict that makes the Marxist notion of ideological conflict seem far more appropriate.[14]

Consider, for example, the fact that oligarchs "now" commonly take the following oath: "I will be hostile to the people and shall plan whatever evil [*kakon*] I can against them" (V.9 1310a9–10). Or consider that a distinctive characteristic of any oligarchic constitution is "to ill-treat the multitude, drive them out of the town, and disperse them" (*Pol.* V.10 1311a13–14) and that of any democracy "to make war [*polemein*] on the notable people, destroying them secretly and openly, and banishing them as plotting against it and obstructive to its rule" (a15–18).

Again, recall Aristotle's hair-raising explanation at the end of IV.11 of the fact that most constitutions are either democracies or oligarchies: if a *polis* does not have a middle class, it is a more or less foregone conclusion that the city will become either a democracy or oligarchy since the poor or rich will always strive to "conduct the constitution to suit themselves" (1296a26). After all, because there are constant civil wars [*staseis*] and violent fights [*machas*] between them, they "establish neither a common constitution nor an equal one, but take their superiority in the constitution as a reward of their victory" (a29–31). The result is that "the middle constitution either never comes into existence or does so rarely and in few places" (a36–38).

Yet, even in the rare event of its creation, a "middle constitution" would not be able to extinguish the antagonism. Aristotle makes many recommendations for incorporating oligarchs and democrats into "mixed" constitutional structures: as I will discuss at some length in the following chapter, he imagines institutions in which some democratic features (e.g. juries selected by lot) are coupled with oligarchic features (e.g. property qualifications for high offices), and he even theorizes a special deliberative tool whereby votes of democrats and oligarchs for a proposal could together be weighed against democratic and oligarchic votes against the proposal. But what he never does is to recommend mixing *character traits within individual citizens*. I see no textual evidence to suggest that the oligarchs who inhabit Aristotle's mixed regimes are psychologically democratized or that his democrats will become in any way sympathetic to oligarchy. To emphasize this point, let me here quote the full passage about the "middle-regime" that I cited in the last chapter:

> And where the multitude of those in the middle outweighs either both of the extremes together, or even only one of them, it is possible to have a stable constitution. For there is no fear that the rich and the poor will conspire together against these, since neither will ever want to serve as slaves to the other; and if they look for a constitution that is more common than this, they will find none. For they would not put up with ruling in turn, because they distrust one another; and an arbitrator is most trusted everywhere, and the middle person is an arbitrator. The better mixed a constitution is, the more stable it is. (*Pol.* IV.12 1296b38–97a7)

The basic strategy being recommended here is *not* to transform the hearts and minds of democrats and oligarchs; there is no suggestion that oligarchs and democrats sit down together and search for intellectual compromise or engage in constructive deliberative dialogue. On the contrary, the "middle" constitution works because it simply *swamps* oligarchs and democrats with middle-class characters. Even though they inhabit the same constitutional order, both the rich and the poor are here treated as unalloyed blocks that simply cannot cooperate, trust one another, or even conspire together. Instead of transforming their identities, Aristotle pins his hopes on introducing an entirely new type of citizen into politics (a multitude of those in the middle) who can act as a buffer between them.[15]

We can make a similar point with regard to the constitution Aristotle claims is the best kind of democracy. We might hope that in the best sort of democracy citizens overcome their differences, learn to work together, and engage in some sort of high-minded cooperation. That, however, is not Aristotle's version. Even in the best democracy the poor and rich remain separate groups; what makes the constitution a better species of democracy is merely that "the poor enjoy no more superiority than the rich" (IV.4 1291b32).

In short, to characterize the conflict between oligarchs and democrats as little more than a negotiable difference on justice seems to turn a blind eye to what we actually find in the *Politics*. What we need is an account that will explain why, exactly, democrats and oligarchs are so ready to launch a violent attack upon one another because of their disagreement over justice. We need an explanation of why democrats and oligarchs remain so opposed to one another even when they find themselves in political structures designed to keep them at bay. While a Marxist reading may be wrong because it overvalues the economic component of identity, the pluralist reading cannot adequately explain the unbridled hostility that shapes the identity of these two groups.

II.1. The Inadequacy of Greed

I do not believe that we can turn to *greed*, understood as a misconceived view of the good caused by unrestrained bodily desire, for an explanation.[16] No doubt, greed often causes problems in political society: Aristotle says "human greed [*ponēria*] is an insatiable thing" (*Pol.* II. 1267b1), and on many occasions he documents how greed leads to political turmoil.[17] But that fact, by itself, does not mean that greed is the *explanans* for democratic and oligarchic enmity, and I believe there are at least three reasons to doubt that Aristotle understood greed as an adequate explanation.

First, a greed-based explanation of antagonism is at odds with Aristotle's explicit declaration in *Politics* V.1 that a feeling of injustice is the major cause for democrats and oligarchs being *stasis*-prone (1301b26–29), and it overlooks the fact that in Aristotle's ornate description of all the triggering events and long-term causes of *stasis* (which I described in the last chapter) greed never appears.[18] Indeed, once again recall Aristotle's charge that the Platonic attempt to trace political conflict to uncontrolled appetite is "absurd" [*atopon*]: such an explanation ignores agents' beliefs about justice. Second, while this greed-based interpretation essentially collapses the distinction between democrat, oligarch, and tyrant, Aristotle seems far more interested in distinguishing these types of people and the respective constitutions they control. Third, and finally, I see no reason to think that greed can adequately explain the level of uniform hostility that Aristotle attributes to these two groups. Greed, one would think, respects no borders, alliances, friendships, or enmities: it only respects getting more for one's own bodily desires. But if it is greed that motivates democrats and oligarchs, then we would expect to find them cooperating just as often as fighting: they would tear each other apart when that was the only way to get more, but they would also band together like pirates when that tactic would benefit them. But, as the oligarchic *oath* to bring evil to democrats dramatically suggests, that is not what we find in the *Politics*.

II.2. Two Emotions, a Distinctive Fallacy, and the Derivation of Despotism

Instead of turning to greed, Aristotle attempts to explain this hostility by two other traits. First, consider Aristotle's descriptions of the rich and poor in *Politics* IV.11 and V.9. Because of the license they were given during an excessively privileged upbringing (IV.11 1295b16–18), oligarchs characteristically suffer from the emotional vice of hubris (b11) or arrogance (b22–23). Likewise, the democrats' poverty and humble origins lead them into habitual malice and envy (b10).

These emotional traits are not presented to the reader for the sake of adding colorful "thickness" to supplement an otherwise "thin" conception of democrats and oligarchs. On the contrary, these emotions play a fundamental role in describing oligarchs and democrats as such—for it is precisely the presence of these emotions in oligarchs and democrats that makes it possible for Aristotle to draw a contrast between them and those in the middle. In *Pol.* IV.11 such middlings are *defined* in terms of their "reasonableness," their pronounced lack of emotional defect, and their correspondingly high aptitude for calm deliberation. If oligarchs are not defined by their arrogance and democrats by their envy, then the impetus for theorizing the middle constitution of IV.11 altogether disappears.

The interpretive benefit of understanding these emotions as central to identity, however, is not only that it motivates the middle constitution: these emotions also provide us with an explanation for the mutual antagonism that seems constantly to bedevil democratic and oligarchic interactions. Here, for example, is Aristotle's description of the sort of relationship that can exist between citizens with these emotional vices:

> This results in a city coming into being that is made up of slaves and masters, rather than free people: the one group full of envy and the other full of arrogance. *Nothing is further removed from a friendship and a community that is political.* For community is

friendly; when people are enemies, they do not wish to share even a journey in common. (*Pol.* IV.11 1295b21–25)

Arrogance and envy help to explain why oligarchs and democrats act more like oil and water than disinterested citizens who simply disagree with one another and could engage in constitutional debate.[19]

These emotional aspects of oligarchic and democratic identity are not portrayed as symptoms that these political actors develop because of their different conceptions of merit. On the contrary, if there is any connection to a trait I have already discussed, it is the (incidental) trait of economic status. *Pol.* IV.11 describes the way in which growing up in opulence or poverty leads to emotional defect. Yet even this causal relationship is precarious, and we find plenty of evidence in the *Politics* that a person's emotions are not straight-forwardly determined by economics.[20] Notice, for example, that in the "city of our prayers" it *is* possible to raise well-off children in a nonoligarchic manner (it just takes virtuous parents, an exceptionally zealous educational system, as well as a few years in the military to set young citizens straight).[21] Again, we find cases where people's economic status changes drastically, but their character remains firmly unchanged: for example, Aristotle claims that there are many workers [*hoi polloi tōn technitōn*] who become rich (III.5 1278a24–25), but this financial success in no way alters his judgment that they should not participate in ruling because they lack ethical virtue.

Just as these emotions cannot be set aside as mere symptoms of how oligarchs and democrats conceive of merit, it also seems that Aristotle does not consider beliefs about merit to be mere verbalizations of how they feel. No doubt being habituated to feel envy and arrogance primes the pump for children to adopt mistaken views at a later stage of their rational development. But Aristotle seems to think that the belief about who deserves what in political life is specifically inculcated by parents during a phase in children's education that suits them for a particular kind of constitution (*Pol.* V.9 1310a12–18). Aristotle complains that most parents do a rather poor job of this: either they superficially believe that raising children for the constitution means preparing them to do whatever pleases the rulers, or they insist on having complete control over their own children's education and end up raising them either without political science or in a way that is too oriented toward private family life (*NE* X.9 1180a18–b7). At any rate, whether done well or poorly, this legislative aspect of upbringing is distinct from emotional habituation. So though emotions and beliefs about merit arise out of the same educational milieu, it is reasonable to think that Aristotle considers these two traits to be distinct.

But in addition to these two traits, we need to add another: Aristotle repeatedly mentions a distinct *conceptual* mistake made only by democrats and oligarchs. This idiosyncratic error is what I will call the "*haplōs*" mistake. In both *Politics* III.9 and V.1, we find the same succinct description of the origin of democratic and oligarchic beliefs: democracy originates from the inference that since people are equal in some *one* way, they are equal, period [*haplōs*]; similarly, oligarchs think that inequality in one respect means inequality in all respects (III.9 1280a7–25; III.13 1283a26–29; V.1 1301a28–33).[22] Here we are being shown that oligarchs and democrats are identifiable not only by the fact that they pick the wrong criterion of worth (respectively wealth and freedom, rather than virtue), but also by their predilection for making a particular invalid inference to reach these conclusions about justice.

This conceptual error is not a corollary or product of any other traits I have discussed so far. First, Aristotle attributes the mistake to the fact that "most people are rather poor judges about their own affairs" (III.9 1280a15–16) instead of saying that it is the result of wealth, group size, conceptions of merit, or emotion. He also points out that mistaking inequality in one respect for inequality absolutely is a general mistake of which inequality in wealth is but an example ("*hoion chrēmasin*" at *Pol.* III.9 1280a23); similarly, equality in freedom is but one trait a person could use to mistake equality in one respect for absolute equality ("*hoion eleutheria*" at 1280a24).[23]

If, then, this conceptual mistake is its own distinct trait, unconnected to beliefs about merit or emotion, why does Aristotle repeatedly insist that democrats and oligarchs are guilty of it? What work is the *haplōs* mistake performing in Aristotle's description of these political actors? I propose that both the *haplōs* mistake and the emotional trait are introduced by Aristotle to explain the attitude that plays such a fundamental role in the classifications of constitutions: being despotic.

Recall that in *Politics* III.7, Aristotle lays out his six-fold classification of constitutions by making use of the numerical distinction among rule by one, few, or many, as well as a distinction between "correct" and "incorrect" rule. The latter distinction is explained in III.6 as follows. If rulers benefit themselves first and foremost, and the community only coincidentally (if at all), then their rule resembles that which a master takes toward his slave and is "incorrect" in a community of equals. On the other hand, if rulers look after themselves coincidently (if at all) and look to the welfare of the community first and foremost, then their rule is political and "correct" among equals. Aristotle claims that both oligarchy and democracy are incorrect constitutions.

Now by classifying these constitutions this way, Aristotle is clearly attributing a *despotic* attitude to both democrats and oligarchs, not what we might think of as a viciously *selfish* attitude.[24] Such selfishness best describes an individual who looks out for himself or herself with disregard for others: by contrast, Aristotle's description in III.6–7 depicts oligarchs and democrats as people who look out for their ruling *group* with a disregard for others outside of it.[25] Rather than call them "selfish," we do better to call them "cliquish." In fact, since they are looking out for a group that is a distinct *part* of the community, rather than the whole of the community, the best term of all is probably "partisan."

Why, however, does Aristotle think that democrats and oligarchs have this proclivity for despotism? He gives no explanation in *Pol.* III.7, and I doubt that Aristotle thought that these actors' respective conceptions of merit could alone justify the charge. After all, a citizen who merely endorses arithmetic justice need not push for a tyranny of majority over minority.[26] Likewise, a person can endorse oligarchic justice without thinking that the rich should take the less fortunate for granted (for example, many university administrators embrace this type of nondespotic oligarchic justice when—keenly aware that some departments generate millions of dollars for the school while others only spend money—they let some departments have more say in university decisions than others). This kind of justice may be misguided or incorrect, but that does not make it *despotic*.

But a rather different story emerges if we also include both the *haplōs* mistake and an emotional defect as traits of partisan identity. Consider the oligarch who begins with the incorrect belief that rule should be proportioned to financial contributions to the city. As I just indicated, we have no reason to accuse such a person of despotism. But now let us imagine that this same person is so wedded to the *haplōs* fallacy that he quite honestly cannot think of a *single* respect in which he and his fellow oligarchs are not better than nonoligarchs. Go on to couple this inability to conceive of equality in *any* respect with an exceptionally strong dose of emotional arrogance. What will be the result? Perhaps this is a case in which an astoundingly large "difference in degree" becomes "a real difference in kind."[27] For when a belief about wealth-based merit is coupled in a person's mind with the *haplōs* mistake and emotional arrogance, surely it becomes likely that he will assume that the group of ruling oligarchs is different *in kind* from those who are not so privileged—and it is the belief that the ruling element is different in kind from the ruled element that would make an attitude resemble that which a master adopts toward a slave (*Pol.* I.5 1254b16–20).

We can construct a similar account to explain why Aristotle attributes a despotic outlook to democrats. Unable to acknowledge a *single* respect in which any citizen is better than another, and feeling extreme envy for anyone who does apparently exhibit something better, Aristotle's democrats end up utterly devoted to majority rule, firmly committed to the belief that whatever the majority believes is better in *kind* than any position held by the minority.

In conclusion, oligarchy and democracy are labeled "incorrect" constitutions in III.7 because oligarchs and democrats have a proclivity for despotism. But to explain *why* they would act this way, we need a complex set of character traits. A mistaken belief about merit is not a sufficient explanation of despotic behavior, even when coupled with emotion. Rather, it is only when these two traits are coupled with the *haplōs* mistake that we have properly accounted for the partisan despotism that defines rule by oligarchs and democrats.

II.3. The Overarching Goal of Partisan Life

We may still worry that this tripartite depiction of the partisan outlook fails to explain adequately the prevalent and entrenched nature of the conflict between democrats and oligarchs. For example, if the belief about merit, the emotion, and the *haplōs* mistake are independent aspects of partisan psychology, why should these be frequently found together? Again, if they are separate, why should it not be relatively easy to dislodge one of the traits and thus quickly "defuse" despotic attitudes? Earlier I characterized the fight between oligarchs and democrats as thoroughly entrenched; but my own account makes it seem as if it should be very easy to create reasonable or moderate oligarchs and democrats.

These are credible worries, except for the fact that the account I have offered so far is incomplete in one crucial respect: according to Aristotle, democrats and oligarchs do not simply base their respective conceptions of *justice* on freedom and wealth, but they also base their conceptions of *happiness* on these as well. This, as we shall see, is an important fact about partisans that makes them far less flexible than a well-intentioned political scientist might hope.

That oligarchs and democrats have different conceptions of happiness is fairly clear. The overarching good for oligarchs is wealth acquisition (*Pol.* V.10 1311a9–11), while the democratic conception of happiness is to do whatever one likes, each living "according to his fancy" (V.9 1310a33). As is widely noted,[28] Aristotle is here identifying an aspect of democratic and oligarchic identity that is distinct from the belief about merit. How these groups think about happiness has to do with their beliefs about the highest human good; how they think about merit concerns their respective conceptions of distributive justice.

Because a conception of happiness is different from a belief about merit, what role does Aristotle take these divergent versions of happiness to play in the political lives of oligarchs and democrats? Suppose Aristotle had never mentioned their respective conceptions of happiness, and we were left only with beliefs about merit, the *haplōs* mistake, and emotional traits to describe them. Since these traits taken together can already explain their despotic attitudes, what aspect of Aristotle's political theory would have been left unexplained? I believe that there are three answers to this question.

First, the fact that democrats and oligarchs have different conceptions of happiness helps to explain the origin and, more importantly, the *persistence* of their different conceptions of merit. It is not clear that adopting a given conception of justice tells us much about a person's conception of happiness, but Aristotle certainly believes that knowing a person's conception of happiness helps to explain her conception of justice. Consider, for example, the following claim about democrats: "In this way the [goal of living as one likes] contributes to freedom based on equality" (*Pol.* VI.2 1317b16–17). Note the direction of the causality: a conception of justice does not lead one to live as one likes; rather, living as one likes leads one to the democratic conception of justice. Telling the reader about the respective conceptions of happiness is a way of explaining why oligarchs and democrats have the conception of merit that they do; conceptions about merit emerge from broader beliefs about who is flourishing as a human being.

Second, these conceptions of happiness act as a final cause, a *telos*, for *all* aspects of citizens' life together. Conceptions of justice influence decisions about who gets which honors and offices, and how rectificatory disputes should be resolved, but conceptions of happiness govern a far wider class of political considerations. For example, to which activities should citizens devote their leisure? In what pursuits should young citizens be educated? At which target should political deliberators aim their policies? As is clear from his description of the ideal city described in the books traditionally labeled as VII and VIII[29] and his repeated criticisms of the Spartan constitution, which aims at little more than victory in war, Aristotle believes that different conceptions of happiness lead to better or worse answers to these overarching political questions that fall beyond the concerns of justice. Democrats and oligarchs are not merely advancing divergent policy positions on a narrowly defined subject, but they are embracing entirely different outlooks about the basic orientation of the *polis*.

The third point is the most important for my project in this chapter: Aristotle wants the reader to recognize that democrats and oligarchs are aiming for an ultimate goal that can provide no *internal* constraints on, or checks against, their behavior. If someone takes virtue as a goal, she is aiming at something that is a mean; striving to engage in virtuous activity requires attention to limits, boundaries, and avoiding excess (*NE* II.6). The same, however, will not be true of an oligarch. If a person takes wealth acquisition as the highest goal a human being can have, it will be difficult indeed to convince him that he should refrain from promoting some shameful, provocative, or even unjust action that would vastly increase the city's fortune. But, perhaps even more worryingly, it will be impossible to convince him that the city has ever reached the point of being sufficiently rich—that a specific goal had been attained and that the pursuit for increasing wealth could stop.

I believe Aristotle has basically the same worry about democrats: if freedom is the highest goal, it will be difficult to recommend a course of action that makes any imposition on the majority, even if the majority is running afoul of legitimate norms and reasonable requests. Again, the majority will never be convinced that their goal of freedom has been reached—that the bonds and constraints for each and every whim have been sufficiently removed.

As political actors operating under such a limitless conception of happiness, we might thus compare democrats and oligarchs to drivers who can always find new reasons to give the car more gas, but can acknowledge fewer and fewer reasons to step on the brake.[30] In either case, the result is that the partisan political car is doomed to meet a curve at too great a speed. It is thus no surprise that a major theme of the middle books of the *Politics* is that unchecked democrats and oligarchs will always run their constitutions off the road. In the purist sort of democracy (IV.4 1292a4–30), the multitude alone dominates deliberation and lawsuits, all offices that could check the many are gutted, decrees [*psēphismata*] and demagogues proliferate, and the resulting mess and disorder does not even deserve the name "constitution" (a31). The situation is no better in the purist oligarchy where only the richest of rich have power; law disappears, and the regime solidifies into a tyrannical "dynasty" (IV.5 1292b10).

Such troubles are not caused by anything peripheral to partisan identity, but are rather the result of trying to make the constitution embody a democratic or oligarchic conception of happiness. Aristotle is quite adamant about this: the democrats who think that democratic virtue (i.e. freedom) is the only virtue (i.e., the highest good, happiness) and the oligarchs who take oligarchic virtue (i.e., wealth) to be the only virtue are the ones who "push the constitution to extremes" (V.9 1309b22). This also explains why the heart of Aristotle's advice to oligarchic and democratic partisans is that they abandon the attempt to make their constitutions as wealthy or as free as possible and instead act more strategically to do "the things that will enable [them] to *govern* oligarchically and . . . have a democratic constitution" (1310a21–22; cf. VI.5 1319b33–20a4).

Notice, however, that this will be easier said than done; Aristotle is making a recommendation that *cuts against* the course democrats or oligarchs will want to take *qua* democrats and oligarchs. He is recommending that they act strategically *despite themselves*.[31] This is why Aristotle thinks there are no good democracies or oligarchies, but only types that are less bad (IV.2 1289b5–11), and it explains why Aristotle takes the most lawful forms of democracy and oligarchy (which Aristotle thinks are the better forms of these constitutions—*Pol.* IV.4 1291b30–92a4, IV.5 1292b4–7) to be those that do the best job of isolating their respective democrats and oligarchs. Aristotle's statement in VI.5 that legislators "should not consider something to be democratic or oligarchic because it will make the city as democratic or oligarchic as possible, but because it will make it so for the longest time" (1320a2–4) reiterates the same theme: if you want a successful democracy or oligarchy, make sure that the answer to the question Who is the constitution here? is *not* simply "democrats" or "oligarchs."

While oligarchs and democrats have profoundly different conceptions of happiness, the role of happiness in their lives has similar effects for their social and political identity: it enforces their sense of justice, guides their wishes for citywide policy making, and sets them down a destructive deliberative path that *always* concludes with a recommendation for more wealth or more freedom.

III. Partisanship as Discriminatory Elitism

What picture emerges from these diverse considerations? Who are Aristotle's democrats and oligarchs? Over the course of this chapter, I have argued against several ways of answering this question. They are not Marxists class warriors: constitutional conflict and change are not determined by economics, and economic status per se is merely incidental to their political identity. Again, they are not political pluralists with different conceptions of justice: democrats and oligarchs are committed to, and entrenched within, their position in such a way that the conflict between them is something deeper than quasilegal disagreement. Finally, they are not selfish and greedy Platonic tyrants who are slaves to uncontrolled appetites.

I have argued that any sketch of Aristotle's partisans must include four distinct traits that, taken together, can serve as an *explanans* for the *explananda* of partisan despotism and destructiveness. Democrats and oligarchs have incorrect conceptions of merit, are plagued with specific emotional defects, are habituated to the "*haplōs*" mistake, and aim at a *summum bonum* that entrenches these traits and involves no mean. So what sort of person is Aristotle is trying to describe by pinpointing these specific traits?

III.1. A New Brand of Elitism

For the sake of comparison and contrast, consider the figure of Cylon who reportedly took an Olympic victory as a reason to aim at becoming tyrant of Athens in 632 BC.[32] Here we have someone who is guilty of a particular kind of political fallacy: he begins with his success in one realm of activity—his superior ranking in the realm of sport—and then incorrectly infers that higher standing in this nonpolitical realm should translate into increased importance in politics. Now elitism in general is simply the idea that a special group (the elites) deserves increased power and privilege in political life. But the fallacy of Cylon is to engage in a special sort of *discriminatory* elitism in which one sets oneself above others in the political arena because of one's higher ranking in a realm that has little to do with politics.[33]

I propose that Aristotle constructs democratic and oligarchic identities from the four specific characterological and intellectual properties discussed in this chapter because he conceives of partisans as leading Cylonesque lives. First, both groups have a conception of human flourishing that blinds them to the fact that the realm of politics, properly speaking, exists to serve virtue—a good that is *different in kind* from those sought in the realms of finance and personal freedom.[34] The oligarch takes his success in matters of wealth acquisition to mean that he is an excellent human being, since for him this is virtue. And the democrat, too, takes his ability to do whatever he wants to mean that he has achieved the pinnacle of human success. As we have seen, these mistaken *telē* then lead to, and enforce, an equally mistaken conception of civic goals and political merit. Thus, both oligarchs and democrats, much like Cylon, end up mistakenly transposing the very high value they possess in realms defined by nonvirtuous goods, into the realm of politics, where superiority is properly merited by virtue.

In fact, because Aristotle also defines oligarchic and democratic identity in terms of emotion and the *haplōs* mistake, he paints them as exhibiting a brand of discriminatory elitism that is, in one way, even more extreme than that exhibited by Cylon. The *haplōs* mistake leads oligarchs from the premise of their inequality in wealth to the conclusion that no one could conceivably be their equal in *any* realm; it is as if Cylon were to take his inequality in athletic prowess to entail his superiority in everything from sailing, to philosophy, to political decision making. Oligarchic arrogance then intensifies this elitism, and oligarchic happiness gives these partisans reasons to act without constraint. Similarly, Aristotle's democrats entrench themselves in the view that no one could possibly be better than the multitude. The *haplōs* mistake leads democrats from the premise of their equality in freedom to the conclusion that no one could conceivably be better than the majority in *any* realm. Their sense of envy toward anyone who appeared better would then only enforce this view, and their conception of happiness steers them down this road without any hesitancy. Indeed, according to Aristotle, in democracies at their most democratic, "the people become a monarch" (*Pol.* IV.4 1292a11) and, in particular, "the analog of tyranny among the monarchies" (a17–18) because they "act like masters toward the better people" (a19, cf. V.11 1313b32–39).

If oligarchs and democrats engage in this kind of *categorical* discriminatory elitism, these partisans are a rather reprehensible lot. Indeed, Aristotle's partisans seem so obdurately irresponsible that we can think of them as caricatures: for no matter how starkly opposed democrat was to oligarch in the tumultuous fifth century, the identities and relationships of these partisan groups in the fourth century, while no doubt chilly and problematic, were certainly more complex than Aristotle's stereotypes suggest.[35]

Because these elaborate sketches do not seem to be carefully rendered historical portraits, one cannot help but think that Aristotle is crafting these identities in the service of a theory. A final observation gives us some indication what that theory might be. Insofar as they are discriminatory elitists, both democrats and oligarchs resemble Cylon, and insofar as they are categorical in their discrimination, somewhat worse. Nevertheless, these partisans possess an important quality that Cylon lacks: "The dispute [over who should rule] must be based on the things from which a *polis* is constituted. Hence the well-born, the free, and the rich reasonably lay claim to office" (*Pol.* III.12 1283a14–17). The reader is supposed to understand this claim in both a normative and descriptive sense: not only would a group basing its claims upon complexion, height, or running speed (1282b27–30, 83a9–14) lack legitimacy in a bid for power, but, as a matter of fact, such a faction is simply irrelevant for political description and analysis.[36] So while free democrats and rich oligarchs can be party to civic dispute, figures like Cylon cannot.

Why does Aristotle stipulate that only functionally efficacious political groups can enter into fights for political control? Why couldn't a deluded would-be monarch crash into the politics of a city and enter the "dispute"? He does not explain his comment, but it could well be that Aristotle is here tacitly suggesting that, in fourth-century Greece, only political groups who could provide widely recognized, credible evidence for their claim to rule have a chance to survive.

Cylon believed that what Athens most needed was rule by one strong man—and, in archaic Greece, this view may have been widely shared (III.15 1286b8–22). What is striking about Cylon, however, is that he also seems to have genuinely believed that his Olympic victory justified the conclusion that he, in particular, should be that strong man. Perhaps Cylon's murder shows that this sort of justification was already losing force in the seventh century. At any rate, I suspect that Aristotle believed it was impossible by the fourth: the Classical Greek political milieu could no longer fathom random actors like Cylon seizing power on the basis of a beauty contest or horse race; such people could no longer "reasonably lay claim" to power.

Therefore, Aristotle's categorical, discriminatory elitism has a distinctive feature: instead of being grounded in unpredictable events and erratic, solitary aristocrats, it is anchored upon predictable and foreseeable political phenomena. Both oligarchs and democrats desire to see a certain sort of person rule because of a *plausible* (though mistaken) conception of the human good (these conceptions, after all, are ethical *endoxa*). While their emotions are politically problematic, these feelings are the result of very *typical* and *common* types of upbringing in different economic strata. And while it is true that Aristotle's partisans commit the *haplōs* fallacy, it is also the case that this is a mistake that could readily be made by many people. Finally, and most importantly for the contrast with Cylon, the erroneous partisan conception of justice, which dictates to the rich and poor that they themselves deserve to rule, is nevertheless supported by a constant stream of evidence. Cities really do require wealthy citizens (*Pol.* III.12 1283a17–18, IV.4 1291a33–34, VII.8 1328b10–11, VII.9 1329a17–19), and thus oligarchs are always positioned to launch a plausible (though weak) argument about the merits of the rich. Democrats, too, will always have available material that they can use to build their (admittedly weak) case: there really is "truth" (III.11 1281a42) in the claim that a multitude can make some sort of contribution to the quality of civic authority; large numbers of men are in fact necessary for military strength (VII.6 1327a40–b15); and every kind of citizen wishes to avoid being a slave and thus wishes to be free. Instead of emerging from somewhat ridiculous actors like Cylon, Aristotle's fourth-century brand of discriminatory elitism is now backed by a certain level of rationality and thus worthy of being theorized in terms of principles of political science.[37]

These theoretical political actors are not hopelessly arrayed against one another because of insatiable greed, blinkered class ideology, or selfishness. Their fight stems from divergent beliefs about human happiness and distributive justice, which are bolstered by actual political conditions. Moreover, we have seen that these divergent beliefs lead to something worse than disagreement because their misconceptions are galvanized by intellectual and character flaws, and their conceptions of the highest good fail to provide any reasons for restraint.

The result is that Aristotle's oligarchs and democrats are unique actors who assume that the entire swath of the adult population outside of their partisan clique is incapable of offering the right kind of answers to pressing problems. Convinced that they are saviors of the city, and confronted with constant evidence that supports their view, emotional partisans will fight unstintingly to ensure that the types of people they deem to be inferior are pushed out of the *politeuma*.

III.2. The Incompatibility of Partisanship and the Best Sort of City

With a full account of who the partisans are, we can appreciate why Aristotle was convinced that they are perpetually hostile and particularly prone to engage in civil war. Recall that among the long-term causal factors that nurse a *stasis*-enabling sense of injustice, we find the following sorts of spectacles:

witnessing unfair allocations of profit or honor, seeing arrogant behavior in officials, and feeling a sense of fear of, superiority to, or contempt for those in charge. If we take a moment to imagine an oligarch living in a democracy, or contemplate the probable observations of a democrat living in an oligarchy, it is clear that *all* of these long-term causes of *stasis* would take place on a regular basis.

Moreover, we see that Aristotle has portrayed these partisans in a way that implies that they will not only push for civil war when they find themselves in a city ruled by opposing partisans; they will also conclude that a city devoted to virtue is unfair. Their limitless conceptions of happiness, their misguided views on justice, their inappropriate emotions, and their proclivity for the *haplōs* mistake will prime these partisans for *stasis* in even ideal conditions.

It is thus no coincidence that neither oligarchs nor democrats are depicted as citizens in books VII and VIII of the *Politics*. For it is here that Aristotle attempts to describe a *polis* that is the best for which one could hope: with excellent resources, virtuous citizens, and well-planned and thought-out laws, this city is supposed to exhibit how good political life could be if only it were shorn of the all the typical shortcomings, unlucky breaks, and limited starting points that hobble average cities. Given his analysis of democratic and oligarchic characters, we can understand why Aristotle takes the presence of partisans to be the sort of problem from which the best *poleis* should be spared.

Chapter 3

Managing Mistrust in Average Cities

Stasis is a catastrophe for any city. Whether conducted with force or fraud, it is undertaken with social enmity, destabilizes the life patterns of a city, and takes place in an environment that is antithetical to human flourishing. That said, there could be times when such destruction is justified. All things considered, it may be best for a city to undergo *stasis* if it has been horribly governed by corrupt leaders, and Aristotle believes that virtuous people should be ready to engage in civil war if (though quite unlikely) that is the course prudence demands (*Pol.* V.1 1301a39–40).

But however appropriate it may be for a city gone awry, *stasis* will not take place in the very best kind of political environment. Indeed, in a "city of our prayers"—a city without any of the typical shortcomings in natural, educational, or social resources—it would even be difficult to find the short- or long-term causes of civil war at work. Citizens in such an untroubled community will have no reason to think that the basic civic order is unjust, for they will never have witnessed any of the spectacles that, as I argued in the first chapter, Aristotle takes to inspire such suspicion. They will not have witnessed officials acting arrogantly, nor will they hold rulers in contempt. Again, these citizens will not have seen honor or money distributed inappropriately, will not think that some citizens possess threatening levels of superiority, and will not live in fear of arbitrary punishment. In short, the best sort of city is well-run, and, just as importantly, it houses virtuous citizens who have the psychological repertoire to recognize and appreciate a well-run city.

Average cities, by contrast, are not so fortunate. The difficulty is not only that, from an abstract, metacivic perspective, we would expect a "dispute" [*amphisbētēsis*] (*Pol.* III.13 1283b3) among all the different groups typically present in a city—"for example, the good, the rich, the well-born, and a political multitude" (b1–3)—about who should rule. In addition to such debates about who deserves to rule, which can easily lead to perceptions that a given constitution is unjust, average cities will also be hobbled by conditions of scarcity and other kinds of imperfection. Defective rulers will frequently offer fodder for disappointment even among those who are otherwise supportive of the constitution, offices will not be governed optimally, and other citizens will have many different kinds of shortcomings. So, even if a given average city is not engulfed in all-out civil war, there will be flaws among rulers and ruled alike with the potential to agitate inhabitants and set the stage for *stasis*. In this chapter, I wish to examine the contours of this stage and explore how Aristotle conceives of the discontent that haunts flawed, yet *stasis*-free, cities.

Not surprisingly, the obdurate, partisan animosity that motivates democrats and oligarchs features prominently in the following account. As I argued in the last chapter, their respective psychologies not only ensure that they will be upset with any constitution ruled by opposing partisans, but make it likely that they will also be disgruntled in even well-run *poleis*. Partisans will mistakenly believe correct rule to be arrogant, will see distributions that reward excellence as unfair, will find magnanimous citizens threatening, and will feel both fear and contempt for those who rule virtuously.

But Aristotle's tricausal account of *stasis* allows us to see how this predictable partisan discontent is only one part of a far broader and more diverse geography of political dissatisfaction. Different combinations of the seven long-term causes of *stasis* can cause unhappiness among inhabitants who are neither democrats nor oligarchs, and (as I will argue) even the discontent of partisans can take different forms depending on the specifics of the political environment.

Moreover, whenever the inhabitants of a particular regime disapprove of the constitution in which they live, it isn't as if the rulers will always remain oblivious to, or dismissive of, these frustrations. On the contrary, rulers can adopt tactics to dampen disaffection and do their best to make civil war less likely. Thus, when we imagine a *stasis*-free city in which the long-term causes of *stasis* are nevertheless present, we should not focus exclusively upon the motivations of restless inhabitants, but we also need to step back and take stock of the uneasy tension that will emerge between rulers and those unhappy with them. In each case, we should document the displeasures of those who would take issue with a given constitution but then go beyond this diagnosis and explore ways others in the constitution might respond. This approach will allow us to appreciate Aristotle's full conception of pre*stasis* political conflict—a type of conflict I will call "managed mistrust."

As I read him, Aristotle thinks of managed mistrust as exhibiting three basic patterns.[1] First, there is a distinctive brand of mistrustfulness that arises in both kingships and tyrannies and that, in turn, recommends a characteristic response; the managed mistrust haunting rule by one constitution has a definite shape and danger. Second, though the constitutions of democracy and oligarchy are quite different from one another, Aristotle believes these constitutions inspire remarkably similar kinds of mistrust and call for many of the same tactical palliatives. So, not only are the internal psychological repertoires of both rich and poor partisans similarly structured (as I argued in the last chapter), but in this chapter, we will see that Aristotle views the intra*polis* challenges faced by partisans to be similar as well. Third, and finally, Aristotle offers a celebrated candidate for a constitution that would, all things considered, best handle the conditions faced by rulers in most political environments. Aristotle calls his candidate the "mixed constitution," and the mistrust generated by this type of rule is as distinctive as Aristotle's favored tactic for managing it.

I. The Challenges of Rule by One

When a single human being has complete control over civic authority, the politics of the community takes on a certain pattern: whether the ruler is average, vicious, or even divinely virtuous, political rule has an agreed-upon focal point. Indeed, it is the simplicity of monarchy that will probably always attract praise from those who tire of the inefficiencies, frustrations, and disappointments that arise when many people are involved in political decision making.

But however appealing the elegant simplicity of monarchy may be, this feature does not spare it from threats and problems—even when the single ruler is supremely virtuous. Indeed, Aristotle believes that monarchy is effectively doomed as a form of political rule because it will always generate near-unmanageable levels of mistrust.

I.1. *The Congenital Defects of Rule by One*

Technically, according to Aristotle's division of constitutions into six types, there are two forms of monarchy. Correct rule by one is kingship, while incorrect rule by one is tyranny. But we should note that Aristotle isn't entirely comfortable calling tyranny a "constitution"—"it is least of all a constitution" (IV.8 1293b29)—since in the *Politics* he time and again portrays this type of government as being nothing more than a vicious human being using everyone and everything in the city for his personal pleasure and profit.[2] Indeed, even that dour description leaves out the unpalatable detail that a tyrant is almost always someone who has come to power by tricking fellow citizens into trusting him and who then has later turned his back on those who brought him into power (V.10 1310b14–16).[3] Characterized thus, tyrants are not only abusive and predatory: they are often where they are through deception.

Against this backdrop, it is hardly surprising to learn that tyrannies are among the least stable of constitutions (V.12 1315b11–12). Those who live under a tyrant will almost certainly believe that the regime is unjust, for many of the long-term causes of *stasis* will appear as constant features of their lives. Inhabitants will continually see the tyrant acting arrogantly, they will always feel afraid that the tyrant could seize them or punish them at any moment, and they will persistently feel contempt for the fact that someone so treacherous and unworthy could have so much power (V.10). With the unceasing influence of these three long-term causes of *stasis* at work, the tyrant will always find himself ruling over a toxic brew of mistrust, which very easily can break out into active rebellion.

Aristotle does not, however, trace all the troubles facing tyrants back to their lack of virtue. On the contrary, even if a city were ruled by a totally virtuous individual, there would still be three *structural* problems causing inhabitants to feel worried about their regime. No doubt virtuous kings reliably run their cities in such a way that these congenital defects are minimized, and tyrants predictably exacerbate such flaws. But, in either case, Aristotle believes there to be problems endemic to monarchy per se that will have to be addressed by whoever rules.

First, consider Aristotle's insistence in *Politics* VII.4 that the best sort of city needs to be limited in size. One reason cities need to be small is technological: the words of orators can only reach so many people, and thus there is an upper bound on the number of people who can participate in an assembly. But the more important reason Aristotle gives in this chapter for limiting the size of the best sort of city is that citizens will want to be familiar with the character of those to whom they entrust political authority: for they not only desire rulers who agree with them about this or that issue, but they want rulers in whom they can place their trust. Yet getting to know people's character takes a lot of time, and it also requires seeing how people handle themselves in different kinds of situations. These basic facts of city life thus generate a structural problem for any large city: when it reaches a certain size, many citizens will find themselves turning power over to people whom they do not know very well. Aristotle's concern with such a lack of familiarity in VII.4 is surely not merely that power might fall into the hands of someone vicious (that is well-nigh impossible given that this is a "city of our prayers") but also that this arrangement unsettles the natural and rational desire of citizens to understand those who will rule over them.

This idea, I propose, motivates one of Aristotle's fundamental structural worries about monarchy: when either a king or tyrant rules, all of this natural curiosity ends up being focused on a lone human being, and this results in every aspect of his life being noticed, recorded, and considered. We can detect this apprehension in the specific recommendations Aristotle offers to tyrants in *Pol.* V.11. He advises them to behave more like kings because the inhabitants of the city will be paying careful attention to how lavish their lives are, whether they seem dignified or not, whether they seem capable of fighting or not, whether they are appreciative of beauty or not, how zealous about the gods they are, not to mention whether their achievements are as impressive and important as those of other inhabitants! This advice is quite striking in two respects. On the one hand, it suggests that Aristotle thinks of monarchs—no matter how virtuous—as living under the concentrated and constant scrutiny of all the other members of the *polis*. He is here advising tyrants to behave as kings because he believes they will be scrutinized in the same ways as, and to the same degree as, kings are scrutinized. On the other hand, this advice is noteworthy because Aristotle never offers similar advice to the rulers of other kinds of constitution. For example, he never advises oligarchs to "appear very zealous about the gods" and never asks poor democrats to forgo debauchery for the sake of appearing respectable. Kings and tyrants seem subject to a heightened level of inspection that exceeds that experienced by rulers in other constitutions.

Of course, this "spotlight problem" (as I will refer to it) can be easily mitigated if a monarch happens to possess superhuman levels of virtue or if the inhabitants of a city are so lowly, and think so little of themselves, that no shortcoming or mistake of the monarch would be noticed. But average cities do not feature such extreme conditions, so fallible monarchs will find themselves walking upon a political tightrope with all the fallible inhabitants noticing every hesitation, slip, or awkward step.

Being in the political spotlight is all the more perilous because of the second great problem faced by monarchs—what I will call the "degree/kind" problem. Aristotle treats ruling and being ruled as activities that differ in *kind*, and so he thinks of the rulers and ruled as exercising different virtues (III.4 1277b7–16). Successfully ruling over human beings requires skills that need not be exercised by those who are merely ruled. Moreover, these skills of ruling are not the developed capacities of a contingent and obscure craft: on the contrary, Aristotle christens the developed capacities of political rulers as being among the core virtues of practical reason. He claims that if you are ruling, then you are exercising distinctively human virtue: "Bias seems to have been correct in saying that ruling will reveal the man" (*NE* V.1 1130a1–2). He also believes that if you are fully exercising practical reason, then you are ruling: "[P]ractical wisdom is the only virtue peculiar to a ruler" (*Pol.* III.4 1277b25–26). Ruling is thus a very great good, a highest good that can make a human life flourish.

But because ruling is such a great good, human beings in political community will inevitably form opinions about who deserves to rule and be ruled. After all, though there may be different conceptions of merit, everyone believes that the amount of a good given to a person should be proportional to her merit (*NE* V.3 1131a25–26). So, whatever their views on merit may be, all members of a community will agree that someone who receives a preeminent good like total and complete authority in politics should also possess a level of preeminent merit.

But it is on exactly this point that monarchs will face an intractable problem. In most real-world cities, will most inhabitants believe that the monarch has such outstanding merit that he deserves a *permanent* lock on *all* political authority? Will most inhabitants of a city believe that only the monarch deserves the very high honor of exercising civic rationality *tout court?* Aristotle consistently uses the word "contempt" [*kataphronēsis*] to describe how the inhabitants of a city regard a person who is not worthy of the position he holds—and I am confident that Aristotle thinks that most inhabitants of average cities, at least in fourth-century Greece, would hold *any* monarch in contempt.

This is not because monarchs are always vicious tyrants. On the contrary, let us suppose that a given king not only possesses virtue but even that he possesses the *most* virtue of any person in the city. Even so, if all the other inhabitants of the city are themselves to some extent virtuous, then they will consider the superiority of the king to be only a matter of degree—not a difference in kind that would justify a permanent lock on power. This, according to Aristotle, was the very situation in ancient Greece that led to the demise of monarchy, since "many people who were similar in virtue . . . no longer put up [with kingship], but sought something communal and established a constitution" (*Pol.* III.15 1286b11–13). It seems, too, that a king cannot avoid this problem. When we read through the list of arguments that Aristotle says are commonly made against kings, we find that kings will have to surround themselves with virtuous advisors (*Pol.* III.16 1287b8–9); but by needing such advice, the king betrays that he is a ruler who possesses total authority but lacks faculties that are better in kind. Worse still, consider the plight of a truly virtuous king who rules over a city filled with the usual blend of mildly virtuous citizens, the poor, the rich, and some in between. In this situation, the amount of contempt among inhabitants will increase dramatically. For rich and poor partisans have conceptions of merit that will not even track the virtue of the king. Yet this imagined situation is still a best-case scenario—we are here assuming rule by an upstanding and virtuous king. There will be that much more contempt among the ruled if it turns out that the king is less virtuous than other citizens.

This line of thought brings us to the last great structural problem of rule by one: in addition to the spotlight and the degree/kind problems, Aristotle believes that anyone in this unique position will probably govern in a way that will strike other inhabitants as arrogant and fearsome. Obviously, if a given monarch is implacably vicious, this would be an expected result. But we can infer from Aristotle's discussion in *Pol.* III.15–16 that even upstanding kings will be viewed this way, especially if they find themselves with limited or diminishing influence over their communities.

First, note that it is when Aristotle is reporting upon the common criticisms made of absolute kingship (*not* tyranny) that he claims that "someone who asks a human being [to rule] asks a wild beast as well" (III.16 1287a30). Similarly, it is when Aristotle is discussing rule by the best man (not the worst) that he repeats the argument that "a large quantity is more incorruptible" (III.15 1286a31–32). Aristotle is here repeating the kind of worries that are expressed about even good monarchs—worries that betray a typical, low-level fear of what any given monarch may do.

Second, to preserve law and order, a king will inevitably take actions that will make him seem arrogant. On the one hand, every monarch—virtuous kings included—will need to have bodyguards who can impose order: "For even if he was exercising authority in accord with the law, and never acted in accordance with his own wishes contrary to the law, it would still be necessary for him to have some power with which to protect the laws" (III.15 1286b31–33). Unfortunately, though this is a step all monarchs must take, being surrounded with bodyguards plays into traditional stereotypes about those who use force for unjust compulsion. Indeed, this is why Aristotle recommends that the force should be "stronger than an individual, whether by himself or together with many, but weaker than the multitude" (b35–37)—for Aristotle is keenly aware that bodyguards will remind people of tyrannies. Furthermore, such stereotypes will only be reinforced when the king announces how rule will be preserved in the long term. Aristotle says that it "demands greater virtue than human nature allows" (b27) for a king to hand over his monarchy to someone other than his children—and he writes this knowing full well that kingship based on lineage generates contempt and strikes people as arrogant (V.10 1313a10–14). For these reasons, all human kings will strike the ruled as arrogant to some degree.

Taken together, these three structural problems of rule by one show it to be an incredibly difficult type of political organization to run effectively. All of the monarch's behaviors take place under the spotlight of the public's constant attention; many inhabitants will hold the king in contempt because they will see that his kind of absolute power is not merited by his degree of virtue; and many of those he rules will find him arrogant and worthy of fear. No wonder Aristotle has such pessimism about kingship among his contemporaries:

> [K]ingship is rule over willing subjects and has authority over important matters. But nowadays there are numerous men of equal quality, although none so outstanding as to measure up to the magnitude and dignity of the office [of king]. Hence people are unwilling to put up with this sort of rule. And if someone comes to exercise it, whether through force or deceit, this is immediately held to be tyranny. (V.10 1313a5–10)

Note that no matter how objectively virtuous a given monarch may be, people "nowadays" will *perceive* him to be a tyrant rather than a king. All three structural problems are here at work to explain why this would be so. In a world where there are a number of people of (relatively equal) quality watching his every move, whatever degree of superiority the monarch may possess will not justify the kind of imperial authority residing in "the magnitude and dignity" of the office of king. As a result, if anyone—even someone of objectively great virtue—attempted to exercise such an office, it would be "immediately held to be tyranny" and cause trepidation. Deserved or not, the very form of governance of rule by one produces a shroud of pessimistic distrust among the ruled.

I.2. Mitigating the Problems of Rule by One

Can anything be done to compensate for these endemic defects? In the last quotation, and at other places in the *Politics* (e.g. III.15 1286b8–22), Aristotle suggests that contemporary conditions of fourth-century Greece make monarchy virtually impossible. Nevertheless, even though this is an incredibly precarious form of rule, Aristotle identifies steps that monarchs might take to manage the mistrust they will inevitably confront. Though the specific tactics he recommends are many, I think we can interpret them as being offered in the service of two general strategies.

The first major strategy offered by Aristotle is rather simple: monarchs must accept that the public is constantly forming judgments about their character and then work to make a point of appearing moderate to shape these impressions. For a virtuous king, such stagecraft would surely not require any great effort, and for a tyrant, this will take a great deal of effort and "spin." But in either case, Aristotle's point is the same: a person possessing total control of a city should make an effort to strike everyone as a moderate character who rules moderately.

This recommendation to appear moderate might strike us as stale pabulum, and surely little insight is needed to realize that avoiding debauchery and extreme displays of arrogance might help a monarch with public relations. But there is more to Aristotle's moderation strategy than this. In *Pol.* V.11, where Aristotle recommends the strategy, he clearly takes himself to be describing the path less frequently taken, and he hopes that his moderation strategy will be contrasted with the way most rulers respond to mistrust. Most monarchs simply *ignore* the perceptions of the ruled and instead devote all their energy to discovering ways of depriving people of the material and psychological means by which they could act upon their misgivings. Aristotle also thinks that many monarchs make the mistake of stabilizing their rule by decisively casting their lot with only one of the major sociological groups of the city, making common cause, say, with the poor, or taking the side of the rich, or bonding with the noble elite of old families. By contrast, by taking a moderate path, the king will lead all these groups to believe that he is someone with whom they have some sort of tie and is someone concerned for their safety (V.11 1315a3–40, b4–7). This, I suppose, is another reason Aristotle advises monarchs to be seen appreciating honor, beauty, and military service: such perceptions show the monarch to be looking out for higher things than the narrow interests of this or that partisan clique.[4]

The second major strategic recommendation Aristotle offers monarchs is to limit the areas over which they attempt to exercise control. In other words, monarchs can mitigate mistrust by consistently recognizing boundaries and then ruling in such a way that these boundaries are taken seriously and not violated. His theory seems to be that this is the best mechanism for thwarting perceptions that one is arrogant (and hubristic) because observing boundaries makes the ruler seem more like a steward rather than a looter (1315a41–b2). After all, a ruler who recognizes boundaries is also cognizant that there are settled norms by which those in the community are leading their lives. Moreover, Aristotle says that kings who restrict themselves to traditional realms will be perceived as "more equal in their characters" (1313a22–23), and by this he means that the monarch will be seen as less masterly and more like every other citizen who is expected to stay within limits.

Aristotle goes on in V.11 to recommend a number of specific tactics monarchs can employ in service of this boundary-keeping strategy. Monarchs should avoid taking people's property (either by direct seizure or high taxation). They must refrain from publicly dishonoring people (for example, by using humiliating punishments or by engaging in sexual exploitation). They should show they are following accepted norms in how public money is spent (offering a public accounting of funds received, showing that taxes are used effectively, etc.). By adhering to these property boundaries, cultural boundaries, and public boundaries, a monarch decreases the perception that he is arrogant or worthy of fear.

II. The Problems of Partisan Rule

Simply put, democracy is incorrect rule of the many, and oligarchy is incorrect rule of the few. However, as we saw in the last chapter, Aristotle offers an elaborate personality profile of the democrats and oligarchs who rule such constitutions, and he portrays them as having diametrically opposed views and character traits. Indeed, his portrait of these partisans is so stark, and the contrasts he draws between the rich and poor are so perfectly mirrored, that it is not unreasonable to worry that Aristotle allows the subtle differences that exist among actual human beings to be overshadowed in his efforts to create a theory of politics.

But when we turn to his analysis of the problems faced by democracies and oligarchies and consider his recommendations for how these two constitutions can be stabilized while preserving their identity as partisan regimes, we find something rather surprising: Aristotle believes that these constitutions possess surprisingly common congenital defects, share systematic threats, and even require similar solutions to address their problems. There are some differences; in particular, oligarchies face a number of challenges from which democracies are free. But these differences are exceptions to the rule. When partisans of either stripe control a constitution, a readily recognizable dynamic appears that, left unattended, will continually increase mistrust and destabilize the regime.

II.1. The Congenital Defects of Rule by Partisans

The level of mutual hostility between democrats and oligarchs is the key congenital defect of any partisan constitution. Since there will be both rich and poor in every average city, every democracy will have to deal with its rich inhabitants, and every oligarchy will be confronted with poor democrats who find themselves blocked from power.

In either case, Aristotle claims that members of the partisan group who are unable to rule will feel *stasis*-causing contempt for those in charge. In oligarchies, contempt appears among the poor majority for the same reason that contempt exists among the ruled in monarchies: even if they were to believe that property entitles one to a greater degree of influence in public deliberation (which they do not), the multitude would still not believe that wealth entitles a small number of people to exercise *total* control over the city. Moreover, Aristotle points out that the majority is always aware of its own physical power and is acutely aware of the city's dependence on this power for success in military matters (II.12 1274a12–15, III.13 1283a40–42, V.3 1302b25–27, VI.7 1321a13–14). Thus, in the eyes of the ruled, the oligarchic rulers who prevent the majority from participating will inspire contempt in two ways: they hold a position that betrays an overvaluation of their own merit, and they undervalue the contribution to the city made by the other inhabitants. Democracies also inspire contempt, but for different reasons: they inspire contempt among the rich because it seems to these elites that democratic rule promotes "disorganization and anarchy" (V.3 1302b28–29).

As we saw in the last chapter, contempt is not the only long-term cause of *stasis* that appears when the rich and poor live with one another. Oligarchs are habitually arrogant and prone to display their superiority, so we can expect oligarchies to feature these two long-term causes of mistrust in addition to inspiring contempt. In democracies, the ruled rich not only feel contempt for the disorganization of the regime, but they also fear that whenever a poor multitude rules, it will punish and penalize those with wealth (V.3 1302b21–24).

However, despite these slight differences in the etiology of mistrust, Aristotle believes that the causes of *stasis* in both partisan regimes result in a tenor of mistrustfulness that has a shared and distinctive character. In oligarchies and democracies, inhabitants' mistrustfulness of one another leads partisans to focus exclusively on money and to ignore honor: "[S]ince they [oligarchs] will seek profit no less than honor, we are justified in calling oligarchies small democracies" (VI.7 1321a41–b1). In democracies, Aristotle believes, the ruling poor will think exclusively of the money they can reap with their new-found political power, while the ruled rich will think solely of the money they could lose with the poor in charge. In oligarchies, the rich will concentrate on the amount of money they can make by taking advantage of their elite power monopoly, while the poor will think only of how the rich rulers are abusing their power to pad their own pockets. So, oddly, even though there are so many issues that divide rich and poor, Aristotle depicts both groups as embracing a very similar kind of mistrustfulness: both groups end up being acutely concerned to see that political power leads to fiscal benefits reaped from their partisan opponents.

This fixation on finances leads Aristotle to posit two more interesting similarities between the mistrustfulness found in democracies and that found in oligarchies. First, when partisan democrats take charge in a democracy, or oligarchs ascend to power in an oligarchy, Aristotle thinks that both groups quickly tend to engage in *stasis*-causing plundering—which, of course, makes the mistrustfulness of those being plundered that much more intense.[5]

But, second, once serving in political office is understood as a means to financial gain rather than honor, Aristotle believes that a certain kind of person, one who inspires exceptionally intense distrust among those not in power, ends up being attracted to political rule. In extreme democracies that pay the poor for their involvement, inhabitants show up who are only too happy to spend time participating since "care for their own property does not impede them" (IV.6 1293a7–8). Strikingly, Aristotle makes the exact same observation about the super wealthy who play an increasingly large role in extreme oligarchies. Inhabitants follow law "the more they have neither so much property that they can be at leisure without worrying nor so little that they need to be supported by the *polis*" (IV.6 1293a18–19). In other words, Aristotle thinks that *both* inhabitants of extreme poverty *and* those of extreme wealth will wish to be in politics even though they are largely indifferent to how their political decisions affect the stability of the city. The fabulously wealthy hardly notice losses that most property owners would find ruinous and terrifying, and the exceedingly poor have nothing to lose however things turn out for the city. So, as odd as it may sound, Aristotle conceives of both the desperately poor and the leisured rich as sharing a certain attitude: they view politics as a riskless instrument for making money and are rather careless about how their political decisions may end up affecting the rest of those in the city.

Not surprisingly, Aristotle directly correlates the increased participation of these careless partisans with the rise of lawlessness and political instability. As democracies become more extreme, the requirements for participating become "looser" and include ever-increasing numbers of such participants; as oligarchies become more extreme, requirements become "tighter" and there are fewer and fewer people who are careful rulers. Thus, even though these partisan constitutions are in one sense taking opposite paths (one becoming looser, one becoming tighter), they share the same dynamic: in both cases careless partisans exert an ever-growing influence over decision-making, and their plundering and lawless rule produces an ever-growing feeling of contempt. This is why Aristotle thinks of extreme democracy and oligarchy as "corresponding" to one another (IV.6 1293a33), sees the devices they use as mirrored opposites (IV.13 1297a35–38), and thinks of their destructive causes as generally similar (V.10 1312b34–37). In both constitutions, the contours of mistrustfulness that set a stage for outright *stasis* are similar.

II.2. Mitigating the Problems of Rule by Partisans

Given the implacable mistrust that will be generated from these long-term causes of *stasis*, how is it possible to manage partisan constitutions in such a way that they do not swiftly spiral out of control into outright civil war? How, if we wish to preserve a democracy as a democracy, can we prevent the rich from becoming ever more contemptuous and fearful of democratic rule that threatens to become lawless? How, if we wish to preserve an oligarchy as an oligarchy, can we prevent the large number of ruled inhabitants from becoming ever more repulsed by the arrogance, superiority, and carelessness of the elite rich who rule in this sort of regime? Aristotle offers surprisingly similar answers to these daunting questions: "each oligarchy should be assembled from its opposites, by analogy with the opposite democracy" (VI.6 1320b19–20). There are, I think, two broad strategies Aristotle offers for assembling a partisan constitution "from its opposites" that induce stability.

We might call the first strategy "opposition outreach." Aristotle recommends that rulers openly show their support for opposing partisans who are not part of the constitution. For example, rulers in democracies should champion oligarchs who might thus be led to think more highly of the multitude (V.9 1310a4–6). Similarly, ruling oligarchs need to stick up for those who are not able to serve in government because they fail to meet the minimal property qualifications (a6–8), and they should go out of their way to decorate and beautify the city in such a way that poor inhabitants feel appreciated (VI.7 1321a35–39).

Aristotle is aware, however, that such attempts to appease rival partisans have little chance of success.[6] After all, these gestures do precious little to alter the core causes of mistrust. Even if oligarchs heap enormous praise upon the poor, this gesture will do little to convince the large majority that the rich deserve a total lock on power. Similarly, even if the poor who rule a democracy celebrate this or that rich oligarch, it is difficult to see how this will change his opinion that democracies are unorganized, or ease his worry that while he may be held up for praise today, he might very well be set up for confiscation tomorrow.

It is the futility of this approach, I think, that leads Aristotle to put so much more effort into developing the second main strategy for stabilizing partisan regimes. The core idea of this latter strategy is to identify mechanisms by which more dangerous varieties of partisan constitutions might be transmuted into more benign forms. We can see that Aristotle has such a structural strategy in mind from the moment he first turns to consider the question of variation among partisan constitutions: "[A] statesman should also be able to help existing constitutions, as was also said earlier. But this is impossible if he does not know how many kinds of constitutions there are. As things stand, however, some people think there is just one kind of democracy and one of oligarchy. But this is not true" (IV.1 1289a6–10). Elsewhere, Aristotle recognizes different types of monarchy, aristocracy, and polity—but it is only when discussing oligarchy and democracy that he emphasizes right from the start of his analysis the link between understanding their different varieties and their preservation.

Why are there different varieties of democracy and oligarchy? Aristotle's explanation in *Pol.* IV.4–6 and VI.4–6 has three main parts. First, any city, much like any animal, must successfully exercise a number of separate functions if it is to survive. Although Aristotle may have been thinking of his own biological sciences, he is here repeating an old political idea: when Socrates attempts to identify civic virtues, his first step is to identify the jobs that must be performed if a city is to exist (*Republic* 369b–72d). There is nothing particularly novel in Aristotle's second idea either: different kinds of political constitutions emerge when these different civic functions are carried out by different sociological groups. Here again, Plato is an obvious influence: the entire dystopian history of imperfect regimes in *Republic* VIII is a portrait of how constitutions change when different kinds of people end up exercising the ruling functions of a city. Aristotle's portrait of oligarchy and democracy follows in this vein. Democracy results when ruling belongs to the "poor" (i.e. partisan democrats), and oligarchy results when the "rich" rule (i.e. when partisan oligarchs are the decision makers).

But I take it that Aristotle imagines himself to be offering something novel with the third component of his theory for the cause of partisan variety. He believes there are significantly different sociological species within the genera of rich oligarchs and poor democrats. In *Pol.* IV.3–4, Aristotle introduces us to the different types of poor (farmers, *banausoi*, traders, laborers), and he also distinguishes different kinds of rich inhabitants (those with and without weapons, horses, and large estates). But with respect to classifying regimes, the most relevant political distinction among all these subgroups ends up being that which we have already discussed: the careful rich of moderate wealth should be sharply distinguished from the careless partisans of vast dynasties; similarly, the careful poor, who must worry about running a farm or tending a herd, need to be clearly differentiated from the careless poor who are not responsible for the maintenance of any sort of property. It is this difference between careful and careless partisans, Aristotle believes, that best explains why we find different varieties of democracy and oligarchy.

This political analysis then inspires Aristotle's structural strategy for transforming dangerous forms of democracy/oligarchy into safe ones: wise politicians should take steps to ensure that the careful partisans who possess worry-inducing levels of property end up dominating the constitution's decision making. Remarkably, Aristotle thinks that the best way of producing such an arrangement is more or less the same in both democracies and oligarchies: exploit the fact that both rich and poor partisans care more about money than honor and take advantage of the fact that they will respond to economic incentives.

In the case of democracy, this means eliminating or lowering payments for attending assembly or jury and transforming most civic offices into honorific positions won through competitive elections instead of being paid positions assigned by lot (VI.4 1318b27–33). *Politics* VI.5 vividly explains how organizing a regime in this way creates incentives to promote a safer form of democracy. First, since no payment is rendered for serving, the careless poor who must work to eke out a living are altogether pushed out of the ruling class. Moreover, even the poor of more moderate means will wish to participate in the assembly only rarely and apathetically. Finally, while the careful poor will still insist upon holding ultimate power of the constitution—this is, after all, a democracy—many citizens who are not democrats may nevertheless end up being elected to the offices of the democratic constitution. By simply removing the economic incentives of political participation, a species of democracy is created that is dominated by citizens who would prefer not to waste their time in politics and who are not overly concerned to block those who can afford to seek such honors.[7]

It is not difficult to understand why Aristotle thinks that this variety of democratic constitution would better manage mistrust than alternative forms. Consider, for example, the rich oligarchs who find themselves stuck in a democracy; they fear having their money confiscated by a demagogue-led mob, and they find the disorder of democratic politics worthy of contempt. Aristotle's recommendations for democracy address both worries. In the safer form of democracy, there is no careless "mob" in a position of authority who might soak the rich with little appreciation of the long-term effects such action may have upon the city; instead, the assembly and juries feature busy farmers who regret having to be away from work or modestly wealthy honorees who have been elected to represent these farmers and herders.[8] Thus, not only will confiscatory lawsuits disappear, but the financial burden of paying people for service in civic offices will decrease. Moreover, because the assembly will meet infrequently and because the careful democrats who dominate this constitution are too busy to think about plundering or political change, this constitution should be more predictable, less chaotic, and thus perhaps less worthy of contempt.

The key to creating oligarchies that better manage mistrust is also found in creating the right sort of financial incentives. First, Aristotle recommends that oligarchies adopt low property qualifications that are, all by themselves, sufficient for participating in the constitution. This one change ensures that a rather large group of moderately wealthy citizens with an oligarchic character will end up participating (VI.6 1320b22–29). After all, as oligarchs, such wealthy citizens will view the constitution as a way of entrenching the power of the few, so they will all want to belong to that small ruling group.

But the fact that the "few" ends up including a rather large number of rulers makes this *politeuma* far more cautious than it otherwise would have been. For even though these rulers are wealthy, they are not so rich that they will be able to pursue reckless goals with little regard for mistakes or unintended outcomes. On the contrary, a larger class of partisan oligarchs will be more averse to risk, and will avoid radical calls for change that risk financial turmoil. Moreover, even if one careless oligarch did wish to embark on some wild scheme of plunder, the fact that there are many rich citizens participating in this sort of oligarchy will make it more difficult for him to confiscate the city's wealth and thereby shrink the ruling class into a more extreme oligarchy of fantastically rich rulers.[9] For the same reason, the families of dynastic wealth, who find themselves swamped by a relatively large number of cautious citizens, will also find it more difficult to exert control over an expanded oligarchy.

Poor democrats who find themselves stuck in this kind of large oligarchy should be less contemptuous of rulers than they otherwise would be: for even though there will still be only a few people governing this type of constitution, the degree/kind problem will be less intense than it would be in an oligarchy with a dynastic ruling class. And, again, while the poor will still be annoyed by the arrogance and superiority of the oligarchs, Aristotle's proposal should appease the poor on both counts. On the one hand, by having low wealth qualifications, the ruling oligarchs will not be as financially superior as they would be in extreme oligarchies. On the other, remember that Aristotle recommends that the low wealth qualifications for ruling in an oligarchy not be accompanied by any other restrictions. If a city follows Aristotle's advice, inhabitants who were not raised as oligarchs will still be able to participate in the regime as soon as they possess sufficient wealth. In other words, people who were never firmly habituated with an oligarchic character as children will nevertheless end up in the class of ruling oligarchs! Thus, though there will still be arrogant rich in Aristotle's recommended variety of oligarchy (it wouldn't be an oligarchy if this sort of person did not dominate the decision making), the poor who are locked out of power will nevertheless find themselves ruled by citizens who not infrequently possess an intellectual and emotional repertoire somewhat familiar to them.

III. The Problems of Mixed Rule

I have yet to address what is perhaps Aristotle's most famous contribution to "nonideal" political theory. Because "good birth and virtue are found in few people" (V.1 1301b40–02a1), and "nowhere is there a hundred good and well-born men" (02a1–2), aristocracy is simply too dependent on improbably perfect conditions to play a major part in that analysis (IV.11 1295a31–34).[10] Moreover, we have already reviewed Aristotle's strategies for how monarchies and partisan constitutions might manage the mistrust endemic to the average, real-world cities that they control. But we have yet to discuss the constitution that Aristotle claims would do a better job managing common problems than would any other. Aristotle calls this "constitution" [*politeia*]—a type of ruling most scholars refer to as "polity" to avoid confusion.

We know from Aristotle's six-fold constitutional schema that polity is correct rule by the many (III.7 1279a37–39). What we will investigate here is how Aristotle conceives of the mistrust endemic to polity, the tactics he recommends for dealing with these threats, and then his argument for the claim that polity manages mistrust more effectively than any other type of constitution.

III.1. The Intractable Problem of Mixed Government

Formally, democracy counts all minimally qualified inhabitants as citizens, and formally, all these citizens are equal. However, as we have seen, Aristotle believes that democracies are in fact run by a partisan clique with a very specific character repertoire. Democracy is incorrect rule by many precisely because this constitution is dominated by a problematic group of poor people whose attitudes ensure domination.[11]

By contrast, Aristotle offers polity as a way of organizing a constitution in such a way that all minimally qualified inhabitants not only formally belong to the constitution, but they also, in some real sense, are making substantive contributions as proper citizens. In other words, polity, like democracy, is a constitution governed by a majority, but unlike democratic regimes, it exhibits a version of rule by many that avoids domination by the poor. This is why Aristotle calls polity a "mixed constitution": neither of the two major partisan cliques achieves a total lock on decision-making power in this community, so neither rich nor poor alone defines the government with their own principles. As Aristotle explains, "polity, to put it simply, is a mixture of oligarchy and democracy" (IV.8 1293b33–34).

This simple formula, however, is misleading. First, Aristotle makes it clear that the mixture that is constitutive of polity is not just *any* mixture that happens to include both oligarchs and democrats. In the abstract, a political theorist could imagine a great number of constitutions in which democrats, oligarchs, and others participate. But when Aristotle is theorizing polity, he explicitly restricts his attention to mixtures that lack a large group of virtuous people who, by dint of their participation, would alter the type of regime: "Hence it is evident that the mixture of the two, the rich and the poor, ought to be called polity, whereas a mixture of the three [rich, poor, and virtuous] . . . deserves to be called an aristocracy" (IV.8 1294a22–24). In other words, polity mixtures are a subset among the class of all conceivable mixtures, blending rich and poor in some distinctive way that results in a constitution that could be spoken of as either an oligarchy or democracy (IV.9 1294b13–16).

Aristotle describes three main strategies according to which distinctively rich/poor mixtures might be created. First, there is the strategy of simple inclusion: a city might offer a blend of incentives (e.g. paying the poor, fining the rich) to ensure that members of both classes show up to participate in group deliberations (IV.9 1294a36–b2, IV.13 1297a38–b1, IV.14 1298b11–26). Aristotle even outlines specific tactics for how both classes could meaningfully participate together to make such inclusion substantive. For example, instead of trying "to mix everyone together as much as possible and break up their previous associations" (VI.4 1319b25–27) as is done in extreme democracies, a city might instead arrange a system whereby the poor and rich vote as separate blocks, thus allowing each group to preserve a sense that their group's unique interests are being factored into decisions. If a proposal is accepted by a majority of the rich, as well as a majority of the poor, then the proposal has authority. For those problematic cases in which a proposal is accepted only by one of these majorities, Aristotle suggests that the total wealth of those supporting the proposal could be compared to the total wealth of those against it and that the position supported by the greater amount could be adopted (VI.3 1318a32–b1).[12] In any case, the general strategy at work here is to create a mix by having groups of both rich and poor actively involved in deliberation in a meaningful way.

The second main strategy for creating a rich/poor mix might be called "trimming the extremes" (Aristotle calls this a mean between "organizations"). By adopting medium property qualifications, or differential qualifications for different offices, a city can ensure that no large group of extremely rich or extremely poor inhabitants achieves domination over all the participants and ends up defining the constitution. On the one hand, a successfully trimmed constitution will not end up as some sort of democracy, because a great number of poor inhabitants will fall below the property qualification and be excluded (IV.9 1294b2–6; VI.7 1321a26–31). On the other hand, because the wealth qualification is rather low, this constitution could not end up as an oligarchy run by the rich; as Aristotle puts it, once an oligarchy drops its property assessments low enough, the resulting constitution becomes "one with the character of a polity on account of its moderateness" (IV.14 1298a39–40).

The third sort of strategy discussed by Aristotle is that of proceduralism: he recommends incorporating into a constitution both oligarchic and democratic procedures that will decide who engages in civic deliberations. For example, a constitution may refrain from instituting any property qualifications for citizenship and, in this respect, resemble a democracy. But this same constitution may also make winning an election necessary for being a decision maker, and this makes the constitution resemble an oligarchy (IV.9 1294b6–13). Or, for another example, a constitution may allow all citizens to make some decisions, just as they would in a democracy, but then reserve other decisions for a select group, as would be the case in an oligarchy (IV.14 1298b5–11).

We should note that Aristotle does not reserve these three strategies for creating mixes of *rulers*; he also discusses ways in which they can be used to incorporate both rich and poor into other officiating and judicial activities of a city. For example, in order to mix the offices of a constitution, an oligarchic board could be created to pick the topics of discussion for the democratic assembly (IV.14 1298b26–32); or (less ideally in Aristotle's opinion) a democratic assembly could make decisions subject to a veto by oligarchs who hold special offices (b32–99a1); or, even more elaborately, there could be one democratic office of preliminary deliberation that prepares material for the assembly and then another office of oligarchic preliminary councilors who act as a check upon this democratic office (IV.15 1299b30–38). Again, Aristotle describes how offices might be mixed by using procedures that, in one sense, are democratic, but in some other sense are oligarchic. For example, perhaps only a few people might be made responsible for selecting civic officials (which is oligarchic), but then the pool of the possible selectees may extend to the entire citizenry (which is democratic) (IV.15 1300a34–38). Or, for yet another example, some offices may be made elective, while others may be filled by lot (VI.5 1320b11–16). Mixed courts could be created in similar ways: a city could fill some of its courts with jurors selected from the entire population but then fill other courts more selectively (IV.16 1301a13–15), or a city could ensure that some of the jurors in a given court are taken from the many, while other jurors in that court come from the few (VI.3 1318a14–17).

In any case, the strategies of inclusion, trimming, and proceduralism, whether applied to rulers, officials, or courts, allow Aristotle to conceive of many possible constitutions that would be marked by their incorporation of both rich and poor. Here, however, we come to a second way in which the simple formula that polity "is a mixture of oligarchy and democracy" (IV.8 1293b33–34) is deeply misleading. By itself, that formula makes it sound as if any time oligarchs and democrats are mixed a stable and correct regime of rule by many results. Yet, given Aristotle's portrait of partisans, such a positive outcome would be a surprising result. Why would Aristotle's partisan democrats see the mixed constitution as anything but an unworkable concession to an arrogant, contemptuous, unjust gang? Again, why would partisan oligarchs think of a rich/poor combination as anything other than a frightfully precarious arrangement tempting an envious "mob" to promote chaos? Bringing these two groups together into a constitution does not make the long-term causes of *stasis* any less salient. The rich will still fear poorer citizens and hold them in contempt. The poorer citizens will still feel contempt and witness (now at very close quarters) the arrogance and superiority of the rich. Moreover, both partisan groups will be constantly observing distributions of money and honor with which they disagree. In short, without being given more information about how these mixtures lead to stability, there is little reason to believe that strategies for mixing poor and rich—whether by inclusion, trimming, or proceduralism—could be anything other than a recipe for catastrophic levels of mistrust and inevitable *stasis*.

Therefore, when Aristotle describes a polity as "a mixture of oligarchy and democracy," he is picking out far fewer constitutions than we might have initially assumed. Polities only refer to constitutions that mix rich and poor while being bereft of contributions from significant numbers of virtuous citizens, and, even within that smaller set, polity only picks out those constitutions that somehow hit upon a *good* way of mixing the sociologically unmixable, not merely *any* conceivable mixture whatsoever: "For what begins the process [leading to *stasis*] in a polity is failing to get a *good* mixture of democracy and oligarchy" (*Pol.* V.7 1307a7–9; cf. IV.9 1294b14–17).[13] That leaves us with the following question: Among all the possible mixtures, how is the good mix that renders a stable constitution of polity achieved?

III.2. Mitigating the Problem of Mixed Government with Those in the Middle

As I already indicated in the last chapter, Aristotle's answer to this question is remarkably pessimistic: there is, he thinks, *no way* to create a pure mixed duopoly of democrats and oligarchs. There are no democratic features we can include in a mixed constitution that will completely appease the poor, and there are no oligarchic aspects that will fully convince the rich that the mixed constitution is safe.[14] On the contrary, the *only* way to solve the great congenital defect of polity in mixing rich and poor is to introduce an entirely different sociological group, namely, "those in the middle." So it is that when Aristotle speaks of a "better mixed constitution" (IV.12 1297a6–7), he clarifies that he is referring to one, and only one, constitution: a more stable constitution with a large group of middlings.[15]

But why is Aristotle convinced that those in the middle will make a successful mix possible? Who, exactly, are these people? At one point these inhabitants are referred to as "those with hoplite weapons" (II.6 1265b28–29), and elsewhere they are described as "those in between" the very rich and the very poor (IV.11 1295b3). They thus possess a degree of wealth, status, and resources that are not like those of the "careless" partisans who are either so rich, or so poor, that they need never worry about the maintenance of anything; these are people who would still be included in a constitution after the extremes were trimmed.

Based merely on this description, we might be tempted to think of this group as Aristotle's political "moderates." But this would be misleading. A political moderate may well identify with those who are extreme partisans but be too fearful to act. By contrast, when Aristotle refers to "those in the middle," he is not talking about democrats or oligarchs who happen to be cautious. Rather, he is identifying a group that psychologically differs *in kind* from partisans.

First, members of this middling group have a distinct emotional repertoire that differs greatly from that of democrats and oligarchs: rather than suffering from the kind of arrogance or envy that leads to vice, they are at least continent enough to obey reason (IV.11 1295b5–9). Second, although they do not possess complete virtue (which would render their rule aristocratic), they nevertheless share in virtue by possessing "military virtue" [*aretēn . . . polemikēn*] (III.7 1279b1–2). Unlike the elite virtue of aristocrats that can only be possessed by a few (let alone the almost superhuman level of virtue that might belong to a quasi-divine king), this middling excellence can be possessed by "a number" (b2) of people and is typically found among "the fighting class" [*to propolemoun*] (b3) that possesses weapons (b4). Importantly, such excellence motivates those in the middle to govern for the common benefit (1279a37–38), so it saves them from embracing a political identity based upon a mistaken and partial conception of the human good. Unlike oligarchs, they do not believe that endless wealth acquisition makes citizens' lives flourish, nor do they consider "doing as one likes" the complete and self-sufficient good that would be best for citizens. And, finally, this middling group does not make the *haplōs* mistake that leads rulers into thinking that they differ from the ruled in the same way that masters differ from slaves. On the contrary, Aristotle says that those in the middle are content to rule but that they are not inclined to do so (1295b12)—for they do not believe their rule should, in fact, resemble that of a master (b19–23). Thus, not only are these inhabitants "in the middle" with respect to wealth and status—but, more fundamentally for their political identity, they do not possess a psychological disposition that resembles what I diagnosed in the last chapter as discriminatory elitism, even on behalf of their own middle-range status group that is neither rich nor poor.[16] Though not virtuous per se, those in the middle nevertheless "pass" as virtuous, at least in the aggregate and for the purposes of city planning.[17]

Aristotle has astonishing confidence in the palliative effects of this middling group. He suggests that adding those in the middle is virtually a necessary condition for stabilizing mixed constitutions: "[C]onstitutions also change when parts of a city-state that are held to be opposed, such as the rich and the people, become equal to one another, and there is little or no middle class" (V.4 1304a38–b2). He also claims that adding those of passable virtue is usually sufficient for making mixed constitutions stable: "[C]onflicts and dissensions seldom occur among citizens where there are many in the middle" (IV.11 1296a8–9). What are Aristotle's arguments for thinking that this group so effectively stabilizes cities?

First, even though the presence of passably virtuous people will not completely dissolve mistrust, they can render it ineffectual. Here Aristotle engages in a bit of brute realism. No matter how upset and mistrustful partisans become, *stasis* will not take place when "those in the middle are numerous and stronger, preferably than both of the others, or, failing that, than one of them" (IV.11 1295b37–38). Partisan oligarchs and democrats are not like those who would throw away their lives in the name of honor,[18] and since they would never consider working with their ideological opponents (IV.4 1296b40–97a3), this means that the presence of a large group of those in the middle in a city effectively ends the possibility of a partisan revolt. Indeed, this is especially true since Aristotle suggests that these middle inhabitants do not merely stand around, passively hoping that their sheer bulk will prevent an attack from an energized minority: "For it [the group of those in the middle] will tip the balance when added to either and prevent the opposing extremes from arising" (IV.11 1295b38–39). Middlings behave as an anti*stasis* party, always willing to add themselves to an opposition and ready to take active steps to prevent partisan revolt.[19]

However, because these middlings do not have a partisan psychology, they will not make the *haplōs* mistake of thinking that such a position of strength justifies the rule of middling masters over the rich and poor as slaves. Rather than assume a despotic outlook, these citizens of passable virtue will look for ways that both rich and poor can be brought into the constitution safely—and it is in this way, I believe, we can best appreciate how Aristotle conceptualizes the strategies of inclusion, trimming, and proceduralism. In the abstract, these are three ways to mix the rich and poor. But in actual constitutional life, they only constitute a "*good mixture*" when they are deployed by middling citizens who wish to avoid becoming masters over rich and poor in a city that they would otherwise dominate.[20]

Moreover, when used by the middle class in a polity, these mixing strategies will go some way to dampening the distrust of both rich and poor by lessening the egregiousness of *stasis*-causing spectacles. Poor citizens, for example, will know full well that they do not live in a democracy. Whether a polity mixes in its rich by incentivizing inclusion in assembly and court, or by adopting procedures that promote rich citizens to high-profile offices, poor democrats will certainly be annoyed at the superiority and the arrogance of these rich voters and officials who focus upon issues of wealth. Nevertheless, with so many people from the middle group participating, it stands to reason that this superiority and arrogance will be less frequently displayed in an overt manner: fewer offices will be held by rich oligarchs, fewer speeches will belong to the rich, and fewer decisions in the courts and assembly will be solely attributable to the rich. Even when there are decisions that benefit the rich, we should expect that in a polity such benefits will be modest, will be accompanied by benefits to other groups, and will certainly not be acts of dynastic plundering that would undercut the interests of the middle class. An analogous argument could be made for how the rich will interpret the operations of a polity: the acts that tend to provoke fear and contempt among economic elites will be less frequent, and distributions of wealth and honor will not be as egregiously tilted toward the interests of the partisan poor who seek freedom. In either case, when those in the middle mix rich and poor, they act as a kind of depressant that does not erase, but nonetheless modulates, the sense that the foundations of the polity are so unfair that *stasis* is immediately required.[21]

When we combine these considerations—the role of the passably virtuous in reducing the visibility and gravity of the spectacles that cause mistrust and the way in which they act as a powerful "anti*stasis*" party that is ready to fight for the status quo—we can better understand Aristotle's confidence that the presence of those in the middle is both necessary and even sufficient for the stability of polities. It also helps to explain why Aristotle believes that their effect will be salubrious in so many political environments: he claims that large cities are more stable than small cities because of the passably virtuous, that democracies are more stable than oligarchies because of their presence, and that the best legislators in any constitution usually arise from this group (IV.11 1296a8–21). Moreover, when Aristotle proposes a test for determining whether a political environment is more naturally suited to a democracy or an oligarchy, he ends his discussion by claiming that, in either case, "the legislator should always include the middle: if he is establishing oligarchic laws, he should aim at those in the middle, and if democratic ones, he must bring them in by these laws" (IV.12 1296b34–38).

IV. Why Polity Is Usually Best

There is one more subject that we should address on the topic of simmering constitutional conflict in average cities. We have reviewed Aristotle's recommendations for how a polity can successfully manage the mistrust generated by mixing partisans, but we have not explained why Aristotle takes this management to be superior to that which can be carried out in other constitutions. Why would polity be a better solution for most nonideal conditions than an oligarchy that is successfully mitigating its mistrust? Or a democracy that has prudently modified its defining principles? Or a monarchy that is actively cultivating ties with all the groups in the city and sticking to traditional areas of rule? Polity, remember, is a constitution that successfully manages the mistrust of mixed partisans—so, for a fair comparison, polity should be compared to other constitutions that are also taking productive steps to manage their respective forms of mistrust successfully.

Aristotle does not answer this question explicitly, but I believe we can reconstruct a three-part argument for the conclusion that polity is the regime best suited to most average cities. The first claim is what, at several points, he calls "the most fundamental principle" (V.9 1309b16): namely, that the part of the constitution that wishes for its continuation must be stronger than the parts that do not (IV.12 1296b14–16).[22] By "strength" Aristotle does not simply mean physical force. Rather, he thinks of strength in terms of physical force organized by people of a certain quality—people who are free, have wealth, have education, and/or are of good birth (1296b17–18). We could thus think of strength as the means to project some amount of force with effective composition: a small force that is very well organized might be stronger than a large force that lacks cohesion—even though there will be a point at which sheer numbers will overwhelm such a superior force.[23] Aristotle uses this "most fundamental principle" to explain why certain types of constitutions tend to develop in certain environments (e.g., a city with a powerful cavalry or hoplite force will tend toward oligarchy, VI.7 1321a5–11), and it is this same principle that motivates Aristotle's quality/quantity test in IV.12 for recommending whether a particular city is better suited for a democracy (where the strength of the disorganized many exceeds that of the organized few) or an oligarchy (where the strength of the organized few exceeds that of the disorganized many).

Aristotle seems to think that only two constitutions can regularly live up to this "most fundamental principle" in fourth-century Greece: democracy and polity. Generally speaking, neither rule by one nor rule by few will be able to manage large, mistrustful populaces over the long term. Consider, for example, how much pessimism Aristotle openly expresses about the viability of kingship, tyranny, aristocracy, and oligarchy in average conditions. "The shortest-lived of all constitutions are oligarchy and tyranny" (V.12 1315b11–12),[24] monarchies were only feasible in archaic Greece (III.15 1286b8–22), and aristocracies are simply out of reach (IV.11 1295a31–34). It is hard to escape the impression that he thinks of all of these constitutions as being exceptionally fragile.

Moreover, considered in the abstract, it seems quite unlikely that the rulers in any of these regimes—even if they were taking proactive steps to manage mistrust—would be able to retain a position of superior strength over a long period of time. After all, if strength is conceived as being the product of a group's size with its quality, then surely larger groups will tend to be stronger over the long term. For the amount of freedom, wealth, education, and pedigree belonging to a particular group depends on a great deal of work and can easily rise and fall for any number of reasons (not to mention that these traits are difficult to cultivate and rare to find in the first place). By contrast, barring some unusual natural disaster or epidemic, the sheer number of human beings in a group will remain fairly constant with little or no effort.

[I]n light of Aristotle's insistence that this is the *most* important principle, perhaps we should even wonder how seriously Aristotle takes his own recommendations for preserving monarchies or oligarchies in average conditions. Given the vast disparities in strength, what are the odds that a king—let alone an arrogant tyrant—will be able to manage avoiding revolt? And, over the long term, how likely is it that a huge number of envious poor, filled with contempt for being ruled by so few, could be appeased by rulers they will see as arrogant and annoyingly superior? Aristotle no doubt makes his recommendations in good faith—but he also must realize that these are very unlikely fixes.

The real question, then, is why Aristotle chooses polity over well-managed democracy as the constitution that would best survive in most nonideal environments—for these are the only two constitutions that could regularly satisfy "the most important principle." Since both polities and well-managed democracies are rare, Aristotle cannot be reaching this judgment on the basis of which constitution is more commonly found in experience.

It is, I think, the "virtue is a mean" argument of *Pol.* IV.11 1295a35–b1 that convinces Aristotle that polity would better serve most political environments than would any type of democracy. He begins this argument by offering a brief summary of his thesis in the *Ethics*: a happy life expresses virtue without impediment, and virtue is a mean. He then applies this ethical claim to his political theory with the statement that "a constitution is a sort of life of a *polis*." The conclusion he would thus have us draw is that a flourishing *polis* is one whose constitution expresses the mean without impediment.

While farming/herding democracies might have an excellent chance at surviving *as democracies*, this argument suggests that, in Aristotle's opinion, such democracies will not have an excellent chance to flourish *as cities*. After all, a farming democracy not only must survive in the face of the powerful mistrust of oligarchs but also survive being ruled by people who are not reasonable, who are not keen on the idea of rotating rule, and who—given the chance—may engage in plotting against those with more wealth. As we have seen, Aristotle believes that well-run democracies manage these threats by incentivizing absenteeism among farmers burdened by apolitical cares. But this solution implies that, even in the best of times, Aristotelian farming democracy is a kind of political triage—an ongoing emergency operation to counteract the enduring shortcomings of a flawed constitution. By contrast, polity is ruled by those of passable virtue who have enough continence to follow reason, who are neutral to ruling, who are willing to rotate, and who are neither the agents nor the victims of plotting and plundering. In short, not only does such rule express a mean, but it does so with less impediment.

Part II

Conflict among Perfect Citizens

Prelude

Aristotle, as we saw in the first chapter, carefully describes *stasis* as an ugly type of internal war marked by enmity, a deep-seated sense of injustice, force, and fraud. The second chapter revealed that the problem of partisanship is also remarkably well defined: partisans possess a zealous hostility for one another and are reliably agitated in constitutional life because they possess distinctive partisan identities that emerge from the unique confluence of four character traits. In the last chapter, I explored Aristotle's conception of the sort of conflict that is nursed by the long-term causes of *stasis* but that is nevertheless distinct from an outbreak of civil war—a many-formed condition of managed mistrust that haunts average cities.

Though these three forms of conflict are distinguishable from one another, they nevertheless share a common feature: at least one party in all these types of political conflict lacks virtue. Whether it is a lack of virtue in the rulers (as in tyranny, oligarchy, and democracy) who inspire reasonable distrust or partisan animus, or a lack of virtue in the ruled who are piqued by their own misinterpretations of excellent rule, or a lack of virtue in both rulers and ruled—in all such cases a lack of excellence helps to explain why a given type of political conflict takes place. As a result, civil war, partisan animus, and the tensions of managed mistrust would find no place in an ideal city, which features both virtuous rulers and excellent ruled citizens.

We need not assume, however, that these three specific types of intra*polis* conflict exhaust all the ways in which human beings who live together might possibly be at odds. People find themselves at variance with one another and struggle against one another in all sorts of ways. While the conflicts considered so far feature acrimony and the kind of distrust that threatens to lead to violent rebellion, experience suggests that people can also struggle with one another in peaceful rivalries, thoughtful debates, and good-natured competitions. Indeed, these familiar forms of struggle appear to take place among people who genuinely admire one another's objective excellence—even when the conflict involves significant pain for those who lose a contest to their rivals or find themselves bettered in an argument. Like boxers who embrace one another in mutual admiration after the final bell has rung, so too it seems conceivable that citizens could be civic friends at the very same time that they struggle against one another and even land painful blows in the legal and political ring.

Does Aristotle recognize this possibility? As I discussed in the first chapter, there are those theorists who would deny that such communal conflict can really take place: for them, *all* forms of political conflict are degrees of civil war, so all conflict is deeply and profoundly antisocial. But there is no reason to assume that Aristotle likewise adopts this view. To decide whether Aristotle recognizes forms of peaceable and sociable political conflict, we should turn to his texts and try to tease out his thoughts about such things. When contemplating the best sorts of political arrangements—cities in which inhabitants possess excellent intellectual traits and outstanding characters—does Aristotle imagine citizens struggling with one another in some way? If so, why? If not, why not?

One way we might argue for the possibility of conflict among the virtuous would be to turn to book II of the *Politics* and point out that there, in the course of critiquing the theories of ideal political life posited by his predecessors, Aristotle explicitly criticizes the proposal that well-run cities should be maximally unified. This is the civic goal that he finds Plato advocating in the *Republic* (462a–e), and Aristotle insists that it must be incorrect: a city is, he claims, by its very nature not a unity. Indeed, if one were to enforce ever-greater levels of unity, the city would be destroyed, and this community would begin to resemble a household or even a single human being rather than a genuine civic community (II.2 1261a13–22).

Aristotle's belief that any given city must possess a higher degree of disunity than is found in either a household or an individual rests upon two metaphysical claims. First, the citizens who make up a city are fully developed human beings who are unified substances in their own right; thus, they are unlike the internal organs of a creature that are mere capacities, and whose being is *entirely* defined by the contribution they make to the function of the whole upon which they are *utterly* dependent.[1] Fully developed human beings, though they are certainly parts of the whole city to some extent (*Pol.* I.2 1253a1–29), do not have a being that is defined exclusively by what they contribute to the civic whole, so they possess a degree of independence from others in the city.[2]

Second, unlike household communities, cities are formed by humans who are natural equals (*Pol.* III.4 1277b7–9). In a household, Aristotle thinks there will be a Greek male who is naturally superior to his spouse, children, and any slaves, and who will thus deserve to rule and order that household in perpetuity. By contrast, in a city, citizens are natural equals, so they will have to find other ways to determine hierarchical relationships of rulers and ruled.

It is tempting to cite this argument from *Pol.* II.2, as well as the claims upon which that argument depends, and to conclude that these are sufficient to show that Aristotle attributes conflict to even well-run cities filled with virtuous citizens.[3] But this, it seems to me, is too quick. It may be that cities are necessarily disunited because their parts are independent and their civic hierarchies unfixed by nature, but such *metaphysical* disunity is something quite distinct from *political* disunity. Nothing in Aristotle's metaphysics would prevent independent and naturally equal people from always agreeing on who should rule the city, and always approving of the decisions made by the city's rulers. Of course, the metaphysical disunity of the city is compatible with tension, dispute, disagreement, and other sorts of conflict among citizens. But the metaphysical status of the city's unity does not settle this political question one way or the other.

For similar reasons, we cannot turn to Aristotle's claims that cities are made up of "people of different kinds" (II.2 1261a23–24, cf. III.4 1277a5–12) and take such differentiation as proof that Aristotle accepts a role for conflict in well-run cities. Aristotle believes that all cities require a number of different "parts"—people filling a number of different functions—if they are to survive and flourish. There are rulers, office-holders, judges, and a number of other roles that must be filled by those who are ruled. But none of this differentiation, by itself, need be divisive, nor need it act as a recipe for dispute among the virtuous people who might inhabit different functions. Aristotle might conceive of excellent cities as places where all such differences are harmonized and reconciled through civic collaboration. We have to go beyond merely citing differentiation and instead try to determine whether and how virtuous citizens may be at odds with one another regardless of the civic functions they serve. By themselves, these distinctions among civic functions cannot do that work for us.

Finally, consider the intellectual virtue of *phronēsis*. This virtue consists of a number of different aptitudes, one of which allows virtuous agents to grasp properly *eudaimonia* and the generalities that help orient practical action.[4] *Phronēsis* also yields nonuniversal, particular ethical judgments that cannot be codified ahead of time. Indeed, for some scholars, Aristotle's analysis of *phronēsis* hints at an early version of "particularism."[5]

This scholarship exploring the "particularist" aspect of *phronēsis* cannot help us answer questions about conflict in the city, for it focuses only on how the *individual* ethical agent arrives at a decision in a specific set of circumstances. If the subject of conflict gets raised at all, it is the *intra*personal issue of deliberative conflict that gets addressed—not the *inter*personal question of whether and why multiple *phronimoi* would dispute over a decision that needs to be made. These are distinct issues: from the fact that an agent cannot choose between two incommensurable goods without loss or remainder or engage in some required action without tragedy or "dirty hands," it in no way follows that virtuous agents would disagree over which choice an agent should make.[6] Again, from the fact that two utterly confident agents have no deliberative or pleasure-based conflicts within themselves when they confront a given situation, we should not leap to the conclusion that they will agree on what should be done.

Moreover, however one answers the question of whether Aristotle is a "particularist" or not, this cannot settle the question of whether Aristotle acknowledges dispute among the virtuous. The fact that particular determinations of *phronēsis* cannot be captured by a set of principles is certainly compatible with the thesis that there is disagreement among agents. But it is also possible that *phronēsis* in each agent precludes disagreement: *phronimoi* confronting political situations might resemble those with 20/20 vision who are asked to read off a series of randomly generated letters on an eye chart. In that case, even though the content of what excellent vision reveals cannot be determined ahead of time by some algorithm, there will be no disagreement among the participants concerning which letters appear before them. The mere unpredictability of what *phronēsis* recommends will not settle this issue one way or another, so we cannot simply take it for granted that *phronēsis* allows or forecloses the possibility of conflict among the virtuous. We need an argument that explains why and how *phronēsis* is, or is not, compatible with interpersonal conflict.[7]

This is the argument I will undertake over the next two chapters, and I will attempt to show that Aristotle does indeed imagine political conflict taking place among perfectly virtuous citizens who are fully and successfully exercising their rational capacities. In chapter 4, I will argue that Aristotle's account of *phronēsis* allows for the possibility of upstanding citizens disagreeing with one another before, during, and even after political deliberations. In chapter 5, I will argue that Aristotle conceives of the metaphysical disunity and social differentiation of the city as a platform upon which virtuous citizens struggle against one another for honor, influence, and office.

Chapter 4

Dispute and Disagreement

Consider two separate *phronimoi*, both of whom are citizens involved in the civic deliberations and decision making of a given *polis*. Could these two end up concluding, even after a great deal of civic deliberation, that different courses of civic action were best?

At first blush, it may seem impossible that this could happen. The following argument—which I will call the "Agreement Argument"—seems persuasive.

1. In any given situation a city faces, either the evidence available to citizens favors one course of civic action as best, or the evidence available to citizens does not favor one particular action as best.

2. If the available evidence favors one course of civic action as best, *phronimoi* will agree that this is the best course of action.

3. If the available evidence does not favor one course of civic action as best, *phronimoi* will recognize the inconclusiveness of this evidence, agree that any of the leading options would be equally well chosen, and then pick one of the leading options using admittedly arbitrary criteria.

4. Thus, in any situation, *phronimoi* will agree on the civic course of action.

5. Thus, it is impossible that *phronimoi* could disagree over political decisions.

The argument is valid; but is it sound? I have no reason to doubt the truth of the first premise: in any given situation, the evidence to which *phronimoi* have access will be either adequate for the intellectually virtuous to reach the best decision, or not. The second premise is also surely true: with sufficient determinative evidence, the intellect of each *phronimos* will arrive at the same conclusion, and, since this is an exercise of prudence rather than mere cleverness (*NE* V.12 1144a29–b1), *phronimoi* will settle on the option that is best for the common good of the city even if that option requires some kind of personal sacrifice by this or that virtuous individual.[1]

However, I deny, and will spend the rest of this chapter arguing against, the claim that Aristotle would find the third premise to be true. To see why the third premise is problematic, let us begin by distinguishing a number of different ways in which evidence could be insufficient for determining the single best course of action. There could be insufficient evidence because

3i. the situation itself presents only limited information (the situation is objectively inscrutable);

3ii. mere human faculties are inadequate to gather and process all the information available in a situation in a given time (the complexity of the situation outpaces the rational capacity of agents);

3iii. there is not, in fact, a single best course of action for the city to take (the situation offers multiple actions that are as good a choice as can be made).

It seems to me that the third premise of the Agreement Argument has prima facie plausibility only because of the first case—[3i] objectively inscrutable situations. In such situations, agents face a choice among civic options that resembles a choice between identical closed doors, behind only one of which sits a prize. Because the doors are identical, the agents (no matter how intelligent, virtuous, or perceptive) have no way to determine which door should be opened. *Phronimoi* would realize that this situation was simply a "toss up" and would then agree on any arbitrary procedure (e.g., a coin flip) to pick an option. Thus, if all situations in which *phronimoi* had insufficient evidence resembled this first case [3i], premise three would be true, and the Agreement Argument would be sound.

The problem, however, is that Aristotle does not take all situations of insufficient evidence to resemble a choice among identical doors.

I. Epistemic Limitations of the *Phronimoi*

Let us imagine an extremely complex political situation in which there is, objectively, a single best course of action for the *polis* to take, and two citizen *phronimoi* are engaged in civic deliberation about what the city should do. Does Aristotle recognize situations where, even though enough exploration could in theory yield a preponderance of evidence for the best course, *phronimoi*, because of their limited rational capacities, have access only to considerations that fail to make clear which course of action is best [3ii]?

I.1. The Epistemic Limitations of Political Decision Making

First, recall Aristotle's description of lawgivers. Even though politicians who exercise prudence in dealing with particulars monopolize the name "political science," Aristotle insists that when excellent legislators craft laws, they, too, are exercising a kind of *phronēsis* (*NE* VI.8 1141b24–33) for the purpose of increasing or sustaining the excellence of citizens (*Pol.* VII.13 1332a32–b8). Note, however, Aristotle's frank admission of the epistemic limits of legislative science:

> [A]ll law is universal, but in some areas no universal rule can be correct; and so where a universal rule has to be made, but cannot be correct, the law chooses that which is usual, well aware of the error being made. And the law is no less correct on this account; for the source of error is not the law or the legislator, but the nature of the object itself, since that is what the subject matter of actions is bound to be like. (*NE* V.10 1137b13–19)[2]

The point I wish to make about this oft-quoted passage is that legislators are cleared of *any* blame, and the "error" is attributed *entirely* to the complexities and particularities of the situations to which the laws will apply. In other words, the point Aristotle is making here is meant to apply to legislators with *phronēsis* just as much as it is meant to apply to average legislators. Indeed, when Aristotle continues on after this passage to suggest a remedy for fixing laws where "the legislator falls short," it is striking that he does not conjure up the figure of an even smarter or more virtuous legislator, but rather he introduces us to the person who is decent [*epieikēs*] and who, at a later time, determines that "this is what the legislator would have said himself if he had been present there, and what he would have prescribed, *had he known*, in his legislation" (1137b23–24). In short, Aristotle's description of lawgivers shows us that *phronēsis* is not shorthand for practical omniscience that allows lawgivers to foresee every consequence, exception, and ambiguity of a given law. Therefore, since Aristotle has no interest in shielding lawgiving *phronimoi* from epistemic limitations, it seems reasonable to think that Aristotle's *phronimoi* politicians will also be working under epistemic limitations when they wrestle with particular decisions. Indeed, we find something close to an acknowledgment of the epistemic limitations of both lawgivers and decision makers in one of the arguments Aristotle cites as being commonly used against kingship: "[T]he sort of things at least that the law seems unable to decide could not be discovered by a human being either" (*Pol.* III.16 1287a23–25).

I believe we can build an even stronger case for the epistemic limitations of political decision makers by considering Aristotle's account of *phronēsis* itself. Principles are universal, but actions involve particulars (*NE* VI.7 1141b16), and because ethical principles are often inexact (I.3 1094b11–95a2),[3] virtuous agents must use *phronēsis* to make a decision about how to act in a particular situation.[4] Aristotle explains that this use of *phronēsis* includes both taking stock of the relevant features in the situation and also deliberating over the best route to take. Aristotle's analysis of both these skills, I believe, reveals epistemic limitations of *phronimoi*.

Let us begin with Aristotle's account of deliberation. The excellent deliberator begins with a rational wish [*boulēsis*] guided by an understanding [*nous*] of happiness, and then, working his way back from the ultimate goal to the action token he should embark upon now, he ends his deliberation with an awareness that "if, right now, I perform this action token (a_1), then that would lead to this outcome (o_1); that outcome (o_1), in turn, would lead to outcome o_2 (or would allow me to perform another action token a_2, which would lead to outcome o_2); outcome o_2, in turn . . . [and so on] . . . would lead to the final outcome (o_f) which is the end of my action." Civic deliberation will work the same way. When a *phronimos* enters into the assembly and defends why he takes an action a_1 to be the best option for the city to attain a given final outcome o_f, he will need to announce some deliberative train of thought like this one in an attempt to convince his peers.

But what, exactly, is the strength of the epistemic connection between the a_1 and o_f featured in the deliberation of an individual *phronimos*? Aristotle calls such a deliberative train of thought a "practical syllogism," but this is somewhat misleading since a_1 cannot lead to o_f with the unconditional necessity we associate with a strong deductive argument. Aristotle explicitly denies that deliberation deals with universals and their necessary relations and insists that, since it deals with things that could be otherwise, it cannot be any sort of demonstration [*apodeixis*] (*NE* VI.5 1140a31–b4). In fact, deliberation cannot even securely establish that a given action a_1 will lead to the final outcome o_f "for the most part" [*hōs epi to polu*]. For predictable regularities that hold "for the most part" resemble those one finds in beings that exist, or come to exist, by nature, and Aristotle insists that we do not deliberate about things that come about "from necessity or by nature" (*NE* III.3 1112a24–25). Moreover, Aristotle explicitly contrasts the sorts of regularities that allow natural beings to be defined and delimited with the regularities that serve as the subject matter of deliberation: "Deliberation concerns things holding for the most part—*but things unclear in their outcome and for which there is no definition*" (1112b8–9). This lack of clear regularity renders deliberation difficult: "[W]hat sorts of things should be chosen instead of which other things, is not easy to answer; for there are many differences in particulars" (III.1 1110b7–9).

But if the deliberation that links a_1 and o_f involves neither the unconditional necessity of a demonstration, nor even a probabilistic connection worthy of much natural science, what type of epistemic connection could there be between actions and outcomes in deliberative trains of thought? How can an agent deliberate over "things holding for the most part" that are "*unclear* in their outcome"? Deliberation is not mere guesswork (*NE* VI.9 1142b2) and requires reason (b12), so there must be more to the connection than an irrational association of one brute fact with another.

Aristotle's ethical works do not shed any light upon this minimal epistemic connection, but this may be because he thought that the subject had already been adequately addressed in the *Rhetoric* during his discussion of "enthymemes"—those vaguely syllogistic pieces of reasoning of a sort [*sullogismos tis*] (*Rhet.* I.1 1355a8).[5] The term "enthymeme" is so broad that it can refer to inferences in which likelihoods require that some other conclusion is likely, as well as arguments in which universal necessities require a necessary conclusion (such enthymemes are "infallible sign" arguments, which Aristotle calls "*tekmēria*"). But of particular interest for my purposes here are the enthymemes Aristotle thinks of as "refutable sign" arguments such as this:

1. this man strikes his father;

2. men are less likely to strike their fathers than to strike neighbors;

3. thus, this man also strikes his neighbors. (*Rhet.* II.23 1397b14–17)

This argument is obviously invalid, and it isn't even a strong inductive argument since the truth of the premises would not require the conclusion to be probable. Nevertheless, Aristotle doesn't think it a fallacy: rather, he seems to think that in such an argument the premises probably lead to the conclusion and that this minimal sort of connection should be counted as a rational inference, unlike the completely bogus connections found in sham enthymemes he describes in *Rhetoric* II.24.[6]

Now I grant that Aristotle does not explicitly mention the rationality of "refutable sign arguments" in his discussion of deliberation; but these do help us to appreciate how Aristotle might conceive of minimal epistemic connections that reside below the level of probabilistic laws. In particular, they show that we are well off the mark if we assume that the *phronimos* is that citizen who can always stand up in an assembly and explain to his peers that the city should do a_1 since it will *necessarily* lead to o_f, or that a_1 will *certainly* make o_f probable. On the contrary, in situations that demand a great deal of deliberation, Aristotle believes the *phronimos* would only be able to argue that there are (refutable) signs that a_1 will lead to o_f. With the previously cited example in mind, we can easily imagine a politician making an argument like this:

1. Phillip has struck Thessaly;

2. a military power is less likely to rest content with abolishing a single threat than to seek the elimination of all possible threats;

3. thus, Phillip is beginning an attack on all those in Greece who threaten him.

An Athenian politician who made this argument could not claim that (1) and (2) necessitate (3), or even that (1) and (2) necessitate that (3) is probable. But there is some sort of rational inference at work here—that which takes (1) as a sign of (3) in light of (2).

Aristotle's theory of how agents take stock of the particulars of their situation reveals additional limitations. While Aristotle does say at one point that *phronēsis* is the "eye of the soul" (*NE* VI.12 1144a29–30), this cannot mean that the *phronimos* has some global ability always to "see" particulars in such a way as to make the best course of action obvious. Such an ability would make deliberation dispensable; yet, as we have been discussing, deliberation is a key component of *phronēsis* in many situations. Moreover, any metaphor relying upon "eyes" and "seeing" obscures the fact that, according to Aristotle, even giving a piece of factual information the status of evidence is itself the result of intellectual activity. For example, anyone can see Peisistratus's wounded hand and see that he is requesting bodyguards in the assembly—but few would realize, as did Solon, that this was evidence of a tyrannical plot (*Ath.Pol.* 14.1–2).

I see nothing in Aristotle's account that calls into question his brief explanation of how, when, and why *phronimoi* are able to comprehend pieces of information as evidence. His cursory explanation is simply that this ability is the result of previous experience and training (*NE* VI.7 1141b14–23, VI.8 1142a14–15)—that is, the excellent aptitude of *phronēsis* results from a process that resembles the sort of training and habituation that helps an agent to develop any sort of ethical virtue. Yet, if this is so, then this ability to comprehend a fact as evidence will be relativized to the realm of experience and training from which it arose. Just as playing the harp leads to being an expert harpist (not being a musician who can play all instruments well), and experience in building leads to being an expert builder (not being a craftsman of any product), so too the ability to take stock of particulars in bread baking, navigation, medicine, or anything else will be relativized to specific domains; it will not be an aptitude to "see" evidence in general in any situation. This is certainly what Aristotle means in *NE* I.3 when he says that "each person judges well what he knows, and is a good judge about that; hence the good judge in a given area is the person educated in that area, and the unqualifiedly good judge is the person educated in every area" (1094b27–95a2).[7] There is no one ability we can develop to possess global judgment; rather, the extent of our judgment is simply equal to the sum of the areas in which we have been educated.

Moreover, we have no reason to assume that a virtuous person is one who has been educated in every realm of the human condition. Aristotle's famous claim in *Pol.* III.11 that the "part [*morion*] of virtue and practical wisdom" (1281b4–5) belonging to each average person can be combined with that of others to achieve a level of virtue exceeding that of a single excellent individual suggests that the practical wisdom possessed by each *phronimos* will be relativized to some finite (albeit large) number of limited domains. Even though superior people "bring together what is scattered and separate into one" (b12–13) and are able to deliberate well about "about what sorts of things promote living well in general" (*NE* VI.5 1140a28), Aristotle believes that the multitude will possess wisdom about some number of realms—some number of "parts" of practical wisdom—that the *phronimos* lacks.

Thus, in summary, both Aristotle's account of deliberation and his account of how agents take stock of particulars portray *phronimoi* as limited rational creatures whose epistemic handicaps can prevent them from accessing evidence that decisively recommends a best course of civic action [3ii]. On the one hand, because they can only successfully take stock of particulars that resemble those of their previous experience and training, situations presenting utterly novel particularities will not easily be comprehended as evidence by all *phronimoi*. On the other hand, even when they are able to take stock of particulars, *phronimoi* may still find themselves in situations where they must deliberate their way to a conclusion, and this deliberative path is constructed by something like refutable reasoning that offers minimal epistemic support for its conclusion.

I.2. Initial and Persistent Disagreement over Political Decisions

Do any of these considerations show, however, that Aristotle imagines *phronimoi* disagreeing over which course of action should be taken in a particular situation? Several passages suggest that perfectly excellent deliberators may initially, in isolation, reach different tentative conclusions about what the city should do. For example, note how Aristotle follows his claim that deliberation concerns what is unclear:

> Deliberation concerns things holding for the most part—but things unclear in their outcome, and for which there is no definition. And we enlist partners in deliberation on large issues, distrusting ourselves as not being able to discern to the proper degree. (*NE* III.3 1112b8–11)

Note three elements. First, this passage is not merely describing average, *non*excellent deliberators: "distrusting ourselves" suggests that Aristotle is even including people like himself among those facing "large" issues. Second, since it would be pointless to "enlist partners" if everyone had identical thoughts, this statement tacitly acknowledges the possibility for *phronimoi* to have different thoughts and arrive at different deliberative conclusions before interacting with one another. Third, and finally, we see Aristotle here highlighting the weakness of the epistemic connections in deliberation that I discussed in the last section: even excellent agents cannot "discern to the proper degree" on these large issues. Similarly, Aristotle describes a common argument against kingship thus:

> Yet, it is certainly not easy for a single ruler to oversee many things; hence there will have to be numerous officials appointed under him . . . Besides, as we said earlier, if it really is just for the excellent man to rule because he is better, well, two good ones are better than one. Hence the saying "When two go together . . . ," and Agamemnon's prayer, "May ten such counselors be mine." (*Pol.* III.16 1287b8–15)

Once again, this passage concerns the advice of "excellent" men; once again, this quotation only makes sense if these excellent people arrive to counsel the king with different views on what the city should do. Similarly, consider the comparison made between multiple advisors and different body parts a few lines later:

> And it would perhaps be accounted strange if someone, when judging with one pair of eyes and one pair of ears, and acting with one pair of feet and hands, could see better than many people with many pairs, since, as things stand, monarchs provide themselves with many eyes, ears, hands, and feet. (*Pol.* III.16 1287b26–30)

If the "many pairs" of eyes and ears that inform judgment were simply reporting the same things to the king, over and over again, then the point of this passage would be lost.

Aristotle's characterization of the virtue of "friendliness" in *NE* IV.6 provides yet more evidence. In this chapter, we are given a description of how virtuous people who are not close friends interact with one another when living and conversing together. Tellingly, Aristotle criticizes those who are always trying to agree with others as "ingratiating" (1126b12) and criticizes those who "praise everything to please us and never cross us" (b12–13). Of course, he is also critical of those who are deficient in friendliness and "oppose us in everything" (b15)—but the portrait Aristotle is painting here is certainly not one of unceasing unanimity.

Nevertheless, all of these passages only support the conclusion that *phronimoi* can have tentative differences in opinion *before* they come together to engage in civic deliberation. We must ask, however, whether Aristotle believes that such differences among agents can *persist* as political disagreements even *after* they have come together into the assembly and discussed the matter at length.

Two arguments suggest that the answer is "yes." First, an argument for persisting disagreement can be made based on Aristotle's account of rhetoric. Rhetoric tells us something about the way Aristotle imagines deliberators sharing thoughts with one another, since rhetoric, like deliberation, involves rational animals coming to grips with subject matters for which we have "no arts" (*Rhet.* I.2 1357a2). Yet Aristotle's description of rhetoric gives the reader no reason to believe that group discussion and deliberation inevitably lead to consensus. On the contrary, not only does Aristotle offer an entire chapter devoted to tactics for refuting a speaker's enthymemes, *Rhet.* II.25, but Aristotle characterizes the subject matter as itself being marked by enduring divisiveness: "[Argument and] counter-argument can be derived from the same topics. For the *sullogismoi* proceed from reputable propositions and many of these are contrary to one another" (*Rhet.* II.25 1402a32–34). Indeed, it is the inherently contentious and debate-inducing nature of rhetorical subject matter that leads Aristotle to recommend that speakers be able "to employ persuasion on both sides of an issue" (*Rhet.* I.1 1355a29–30), and he offers this advice not to put an end to disagreement, but only as a tactic for allowing speakers "to grasp clearly what the facts are" (a32).

Of course, one interpretive response to the acknowledgment of enduring and pervasive disagreement in the *Rhetoric* is to dismiss this work as Aristotle's description of how irrational non*phronimoi* interact with one another. After all, if rhetoric is nothing but irrational flattery (as, for example, the figure of Socrates suggests during his conversation with Polus in the *Gorgias*),[8] then the occurrence of disagreement among political rhetoricians is as predictable as clashing appetites, and it sheds no light on the question of whether virtuous *phronomoi* would disagree. But surely we cannot saddle Aristotle with such a dismissive view of rhetoric. After all, it is Aristotle who complains in *Rhetoric* I.1 that all previous writers on the subject have mistakenly thought of rhetoric as a grab-bag of nonessential emotional tricks, overlooking the rationality of the speakers' arguments (*Rhet.* I.1 1354a11–18).

Indeed, far from thinking of rhetoric as the realm of the irrational, Aristotle famously announces in the first sentence of the *Rhetoric* that "Rhetoric is the counterpart of Dialectic" (*Rhet.* I.1 1354a1)—where dialectic is a serious mode of philosophical inquiry that regularly involves ongoing differences about how to work through knotty puzzles, ongoing differences among reputable opinions and first principles, and even ongoing questioner/answerer duels.[9] Dialectic, in short, features not only disagreements, but ongoing disagreements that Aristotle sanctions as being philosophically legitimate. In short, Aristotle chooses to associate, not disassociate, political disagreements with philosophical disagreements: "Dialectic does not construct its syllogisms out of any haphazard materials, such as the fancies of crazy people, but out of materials that call for discussion; and rhetoric, too, draws upon the regular subjects of debate" (*Rhet.* I.2 1356b35–57a1).

My second argument for the conclusion that initial political differences can persist as ongoing political disagreements among *phronimoi* relies upon Aristotle's sketches of political life. As we have seen in previous chapters, Aristotle does an extraordinarily thorough job analyzing the violent and deeply problematic conflicts of faulty cities. But we also find him mentioning quotidian disagreements of political life without the slightest hint that they are always caused by vice and without any obvious effort to shield *phronimoi* from generalizations that seem to include both average and excellent citizens alike.[10]

For example, Aristotle's candidate for the best sort of city, filled with magnanimous *phronimoi*, embraces a principle of majority rule among those who are active citizens[11]—a political procedure that clearly assumes that even after assembly debate, participating citizens may not have achieved consensus. We might try to exclude *phronimoi* from such disagreement by suggesting either that Aristotle only attributes a nonunanimous procedure to the best city for the sake of rare situations where there is no time to deliberate; or we might suggest that less than virtuous people somehow make it into the assembly. Yet such interpretations strike me as strained: after all, Aristotle explicitly offers books VII and VIII of the *Politics* as a description of what a city "of our prayers" would look like.

Again, in Aristotle's characterization of the best city, each citizen owns his own household and is responsible for its flourishing.[12] Because of their private ownership, it will thus be citizens who are responsible for engaging in the economic exchanges that are necessary and natural for any household.[13] But how do citizens (or their representatives) establish the price at which exchanges are to take place? As Aristotle describes it, establishing the value of a given utility is inherently problematic because the seller is aware of those considerations that speak in favor of the high value of the item, while the buyer recognizes considerations that suggest a low value:

> For recipients say that what they got were small matters for the benefactors which could have come from others instead, and so they belittle them. But the benefactors say that they were the greatest things, that they could not be gotten from others, and that they were given in danger or similar need. Since the friendship is for utility, the benefit to the recipient must be the measure. (*NE* VIII.13 1163a12–17)

I think we could plausibly interpret Aristotle here as describing some sort of haggling over price that ends when the buyer accepts a given exchange value. But whether there is overt haggling or not, the more important point is that Aristotle here recognizes persistent disagreement over value. Even if the transaction itself was overtly polite, Aristotle here raises the possibility that both parties inwardly believe, and then later express, that they got a bad deal. Moreover, Aristotle suggests that such disagreements are common occurrences in utility friendships. For in contrast to gifted goods, which are received without expectation (and which, therefore, cannot disappoint), exchanged goods must meet two sets of expectations—expectations that are based on the participants' respective, often conflicting, needs and requirements:

> Friendship for utility, however, is liable to accusations. For these friends deal with each other in the expectation of gaining benefits. Hence they always require more, thinking they have got less than is fitting; and they reproach the other because they get less than they require and deserve. And those who confer benefits cannot supply as much as the recipients require. (*NE* VIII.13 1162b16–21; cf. *EE* VII.10 1243a2–3)

When they are dealing with one another as virtue friends, and thus involved in sequential rounds of gift giving, *phronimoi* need never dispute over the value of a given good.[14] But nothing in the text suggests that *phronimoi* will escape the disagreements over value endemic to exchanging utility goods that Aristotle describes in these passages. Cities exist, in part, to facilitate economic exchange,¹⁵ the agricultural products of citizens' household estates do not announce their own value, and no third party steps in to set the rate at which they will be exchanged for other goods.¹⁶

Again, Aristotle posits that a judiciary is necessary in *every* city, not merely in corrupt *poleis*: justice is the "organization of a political community" (*Pol.* I.2 1253a38), and in every city this will require a judicial part to render "a judgment about what is just" (a38–39); having people "who participate in administering judicial justice" (IV.4 1291a27) is far more important to a city than what is merely necessary; people cannot live in a community with each other when lawsuits do not take place (VI.8 1322a5–8); every city requires "necessary kinds of supervision" (1322b29–30) including "matters relating to the courts" (b34); and, even in the best of cities, citizens need to be armed—not only for the sake of common defense, but to punish "people who disobey" (VII.8 1328b9). In making these general claims, Aristotle never bothers to pause and make exceptions for the virtuous. Lacking any signs to the contrary from Aristotle, such passages suggest that sometimes *phronimoi* have irresolvable disputes that require courts.¹⁷

Moreover, it is worth revisiting Aristotle's conceptions of what, exactly, a judge does in courts. When describing rectificatory justice as an intermediate between loss and profit, Aristotle offers the following description:

> That is why when people are involved in dispute [*amphisbētōsin*] they take refuge in a judge. Going to a judge, however, is going to justice, since a judge is meant to be, as it were, justice ensouled. Also, they seek a judge as an intermediary—in fact, some people call judges "mediators," on the supposition that a person who can hit the mean is the one who will hit what is just. (*NE* V.4 1132a19–24)

Notice that the reason the disputing parties agree to consult a judge is that they take the judge to be a mediator: Aristotle is *not* here describing a situation where one party wishes to abscond with unjust booty, while a victimized party uses the force of the city to haul this guilty person before a judge. The parties described here wish justice to be done; the parties are virtuous. This, too, is why Aristotle does not describe the judge as one who determines which party is vicious and which party is virtuous; rather than focusing on character, the judge is only searching for a rectification that allows both parties to profit (or avoid loss) equally . . . which is that for which the disputing parties were hoping.

Again, consider that every city needs officials who will handle deliberative issues: "[T]he law should rule universally over everything, while offices and the constitution should decide particular cases" (*Pol.* IV.4 1292a32–34),[18] and in better cities, more virtuous people are office holders—especially those offices that are "ranked higher in dignity" (*Pol.* VI.8 1322a31–32). Yet when such high office is held by someone of virtue, this apparently does not make an inspection [*euthuna*] of that office unnecessary. During Aristotle's criticism of the claim that only experts should inspect experts and that "the multitude should not be given authority over the election or inspection of officials" (*Pol.* III.11 1282a12–14), he never calls into question the assumption upon which his entire discussion rests, that experts should be inspected by someone. Never does he hint that when the office holder is virtuous, the inspection becomes unnecessary. Instead, Aristotle devotes himself to showing that average citizens are capable of rendering better judgments than some may think.

In conclusion, summarizing the argument that I have made so far, Aristotle portrays *phronimoi* as being epistemically limited; he suggests that *phronimoi* may arrive in the assembly having reached different tentative conclusions about the best course of action; and his descriptions of both public dialogue and political life give us reason to think that these differences can persist. To imagine that the *phronimos* is someone who, by dint of his *phronēsis*, always hits upon the best action, and unfailingly accesses a line of impartial reasoning that will convince any rational interlocutor about which civic action is best, is to imagine ethical and political life in a way that Aristotle does not describe.

Rather than resembling two patients with 20/20 vision who can unerringly read off a series of unexpected letters, there can be situations in which Aristotle's citizen *phronimoi* rather resemble leading medical researchers who have different (refutable) theories and research programs about how to cure cancer. At this point in history, cancer is not cured; the best course of research is not known; and researchers disagree about which research program is best. But these epistemic limitations, shortcomings, and disagreements in no way suggest that these scientists are poor scientists or that they lack excellence.

II. The Problem of Multiple Best Actions for the *Polis*

When we consider an individual deliberating over which course of action he should pursue in a given situation, it can certainly turn out that there are several options better than the others but that are equally good for him. In such a situation, if the *phronimos* tries to uncover evidence that will reveal the single best option he can take, he will not find it: for here there are, objectively, multiple "best" actions available. It will not matter, therefore, which of these best actions he chooses; this will be a choice that he could decide with a flip of the coin or a toss of dice.

But when a *city* confronts such a situation in which there are multiple actions that would be best for it [3iii], there arises the possibility of a uniquely political problem that does not arise in the case of an individual agent. For even though, with respect to the good of the city, there may be no great difference between taking option A rather than option B, there may be a very great difference between A and B in terms of the respective costs and benefits rendered to two citizens, $citizen_A$ and $citizen_B$. It could happen that if the city pursues A, $citizen_A$ will greatly benefit and $citizen_B$ will not; while if the city pursues B, $citizen_A$ will suffer, and $citizen_B$ will prosper.

II.1. Virtue and Zero-Sum Environments

Aristotle believes not only that such winner-loser situations take place in cities but that virtuous citizens, in particular, will be dealing with them. First consider how, in his discussion of friendship, Aristotle repeatedly brings readers' attention to zero-sum situations in which a virtuous person will have to decide whether it will be he or his virtuous friends who receive the greater good.[19] For example, here is one of Aristotle's recommendations:

> [A friend] may even give up actions to his friend; it may be nobler to become the cause of his friend's acting than to act himself. In all actions, therefore, that men are praised for, the good man is seen to assign to himself the greater share in what is noble. In this sense, then, as has been said, a man should be a lover of self; but in the sense in which most men are so, he should not. (*NE* IX.8 1169a32–b2)[20]

Note how Aristotle assumes that there are situations in which the opportunity for virtuous action among friends is scarce—situations in which a city may be equally well served by the actions of a good man or his friend, but where it is impossible for both to take action. If even virtue *friends* run into such zero-sum situations, we can infer that zero-sum situations among virtuous citizens will be even more frequent. After all, virtue friendship takes place only among a small number of people, whereas a far larger group of virtuous citizens can be involved in shared political life. If there are not even enough available virtuous actions for a few friends, then there will certainly not be enough to go around for more numerous virtuous citizens.

Presumably, it is also on account of such situations that Aristotle describes one of the difficulties of expanding character friendship this way: "It also becomes difficult for many to share one another's enjoyments and distresses as their own, since you are likely [*eikos*] to find yourself sharing one friend's pleasure and another friend's grief at the same time" (*NE* IX.10 1171a6–8).[21] Why would it be "likely" for character friends to face this difficulty "at the same time"? The implication is that cities regularly put people, including the virtuous, in situations where there are winners and losers.

Another way in which virtuous citizens often inhabit a zero-sum environment with one another is implied by Aristotle's conception of correct civic merit:

> So political communities must be taken to exist for the sake of noble actions, and not for the sake of living together. Hence those who contribute the most to this sort of community have a larger share in the *polis* than those who are equal or superior in freedom or family but inferior in political virtue, or those who surpass in wealth but are surpassed in virtue. (*Pol.* III.9 1281a2–8)

The language of "a larger share" implies that there is a meaningful notion of the sum total of virtuous contributions that have been made to the city, and Aristotle here proposes that the greater the contribution an individual makes to this virtue total, the greater is his merit. But this conception implies that as I perform more virtuous action that contributes to the city, then the percentage of your "share" in the total virtue performed must decrease. All virtuous citizens are thus in a zero-sum relationship with one another in respect to their civic merit.

Finally, in addition to conflicts caused by scarce opportunities for virtuous action and a zero-sum conception of political merit, Aristotle recognizes difficult situations where the attachments of virtuous citizens to their private estates leads to disagreements over benefit and loss. For example, in the midst of his description of the best city, he insists that each citizen should own two plots of land. The explanation of why each virtuous citizen should have part of his private property "near the frontiers" and another part "near the *polis*" is revealing:

> This not only accords with justice and equality, but ensures greater concord [*homonoētikōteron*] in the face of wars with neighbors. For [*gar*] wherever things are not this way, some citizens make light of feuds with bordering city-states, while others are overly and ignobly concerned about them. That is why some city-states have a law that prohibits those who dwell close to the border from participating in deliberations about whether to go to war with neighboring peoples, because their private interests are thought to prevent them from deliberating well. For these reasons, then, the land must be divided in the way we described. (*Pol.* VII.10 1330a16–25)

There are two important features in this passage. First, Aristotle uses the comparative adverb "*greater* concord" [*homonoētikōteron*], instead of speaking of "concord *tout court*" [*homonoētikōs*] or using a superlative to indicate maximal similarity of mind [*homonoētikōtata*]. This suggests that while this two-plot policy may mitigate dispute, disputes are endemic to these sorts of situations; the recommended two-plot tactic will mitigate, but not erase, the endemic conflict. Second, while Aristotle is surely not suggesting that the best sorts of citizens act exactly like the typical citizens of defective cities (who are here portrayed as lacking sensitivity, having ignoble possessiveness, and lacking excellent deliberation because of private concerns), he does think that these average citizens illustrate a principle that justifies (note the "*gar*" at a18) the two-plot arrangement in even the *best* city: virtuous citizens too are more deeply attached to their own private estates than they are to those of others.

From this observation, it in no way follows that Aristotle takes virtuous citizens to be slightly vicious, and we cannot assume that the best explanation for a lack of perfect concord is that there is always some "bad thing that exists in every human being" (*Pol.* VI.4 1318b40–19a1). It may be tempting to assume that truly virtuous people are free of private commitments, which then invites the conclusion that disagreements caused by attachments are symptoms of vice and poor judgment. But remember that Aristotle does not equate virtue with freedom from attachment: in *Pol.* II.2–5, he explicitly rejects the *Republic*'s conception of the best city as something that desires and feels as does a single human, where ruling decision makers neither distinguish between "mine" and "not mine" (461e–62e) nor own private property (415d–17b). His critique is not that the *Republic* describes the best sort of city, but, regrettably, this world is too fallen to achieve that ideal; rather, Aristotle's critique is that the *Republic* is not describing the best city. At the very time virtuous citizens work together for common civic ends, they retain their dissimilar commitments: "[T]he citizens too, even though they are dissimilar, have the safety of the community as their task" (*Pol.* III.4 1276b28–29). Truly virtuous citizens have private attachments; *phronimoi qua phronimoi* deploy a relativized "mine" that is partial to their own.[22]

II.2. Unsatisfactory Counterarguments

The reader might protest, however, that I have moved too quickly from discovering winner-loser situations and private attachments in Aristotle's political theory to the conclusion that *phronimoi* will dispute with one another. I anticipate two counterarguments, both of which I believe to be unsatisfactory.

First, one might counterargue that Aristotle's *phronimoi* will respond to winner-loser situations by resorting to chance. Perhaps the other virtuous members of the assembly would say something like this: "In this situation, we all realize that citizen$_A$ or citizen$_B$ will suffer (or gain) unequally, and we wise citizens agree that the city will be making the best decision regardless of whether it chooses A or B. Thus, despite the protests of citizen$_A$ and citizen$_B$, let us cast lots to see who it will be." This response strikes me as unsatisfactory in two respects. First, this procedure might work when there are only two citizens who will be affected, but the problem of attachments has simply been delayed rather than solved. Nothing prevents a situation from arising in which *all* citizens will be affected by a civic decision—a situation where the city faces a choice between harming (or benefiting) one large group of the citizenry at the expense of the remaining large group. More importantly, this response simply admits the truth of the thesis for which I am arguing, that *phronimoi* disagree. Rather than showing how *phronēsis* would resolve the clashing claims of citizen$_A$ and citizen$_B$, we are given a purely pragmatic procedure for reaching a political decision.

The second strategy one might try is to admit that Aristotle's citizens will inhabit zero-sum situations and that they will have differential attachments, but then to argue that the shared virtue of citizens will overwhelm such problems and ensure unanimity in spite of them. More specifically, the argument could go like this: before Aristotle's *phronimoi* even had families and estates, and before they had matured enough to participate in the assembly, they possessed similar natural virtues in their adolescence that were later similarly cultivated in a common civic education. Thus, as adults, they will end up with shared excellent characters and similar desiderative repertoires. Even in problematic situations, such shared character would suppress disagreement because Aristotle believes that desiderative homogeneity leads to convergence in decisions. After all, virtuous character, as "the intermediate and best condition" (*NE* II.6 1106b22), prepares agents for "having feelings when one should [*dei*], about the things, toward the people, for the end, and in the way one should [*dei*]" (b21–22).[23] That shared virtues lead to converging opinions is furthermore suggested when Aristotle follows this description with the claim that while there "are many ways to be in error [*hamartanein pollachōs*]" (b28–29) there is "only *one* way to be correct [*katorthoun monachōs*]" (b30–31).

This second counterargument, however, does not deliver the desired result: such shared virtue among *phronimoi* need not lead to complete political consensus, will not make zero-sum situations any less prone to dispute, and will not erase property-based disagreement. While I admit that shared character virtue requires *some sort* of convergence, and that similar character virtue prevents the kind of quarrels that break out when people have fundamentally different aims (e.g. those described in *NE* IX.1), I deny that Aristotle believes convergence among *phronimoi* always takes place down at the level of particular beliefs, decisions, and action tokens.

First, a proper state of character merely ensures the true view of what is fine and pleasant (*NE* III.4 1113a31–33) and "acting correctly" is action, decided upon for its own sake and motivated by virtue, that deals well with the objects of choice: the fine, the expedient, and the pleasant (II.3 1104b30–34, VI.12 1144a13–22). While this may mean that there is only one *way or manner* one should conduct oneself, i.e. nobly, there is no reason to think that each situation bears but one noble (correct) action token upon which all excellent agents must embark. Like MPs in the House of Commons, two citizens can disagree with one another while being and thinking of one another as "right honorable" agents conducting themselves well.

Moreover, such shared desires and feelings only ensure that agents will have the same kind of enduring *wishes* for similar kinds of things. As Aristotle puts it, the virtuous are "in concord [*homonoousi*] with themselves and with each other, since they are practically of the same mind [*epi tōn autōn ontes hōs eipein*];[24] for their *wishes* are stable, not flowing back and forth like a tidal straight" (*NE* IX.6 1167b5–7, cf. IX.4 1166a10–29). It is true that these excellent agents share a wish for the common good, a wish for citizens to have *eudaimonia* properly understood, and a wish for a civic order based on correct justice and friendship. But such overarching rational desires vastly underdetermine which action token should be undertaken here and now. This is why Aristotle's virtue-based description of political "concord" [*homonoia*] only delivers "consensus among citizens about the fundamental terms of their cooperation."[25] Indeed, as his own examples show, a *polis* can possess concord when citizens agree to make offices elective (which allows for disagreement over who should hold office), agree to make an alliance with another city (though they may disagree over terms), or agree to have a certain person rule (though citizens may still dispute over what, exactly, the ruler should do). That concord is a kind of fundamental sympathy rather than policy or action consensus also explains why Aristotle does not describe the opposite of concord as disagreement but rather the catastrophic condition of civil war in which citizens make one another an "enemy" (*NE* VIII.1 1155a26).

All of this, then, goes to show that the shared virtue of Aristotle's upstanding citizens in no way guarantees unanimity in specific winner-loser situations or in the face of differential attachments to estates, families, and children; the similarity of their stable wishes, their concord, will not translate into exactly identical feelings or actions in particular situations.

In conclusion, the eye-chart analogy again fails us. First, since there is never more than one correct answer to the question Which letters are on the third row? the analogy ignores the political problem of there being multiple best actions. Second, nothing in the analogy captures the possibility of zero-sum circumstances, since all the patients view the chart autonomously. Finally, it would be bizarre to think that different agents could have differential attachments to different letters.

Rather than picturing patients at an eye clinic, imagine parents trying to get their child into a good school. It would not be the rational wish of a virtuous parent to want to get his or her undeserving child into a school at the expense of a child who was more deserving but from a different family. But when two children from different families are both deserving and would both do a good job, and yet there is only one spot, there is nothing bizarre about a parent desiring that it be his or her child, rather than the other, who gets accepted.

III. Too Much Pessimism for the Best of All Cities?

The Agreement Argument, then, is unsound. The third premise rests on the false assumption that when *phronimoi* lack compelling evidence for a single civic option being the best, they will then also agree that one option would be as good as the other. There can indeed be situations like this—inscrutable situations where the options resemble a choice among identical doors [3i]. But I have argued in this chapter that there is a broader class of scenarios that must be considered. There can be situations in which it is not clear which option is best, but where some *phronimoi* believe that there is more evidence for one option, other *phronimoi* believe there is more evidence for another, and the deliberative train of thought that justifies any conclusion is too epistemically weak to rule out either [3ii]. Again, there can be situations where reason reveals that multiple options would be optimal for the *polis*, but where these options affect different *phronimoi* in different ways and in which their private attachments lead them into dispute [3iii]. Moreover, nothing would prevent situations from arising in which both of these dispute-causing features [3ii and 3iii] were at work at the same time.[26]

Nevertheless, even if I am correct in thinking that Aristotle would reject the Agreement Argument and correct in claiming that *phronimoi* could disagree in the sorts of situations I have outlined in this chapter, is any of this enough to establish my claim that Aristotle imagines virtuous citizens as being engaged in political conflict in even the best of cities? Some interpreters might still balk at drawing such a conclusion.

For those who believe that genuine conflict in politics must always involve bitterness, profound clashes of "worldviews," or some other sort of deep-seated split, the disagreements I have outlined in this chapter might simply seem too innocuous to count as genuine conflict at all. After all, prudent citizens would surely find polite ways to work around any enduring disagreements, and such responsible citizens would also do their best to accommodate persistently opposed interests in such a way that any potential for fighting would be defused.

Notice, however, that this line of thought seems to assume that any form of political conflict worthy of being called "conflict" must resemble, in some way, civil war. However, barring some strong argument to the contrary, I see no reason we should build such an assumption into the very definition of conflict, and (especially in light of his carefully delimited use of the word "*stasis*") I see no reason we should attribute such a view to Aristotle.

Even if Aristotle's ideal citizens are not warring with each other, it still is worth asking whether they can part ways. For there is a profound difference between a political philosophy that allows for opposition in even the most optimal of circumstances and a political philosophy that insists that the best sort of civic conditions would prevent all forms of conflict from arising in the first place. While both views will predict an absence of enmity, feuding, and violent rebellion in perfect cities, these philosophies will nevertheless differ in terms of which navigational skills excellent citizens will deploy as they lead the best sort of political life. A life spent virtuously reconciling oppositions is different than one spent reveling in unanimity, and, as a matter of scholarship, it matters which of these views we attribute to Aristotle.

This rejoinder may lead to another kind of worry about my interpretation. If we allow that *phronimoi* can disagree and find themselves with opposed interests in communal life, and if we also conceive of these oppositions as genuine forms of political conflict, have we not thereby committed ourselves to an interpretation that casts Aristotle as a pessimist who offers no normative ideal for politics? A critic could protest that such dark pessimism is in tension with other important elements in Aristotelian political theory. After all, Aristotle himself states that political science must study "what the best constitution is, and what it would be like if it was *most* [*malista*] like what is prayed for, lacking external obstacles" (*Pol.* IV.1 1288b22–24). How could a conflict-ridden city be *most* like what we would pray for? How could a city with ineliminable oppositions serve as an ultimate goal for political life?

To this sort of critic, I ask the following: Why would admitting debate, disagreements, and on-going oppositions among *phronimoi* be too pessimistic for an ideal of human community? Suppose someone declared, "I am an idealist: by pulling together, I believe we can solve the problem of world hunger," and was then met with the response, "You call *that* idealism? The ideal would be if people were not burdened with stomachs that had to be filled in the first place." We can, I think, complain that this response too briskly sets aside realistic standards that inform our political goals and protest further if someone then called us a "hardened realist" or "pessimist" for our complaint.

The challenge of political decision making in a complicated world of scarcities that regularly features sui generis situations is merely an analog to stomachs needing to be filled. Acknowledging that citizens with different attachments stake out positions at odds with one another, or that citizens face difficult situations that resist conclusive determinations, is not submission to nonidealistic pessimism, but a recognition of the demanding state of affairs that we find as part and parcel of the human condition. Aristotle, I think, is incredibly optimistic about what human beings can accomplish in the face of this challenge. In situations where only conflicting indicators are available for nonomniscient humans, he believes that prudent people will register these conflicting signs into a productive dispute that will bring forth whatever truth is accessible to them. Moreover, he is confident that virtuous people can handle such debate in stride, and he seems to have no difficulty conceiving of dispute and disagreement as part of a political life well lived. He avoids what I take to be the far gloomier view that disagreement always arises from greed and blind ambition and that human beings are so brittle and combative that anything short of consensus must lead citizens down the path of civil war.

The reason we never find Aristotle worrying about disagreement among citizens or celebrating consensus in any of his lists of human goods is probably best explained by the fact that Aristotle never conceived of civic stability as resting upon consensus among inhabitants in the first place.[27] As I will address in a later chapter, for those working in the Hobbesian tradition (wherein the Sovereignty that makes political community possible depends upon a large group of people in the state of nature *deciding together as one* to transfer their authorship to a figure or body), such insouciance about disagreement might seem a dangerous flirtation with an anarchic, warlike state of nature. But for Aristotle, a city is first and foremost a place where people come *to live* together rather than to agree together. Cities arise from large villages because such arrangements make it easier for family estates to procure external goods, and then cities also expand opportunities for citizens to engage in virtuous actions (*Pol.* I.2 1252b27–30)—actions that will allow cities to be a community "whose end is a complete and self-sufficient life" (III.9 1280b34–35). Such living together may involve agreements and disagreements and may require both consensus and dissensus.

Indeed, it is striking that when Aristotle briefly focuses his attention on the subject of increasing unity in the city, he does not outline strategies for finding shared terms of agreement or search for ways in which citizens' views could be accommodated to one another. Rather, the theme he stresses is that a city "should be unified and made into a community by means of education" (II.5 1263b36–37, cf. VIII.1 1337a21–32). The source of citizens' unity is the education they received in childhood, not some conceptual norm or institutionalized procedure that will ensure agreement among adults. Citizens with a common education will have similar characters and aspire to act in accordance with similar virtues. However, as we have seen in this chapter, such psychological similarity, even among perfectly virtuous *phronimoi*, is compatible with dissonance.

Chapter 5

Contending for Civic Flourishing

Aristotle's virtuous agents are not omniscient gods, and they do not inhabit a world that presents itself in complete transparency and offers endless situations in which everyone can enjoy equal benefits and suffer equal costs. Such difficulties would never lead *phronomoi* to engage in *stasis* against fellow *phronomoi*, nor would such citizens be tempted to avoid these difficulties by adopting the discriminatory elitism of partisans. Nevertheless, because of limitations inherent to deliberation, recognition of evidence, and zero-sum situations, we have seen that even the most virtuous of people can disagree.

Yet while these disagreements will play themselves out *in* political realms with virtuous citizens, the disputes diagnosed in the last chapter still have a distinctly apolitical etiology. They arise from epistemic and metaphysical facts of human life that obtain independently of which political order we happen to be considering. Indeed, such disputes could easily arise in associations where quintessential "political" activity is entirely absent: the argument I made in the last chapter could be used to show that disputes will take place in close-knit families with virtuous elders, among virtuous advisors to a tyrant, and among virtuous friends who live among the ruled rather than ruling.

By contrast, in this chapter, I would like to address a type conflict that is more squarely political. We have seen that *phronomoi* will disagree in conditions of group decision making, but will they also engage in conflict that is not just a matter of deliberation and debate? In particular, does Aristotle conceive of virtuous citizens as contesting and competing with one another in a way that is not forced upon them by unavoidable epistemic limitations?

I believe that Aristotle does indeed envision *phronimoi* engaging in competitive political behavior, and in this chapter, I will argue that he reaches this conclusion by making a normative commitment to political competition as a *goal* at which excellent communities should aim. In other words, for

Aristotle, there are kinds of competition among citizens that do not creep into politics as conditions deteriorate or because of citizens' limitations but rather take place because a certain kind of competition is part and parcel of the virtuous life that should be promoted in the best of cities.

I. Virtuous Citizens Wish for Honor

When investigating the topic of competition in Aristotle's political theory, we can do no better than to begin by analyzing the notion of honor, *timē*. This good belongs to a special group that "can be divided among members of a community who share in a political system" (*NE* V.2 1130b32); like both money and safety (1130b2), Aristotle says that honor is a good that must be distributed among different citizens on the basis of justice. But even among this class, honor is unique. For when we carefully consider the specific decisions that must be made to divide and distribute such goods, we realize that honor is particularly competitive: not only is it a good that is inherently zero-sum (as is a pot of money or a fixed number of shields), but it is also a good that cannot be distributed in (arithmetically) equal shares (and in this respect it is *unlike* money or safety items). Receiving a specific honor, by definition, requires beating out another person or group who will *not* receive it; for example: "offices are positions of honor, we say, and when the same people always rule, the rest must necessarily be deprived of honors" (*Pol.* III.10 1281a31–32).[1] Even when large numbers of people receive an honor, this still depends upon the existence of others who fall outside the group.[2]

Such inherently competitive honor played an inescapably large role in ancient Greek culture. Especially among aristocrats, contests were common and incorporated into an exceptionally wide range of activities.[3] In politics, in particular, competition for honor among elites played such an important, enduring, and even essential role that there was a special word coined to capture its energetic pursuit: *philotimia*.[4]

Of course, we cannot argue that since *philotimia* played a major role in ancient Greek society, Aristotle too must have wholeheartedly embraced it. That move not only would betray a sort of naive historicism but also would run afoul of the disapproval Aristotle frequently expresses in his writings. In the *Eudemian Ethics*, those who love honor seek flatterers more than friends (VII.4 1239a21–27); in the *Rhetoric*, it is the hot-headed youths who are honor-loving and desirous of victory (II.12 1389a11–13); in the *Nicomachean*

Ethics, Aristotle not only explicitly rejects the life devoted to honor as being highest because it is "too shallow" [*epipolaioteron*] (I.5 1095b24), but he also classifies *philotimia* as a vice (IV.4); in the *Politics*, he even claims that most of the voluntary injustices perpetrated among human beings are the result of *philotimia* and money-loving (II.6 1271a16–18).

Such passages, however, do not tell the whole story. For though they clearly exhibit a critical attitude toward excessiveness in competition, they do not suggest that Aristotle hoped to dissuade people from seeking honor altogether. On the contrary, the texts show quite clearly that upstanding and virtuous people are supposed to be honor-seeking in two important respects.

First, and most obviously, honor for Aristotle is something that is a good rather than an evil or an indifferent. He is not a Stoic who takes virtue to be the only good, nor a Christian who conceives of honor-seeking as indicative of pride. On the contrary, for Aristotle, honor is worth pursuing for its own sake:

> Honor, pleasure, understanding, and every virtue we certainly choose because of themselves, since we would choose each of them even if it had no further result; but we also choose them for the sake of happiness, supposing that through them we shall be happy. (*NE* I.7 1097b2–5)

Clearly, honor is not as great of a good as happiness, the activity of the highest rational virtue over a complete life. But honor is a good to be pursued for its own sake. There are many other places where Aristotle expresses the same idea: in the *Rhetoric*, he includes honor as a component of a happy life (I.5 1360b22) and an external good (b28); in the *Eudemian Ethics*, honor is listed as one of those "things fought over and thought to be greatest goods" (VIII.3 1248b27–28) that are "good by nature" (b30); the *Nicomachean Ethics* goes so far as to claim that "honor . . . is the *greatest* [*megiston*] of the external goods" (IV.3 1123b20–21).[5]

However, besides thinking of honor as one good among many, Aristotle makes a deeper commitment to the importance of honor in his depiction of the virtuous life. Regardless of whether one adopts an "intellectualist" interpretation of Aristotle's theory of *eudaimonia*, it is clear that a life of complete ethical virtue should be counted as happy (*NE* X.8 1178a9–10). Such a life, we learn as we read through Aristotle's articulation of the individual ethical virtues, is also to be characterized as magnanimous since "greatness in each virtue also seems proper to the magnanimous person"

(*NE* IV.3 1123b30). And magnanimity is a state of seeking and valuing honor: "[E]ven without argument it appears that magnanimous people are concerned with honor; for the great think themselves worthy of honor most of all, in accord with their worth" (1123b22–24).

But why would Aristotle have truly virtuous people valuing honor at all? Such an idea will seem quite far-fetched if we take "honor" to mean nothing but "fame" or "recognition," unhinged from any notion of the good. I believe, however, that Aristotle thinks of people who simply identify honor with fame as being deeply misguided. He distinguishes the way in which most people "enjoy being honored by *powerful* people because of what they expect, since they believe they'll be provided *whatever they need* from them" (*NE* VIII.8 1159a18–21) and the manner in which virtuous people "want honor from *decent people* with *knowledge*" (a22). In other words, honor, when it is properly conceived, is a sign of having a good reputation for "good work" (*Rhet.* I.5 1361a28), and it "is the prize of virtue, and is awarded to good people" (*NE* IV.3 1123b35–24a1). Indeed, notice that when Aristotle critiques the agent who takes honor to be the highest good in *NE* I.5, he does so by *tying* honor to virtue: honor cannot be the highest good because notables "pursue honor to convince themselves that they are good; at any rate, they seek to be honored by prudent people [*tōn phronomōn*], among people who know them, and for virtue" (*NE* I.5 1095b26–29).[6] Conceived of in this way, honor is not simply praise from any random group; it is not empty fame won from powerful cohorts for some trifle. Rather, honor is rational esteem from the *phronomoi* for virtue.[7]

Given that such properly regarded honor-seeking is a kind of crowning achievement to a life of ethical virtue, it thus comes as no surprise that Aristotle is willing to criticize as pusillanimous those who fail to value honor (*NE* IV.3). We can also appreciate why he claims that honor "comes naturally to the ruler" (*EE* VII.10 1242b19–20), that "honor . . . is more or less the end [*telos*] of the political life" (*NE* I.5 1095b23), and why he says of the lives of both politicians and philosophers that "these are the two modes of life principally chosen by the men who are the *most honor-loving* with regard to virtue [*philotimotatoi pros aretēn*], both in past times and at the present day" (*Pol.* VII.2 1324a29–31). He is not injecting shallow pride into lives devoted to contemplation and civic-mindedness; rather, these lives place value upon the praise of *good* people who really know what is ethically or intellectually excellent.[8]

All of this textual evidence suggests that Aristotle has two rather distinct attitudes toward honor-loving. On the one hand, there is a reprobate *philotimia* that is unmoored from prudence and leads to all sorts of trouble. But there is also a proper mode of competitive honor-seeking that plays an important role in a flourishing life of ethical virtue.

Interestingly enough, this dichotomous attitude is not unique to Aristotle, and he was hardly the only one to recognize that *philotimia* could, if detached from considerations of the common good, be a very bad thing. Many Greek citizens of the late fifth and fourth centuries felt that the older, elitist norm of "competitive outlay" had too often sacrificed community flourishing for the sake of individual accomplishment. The case of Alcibiades in the late fifth century was widely considered to be a particularly galling example of a citizen seeking honor without proper regard for the civic costs. However, rather than abolishing *philotimia* from the cultural lexicon, democratic citizens began to insist that honor be won via civic benefit:[9] cities even invented a new kind of honorific decree that commended *philotimia*, but specifically that kind won for the community, that is, "*pros to koinon*."[10] Aristotle's own thinking about honor-seeking not only bears a resemblance to this development but is even couched in the new demotic terminology:

> [Magnificence] has to do with the sorts of expenses called honorable [*ta timia*], such as expenses for the gods—dedications, temples, sacrifices, and so on, for everything divine—and there are those expenses associated with good competitions done on behalf of the common community [*pros to koinon euphilotimēta*], if, for instance, some city thinks a splendid chorus or warship or a feast for the city must be provided. (*NE* IV.2 1122b19–23)

Not only does Aristotle here insist that honor be won "*pros to koinon*," but he goes out of his way to insist that it comes from *good* competitions: he adds the prefix "*eu*" to "*philotimēta*." It is also worth noting that Aristotle obviously feels no need to invent a whole new class of utopian competitions that have no basis in previous experience: in this quotation he contentedly adopts the competitive liturgies of choruses, warships, and feasts that were regular features of actual Greek culture.

Will this kind of competition, which embodies a proper regard for honor, exist in the "city of our prayers" described in *Politics*? The citizens of this particular city are magnanimous,[11] and Aristotle repeatedly stresses the need for *all* cities to have wealthy members who can afford to make such competitive expenditures.[12] He never suggests that cities will be better off by making themselves poorer or by doing away with liturgical outlays. Given that the best sort of citizen is both financially well-off,[13] and will have been educated to share the same conception of complete ethical virtue,[14] I do not see how we can avoid the conclusion that competing for honor properly understood will be integral to living well in the best city.

II. Political Competitions

By establishing that Aristotle embraces these competitions for well-deserved social esteem, I have already gone some way toward showing that Aristotle thinks of the best sort of citizens as being involved in political competition. After all, putting on and attending a dramatic festival was an intensely political experience in the ancient world, and public works [*leitourgiai*] were themselves political in that they generated a type of reciprocity among citizens *as* citizens.[15]

But when contemporary readers think of "political competition," they first and foremost think of candidates being at odds with one another for the sake of gaining political power and office. Does Aristotle recognize anything like this type of political struggle that is so familiar to us? I believe so.

II.1. Ruling and Being Ruled

Let us return to Aristotle's claim that a *polis*, by its very nature, consists of people who are of different kinds and parts (*Pol.* II.2 1261a22–24, III.4 1276b27–29, 1277a5, IV.4 1290b23–24). The differences that help to compose a city are themselves of different types. In the weakest sense, cities depend on there being human beings who are naturally different from one another: for example, the households that help to make cities (III.9 1280b40–81a1) are composed of master/slave, husband/wife, and parent/child relationships—all of which Aristotle takes to depend upon differences in nature. But these sorts of differences are tangential to the city, properly speaking. For a city is a political community that differs in kind from the household (*Pol.* I.1) and is made of people who are, as far as their nature is concerned, equals (II.2 1261a39–b1; III.4 1277b7–9). The differences that are more relevant for the city are those that exist among these natural equals.[16]

One sort of difference among natural equals who make a city is found in those who produce tangible goods. As we have already seen, Aristotle believes that a city depends upon farmers, craftsmen, traders, and laborers who are different from one another and who play some role in producing and selling tangible goods (*Pol.* IV.4 1290b23–1291a10). In *NE* V.5 1132b31–33b28, Aristotle describes how a city achieves an important kind of unity by hosting a system of exchange that allows for these goods to change hands in accordance with reciprocal justice.

But even these differences among workmen do not identify the primary sense in which cities are composed of different kinds of people. For while these workers may be the natural equals of all the other Greek adult males in the city, Aristotle believes they possess well-entrenched, inferior habits that ensure they cannot engage in the deliberation and judgment that is essential to citizenship. Just as the soul is a more important part of an animal than the body, so too are the warriors, judges, office holders, and deliberators more important to a city than its craftsmen and farmers. The former are primary parts of a city, while the latter are merely necessary (*Pol.* IV.4 1291a22–28). Indeed, Aristotle thinks that these functions are so inferior to those of the warriors, judges, and rulers that he even suggests that the best sort of city would have such roles filled by natural slaves (*Pol.* VII.10 1330a25–28).

The major dissimilarity within the city proper, then, is not that between those in the political class and those locked out of it, but it is rather found in how citizens divide themselves from one another. For Aristotle, a citizen is "someone who is eligible to participate in deliberative and judicial office" (III.1 1275b18–19), and a *polis* is "a multitude of such people, adequate for life's self-sufficiency" (b20–21). Note that, so described, a person does not have to be an active participant to be a citizen: rather, he is a citizen merely if the regime makes it possible for him to deliberate and judge. So it is that in cities that have not unjustly restricted citizenship to either an ultrawealthy clique or to some one person who pretends to have godlike virtue, there will be a somewhat large number of citizens—a situation making it impossible for all citizens to rule at one and the same time (II.2 1261a32–33). Citizens are therefore divided between the rulers and the ruled, even when they all possess good habits (and are thus free) and are natural equals (III.4 1277a20–25).

The differences between ruling citizens and ruled citizens are not merely formal. First, ruling citizens really do have more power than the ruled: they hold different offices (II.2 1261b5–6), and they seek to distinguish themselves "in demeanor, title, or rank from the ruled" (I.12 1259b7–8). Second, Aristotle believes that ruling citizens will tend to have more practical wisdom than the ruled (VII.9 1329a8–9) and should, in some sense, be considered better by the ruled (VII.14 1332b39). Third, and perhaps most importantly, Aristotle repeatedly points out that rulers and the ruled possess different kinds of virtues.

> Practical wisdom is the only virtue peculiar to a ruler; for the others, it would seem, must be common to both rulers and ruled. At any rate, practical wisdom [*phronēsis*] is not the virtue of one who is ruled, but true opinion [*doxa alēthēs*] is. For those ruled are like makers of flutes, whereas rulers are like the flute players who use them. (III.4 1277b25–30; cf. 77a14–16)

The notion that practical wisdom is unique to rulers is a particularly striking claim, especially when we recall that Aristotle believes that possessing practical wisdom is a sufficient condition for having all of the other character virtues (*NE* VI.13 1144b30–32). Taken together, these two claims imply that rulers should have the full suite of character virtues—and this is, in fact, what we find Aristotle asserting: "Hence a ruler must have virtue of complete character" (I.13 1260a17–18). Indeed, consider Aristotle's description of justice in the general sense—the sense in which it means complete virtue:

> Moreover, justice is complete virtue to the highest degree because it is the complete exercise of complete virtue. And it is the complete exercise because the person who has justice is able to exercise virtue in relation to another, not only in what concerns himself; for many are able to exercise virtue in their own concerns, but unable in what relates to another. This is why Bias seems to have been correct in saying that ruling will reveal the man; for a ruler is already related to another, and in a community. (*NE* V.1 1129b30–30a2)

What these and similar passages show is that Aristotle thinks of ruling as a role in the city that demands deployment of a wide-ranging psychological repertoire,[17] while ruled citizens—though they may certainly have excellent habits and intellects—will be called upon to exercise those traits for the city in a different and more focused way that requires less independent decision making, and more acceptance and obedience.

None of this suggests that ruled citizens lead passive lives that are apolitical. In the best sort of city, ruled citizens will still be exercising many of the character virtues that help the city (e.g., fighting courageously, helping to put on the sort of magnificent events described above, engaging wittily and truthfully with others, etc.). Moreover, though they may not hold elite positions of active rule, the ruled of the best sort of city can make some sort of contribution that is appropriate for any sort of virtuous "multitude." Whether they "participate in deliberation and judgment" (III.11 1281b31) by forming opinions while listening to leading speakers who advocate for new plans or decisions in a majoritarian assembly, or whether they participate merely by helping to elect and inspect officials (1282a26–27), they are nevertheless helping the exercise of "authority over the more important matters" (1282a38) in the distinctive way that a ruled multitude can do.

Cities, then, are not simply composed of people who are different from one another by nature or by virtue of their dissimilar roles in the means of production. Cities, properly speaking, are composed of citizens who are either rulers or the ruled, and it is these two parts that will need to be unified by some sort of reciprocal equality if the city is to be whole (II.2 1261a29–32).

But how does Aristotle conceive of these free and equal citizens sorting themselves into the positions of rulers and ruled? While we have found that even the best sort of city will feature a distinction between the rulers and ruled, we do not yet know how virtuous citizens will sort themselves in accordance with this distinction.

II.2. Competitive Elections for Office

We saw above that virtuous citizens are honor seekers. In the *Politics*, civic offices are themselves depicted as honors. This isn't shown merely by the fact that one of the two Greek words [*archē, timē*] Aristotle uses to refer to these political offices is the same word he uses to discuss honor [*timē*]. In addition, Aristotle announces that "offices are positions of honor" (*Pol.* III.10 1281a31), and he makes it clear that anyone with a sense of honor will want to control (or at least influence) political office (*Pol.*VI.4 1318b14–22). This is no doubt why Aristotle recommends that democracies should create offices as a tactic for pacifying honor-loving aristocrats who would otherwise be alienated from a democratic way of life (*Pol.* VI.4 1318b27–19a4). So we can expect that virtuous citizens will conceive of holding office as one important way in which they can honor themselves.

But we have also seen that Aristotle thinks that it is impossible for a city to have all of its citizens in ruling positions. Some citizens will be rulers, others will be ruled, and even the ruling citizens will be split up among different offices, whereby "some hold one office, some another" (*Pol.* II.2 1261b6). It seems, then, that we will have a kind of bottleneck: in the best city, there will be a great number of virtuous citizens who value the honor of holding office, but there will be fewer offices that allow them to rule. How does Aristotle conceive of the process that ends with some citizens holding different offices and others citizens being ruled?

The answer to this question, I think, depends on one's interpretation of Aristotle's oft-repeated claim that, in a truly political community, equal citizens rule and are ruled in turn. Books II and III of the *Politics* make it clear that the best city will be constructed upon this principle,[18] and Aristotle says that each virtuous citizen must have "knowledge and ability both to be ruled and to rule . . . to know the rule of free people from both sides" (*Pol.* III.4 1277b13–16). So it is clear that there will have to be some sort of rotation among these citizens—some alternation between periods of ruling and being ruled. What is less clear, however, is how this rotation is supposed to take place.

One prominent interpretation of how Aristotle conceives of rotational rule in the best city is what I will refer to as "universal rotation." On this view, because Aristotle's best city is a "utopian"[19] arrangement, and all citizens are fundamentally equal to one another in terms of merit, distributive justice will demand that every citizen rotates though each and every office in the constitution—or, given that there may still be too few offices for each citizen to have a turn, each and every office will be filled by lot.[20] On this view, citizens do not have to *pursue* office in the best sort of city, or *labor* to gain a position of power there; rather, they are assigned a role.

I doubt that this interpretation is correct. Though it may be true that any given virtuous citizen will end up rotating through *some* ruling position or other, "for a year or some other period" (II.2 1261a33–34), it seems implausible to me that each citizen would rotate through every office, or that each citizen would be equally likely to be picked for any given office.

First of all, Aristotle draws a distinction between offices that are "most necessary" (*Pol.* VI.8 1322a30) and those "ranked higher in dignity since they require much experience and trustworthiness" (a31–33) when describing offices that any well-governed city must have. The latter sort of offices will be positions of high honor and will be considered particularly valuable: "[I]n truth, both positions of power and the other good things are honourable and worth caring about inasmuch as they are truly great" (*EE* III.5 1232b21–23). If it is true that every citizen rotates through every office in the city of *Pol.* VII–VIII, or has an equal chance of doing so, then this will mean that each citizen could not only spend time in necessary offices such as market warden (*Pol.* VI.8 1321b12–16) or sacred recorder (b39), but also in more specialized and "truly great" offices such as general [*stratēgos*] (1322a33–b1, cf. IV.14 1298a24–28). According to the "universal rotation" interpretation, Aristotle would ignore the fact that some citizens may, for example, have more military experience and trustworthiness in battle, and he would instead adopt a strict egalitarian procedure that would vault any citizen into even the highest of high-honor positions.[21]

The mere fact that this interpretation portrays citizens as distributing (high) honors by means of a lottery and "arithmetic" justice strikes me as problematic. Even if there are egalitarian results in the best city, it seems unlikely that Aristotle's virtuous citizens, who embrace "proportional justice," would achieve these ends with such means. Indeed, consider Aristotle's explanation for why there must be a limit to the city's expansion:

> And a ruler's task is to issue orders and decide. But in order to decide lawsuits *and distribute offices on the basis of merit*, each citizen must know what sorts of people the other citizens are. For where they do not know this, the business *of electing officials* and deciding lawsuits must go badly, since to act haphazardly is unjust in both these proceedings. (VII.4 1326b14–19)

Rather than finding a description of a rotational procedure, we find Aristotle talking about elections that reward office proportional to merit. What would be the point of such elections on this interpretation?

Moreover, it isn't clear that this interpretation of rotational rule fits very well with the one straight-forward description Aristotle offers of rotation in the best city. In *Pol.* VII.14, Aristotle asserts that while partisan cities determine their rulers by using an ideological criterion of justice, the criterion in the best city is that of deliberative ability. Thus, Aristotle concludes, because this ability fluctuates with age rather than ideology, "nature itself settled" (1332b35–36) the fact that it is the young and old who should be the ruled, rather than the ruling, part of the city. So, it turns out that when Aristotle considers a process resembling universal rotation, he only associates it with the en masse rotation among generations and does not describe it as a process that explains how specific mature citizens of the ruling cohort end up in particular *archai*.[22]

Again, Aristotle considers offices to be honors, and we have seen that honor is a particularly competitive, zero-sum good. Yet how will offices continue to be truly honorable if they are handed out according to a lottery or in accordance with some other indiscriminate procedure? A procedure of universal rotation transforms civic offices into positions that are filled simply as a matter of course and erases the notion that an office-holder must have done something special to be considered worthy of such an honor.

Finally, I believe this interpretation rests upon a fallacy: it makes an illegitimate move from the (true) premise that virtuous citizens are equal to the (false) conclusion that each one would be an equally appropriate candidate for every one of the higher offices. Even if we were to make the *extremely* unlikely assumption that good citizens have the *exact* same level of training and experience and then make the even more unlikely assumption that they all had an *identical* level of ethical virtue,[23] this radical and implausible equality does not support the claim that high offices like *stratēgos* would be filled by lot. For consider the analogous case of deliberation in political decision making: even if we suppose that virtuous citizens have perfectly equal deliberative skill and intellectual training, we would be wrong to conclude that Aristotle's optimal citizens will abandon the deliberative assembly in favor of a single, rotating decision maker. We have seen that citizens with equally high deliberative skill can disagree, and Aristotle's embrace of a majority-ruled assembly in even the best conditions shows that *phronimoi* can offer to their peers considerations that will strike them as better or worse reasons for a particular action on a particular occasion. In exactly the same way, it seems to me, two equally talented individuals could have different levels of "trustworthiness" as *stratēgos* in a particular year or against a particular enemy.

All of these considerations suggest that we should reject the "universal rotation" interpretation, and that we need to identify a different mechanism by which magnanimous citizens pick office holders. *Pol.* IV.15 shows that democracies use lottery, while oligarchies and aristocracies favor voting and elections. Since, as I have just argued, the notion of political rotation among equals does not by itself entail the procedure of lottery, and because virtuous citizens will assign high offices on the basis of virtue (as do aristocracies), I think we should draw the conclusion that the citizens of *Pol.* VII–VIII will fill their higher offices by holding elections.[24] Unlike the "universal rotation" interpretation, this suggestion adopts a procedure that fits well with a commitment to proportional justice, recognizes that Aristotle takes offices to be positions of honor, does not presuppose an impossible equality among citizens, and does not rest upon an argument that would render the assembly superfluous.

As soon as we attribute elections to the best city, however, we must also include competitions for power: there will be events in which multiple candidates stand for office and only one (or a few) is selected. No doubt, competitions in the "city of our prayers" will differ substantially from those in nonideal political life. First, in the best city, those who are truly worthy for the job will not nominate themselves but will wait for others to recommend them: Aristotle says that the best citizens do not ask or beg [*aiteisthai*] for office and divorce considerations about whether they should serve from their own desire (or lack thereof) to be in office (II.6 1271a9–18).[25] Given Aristotle's conception of honor, this is what we should expect: candidates desire the honor of having their worth *recognized by those in the know*, and they do not lust for mere power or fame as do those who possess reprobate *philotimia*. Second, Aristotle says that the best city must be small enough to allow citizens to be familiar with the character of those they put in office (*Pol.* VII.4 1326b11–20).[26] I take this to be a tacit endorsement of the political mechanism used by actual Greek citizens in ancient *poleis*, suitably idealized: citizens will make decisions among contenders for an office based on the lives they have been leading within the city.[27] They will rate the worth of the candidate based on the notable actions the person has undertaken for the city in the past, and they will also rate the worth of the person's intellectual character based on the political conversations taking place in the agora, gymnasia, and assembly.[28]

How will candidates act after being nominated for office? Aristotle's great-souled nominees would not deny their own importance; on the contrary, they will explain why they really are worthy of great honor. That is, they will compete against one another by making "epideictic" orations that produce "confidence . . . in regard to virtue" [*axiopiston . . . pros aretēn*] (*Rhet* I.9 1366a28) and by persuading voters with their ethical character (*Rhet*. I.2 1356a2). Now no great-souled citizen would dream of making such an oration for a merely necessary job or average honor, and any potential candidate who recognized that he could not win would withdraw (*NE* IV.3 1124b23–26). But when magnanimous candidates do face off, they will compete: "[W]hen [a great-souled person] meets people with good fortune or a reputation for worth, he displays his greatness . . . since superiority over them is difficult and impressive . . . and there is nothing ignoble in trying to be impressive with them" (b18–22).

Thus, among well-known and experienced statesmen who are nominated—among those who really do have reason to believe they are the worthiest—we should expect public debate about who should rule. When the best city, for example, is in an existential conflict and about to enter a series of battles that will determine the history of the community for generations to come (that is, in a year when holding the office of *stratēgos* would be the highest of high public honors), it is difficult to imagine that Aristotle's *megalopsychos* would avoid a competitive debate, the value of which was to clarify the objective worth of citizens for meeting that particular exigency.

II.3. A Competitive Reconstruction of Political Rhetoric

Raising questions about how the highest *archai* of the best city are to be filled thus leads us to the spectacle of highly esteemed citizens being judged, being sought out for service, and then playing important roles in civic deliberations. But how does Aristotle conceive of their participatory activity once they do end up in an office? In particular, when virtuous citizens are involved in group decision making (e.g. in assembly or council), how does Aristotle imagine them engaging with one another?

In the last chapter I argued that Aristotle does not conceive of even perfect citizens as living in continual unanimity. *Phronēsis* does not make all the problems disappear, it does not prevent ongoing disagreement, and it does not erase disputes based in opposing interests (however useful it may be in amicably managing such disputes). But at this point, I would like to argue that Aristotle imagines many public disagreements and disputes taking a certain shape. Namely, it seems to me that Aristotle would comprehend civic discussions as *competitions* among proposals, where a competition is an event in which (1) multiple contenders are pitted against one another in some way, (2) the contenders emerge from the event with an ordinal ranking, (3) this ranking is based upon nonarbitrary criteria and agreed-upon rules, and (4) the outcome of the event is not fixed or determined ahead of time.[29]

Notice that the events I have already discussed in this chapter meet all four conditions. For both *euphilotimēta* and *archai* elections we have (1) multiple citizens who are struggling against one another in (2) an event which will rank them. Moreover, the final outcomes are decided by the judgments of virtuous citizens who have (3) a shared ethical outlook and understanding of the good, thus ensuring a nonarbitrary outcome. Finally, in both social competitions and elections, (4) the process of picking a winner is not a sham or "fixed" in such a way that the winner is predetermined.

Admittedly, it is not as obvious that Aristotle's conception of public deliberation itself meets these same four conditions, so I will offer an argument. It is helpful to begin by briefly revisiting the "wisdom of the multitude" argument of *Pol.* III.11 that I touched upon in the last chapter. Concerning the claim that a multitude, rather than a few of the best, should possess civic authority (1281a40–41), Aristotle says that there is some "truth" (a42) as well as a "problem" (a41). The truth is epistemological: many people together can, in some sense, improve the judgments being made in the political realm. The problem is political: in which specific institutions, and by means of which concrete constitutional arrangements, should real-world multitudes be allowed to exercise this judgment-improving aptitude? As I read him, Aristotle never offers any specific solution to the political problem in *Pol.* III.11.[30] Instead, he argues only for the claim—and it is rather minimal—that cities should steer clear of two extreme political arrangements: one that blocks the multitude completely from exercising any influence over any office and one that selects particular individuals from among the multitude to serve in the most important single-person offices (1281b25–30).

In trying to understand how Aristotle conceives of group deliberation among truly virtuous citizens, we can set aside the political problem and focus on the epistemological claim that a multitude improves the quality of political decisions. Famously, to support that proposal, Aristotle relies on an analogy with a potluck and another with a human being who gains an increased number of feet, hands, and sense organs. The former analogy suggests that group deliberators will be able to achieve higher degrees of wisdom because of the increased number of deliberative inputs into the political process; as participation becomes more inclusive, it becomes less likely that some issue will be left out or overlooked in the deliberations. The latter analogy with the genetically modified human seems to emphasize something like the notion captured in our own saying that "two heads are better than one," or as Aristotle quotes Agamemnon, "May ten such counselors be mine" (*Pol.* III.16 1287b14–15).

Unfortunately, because he does not elaborate on how he understands these analogies, it is hard to infer too much from them. How, exactly, does one create the best meal from all those dishes? How, precisely, does the genetically enhanced human navigate among its expanded options? The text provides almost no help in characterizing the deliberative process by which a community actually arrives at any given outcome.[31] The point I would like to emphasize is that, however vague they may be, Aristotle clearly intends these analogies to support the claim that the multitude *improves* the quality of political judgements and that this improvement function implies that Aristotle conceives of proposals as being *ranked* in terms of better and worse. The judgment rendered by a feast of three is likely to be worse than a feast of fifty; the proposal belonging to a humanoid of sixteen senses is likely to be better than one with five.

Moreover, it seems we cannot avoid attributing this ranking process to Aristotle's conception of deliberation in the best of all cities since we are led to patently unacceptable conclusions should we deny its role. If citizens refuse to rank proposals, no citizen must wrestle with a proposal different from the one with which he began, and there will be no reason to think that the adopted proposal will have improved upon the deliberative inputs in any way. Again, if we do not conceptualize this process as one that ferrets out better proposals from worse ones, it becomes unclear how this process could be thought of as being deliberative in any meaningful way. The virtue of *good* deliberation [*euboulia*] requires that it is "the sort that reaches something good" (*NE* VI.9 1142b22). While in nonideal assemblies speakers might succeed because of mere cleverness in reaching the relative ends set by popular morality, surely Aristotle would think of rhetoricians in the best city as succeeding by exhibiting the virtue of prudence [*phronēsis*]—a virtue that discriminates between better and worse courses of action.[32]

The fact that idealized deliberation exhibits prudent discussion or oration highlights another trait that we must attribute to the deliberative process of virtuous citizens: the assemblymen who judge the proposals will not determine the winner by arbitrary criteria—they will not adopt civic proposals at random. On the contrary, they shall choose the winning policy in accordance with the virtue of comprehension [*sunesis*], which uses "belief to discern what someone else says about matters with which practical wisdom is concerned—that is, discern correctly" (*NE* VI.10 1143a13–15), judging in terms of what is actually good. Indeed, even in nonideal conditions, Aristotle insists that those who participate in the process of discernment must be virtuous to some degree: for a multitude that had *no* developed criteria for judgment would in no way be able to improve the quality of its decisions (*Pol.* III.11 1281b15–21).

Notice, then, that by describing the deliberative process in an assembly as one in which (1) proposals and counterproposals are pitted against one another and then (2) given a ranking, (3) in accordance with nonarbitrary ethical criteria, I have already gone some way in reconstructing Aristotelian deliberation as a competitive process. The only missing criterion is that (4) the result of the group deliberative process not be fixed ahead of time.

This fourth and final point needs to be handled with care, and before showing that it is indeed appropriate to attribute this trait to Aristotelian group deliberation, we should pause to note the philosophical problem this fourth criterion presents. In the last chapter, I argued that it is possible for Aristotle's virtuous citizens to arrive at deliberative gatherings with different opinions, and I also made the case that it is possible for such citizens to continue to disagree even after discussion. Now consider the following question: When virtuous citizens first arrive at the assembly with their divergent opinions and proposals, is the ultimate decision they will reach after discussion (whether that be established by unanimity or majority vote) already a foregone conclusion?

I can appreciate how readers might think that the outcome would, in fact, be predetermined. After all, Aristotle's virtuous citizens share the same ethical standards, and, whatever the proposal put before them, they will judge that proposal in terms of these shared standards. Just as a function whose independent variables are assigned definite values will yield fixed values for dependent variables, it seems that a set of shared principles, given a set of initial proposals, will lead to a fixed ranking of those proposals. Or, to give another analogy, consider the case where one person is a much better diver than another: when these two enter an official diving competition, it will be (more or less) predetermined that the former competitor will win. Similarly, when one initial proposal is superior to another initial proposal (in a deliberative realm with shared norms), it will be more or less predetermined that *phronimoi* will decide upon the former. Of course, when deliberators first enter an assembly (or the swimming meet begins, or values are initially plugged into a formula), no one may *know* this predetermined ultimate outcome, and it may take a great deal of time and effort to reach that point. But this initial ignorance does not change the fact that the participants will inevitably arrive at a predetermined ordinal ranking.

I believe this line of thought is mistaken in no fewer than four ways. First, this argument trades upon the notion that there really isn't any difference between a severely lopsided competition, on the one hand, and a competition that has in fact been determined ahead of time, on the other. Practically speaking, it is true that there may not be much of a difference. But in terms of the objective human reality of what is taking place, and in terms of whether we should conceive of a given event as a competition or not, there is a profound difference of kind between them. A fight that has been "fixed" by the mafia *isn't a fight at all*; it is only a pantomime. By contrast, the ultimate victory of a superior participant in a lopsided contest, though it may be probable, is nevertheless the result of an event that could have had a different outcome. In short, even in situations where one proposal is clearly better than all the others, the fact that all the *phronimoi* would settle upon the superior proposal does not, all by itself, show that this outcome was "fixed" and not the result of a genuine competition.

Second, I think this argument too quickly ignores all the textual evidence (which I collected in the previous chapter) suggesting that Aristotle imagines even the best of deliberators confronting situations whose complexity and opacity outpace any exercise of their epistemological virtues. It is true that we can imagine a group of omniscient gods who, even in such complicated situations, perfectly judge which of many proposals best fit relevant deliberative norms; for them, a deliberative forum would indeed be nothing more than a parade of divine citizens engaged in a "chanting of accepted truths."[33] But this consideration tells us nothing about how a proposal will be judged best in an assembly filled with humans. Consider our analogies. It may be that you are an objectively superior diver than me, and it may be that this fact is known to an omniscient being; but we humans may unfortunately be in a situation where we must determine who is the best diver by observing a single dive off a lake pier rather than many dives off an Olympic diving board. Again, it could be that an incredibly powerful computer could, given specific inputs and rules, produce the objectively best calculated output in an astonishingly short amount of time; but we humans may still have to rely on notions of "strategy" and "tactics" when playing chess against that supercomputer and weighing multiple moves that seem equally good. The realm of human deliberation is one in which there are "things unclear in their outcome for which there is no definition" (*NE* III.3 1112b9). *Phronimoi* will suffer that lack of clarity like other human beings, so the outcomes of their actual deliberations will often end up being very different than what the "God's-eye" view would predetermine.

In addition to these two counterarguments against the claim that, for Aristotle, the outcome of all excellent group deliberation is predetermined, I suggest a third, even more radical, argument. This response is more fundamental in that it calls into question the entire framework for how we should think about the process by which proposals are ranked in the first place.

Consider the different ways in which we rank the performances of those who enter into competitions. In what we might call the "standardized" model of competition, the quality of the behavior of a contestant is assessed by measuring it against a predefined, idealized blueprint; the winner of the competition is then that individual whose movements most perfectly measure up to the blueprint. The diving competitions we have considered so far, for example, select a winner in this way. But not all competitions work the same. What I call the "vis-à-vis" model of competition does not lay down a predefined standard of perfect behavior, but it only sets down rules for increasing a contestant's score; the winner is determined by how frequently she scores vis-à-vis her opponents. Consider, for example, a chin-up competition. Here there is no predefined blueprint of the number of chin-ups that needs to be performed; rather, the contestant is simply ranked on whether he has done more chin-ups than the other contender.[34]

I think it is more plausible that Aristotle conceives of political deliberation in such a way that it more closely resembles a vis-à-vis competition than a standardized competition with preconceived ideal outcomes. When citizens step into the *ekklēsia* to determine which of the many proposals for civic action they should follow, it is not as if each citizen performs a dive and then the group decides who came closest to offering "the perfect—10.0—dive." Rather, the analogy is that a citizen shows up and, by making a proposal, begins doing chin-ups; as that citizen then defends a given proposal and argues on its behalf, he is (as it were) looking around and trying to make sure that he is doing more chin-ups than anyone else. Citizens' proposals are ranked against *one another* rather than against the paradigm of a perfect policy, and the winner is determined vis-à-vis *other proposals*. This, I take it, is the sort of comparative ranking Aristotle has in mind when he says things like "[D]ecision is choice, not unqualifiedly so, but of one thing in preference to another; and this is not possible without reflection and deliberation" (*EE* II.10 1226b6–8).

Note that this way of conceiving of ranking in no way suggests that the entire process of deliberation is unstructured, chaotic, and adulterated by the whims of subjective preferences. As long as the criteria for scoring are based on what is objectively good, the result of a vis-à-vis ranking process need be no more adulterated by idiosyncratic perspectives than that reached by a standardized process. Both models of competition can bring out what, in truth, is the best policy the city should take, though they use different procedures to reach the result, and the meaning of "best" will be different. One process deems a proposal best because it most matches a preconceived objective ideal; the other process deems a proposal best because, as it made its way through the process of deliberation, it did better than any of the other proposals offered according to objective rules for scoring.

If Aristotle conceives of public deliberation along the lines of a vis-à-vis competition, what would the criteria for scoring be? In a chin-up competition, there are agreed-upon, objective standards that determine what counts as a successful chin-up, and these successes will count toward the contestant's total. In public deliberation, what is the analog of such standards? It seems to me that this is just the sort of thing Aristotle enumerates in *Rhetoric* I.6–7. While the deliberative situation is far more complex than that in a chin-up competition (for in the latter there is only one way to score, and scores are never partial), the added complexity of Aristotle's account does not alter the basic point. By my count, *Rhet.* I.6 sets out twenty-eight criteria by which a proposal can score in the assembly, ten of which are well-established, and eighteen of which allow for a score that is "more contentious" [*en de tois amphisbētēsimois*] (1362b29–30). For example, a given proposal scores in a well-established manner by furthering the health, wealth, or status of the city; it scores controversially by embodying what Athena would do, or what Sparta would detest. In *Rhet.* I.7, Aristotle articulates forty-three ways by which such proposals should be scored *relative* to one another, not only addressing the issue of how to score different proposals by the same criterion, but also telling us how to compare proposals by different criteria.

Conceived this way, there is no deliberative blueprint or *paradeigma* that is "stored up in heaven" (*Republic* 592b) from which one could (at least in theory) deduce the best policy proposal: the best policy will be that which does a better job promoting objective goods than those others that happened to have been proposed. A proposal that promises to protect the health of citizens for three months will score lower than one that promotes health for a year; a proposal that promotes the splendor of the city for a year at a certain cost will be ranked above that which yields the same civic beauty at twice the cost. Of course, in situations where some goods can only be promoted at the expense of other goods, these deliberations will become increasingly complex. And, as Aristotle identifies twenty-eight such goods, it seems that he had a deep appreciation of just how difficult deliberation could be. But this complexity will not affect the model: anyone who dropped out of politics to hunt for "the perfect proposal" would be as misguided as the chin-up competitor who left the sport to discover the perfect number of chin-ups. There simply is no such thing as a proposal that makes all citizens perfectly happy, virtuous, healthy, beautiful, wealthy, friendly, honored, loquacious, witty, alive, and just (cf. *Rhet.* I.6) for an infinite amount of time without cost.

The fact that there are so many different ways to score brings to light another, fourth, way in which the shared virtue of assembly members does not determine the direction of discussion ahead of time: different strategies for defending a given proposal may elicit different sorts of counterarguments in the assembly that were not even envisioned before the actual meeting. The sort of argument a given speaker uses to defend a proposal may very well change depending on what other proposals have been made. After all, in the vis-à-vis competitive model I am proposing, the norms do not predetermine the outcome, but simply provide agreed-upon rules. Just as the tactics a team might use to win a particular game of basketball are not analytically deduced from the rules of basketball, but instead depend on the unique challenges posed by the opposing team during the game, so too will the path by which a given proposal beats out its competitors in a particular assembly not be analytically deducible from shared ethical norms.

I suppose someone could try to oppose this entire line of reasoning by claiming that it depends too much on the *Rhetoric*—a work that clearly does not limit itself to describing the deliberations of only the best and most virtuous deliberators. Such a critic might claim that the open-ended vis-à-vis structure I'm attributing to Aristotle's conception of group deliberation is only possible among the flawed participants depicted in the *Rhetoric*, who lack clarity in their thinking. Such criticism in unpersuasive. As I already argued in the previous chapter, we cannot simply dismiss this work as Aristotle's collection of irrational tricks and stratagems; Aristotle sees rationality afoot in a great deal of political communication. Moreover, suppose we were to query Aristotle on how his description of everyday rhetoric would change as citizens improved in virtue. I think he would say that as a political environment became better, the more controversial premises and far-flung comparisons would do less and less work. It seems highly unlikely, however, that he would say that rhetoric would disappear *tout court*. As in any competition, we do not decrease the competition by increasing the virtue of contestants and referees. On the contrary, if anything, we make the contest better.

In summary, we have four reasons to believe that, for Aristotle, the results of a group deliberative process among *phronimoi* would not be fixed ahead of time. First, just as we would not want to mistake actors reading their lines with a genuine (but lopsided) debate, or a mafia-fixed pantomime with a genuine (but unequal) boxing match, so too we should not mistake a predetermined decision with a deliberative process in which one proposal is, because of its superior merits, more or less likely to be decided upon. Second, while *phronimoi* are excellent human beings, they nevertheless are mortals subject to the sort of epistemological shortcomings that can render several competing proposals equally plausible and that also render the ultimate outcome of deliberation about such proposals deeply underdetermined. Third, the very structure of the process by which the best proposals are settled upon suggests the outcome is not predetermined: deliberative proposals are in a vis-à-vis competition with one another, ranked according to rules for scoring, rather than being ranked according to how well they live up to a preexisting, paradigmatic, ideal proposal. Fourth, and finally, because the structure of the contest is vis-à-vis, there are any number of different "tactical" paths by which a given proposal may end up beating out all the other proposals offered in an actual discussion.

Conceiving of civic deliberation in this way, we have an explanation for why Aristotle's excellent civic deliberators will not be condemned to "chanting accepted truths" ahead of their shared discussions. To posit open-ended competition among proposals offered by *phronimoi*, we do not need to "de-normalize," "de-essentialize," or "pluralize" Aristotle's conceptions of the good, nature, justice, or friendship.[35] Citizens of the best city will engage in deliberative competition that requires agreed-upon rules and objective criteria for scoring; without these, there would be a chaotic, decidedly non-Aristotelian, deliberative free-for-all. However, as a vis-à-vis competition in a deliberative realm of epistemic limitation, these shared commitments do not predetermine the winning proposal ahead of time, and thus group deliberation meets condition (4) for a genuinely competitive event.

II.4. Jockeying for Political Influence among Deliberators

There is, nevertheless, an important difference between the activity of rank-ordering *proposals*, on the one hand, and the activity of ranking *citizens* who participate in the deliberative process, on the other. It could be that ruling citizens gather to deliberate in full cooperation as a noncompetitive collective but that they merely employ a deliberative process that demotes weaker proposals and elevates better ones in a public ranking. Perhaps the best sorts of citizens would not even keep track of who authored specific proposals. Proposals could be floated, debated, combined, and so on, without anyone being overly concerned to hand out or receive the credit for the proposal that ultimately carried the day.

I doubt, however, that this is how Aristotle imagines assembly deliberation, and I think we would be making an interpretive mistake to conceive of the best city as a place where deliberative proposals compete in the assembly but the citizens advocating for them do not. On the contrary, the best sorts of citizens will be quite competitive with one another in their deliberations, very much desiring the honor of authoring a winning proposal. The two arguments I will use to support this claim are what I shall call the "implausible-disjunction" argument and the "best-of-intentions" argument.

Earlier, I argued that Aristotle conceives of virtuous citizens as engaging in a "good kind of competition" for honor by means of traditional liturgies [*euphilotimēta*]. The honor won from such acts is an important good for citizens because it is distributed by virtuous peers on the basis that an outlay has improved the *polis*. The agent who would shun such public honor, either on the major-league or minor-league scale, is, in the Aristotelian ethical framework, vicious.

The first version of what I am calling the "implausible-disjunction" argument is simply this: there seems to be no good reason for drawing a sharp distinction between activity inside and outside the idealized assembly and then insisting that the *ekklēsia* is an island of noncompetition in a sea of liturgical struggle. Actual aristocrats competed both inside and outside the assembly, and we should expect Aristotle's reconstructed virtue-crats to do the same. After all, the very opportunities for honor that obtain outside the assembly are present inside as well; the ruling *phronomoi* are collected together with rapt attention, ready to bestow rational esteem for virtue, and every speaker stands up to make a proposal for the sake of the common good. The pump for what we might think of as "rhetorical *leitourgiai*" seems perfectly primed.

The most convincing version of the implausible-disjunction argument, however, is based squarely on Aristotle's conception of "whole" or "correct" justice, which requires that human beings be politically valued according to their virtue (*Pol.* III.9 1281a2–8) and that rule itself in some way be proportioned to worth (*NE* V.3 1131a25–29). The macrostructure of the city in *Pol.* VII and VIII reflects this commitment: "[N]atural slaves" who lack a full-fledged deliberative apparatus are made permanent noncitizen farmers, while fully functioning educated Greeks are rulers because of political virtue. Neither oligarchic wealth nor democratic freedom serves as the basis of the constitution; rather, virtuous activity is the criterion of worth.

It would be quite implausible to suggest that while the entire macrostructure of the best city is committed to ranking human beings according to political virtue, civic decision makers brush aside this same approach at the microlevel of the assembly, treating it as either a justice-free zone or a miniature realm of partisan democratic justice. As it is merit-based justice that structures the way of life in the entire "city of our prayers," surely this same justice mandates that citizens who display exceptional acumen in their proposals be ranked above, held in greater esteem, and given more influence in the assembly than those who do not.

Moreover, on the basis of what I will call the "best-of-intentions" argument, I believe Aristotle conceives of virtuous citizens as desiring and actively seeking to exert this influence. I argued in an earlier section that truly magnanimous citizens will wait for their prudent peers to nominate them for prestigious *archai* and that their desire or lack of desire for the office itself has no bearing on whether they serve. Similarly, here in the deliberative assembly, we should expect that virtuous citizens' desire or lack of desire to be held in esteem will not be the factor that explains their behavior. But while the earlier analysis dealt with the issue of how citizens act toward offices *they do not yet have*, here we are examining the behavior of citizens who are *already* serving in the office of the assembly. Thus, just as we would expect the magnanimous *stratēgos* to use that office to do as much good as he could with the power that this role makes available, so too we should expect truly virtuous assemblymen to do as much good as they can with their roles as well. But in this situation, where there are multiple citizens with the best of intentions, I believe it follows that there will be competition for influence that Aristotle takes to be good for the city.

I acknowledge that it sounds strange to say that exemplary public deliberators will be competitive with each other; competitive people often possess the worst motives. We frequently observe competitive behavior motivated by greed, *pleonexia*, selfishness, narrow-mindedness, power lust, and a whole host of dubious desires. I would adamantly reject any suggestion that Aristotle's best city has competition in it because its citizens are somehow stuck with such motivational deformities. On the contrary, *Politics* VII and VIII make it clear that all citizens are raised to be free from such problems; the education that Aristotle sketches in *Pol.* VIII is clearly meant to cultivate ethical virtue. These citizens are motivated by civic-mindedness rather than narrow selfishness, friendship rather than brutish egoism. The reader should not assume that I am attempting to slip in psychological assumptions that will transform Aristotle's *phronomoi* into Mandevillian bees, Kantian devils, nonangels of Federalist No. 10, or Nietzschean dominators.[36]

On the contrary, the premises of the "best-of-intentions" argument that I will now articulate are only (1) that virtuous citizens are motivated to see that the very best proposals are adopted by the polis for the sake of the common good; (2) that citizens must communicate their ideas, arguments, and proposals through speech rather than telepathically; and (3) that participants in the assembly do not have an infinite amount of time in which to make their political decisions. If the reader accepts these premises, she will be hard pressed to escape the conclusion that, for Aristotle, even the best sorts of citizens will struggle against one another for the sake of increasing their share of influence over civic deliberations.

Pol. I.2 1253a7–18 advances the second premise: both the city and household are different from other animal communities in the way that their inhabitants communicate. Humans not only generate vocalized noise like animals, but their noise sets out narratives and arguments in which they attempt to make clear to one another what is beneficial and harmful, just and unjust. Moreover, we can safely attribute the third premise to Aristotle based on his attitude about rule by the majority of citizens. As I noted in the previous chapter, *Pol.* IV.4 1290a30–32 makes it clear that Aristotle attributes majority rule among active citizens to the best city. He rejects the idea that democracy is the only constitution that operates by rule of a majority of active citizens and makes the sweeping claim that "in oligarchies and *everywhere else* the greater [*pleon*] part has authority" (a31–32). Given that democracy, oligarchy, and even aristocracy (*Pol.* IV.8 1294a11–14) work by majority rule, it seems best to attribute it to the city of *Pol.* VII–VIII as well. But why does Aristotle believe that every city is ruled by "the greater part"? He provides no direct justification, but the best explanation is probably that political deliberation nearly always takes place under time constraints and in complex circumstances. Of course, on occasion, one citizen might deliver an oration that convinces every single member of the assembly in a relatively short amount of time. But if we attribute to Aristotle the beliefs that fourth-century Greek political environments were quite complex and dangerous,[37] that life-or-death political decisions are inherently contentious, and that rapidly changing exigencies must be dealt with quickly—and we should note that good deliberation must be done in the right amount of time (*NE* VI.9 1142b26–28)—then we have reason to think that Aristotle would insist on a process of majority rule for any nonsuicidal political community.

The antitelepathy premise (2), coupled with the time-constraint premise (3), forces us to conclude that, even in the perfect-sized *polis* (with, say, five hundred participating citizens),[38] not every member of the assembly will be able to deliver a full-fledged political speech in the time that good deliberation allows. If an *ekklēsia* in the best sort of city is going to remain true to its deliberative focus, then the speeches given must be based in argument and must aim at convincing a rational audience. Moreover, because it would defeat the purpose of the forum if every citizen spoke and merely issued an unpersuasive two-minute harangue, the speeches are going to have to be long, well-articulated, and carefully developed.

But in a dangerous situation when time is of the essence, and the issue at hand is complicated, who, in this group of highly educated, politically astute, well-raised citizens, shall be given the honor and power of being a spokesman? If these citizens want, *above all*, to ensure that the common good is furthered (premise 1), then we know that they will not pick a spokesman for their favored position by lottery. *Ex hypothesi*, these citizens are ethically disposed to ferret out the best arguments and favor the orator who will communicate these arguments in the most effective manner. If they left this communicative element to chance, these outstanding citizens would not be making the strongest case they thought possible.

Once again, there is no direct textual evidence in *Pol.* VII–VIII that describes a process by which the best spokesmen are determined. But it is difficult to imagine that it would be anything other than a suitably idealized version of the behaviors that any politician of the ancient world had to perform in *poleis*: outside the assembly, in the streets, gymnasia, and agora, *even a politician with the purest of motives* had to put himself forward and argue, persuade, recite, and struggle for his cause. After all, in a world where politicians do not rely on the dissemination of positions through any type of media, they themselves must command facts, figures, names, arguments; they themselves must explain and reexplain to their peers the correctness of a position, literally showing themselves to have the leading proposals on the issues of the day.[39]

Thus, on my interpretation, the best politicians do not compete because of greed: rather, they compete for the rational esteem of prudent peers because it is this that allows them to chart the course of the city toward flourishing. They will value this competitive process as one that uncovers the leading truth-tellers and do-gooders for the issue at hand. In fact, this is what I take to be the best explanation for why Aristotle says that "any citizen who is able to should try to pursue [*peirateon diōkein*] the power to rule his own city-state" (*Pol.* VII.14 1333b32–33) and why he also links *all* political action to a lack of leisure:

> But the actions of the politician also deny us leisure; apart from political activities themselves, *those actions seek positions of power and honors*, or at least they seek happiness for the politician himself and for his fellow citizens, which is something different from political science [*politikēs*], and clearly is sought on the assumption that it is different. (*NE* X.7 1177b12–15)[40]

Recall the context of this important passage: at this point in book X of the *Nicomachean Ethics*, Aristotle is arguing that the life of contemplation is happier than a life of complete ethical (i.e., political) virtue. Aristotle's description of politics in this passage thus cannot be referring merely to the grubby politics of average cities. On the contrary, the argument requires that we interpret this quotation as a description of *political activity itself*, including the virtuous politics of the best city. Even the well-intentioned citizen of the best possible city must seek "positions of power and honor," and my competitive interpretation explains why this must be so.[41]

Now it may happen that some citizens are so frequently chosen as spokesmen that the political conversations of the day, in a sense, come to them without much effort. Once a citizen has the status of "go to" person, we can expect his life to look more and more great-souled: he can afford to walk slowly and wait for fellow citizens to beg him to speak for their cause. But the possibility of some citizens reaching this level does not alter the basic realities of political activity: in an arena of group deliberation and public reasoning, you must do an awful lot of arguing to convince an awful lot of citizens that *your* opinion is the one to trust and that it is *your* opinion that is worthy of consideration in pivotal moments when time is precious.

III. Contending as a Fine Activity

By attributing competitions for winning proposals, honors, high offices, and political influence to citizens in the "city of our prayers," I am not suggesting that they partake in the sort of political melees that some scholars attribute to Greek *poleis*—where rivalry had an "all or nothing" quality, and where "ostracism was a symbol of the gentler form, the political trials the common manifestation of a more severe form, assassination the final form."[42] Certainly we should make a distinction between a free-for-all and a competition, and throughout this chapter I have been careful to attribute only the latter type of conflict to Aristotle's perfected city. Any form of rivalry that transgresses the ethical norms set out in the shared education of virtuous citizens would cease to be a competition and become civil war or some other type of vicious conflict.[43]

Indeed, whenever Aristotle explicitly criticizes competitions, it is quite striking that he never worries about the *competitive element itself*, but he worries instead about how such competition could morph into activity that encourages vice. Musical competitions, for example, are criticized thus:

> We reject professional education in instruments (and by professional education I mean the kind that aims at competition

[*agōnas*]). For the performer does not take part in this kind of education for the sake of his own virtue but to give his audience pleasure, and a boorish pleasure at that. (*Pol.* VIII.6 1341b8–12)

Note that if professional education in instruments involved preparing students for competition that increased their own virtue, there would be no problem at all. Similarly, when he criticizes athletic competitions, it is not the competition he condemns, but rather the physical conditioning of the athletes that destroys their health.[44]

In fact, because a competition (unlike a melee) *requires* cooperation about rules and agreement on ethical norms, we can think of these rules as components of the civic consensus and like-mindedness [*homonoia*] that undergird well-functioning cities. As I pointed out in the last chapter, political concord is a condition of secure agreement among citizens on fundamental and final ends, not a condition in which conflict per se is nonexistent. Such agreement about fundamentals is a necessary condition for competition, not a reason to think that it will not exist.

Moreover, rather than thinking that political friendship would quash competition, we have every reason to think that political friendship among virtuous equals promotes competition. If we conceive of political friendship as some form of utility friendship, then it will involve much of the dispute and one-up-manship that we find among buyers and sellers that I described in the last chapter.[45] But even if we think of Aristotelian political friendship as some type of diluted character or virtue friendship, this will not stop competition. Aristotle, after all, describes virtuous people as being engaged in a kind of rivalry with one another:

> [The magnanimous citizen] is the sort of person who does good but is ashamed when he receives it; for doing good is proper to the superior person, but receiving it is proper to the inferior. He returns more good than he has received; for in this way the original giver will be repaid, and will also have incurred a new debt to him, and will be the beneficiary. (*NE* IV.3 1124b9–12)[46]

When one citizen gives another citizen (or group of citizens) a gift, Aristotle conceives of the receiver as being a debtor, under some pressure to retaliate with an even greater gift, and this then pits them in social competition: "For those who are friends because of virtue are eager to provide benefits for each other, since this is characteristic of virtue and friendship, and when that is what people are competing about [*hamillōmenōn*], there can be no complaints or quarrels [*machaí*]" (*NE* VIII.13 1162b6–9). The political implications of such a conception of friendship are also clearly competitive. How, after all, will a community of virtuous citizens respond when one of their peers provides an unusually good dedication, performs with outstanding effectiveness in some office, or offers a particularly good political proposal that is a great gift to the city? It seems plausible to predict that each citizen would strive to escape his indebtedness and throw that much more energy into the competitive political life that animates the city.

Nor will that be the only motivation for entering the contest. Citizens who engage in these competitions will not merely be acting from a desire to pay off a debt or even a desire to promote the common good: truly virtuous people genuinely love fine things, the political life is occupied with fine actions (*EE* I.4 1215b3–4),[47] and "just actions that aim at honors and prosperity are unqualifiedly finest" (*Pol.* VII.13 1332a15–16). Winning a legitimate contest *pros to koinon* is something beautiful, memorable, and pleasurable; public competition for honor is part and parcel of a life that is fine and virtuous:

> Those who are unusually eager to do fine actions are welcomed and praised by everyone: for when everyone contends [*pantōn hamillaōmenōn*] for what is fine and strains to accomplish the very best, everything that is necessary will be done for the community, and each person individually receives the greatest of goods, since that is the character of virtue. (*NE* IX.8 1169a6–11)[48]

When Aristotle here speaks of the virtuous who are "contending" [*hamillaōmenōn*], he is not merely stressing that those who aim for the fine will need to exert themselves.[49] Rather, he is claiming that virtuous citizens enter into a distinctive kind of interpersonal social event: they enter into a political rivalry [*hamilla*] that clearly resembles what we find in sport:

> Victory is pleasant, not only to those who love to conquer, but to all; for there is produced an idea of superiority, which all with more or less eagerness desire. And since victory is pleasant, competitive [*machētikas*] and disputatious [*eristikas*] amusements must be so too, for victories are often gained in them; among these we may include games with knuckle-bones, ball-games, dicing, and draughts. It is the same with serious sports; for some

become pleasant when one is familiar with them, while others are so from the outset, such as the chase and every description of outdoor sport; for wherever there is rivalry [*hamilla*], there too is victory. It follows from this [*dio*] that practices in the law courts [*dikanikē*] and disputation [*eristikē*] are pleasant to those who are familiar with them and well qualified. (*Rhet.* 1370b32–71a8)

The legal and political realms feature the same kind of victory-oriented rivalries that we find in sport; this is why "it follows" that competitive action in those realms is pleasant. In Aristotelian political philosophy, the best communities do not demand that citizens demote themselves for the sake of consensus, but rather they ask citizens to enter fractious institutions and struggle to win competitions for the sake of the beautiful and the pleasure of victory.

PART III

ARISTOTELIAN CONFLICT AND MODERN POLITICAL THOUGHT

Prelude

In the first five chapters of this book, I have argued that Aristotle did not have one theory of political conflict per se and that he never adopted one normative theory of political conflict. Civil war, partisanship, and civic mistrust are treated as different types of clashes, and all three are deemed inappropriate for the type of city Aristotle takes to be best. Yet Aristotle also acknowledges the inevitability of dispute without any sense of regret or pessimism, and, I have argued, he even celebrates civic competition as an important component of virtuous and fine political life. These are five quite different ways in which human beings can be at odds with one another in political environments; the notion of political conflict is multivocal rather than univocal.

Such an analysis of conflict is not, by itself, a complete treatment of Aristotle's political theory. I have made no attempt to offer a comprehensive account of how Aristotle understands concepts such as nature, friendship, justice, and community or how these notions contribute to his theory of civic organization. Rather than developing interpretations of these sources of order, my goal in the last five chapters has been to tease out Aristotle's thoughts on topics that many would consider to be types of political *disorder*.

One way of continuing this book would be to develop a full theory of how these sources of order are to be understood in light of civic disorder. For example, how are we to understand Aristotle's conception of nature, if cities, which exist by nature, are supposed to feature disagreements and competitions? Or again, how are we to understand the bonding that takes place in friendships, if cities do indeed feature political friends who are also rivals? To the extent that the arguments I have offered here are persuasive, interpretations of such familiar ordering principles will need to say something about how they accommodate certain kinds of conflict lest they mistakenly render all sorts of conflict unnatural, unfriendly, or unjust.

However, because fully investigating these topics would take me well beyond the subject of political conflict, I believe it makes more sense to remain on the topic of conflict in politics and turn to offering an interpretation of how Aristotle's way of thinking about human struggle in the civic realm fits into the broader sweep of political philosophy. After all, it is modern political philosophy that is usually associated with themes of conflict, and readers may well wonder how Aristotle's view compares to these modern themes.

Usually when scholars are exploring whether Aristotelian thought is still relevant to contemporary political concerns, they ask whether it can be fruitfully compared to one of the major contemporary theories of political value—that is, one of the theories claiming that some particular value deserves default priority in our political decision making, basic institutional norms, and adopted laws. They may, for example, argue that Aristotle anticipates key elements of liberalism (which, among political values, gives default priority to individual liberty), communitarianism (community), egalitarianism (equality), or republicanism (nondomination).

All these investigations bring out interesting aspects of Aristotle's work, but the subject of conflict need not play a role in any of them. After all, if the goal of such inquiries is to determine which value should serve as an ultimate ideal, then much of the conflict we find in political societies will merely be registered as an aspect of the messy, empirical world that need not play any significant role in philosophical discussion. Or, again, even if conflict is not dismissed as irrelevant for our choice of highest ideals, it will simply show up as an uninteresting and predictable by-product that follows from a given society's embrace of one of these values. For example, in a liberal society that gives default priority to individual freedom, we can confidently predict that individuals exercising their freedom will come to be at odds with one another in various ways. But the types, nature, resolution or management of such political conflict need not be part of the defense of liberalism itself—for such issues of application are "downstream" from the issue of primary concern. So, in what follows, I will set aside the question of how (and whether) Aristotle prioritizes values such as liberty or equality, community or nondomination, and turn elsewhere to look for comparisons between Aristotle's treatment of conflict and more recent approaches.

Given that Aristotle has such a sober and realistic assessment of the problems facing average cities, and because he so clearly appreciates the role that regrettable conflict plays in many real-world communities, it is reasonable to speculate that Aristotle's conception of conflict will show him to have much in common with modern constitutionalists. After all, the constitutional tradition is deeply motivated by the claim that unfortunate conflict among bad actors is an inescapable aspect of political life, and constitutionalism insists that communities must accept, prepare for, and manage such conflict rather than simply wish it away. We will find, however, that Aristotle's conflict theory does not fall into this constitutional mold (chapter 6). While I believe he is aware of check-and-balance strategies, he ultimately concludes that it is the good character of the inhabitants—the sociological virtue of the community—that offers the *only* viable path toward long-term civic stability in average cities.

Rather than constitutional theory, it is democratic theory to which Aristotle's theory of conflict makes him more relevant (chapter 7). However, it is not the familiar notion of democracy as self-government of the people, or even the more recent theory of deliberative democracy, to which Aristotle's views are best compared. Rather, Aristotle's understanding of how human beings can be at odds with one another in political community shows that he anticipates some of the conflict-oriented themes described by Max Weber in his distinct notion of a "leadership" democracy.

Chapter 6

Conflict and Constitutionalism

When we turn to modern political philosophers and ask what role conflict plays in their theories, we probably first think of Hobbes's memorable description of that nasty and brutish condition "which is called War (and such a war as is of every man against every man)."[1] Such war, which Hobbes claims would be found in a state of nature, would be so disconcerting that all rational agents would be motivated to escape it by creating a sovereign who would rule a commonwealth. Again, when considering how conflict is depicted in modern thought, we probably also recall Machiavelli's difficult-to-forget account of how some successful princes need to deploy tactical cruelty at the very beginning of their rule in order to establish their regimes.[2]

In both of these cases, conflict defines the initial stage in a story of political genesis, and conflict so conceived is a species of *pre*-political total war that must take place outside of—or perhaps just beyond the edges of—any kind of order found within communal life. Not only does such conflict resemble a melee without agreed-upon norms, but the actors involved in such violence even lack stable political identities. Unlike the factionalizers that Aristotle depicts in civil war, who take *sides* because they believe their constitution *unjust* or *just*, the human beings depicted in the Hobbesian state of nature (or a Machiavellian founding period) seem to bear more resemblance to those Aristotle calls "either beast or god" (I.2 1253a29). Indeed, Aristotle might even deem such apolitical fighters to be *worse* than beasts since, "as a human being is the best of the animals when perfected, so when separated from law and justice he is the worst of all" (a31–33; cf. *NE* VII.6 1150a7–8).

The terrifying spectacle of pre-political total war is not, however, the only kind of conflict theorized in modern political theory. Many modern thinkers have been well aware that even after political communities are founded and established, citizens continue to struggle against one another. Indeed, the recognition of such intra-communal conflict motivated one of the fundamental critiques of Hobbes's claim that the only way for human beings to escape the state of nature would be to turn over *complete* control to an *absolute* Sovereign. Critics of Hobbes, such as Locke, wondered: what if inhabitants turn over all their authority to such a Leviathan, and then the ruler vested with such authority turns out to be a deeply flawed monster who attacks and preys upon the ruled?[3] While recognizing that some kind of Sovereign power may be necessary for escaping a hypothetical state of pre-political total war, acknowledging the need for such a Sovereign does not erase the possibility of rulers and ruled citizens being at odds with one another.

Hobbes himself was keenly aware of such problems haunting established commonwealths. Yet he was convinced that any attempt to prevent potential abuses by the Sovereign would fatally undermine its power and end up doing more harm than good to the commonwealth.[4] His critics, unconvinced by such a defense of absolutism, and drawing upon historical developments and early contributions to literature about early modern government, set themselves the task of developing so-called "constitutional" frameworks—theoretical accounts of political systems capable of withstanding the threats and challenges posed by imperfect rulers holding Sovereign power over nonideal citizens in a troublesome world. From these efforts emerged many of the principles most associated with modern constitutionalism. Modern articulations of rule of law, theories of limited government, separation of powers, and mixed government were all developed as strategies for preserving modern political communities in nonideal conditions.

Having surveyed Aristotle's understanding of political conflict, we have found that he too was profoundly aware of the threats posed by nonideal political life, and intensely interested in how political communities might handle such risks. Well beyond his brief allusion to the horror of pre-political total war, Aristotle develops an entire theory of how and why civil war erupts in cities, offers an elaborate explanation of typical partisan animus, and gives his readers a detailed account of the mistrust that haunts average cities—a mistrust which, if not managed properly, can lead to civil war. Given that modern constitutionalism was in large part developed to address exactly these sorts of imperfect conditions, it is reasonable to wonder how Aristotle's understanding of managing mistrust compares to the main themes of the constitutional tradition.

I. The Posteriority of the Rule of Law

Let me begin by considering the constitutional notion of the rule of law—the idea that all (or at least most) activities of those in governing positions should accord with general norms that have already been embraced by the political community. Aristotle was quite familiar with this idea. He lists all the common arguments made for the rule of law in *Pol.* III.16, and he was well aware that Plato in his later dialogues had already described and defended the rule of law as a strategy for stabilizing regimes. In the *Statesman*, for example, Plato argued that following laws rather than rulers is the safer course when a city lacks leaders in possession of genuine statesmanship (294d–97e). Moreover, Plato pointed out that even if some wise person *did* appear in the city, most inhabitants would still prefer to live under laws: reflecting on past experiences, residents will worry "that a person in such a position always mutilates, kills and generally maltreats whichever of us he wishes" (301d). Inhabitants not only fear bodily harm, but they fear being exposed to arbitrary and unpredictable power. So, even though living under general laws rather than a gifted leader will inevitably result in clumsy outcomes (294b–c), most people will accept such imperfections when they compare them to the risks of an alternative arrangement. In a challenging world where it cannot be taken for granted that rulers will invariably promote the good of the ruled, the rule of law offers protection and peace of mind to the community at large, so it tends to mitigate the distrust citizens would otherwise possess about those holding power over them.

Aristotle agrees with Plato's "second-best" solution of rule by law to this extent—he too believes that any successful city will need settled laws that are obeyed: "[G]ood government [*eunomia*] does not exist if the laws, though well established, are not obeyed" (IV.8 1294a3–4). Aristotle is especially keen to describe the role law must play in constitutions that include partisan oligarchs and/or democrats. For example, Aristotle characterizes moderate oligarchies as those in which members of the deliberating class "follow the law and do not attempt to make changes that it forbids" (IV.14 1298a37–38) and where leaders consent to having the law rule and not themselves (IV.6 1293a16–17). Similarly, in any kind of mixed constitution, "it is necessary to ensure that laws are in no way broken, and that small violations are particularly guarded against: for illegality creeps in unnoticed" (V.8 1307b31–33). It makes sense that Aristotle, given his conception of *stasis*, would recommend adherence to law for these sorts of constitutions: in such environments, any perceived misallocation of honor and/or money can serve as a spectacle arousing suspicion (or even a trigger for outright civil war), and both the rich and the poor will be prone to interpret distributions as unfair. In a political tinderbox, even the slightest deviation from settled norms can arouse feelings of mistrust.

Aristotle's belief in the importance of law is also on display when he claims that extreme democracies, extreme oligarchies, and tyrannies should not even be counted as genuine constitutions since "where the laws do not rule, there is no constitution" (IV.4 1292a32). Those who rule in such excessive and incorrect regimes make their decisions without proper deliberation; as a result, these rulers struggle to posit genuine laws that are, by their very nature, general in scope, rational, and disinterested. Instead, extreme regimes tend to issue hastily conceived, self-serving decrees that corrode whatever semblance of organization their rule possessed.[5] Indeed, Aristotle so closely associates correct rule with law that, when a ruler who would otherwise be considered a tyrant manages to create some kind of regulation that merely resembles law, that achievement by itself makes him somewhat kinglier (IV.10 1295a14–17).

Nevertheless, though Aristotle acknowledges that creating and following law will play *some* role in any *successful* constitution, the rule of law plays a decidedly minor role in his overall evaluation of how constitutions should manage mistrust among the ruled. For example, as we have seen, when Aristotle considers the challenges facing democracies and oligarchies, his first thought is not that partisan rulers need to stabilize their regimes by embracing law. Rather, his primary recommendation is that they take steps to exclude the careless wealthy and desperately poor from political decision making. In other words, it is improved political sociology, not the generality of law, to which Aristotle gives priority in his recommendations for stabilizing these constitutions. Similarly, we have seen that, when assessing the threats to mixed constitutions, Aristotle stresses how such regimes can only be saved by a large group of "those in the middle," a group composed of members possessing a distinctive suite of character traits. And, finally, while it is true that Aristotle recommends to monarchs (and tyrants in particular) that they stick to traditional areas of control so that they will not appear to be violating the law, we have found that this recommendation is not chiefly motivated by the thought that the ruled will greatly appreciate law-abidingness per se. On the contrary, Aristotle's intuition is that when a ruler follows such laws, he might get credit for improved character: "In character, [the tyrant] will be well disposed towards virtue, or semi-good;

not corrupt, but semi-corrupt" (V.11 1315b8–10).[6] Time and again, it is the issue of character that takes priority over any concern with law as such.

Given Aristotle's deep conviction that the efficacy of law depends heavily on education, perhaps this relatively minor role of law should not surprise us. Laws, in and of themselves, can do little good if the citizens who compose the constitution have not been properly educated to them:

> But of all the ways that are mentioned to make a constitution last, the most important one, which everyone now despises, is for citizens to be educated in a way that suits their constitutions. For the most beneficial laws, even when ratified by all who are engaged in politics, are of no use if people are not habituated and educated in accord with the constitution. (V.9 1310a12–17)

Note the strength of the claim made in this passage: even in the rare case of the *most beneficial* law being ratified *by all citizens*, such universal consent to an objectively good law would come to *naught* without the proper habituation of the citizenry. However worthwhile law may be, it always plays second fiddle to the settled character of the citizens whose traits define the constitution type. As Aristotle elsewhere puts the point, "[L]aws should be established, and all do establish them, to suit the constitution and not the constitution to suit the laws" (IV.1 1289a13–15).[7] In both a normative and a descriptive sense, it is the life of the constitution that drives political success and failure, not the law.[8]

Thus, while Aristotle would not disagree with the claim that defective constitutions need law, the social dependency of law shows that this would be little more than an unhelpful gloss, offered at too abstract a level. Preserving constitutions requires grappling with the constitutional defects that are unique to different kinds of people who possess different kinds of habits. Thinking about the preservation of real-world constitutions requires asking "which constitution, and which kind of it, is beneficial for which, and which kind of people" (IV.12 1296b13), not importing universal laws into social environments for which they may not be suited. In Aristotle's mind, law can serve as a capstone, but not a foundation, for constitutional stability.

It is this primacy of social character that also explains why Aristotle never bothers to discuss law in his account of the best sort of city in *Pol.* VII–VIII and why he claims that there is no law for people who are supremely virtuous because "they themselves are law" (III.13 1284a13–14).

Such statements are not exceptions or qualifications to what would otherwise be a firm commitment to the rule of law.[9] On the contrary, these omissions and claims are only further proof that Aristotle was never committed in the first place to the view that law provides guidance independent of a constitution's character. Law is an instrument for enforcing stability among the patterns of life that citizens have already adopted due to their settled character traits. Such settled custom or second nature is the *only* source of law's force, "for the law has *no* power to secure obedience except with habit; but this can only be developed over a long period of time" (II.8 1269a20–22). Supremely virtuous people are law because their very lives exhibit and induce this sort of stability. In a blessed city where all citizens are virtuous, no separate analysis of law is even needed because a discussion of the temperament of these citizens and the lives they lead is already a description of the constitution's settled character.

Because Aristotle thinks of law in this way—as norms largely dependent upon the stable patterns of life in a city—some scholars have even gone so far as to suggest that Aristotle could not have conceived of constitutions as possessing a legislative function.[10] After all, they argue, a legislative function is one exercised by a body creating *new* laws through frequent acts of a sovereign will, yet Aristotle thinks of laws as stable societal norms that were either never explicitly willed into existence at any identifiable point in time or were enacted in the distant past by a mythic lawgiver. So it is (according to this interpretation) that Aristotle says "the law should rule universally over everything, while offices and the constitution should decide particular cases" (IV.4 1292a32–34): Aristotle, like later medieval theorists, conceives of government as only a judicial instrument that interprets and applies unchanging laws, not an instrument for creating new law.[11]

There is something to be said for such an interpretation. Certainly, Aristotle thinks of laws as being less frequently created and altered than we find in contemporary democracies wherein laws are constantly churned out in accordance with fleeting policy preferences. Nevertheless, such an interpretation goes too far. First, Aristotle is clearly aware that laws can be changed for the better over time (II.8 1268b31–69a12), and he openly entertains the question of whether it is wise to change laws frequently or not (69a12–28). Second, there are many passages in the *Politics* where Aristotle attributes the regular creation of law to a specific part of the constitution. For example, consider the description of the deliberative part of a constitution: "[T]he deliberative part has authority in relation to war and peace, the making and breaking of alliances, and laws; and in relation to death, exile, and the confiscation of property; and in relation to the selection and inspection of officials" (IV.14 1298a3–7). Here, Aristotle places "laws" in a list of conditions that are frequently started, ended, created, destroyed, or altered. A similar idea is suggested by the claim that "laws, apart from those that reveal what the constitution is, are those by which the officials must rule, and must guard against those who transgress them" (IV.1 1289a18–20). While there may be basic, essentially unchanging laws that shape the structure and orientation of the constitution, Aristotle here suggests that there is also a separate class of more mundane laws enforced by the city's officials. Aristotle also seems to have such laws in mind when he states that "nowadays, however, one should also attempt reform by using the law of the Aphytaeans" (VI.4 1319a14) or when he recommends laws against improper confiscations (VI.5 1320a6–9). Indeed, in a very general way, I take it that Aristotle hopes his own analysis of politics will offer deliberators many tools for creating laws that they would not have otherwise considered. He says that legislators

> should make use of our earlier studies of what causes the preservation and destruction of constitutions, and from them try to institute stability, carefully avoiding the causes of destruction, *while establishing the sorts of laws*, both written and unwritten, which best encompass the features that preserve constitutions. (VI.5 1319b37–20a2)

This is hardly a medieval call for citizens of the *poleis* to turn their attention to unchanging natural law and exercise what is largely a juridical function. On the contrary, this is a call to deploy prudence: "[I]t is with this same practical wisdom that one should try to see both which laws are best and which are appropriate for each of the constitutions" (IV.1 1289a11–13).

In conclusion, Aristotle believes that law plays an important role in maintaining the order of average cities, and he thinks that those who legislate should (at least on occasion) create new laws and alter old laws in order to promote civic stability. However, when Aristotle reflects upon the threats, challenges, and problems faced by typical communities in difficult circumstances, he does not imagine law to serve as some kind of beacon that orients all wayward ships around dangerous shoals. Having citizens ready to obey well-made laws is a symptom of flourishing cities, but merely establishing law is no substitute for the sociological and character-based solutions that take priority.

II. External Checks: Aristotle on Limited Government

Because Aristotle does not think of the rule of law as a primary tactic for managing endemic mistrust, it is, perhaps, not surprising that Aristotle never expressly turns to other constitutional tactics that have been offered in the history of political thought as instruments for achieving the rule of law in the face of nonideal conditions—tactics such as limited government and divided government. Indeed, because he never explicitly articulates or embraces such principles, it is surely tempting to assume that nothing like these constitutional tactics was known to Aristotle and that they were only discovered in later historical periods.

But this, I think, is a temptation we should resist. When we reflect upon Aristotle's conception of the mistrust faced by rulers in average conditions, and reconsider his understanding of how rulers might best manage that mistrust, I believe we discover Aristotle entertaining proposals that bear a striking resemblance to these famous principles of constitutionalism. The reason he never develops and champions such ideas is not that he is wholly unaware of them. Rather, it is because he thinks such devices cannot adequately preserve political communities in the face of partisan conflict.

Let us begin by considering the notion that government should be limited. In modern political thought, the core attribute of a limited government is that ruled citizens possess substantive forms of nondelegated political power, which they can use to influence and exert some control over those who govern (that is, the ruled exercise an external "check" on the power of those who rule).

The most familiar modern argument to be made for limiting government in this way is that it helps to promote citizens' freedom. Aristotle would surely be sympathetic. Consider, for example, his description of unaccountable monarchy: "[A monarchy] is necessarily a tyranny of this kind if the monarch rules in an unaccountable [*anupeuthunos*] fashion over people who are similar to him or better than him, with an eye to his own benefit, not that of the ruled. It is therefore rule over unwilling people, since no free person willingly endures such rule" (IV.10 1295a19–23). In Aristotle's mind, there is no way for a ruled person to live freely when he or she is subject to the whims of a tyrant who can in no way be held to account for his choices.[12] For my purposes here, however, I am not interested in exploring Aristotle's scattered thoughts on freedom. Rather, the question I am interested in pursuing is whether he conceives of anything like limiting government as a technique for managing civic mistrust.

Aristotle is certainly worried about the destabilizing effects that can result from flawed rulers possessing wholly unchecked power: "Even if it is very difficult to discover the truth about what equality and justice demand, however, it is still easier than to persuade people of it *when they have the power* to be acquisitive. For equality and justice are always sought by the weaker party; the strong pay *no heed* to them" (VI.3 1318b1–5). In mediocre hands, unlimited power leads to ethical norms being side-stepped or ignored. But does Aristotle, aware of the threat posed by rulers who possess the unlimited "power to be acquisitive," conceive of limited government as a possible solution? Is he aware of the constitutional notion that if ruled citizens possess nondelegated political power and can hold their rulers accountable in some way, even the most acquisitive of rulers has a self-interested reason to avoid the sorts of spectacles and decisions that inspire distrust and sow the seeds for *stasis*?

The basic answer is yes. Aristotle certainly comprehends that giving ruled citizens the power to check ruling citizens can help to make a constitution more stable. For example, Aristotle repeatedly expresses approval for the proposal that cities should conduct an "audit" [*euthuna*] of officials, embracing the idea that those who are subject to rulers should be able to penalize those performing poorly. Indeed, he highlights this ability to check officials as one of the main strengths of successful democracies:

> This is why, indeed, in the aforementioned kind of democracy, it is both beneficial and customary that all elect and inspect officials and sit on juries, but for the holders of the most important offices to be elected from those with a certain amount of assessed property (the higher the office, the higher the assessment), or alternatively for officials not to be elected on the basis of property assessments at all, but on the basis of ability. People governed in this way are necessarily governed well; the offices will always be in the hands of the best, while the people will consent and will not envy the decent; and this organization is necessarily satisfactory to the decent and reputable people, since they will not be ruled by their inferiors, and will rule justly because the others [the common people who are ruled] have authority over the inspection of officials. For to be under constraint, and not to be able to do whatever seems good, is beneficial, since freedom to do whatever one likes leaves one defenseless against the bad things that exist in every human being. So the necessary result,

> which is the very one most beneficial in constitutions, is that the decent people rule without falling into wrongdoing, and the multitude are in no way short-changed. (VI.4 1318b27–19a4)

This remarkable passage shows that Aristotle is aware of the key concept of limited government: even elected officials of great ability—the "best" and the "decent and reputable"—should nevertheless be subject to the constraints of auditing and elections. Aristotle elsewhere makes the same point. He criticizes the Spartan and Cretan constitutions for making senators [*gerontes*] exempt from audit (II.9 1271a1–8, II.10 1272a35–39), and in *Pol.* III.11 he defends the practice of auditing in the face of elitist doubts about whether commoners should be allowed to check their political superiors (1282a25–26). Moreover, as we have seen, Aristotle understands that elections can be used in farming democracies to satisfy those who rarely participate in the politics of a city, but who nevertheless seek the honor of exerting some control over those who will rule (VI.4 1318b21–22). In such constitutions, ruled citizens can effectively block those whom they believe would be inferior rulers from elective "definite" office and can punish those who serve in office and perform poorly. Finally, recall Aristotle's advice to monarchs that they should limit themselves to acting in ways long recognized by their subjects. This is one of the ways in which the rule of law might act as a stabilizing force in monarchies. However, because such laws are norms upheld and expected by those who are ruled, we can also understand Aristotle's advice as a kind of recognition that governments held accountable to the expectations of the ruled tend to be more secure.

Nevertheless, however clear it may be that Aristotle acknowledges the usefulness of procedures and structures that limit rulers in some sense, it is equally clear that he never bothers to develop this idea into anything like a full-fledged doctrine of limited government—a doctrine that could be used as a global strategy for dampening civic mistrust wherever it may arise. Indeed, it is striking that when Aristotle conducts his grand review of all the major principles by which constitutions can preserve themselves (*Pol.* V.8–9), he fails even to mention that constitutions can be made more stable by allowing the ruled to hold rulers to account. He does insist that the multitude wanting the constitution to endure must be stronger than that which does not (V.9 1309b16–18), but he does not go on to say that providing this stronger multitude with a guaranteed power to hold rulers accountable is an effective instrument for ensuring their continued support.

Why would this be so? Since Aristotle is keenly aware of the benefits that auditing and electing public officials might yield, why does he not seize upon the general principle of limited government that lies behind such mechanisms—letting the ruled check rulers—and then systematically deploy it as a technique for minimizing the mistrust felt by those who are subject to rulers' decisions?

One answer to this question, which I will explore later in this chapter, is that Aristotle is deeply committed to preserving a very sharp distinction between rulers and ruled. While modern political theorists may find it easy to think of the ruled as "governors behind the government," Aristotle entertains no such view. On the contrary, as we will see, even in those political communities where citizens are natural equals, he still requires a hierarchy of rulers and ruled to be maintained and insists that the virtues of rulers be plainly distinguished from the virtues of the ruled. In short, it may be that Aristotle never developed the proposal that all rulers, as a group, should be checked by their subjects, as a group, because such an arrangement could undercut the ruler/ruled hierarchy that he took to be fundamental to the operation of all cities.

Another reasonable explanation for why Aristotle never developed limited government as a general tactic for managing mistrust follows directly from the secondary status of the rule of law. Law may be able to stabilize and enforce the settled way of life preferred by most citizens in an existing constitution, but law, all by itself, cannot organize large numbers of inhabitants whose habits are directly at odds with the law. Similarly, when Aristotle considers the efficacy of elections, auditing, and enforcing traditional boundaries, it is likely that he thinks of these devices as aids that can only help constitutions *already* in possession of virtuous, or at least passably virtuous, citizens. Aristotle's defense of allowing average citizens to audit officials, for example, requires that these citizens already possess some degree of human virtue (III.11 1281b15–21). Similarly, Aristotle does not discuss elections as devices capable of stabilizing *any* regime whatsoever but merely suggests that elections can help democratic regimes that already enjoy the stabilizing influence of citizens of moderate means. And when Aristotle recommends to monarchs that they avoid transgressing traditional boundaries, he is certainly not proposing that the ruled wield nondelegated power over their ruler. On the contrary, he is merely suggesting that every city has long-standing norms that a given tyrant would do well to follow for his own self-improvement and safety.

In other words, it is true that some rulers in constitutions can be usefully constrained by audits, elections, and long-recognized traditions. But Aristotle seems to conceptualize such devices as techniques for *reassuring* ruled subjects who are passably virtuous or careful, not as a means by which the ruled, as such, can hold an entire government accountable or force rulers to do their bidding.

III. Internal Checks

Having considered whether Aristotle conceives of external checks on those in power, let us also ask whether he anywhere recognizes a need for *internal* checks on government. Many constitutional theorists who have wrestled with the question of how best to organize government in nonideal conditions have proposed not only that governments should be limited from without by the subjects over whom they rule but also that the flawed actors within government should be able to check one another's activities as well. Such intragovernmental limiting makes it far less likely that any one person (or group) can engage in the reckless and arbitrary actions that then cause mistrust among citizens. In short, internal checks serve as another constitutional tactic for managing mistrust and promoting the long-term stability of average regimes.

In the history of political philosophy, the two primary tactics for establishing this kind of inner regulation are mixed government and the separation of powers. According to both views, the power exercised by government itself should be divided, with no single person (or group) possessing complete control of government. On the mixed theory, such a division is accomplished by allowing all major social interests of a community to share in ruling. For example, when society was conceived of as consisting of the many poor, the fewer rich, and a truly elite few with ancient pedigree, those promoting mixed government argued that all three of these heterogeneous social elements should exercise some degree of government power. By contrast, the separation of powers doctrine was conceived as a way of preventing arbitrary government among people who were all (more or less) homogenous and equal. According to this latter tactic of dividing power, multiple abstract functions of government are identified (e.g., legislative, executive, and judicial), each function is exercised by a distinct agency of government, and then agencies are not allowed to share personnel.

On one reading of the history of political philosophy, Aristotle never even *entertained* the notion that imperfect governments might be internally stabilized through a separation of powers.[13] Rather, the theory of separation was only fully recognized much later during the confrontation between Charles I and Parliament in seventeenth-century Britain and then articulated in the theoretical writings of Locke and Montesquieu. On this view, if Aristotle was cognizant of any tactic for achieving inner regulation of government, it was only that a government including both rich and poor would be more stable than either pure democracy or pure oligarchy. In other words, this interpretation claims that Aristotle embraced a nascent theory of mixed government and that he never considered the notion that equal citizens might establish a government of separate powers.

Aristotle's conception of how mistrust is best managed in average cities, however, gives us plenty of reason to call this account into question—or at least to qualify it in important ways. On the one hand, it is misleading to claim that Aristotle had *no* awareness of the notion that imperfect constitutions might be stabilized by requiring the different, defective, and roughly similar citizens to serve different functions of government. On the other, it is also incorrect to claim that Aristotle is best understood as an early advocate of mixed government in the sense that we find described in the later Roman and English thought. It is more accurate to say that Aristotle considered the possibility of mixed government but then concluded that it would be hopelessly ineffectual.

III.1. Aristotle's Conception of Functional Separation among Rulers

To determine whether Aristotle ever entertained some notion like the separation of powers, let us attempt to answer four more specific questions. Did Aristotle believe that successful governments should exercise multiple, distinguishable functions? Did he believe that governments should be organized so that different institutions (or "branches") of government uniquely serve those functions? Did he believe that citizens should be barred from serving in these different institutions at the same time? And, finally, did Aristotle ever consider the notion that separating personnel in this way would allow each branch to act as a check on the arbitrary actions of the others? If we were going to attribute some version of a separation-of-powers doctrine to Aristotle, then we would need to answer "yes" to all four of these questions.

The answer to the first is fairly straightforward. Like Plato, Aristotle does believe that all cities must exercise a number of differentiated functions. In *Pol.* IV.4 1290b39–91b2, he identifies the following nine "necessary parts":

1. Farmers who produce food
2. Craftsmen who undertake lowly crafts (some are necessary, some for luxury)
3. Traders who engage in selling, buying, trade, and commerce
4. Laborers who provide physical labor when and where it is needed
5. Warriors who make the city militarily self-reliant
6. Judges/jurors who settle disputes and decide what is just in disagreements
7. Benefactors who perform public works with their own property
8. Civil servants who help maintain and run the city's various offices
9. Rulers/deliberators in offices

This is a list of roles or functions that must be served if the city is to operate, not a description of the major sociological groups we should expect to find any given city. We can see that this is so since Aristotle goes on to explain that different democracies and oligarchies exist because different kinds of people end up serving in these abstractly defined roles.

But simply exercising *any* of these roles, however, is not sufficient to effect a change in constitution-type—it is only when different groups of rich or poor inhabitants step into the specific roles of [6] judges/jurors, [8] office-holders, and [9] rulers/deliberators that a city becomes this or that type of partisan regime.[14] Aristotle compares the relation that these three parts have to the rest of the city with that which soul has to body (IV.4 1291a24–28) and claims that it is the proper exercise of these functions that largely determines whether a constitution is going to succeed or not:

> All constitutions have three parts by reference to which an excellent legislator must study what is beneficial for each of them.

When these parts are in good condition, the constitution is necessarily in good condition, and constitutions necessarily differ from one another as a result of differing in each of these parts. One of the three parts deliberates about public affairs; the second concerns the offices, that is to say, which offices there should be, with authority over what things, and in what way officials should be chosen; and the third is what decides lawsuits. (*Pol.* IV.14 1297b37–98a3)

For anyone wondering whether Aristotle entertains some notion of separation of powers, it is rather startling to find him here insisting that there are three different, distinguishable functions that must be served within the soul-like part of the constitution. After all, he might have described these three vital functions as together forming one "controlling" part of the constitution, much in the same way that he collapses all the different crafts of the city into a single "craftsmen" part. But he steadfastly refuses to do this. On the contrary, not only does he repeatedly announce that constitutions must exercise these three particular functions, but when he turns to the project of describing the parts of constitutions, he goes to the trouble of discussing each part separately (*Pol.* IV.14–16) and repeatedly makes it clear that all three of these functions are exercised in both average (VI.1 1316b31–34, VI.2 1317b35–38) and excellent (VII.8 1328b13–15; b20–27) cities. Moreover, it is remarkable that Aristotle insists so strongly on the exercise of the judicial function, conceived of separately from the deliberating and office-oriented part of the constitution. For, in the history of the development of the idea of the separation of powers in later English history, it was the recognition of a distinct judicial power independent of an executive function that was slowest to develop.[15]

I certainly do not mean to suggest that the three parts Aristotle here identifies—the deliberating part, magisterial part, and the judicial part—seamlessly line up with later notions of legislative, executive, and judicial power. As is often pointed out, that is not the case.[16] Exercising a legislative function is only a subset of what Aristotle imagines taking place within what he calls the deliberating part of the constitution. Moreover, there are elements in both the deliberating and office-oriented parts of the constitution that enforce norms and exercise prerogative to meet unexpected challenges, and Aristotle nowhere suggests that such activities are the exercise of a consolidated executive power. But my goal here is not to ask whether Aristotle shares exactly the same conception of separation of powers as we find described in seventeenth-century English pamphlets or in Montesquieu's work, but whether he entertains *some* version of this theory as a way of managing problems in nonideal cities.

At any rate, regardless of how struck we might be with Aristotle's recognition of three separate functions of government, we should not confuse such recognition with the proposal that government should be internally divided. To discover whether Aristotle considered that possibility, we need to examine how he imagines average citizens exercising these functions.

Generally speaking, Aristotle believes that citizens who actively participate in a constitution do so by means of holding "office" [*archē, timē*] of one kind or another. Some offices (like serving on a jury or in assembly) are "indefinite" and put greater emphasis upon deliberating and rendering judgment; other offices (such as serving as general) are "definite" and stress issuing directives. However, in either case, what is "most characteristic" of office per se is that it is a position in the city that allows its possessors to make decisions that will (directly or indirectly) bind other inhabitants through some sort of command (IV.15 1299a25–28). Considered as a whole, these positions of office form a system [*taxis*] that characterizes the ways in which active citizens control one another, so this system, in an important sense, characterizes the entire orientation of the constitution (III.6 1278b8–10, IV.1 1289a15–16). No doubt, this is why Aristotle says that "the question of which offices it is appropriate to combine and which to keep separate should not be overlooked" (VI.8 1321b10–12): for how offices are structured effectively shapes the activity of the city and also ensures that there will be a certain pattern of supervision and management of the constitution's decisions (III.1287b8–9; IV.15 1299a14–24; VI.8 1321b4–12).

During Aristotle's discussion of "which offices it is appropriate to combine," we are offered a good example of the kind of structures Aristotle takes to constitute what we might call the "officiating" dimension of a city.

> Furthermore, officials too should take some actions; in particular, incoming officials should take those imposed by outgoing ones, and, in the case of sitting officials, one should pass sentence and another take the action. For example, the town managers should take the actions imposed by the market supervisors, while other officials take those imposed by the town managers. For the less hatred there is toward those who exact the penalty, the more the actions will achieve their end. To have the same people both pass sentence and carry it out certainly doubles the hatred; and

to have the same people carry out every sentence makes them inimical to everyone. (VI.8 1322a10–19)

Here Aristotle describes a series of procedures and behavioral patterns that define an overarching structure in which individual officials will serve. On the one hand, there is a set of hierarchical relations: there are supervisors, followed by managers, followed in turn by low-level officials. On the other hand, Aristotle draws a distinction between those officials who directly make decisions or "pass sentence" and then different officials who see to it that such judgments are indirectly carried out in the city. Moreover, while this example deals only with issues of town management, Aristotle seems to be suggesting here that these sorts of organizational relationships are only examples of arrangements that could be found in many different areas of the city.

Of particular relevance to the discussion here, Aristotle repeatedly indicates that the deliberating, officiating, and judging parts of the constitution operate within different institutional structures. Consider, for example, Aristotle's claim that "it is neither the individual juror, nor the individual councilor, nor the individual assemblyman who is ruling, but the court, the council, and the people, whereas each of the individuals mentioned is only a part of these. By 'part' I mean the councilor, the assemblyman, and the juror" (III.11 1282a34–37). Similarly, note that when Aristotle considers constitutional types that bear some resemblance to a different type (e.g. aristocracies that bear some resemblance to oligarchies), he simply takes it for granted that there will be institutional parts operating separately:

> For example, where the deliberative part and the part that deals with the choice of officials are organized oligarchically, but the part that deals with the courts is aristocratic; or where the part that deals with the courts and the deliberative part are oligarchic, and the part that deals with the choice of officials is aristocratic; or where, in some other way, not all the parts appropriate to the constitution are combined. (VI.1 1317a4–10)

Again, when he summarizes his thoughts about the kinds of supervisory offices needed in all cities, he describes three different sets of offices carrying out the functions of the deliberative, officiating, and judicial parts (VI.8 1322b29–37).

Now it would surely be misleading to claim that Aristotle imagines the functions of deliberating, officiating, and judging as being housed in "bureaucratic" offices that are "administrative" in the modern senses of those words. Without a doubt, the kinds of arrangements Aristotle attributes to ancient cities are far more rudimentary than governing structures in modern states. Nevertheless, such an anachronistic interpretation would be closer to the truth than one that attributed to Aristotle a view whereby a city is a place of pure spontaneous order in which no conscious effort is made to shape official, institutional structures to ensure that multiple government functions were served. The judging function requires courts with organized juries and systems of arbitration, not simply citizens who render good judgments. The deliberating function will require an assembly or some other kind of organized body, not merely fine deliberators. The officials in a city will need to be arranged into supervisory, managerial, and caretaker relationships, and a city must carefully consider whether (and how) to combine or separate these diverse offices.

However, recognizing three separate functions of government, and even distinct offices supporting each is still not enough to amount to a separation of powers doctrine. That view further requires that political communities prevent their citizens from serving multiple civic functions and that they do so with the goal of preventing arbitrary rule. As a matter of time and space, little would prevent citizens (especially well-to-do citizens) in many ancient *poleis* from sitting on juries, participating in civic deliberations and holding one of the many managerial offices available in a city. Does Aristotle ever entertain the thought that it might be for the best to bar active citizens from wearing multiple civic hats?

Aristotle does believe that the best cities feature citizens who have some specialization in particular civic functions. When speaking about offices in general, he states that "every task is better performed when its supervision is handled as a single matter rather than as one matter among many" (IV.15 1299a38–b1). Moreover, we find Aristotle, besides repeating this general claim about the importance of specialization in several passages (I.2 1252b1–5, II.11 1273b9–15), hinting that among inhabitants in average cities, there will be some who possess specialized knowledge in one particular functional area.

For example, because Aristotle thinks of justice as a type of character excellence, the practice of justice will be limited to those who have already been habituated to apply law with decency (*NE* V.10) and who have enough experience to recognize correctly the demands of distributive, rectificatory, and reciprocal justice (V.3–5). This explains why, for example, Aristotle states that there will be court cases requiring the special skills of arbitrators (II.8

1268b4–22) who exercise a specialized judicial function that regular jurors cannot: "[F]or judgment must be given in these cases too, but it should not fall to a multitude of jurors to give it" (IV.16 1300b34–35).

Again, consider Aristotle's discussion of political prudence in *NE* VI.8. One of the main points he attempts to establish in this chapter is that it is a mistake to lump together a number of different *kinds* of practical wisdom under a single name. He is especially keen to point out that the kind of prudence exercised in the legislative science of crafting universal laws is distinct from the "political" prudence that is exercised when dealing with particulars (1141b24–28). In fact, it turns out that even this latter type of "political" prudence is an abstraction, encompassing the kind of prudence deployed by statesmen who deliberate well, on the one hand, and then the quite different sort of prudence exercised by citizens reaching judicial verdicts, on the other (b32–33).

Given that Aristotle draws these distinctions among legislative prudence, judicial prudence, and the prudence of political action, it seems plausible to conclude that Aristotle also imagines citizens who, in average cities, have more experience or expertise deploying one kind of prudence rather than another. We've just noted that Aristotle recognizes the need for arbiters who possess a distinct kind of judicial expertise. The sorts of advisors and officials that Aristotle imagines surrounding kings (*Pol.* III.16 1287b8–35) probably possess (or aspire to possess) the prudence of political action. And both of these types of citizens seem to be distinguishable from the legislators whom Aristotle describes as coming together to formulate self-consciously universal laws (*NE* V.10 1137b11–29).

III.2. Functional Separation as a Tactic for Thwarting Arbitrary Rule

Aristotle recognizes separate civic functions among rulers, describes different institutions that serve those functions, and believes that well-run cities can feature citizens who specialize in deliberating, judging, or directing the apparatus of officialdom in some capacity. But these three points still fall short of a separation of powers doctrine; attributing that doctrine to Aristotle would require that we also find him championing specialization in separate functions as a means to the end of blocking arbitrary rule.

I believe that those who doubt whether Aristotle ever espoused such a view are, essentially, correct.[17] Although such an interpretation needs to be qualified (as I will discuss below), Aristotle does not think of specialization among ruling functions as general tactic for restraining government, as much as he understands it as a way of dividing labor so that different tasks are given to the sorts of people who would best be able to carry them out. Indeed, two aspects of Aristotle's political analysis would directly counter any suggestion to the contrary.

First, consider Aristotle's lack of trepidation about overreach when discussing the activities of those who deliberate, judge, and officiate. When he offers an exhaustive account of all the offices successful cities possess (*Pol.* VI.8), he is content merely to describe them as tasks that any government must undertake, pays no heed as to whether these tasks can be combined or separated, and entirely ignores the issue of who, exactly, should serve in these official roles. Even when Aristotle offers distinct and extended accounts of the deliberative, official, and judicial parts of constitutions in *Pol.* IV.14–16, he is content to describe how each of these parts may take different forms. He makes no overt attempt to explain how these parts, or how those who serve them, should be related to one another in any given regime. On the contrary, his analysis remains exclusively intrafunctional rather than interfunctional, more similar to the way one would list the diverse functions and varieties of animal organs than to the way in which one would describe different groups jealously guarding a share of governmental power.

Another sign that Aristotle is not particularly distressed by the prospect of one government power encroaching on others can be seen in his description of how some cities need the same people to serve multiple functions. It often happens that the people who are "administering judicial justice" end up being the same as "those who deliberate" (IV.4 1291a27–28). This is especially the case in smaller cities whose officials are like "spit-lamps" because they must serve multiple offices and functions (IV.15 1299b1–10). But Aristotle reports that even in larger cities, where no scarcity of citizens makes it necessary for the same people to serve several roles, most people believe that they have the virtues necessary to serve as deliberators, judges, and capable officials (IV.4 1291b2–6). While Aristotle no doubt thinks that many people exaggerate their own abilities and believes that it would be better not to allow these citizens to undertake so many tasks, it is remarkable that Aristotle nowhere announces a principled, *constitutional* worry about any of these "spit-lamp" arrangements.

Finally, even if we were to overlook this silence concerning intrafunctional infringement, there is also Aristotle's belief that the deliberative part of the constitution possesses supremacy over the others: "[T]he deliberative part has authority . . . in relation to the selection and inspection of officials" (IV.14 1298a3–7). Aristotle seems not in the least bit troubled by an arrangement whereby those who initiate laws and decrees also end up having final control over the offices implementing these decisions. Indeed, he openly embraces such control:

> Besides all these offices, there is the one with the most authority over everything; for the same office often has authority over both implementing and introducing a measure, or presides over the multitude where the people have authority. For it is necessary that there be some body to convene the body that has authority over the constitution. (VI.8 1322b12–15)

The exact makeup and identity of the body that has "the most authority over everything" will differ from constitution to constitution. In democracies, an office convenes and introduces measures to the multitude that then has ultimate authority; in oligarchies, one body both has final authority and implements it.[18] In a monarchy where "someone else has superior virtue and his power to do the best things is also superior . . . he should possess not virtue alone, but also the power he needs to do these things" (VII.3 1325b10–14). In every case, Aristotle posits that there is some *one* office, body, or position that is, or is responsible to, the *sole* source of "authority over everything" and that has "authority over the constitution," but then he expresses no worries that this sort of arrangement might lead to what later thinkers would recognize as "executive" and "legislative" powers being placed in the same hands.

All of this evidence suggests that the standard interpretation of Aristotle as a political thinker who did not embrace the separation of powers is basically correct. While it is true that Aristotle recommends that citizens in both average and excellent constitutions specialize in civic functions (including judging, deliberating, and executing the roles of different definite offices), and though he recognizes that there will be distinct institutional infrastructures that house and support these activities, he is primarily motivated by the idea that such a division of labor will allow for better civic performance, not that such division will prevent rulers from engaging in arbitrary rule.

Nevertheless, I think it is important to recognize a major caveat to this conclusion. Though Aristotle does not advocate separation of powers as a *general* principle for stabilizing all constitutions, he comes tantalizingly close to suggesting that such a tactic can help promote stability in democracies and oligarchies. For Aristotle consistently protests the monopolization of political power that takes place in these partisan regimes, and he criticizes such partisan monopolization not only for compromising efficiencies gained by dividing civic labor but also for preventing ruling citizens from *checking* one another's actions.[19]

First, consider what Aristotle means when he compares "extreme" democracies and oligarchies to tyrannical monarchies (IV.4 1292a11–18, IV.5 1292b4–10). As we saw in a previous chapter, one reason Aristotle thinks of partisan regimes as being tyrannical is that the people who rule in such regimes do not exercise power for the common good, and the character traits of rulers in partisan *politeumata* can resemble those possessed by a tyrant. In addition to such psychological similarities, however, we should here observe that Aristotle also takes partisan constitutions to be tyrannical because of a distinct *structural* transformation that takes place among rulers as partisan constitutions become more extreme. For example, when discussing the path taken by oligarchies as they become more and more oligarchic, he describes a predictable consolidation of political power: rulers' control over the constitution "tightens" [*epiteinōsi*] (IV.6 1293a26) until the members of a single family not only perform all the ruling and judging but also keep all "the offices for themselves" (a28). In other words, the transformation to pure oligarchy brings with it a consolidation of those who exercise control over the three "soul-like" parts of the constitution, and this consolidation is depicted as a problematic development, in and of itself, without regard for who is being excluded.

Aristotle offers a similar description of what takes place in democracies as they become more democratic. Here, too, Aristotle sees a pattern wherein the three soul-like constitutional functions become increasingly monopolized by a single group. For example, Aristotle repeatedly draws a distinction between stable democracies that maintain an institutional separation between the office of council [*boulē*] and the deliberative assembly [*ekklēsia*], on the one hand, and those extreme democracies that fail to uphold such a separation, on the other. The latter type of democracy allows

> for all to meet and deliberate about all matters, while the offices decide nothing, but prepare issues for decision only. This is the way in which the final kind of democracy is actually managed, the one we say is analogous to a dynastic oligarchy or a tyrannical monarchy. (IV.14 1298a29–33)

Here Aristotle is not complaining about a lack of sociological diversity but rather the lack of separation among powers; in extreme democracy, no element within the structure of constitutional offices is able to check the deliberative part housed in the assembly. This sort of political solidification seems to have made a deep and lasting impression upon him: he repeats no fewer than three different times that this managerial consolidation is a cardinal trait of the final kind of democracy (IV.4 1292a25–30, IV.15 1299b38–1300a1, VI.2 1317b28–35).

I believe it is likely that Aristotle has these same partisan consolidations of power in mind when he asserts that, in both extreme democracies and oligarchies, there are no laws but only decrees (IV.4 1292a6–7). No doubt the main reason Aristotle makes this claim concerns character traits: in pure partisan regimes, rulers engage in short-term, reactive thinking rather than the long-term substantive deliberation that is necessary for creating anything deserving of the name of "law." But it could also be that Aristotle thinks pure partisan regimes only pass decrees because they are no longer willing to uphold distinctions among different kinds of official functions. Because doing so would stand in the way of monopolizing power, partisans will refuse to acknowledge meaningful distinctions among the officials who issue specific commands, the judges who are responsible for reaching verdicts about particular kinds of issues, and the rulers who are in a unique position to create self-consciously general laws. In less partisan cities, different officials, even housed in different institutions, would be making different kinds of contributions to the operation of government. But in extreme democracies and oligarchies, such separation is abandoned and the entire structure of constitutional power collapses until it resembles a town manager issuing commands.

Still another sign that Aristotle takes successful cities to be those that maintain institutional separations in order to resist the monopolistic tendencies within partisan regimes is his recommendation to cities that they establish special offices whose function is to thwart citizens from changing the constitution. For example, Aristotle recommends that all "city-states that enjoy greater leisure and prosperity" need an office that devotes itself to "the guardianship of the laws" (VI.8 1322b37–39, cf. IV.14 1298b26–30). This is not a call for a sociological mix of character types; this is a recommendation for the existence of an institution that stands apart from the assembly, and whose function—as the very title of the office suggests—is to check those in the deliberative part of the constitution who might attack and overturn prevailing laws. Similarly, Aristotle recommends that cities establish special courts "concerned with inspection" (IV.16 1300b19–20) that will make it possible to hold officials to account, as well as additional courts that should be devoted to "matters that affect the constitution" (b20–21). In all of these cases, Aristotle is proposing that there be special courts and offices that can block those who serve other functions of the constitution from attaining an unaccountable monopoly on power.

None of this evidence, admittedly, calls into question the traditional conclusion that Aristotle nowhere explicitly theorizes, or openly advocates, a separation of powers doctrine. But it does show us that Aristotle is aware that a monopolization of the distinct, soul-like functions of a constitution can be a grave threat to average cities. Especially for real-world democracies and oligarchies, Aristotle sees merit in the proposal that there should be intraconstitutional hurdles preventing citizens who serve one function of the constitution from exercising the others.

III.3. Aristotle on the Possibility of Constitutional Balance

Because the doctrine of separating powers does not adequately capture Aristotle's understanding of the inner checks that stabilize constitutions, we might wonder whether the tactic of mixed (or balanced) constitution offers a better way of describing his understanding of how stability is achieved in typical regimes saddled with distrust. In fact, many have interpreted Aristotle's analysis of mixed government in this way, portraying him as an early advocate of a view somewhat similar to that espoused by later thinkers such as Polybius, who thought that within government there should be a sociological balance among the kingly elite, the rich, and the people; and Machiavelli, who proposed that republics are stabilized by competing interests of the *grandi* and the *popolo*.[20]

Thinking of Aristotle as an early theorist of mixed government is surely plausible for three reasons. First, like any good theorist of balanced constitution, Aristotle believes in the existence of a prepolitical, heterogeneous population comprising distinct sociological groups that have the potential to be politically efficacious. There are, he thinks, three basic types: "In all city-states, there are three parts of the city-state: the very rich, the very poor; and, third, those in between these" (IV.11 1295b1–3). Among the rich, one tends to find people who are not only wealthy, but who have powerful families and are more educated; among the poor, Aristotle believes we find people who tend to be of low birth and vulgar (VI.2 1317b38–41). Moreover, as we have seen repeatedly in this study, Aristotle offers a well-developed theory of the psychological and political attitudes possessed by these three social groups: in average cities, the rich are oligarchic, the poor are democratic, and those in the middle are passably virtuous.

Second, like other theorists of mixed government, Aristotle believes that average political communities tend to be more stable and safer when they include all major sociological blocks within the operation of the constitution. In my earlier discussion of Aristotle's notion of mixed constitution, I described the three main tactics Aristotle offers as possible ways of bringing both rich and poor into the constitution: statesmen can incentivize participation by using fines and payments, by establishing relatively low wealth qualifications so that neither poor nor rich citizens end up dominating the constitution, and by adopting procedures for selecting rulers and officials that blend democratic and oligarchic norms. These tactics—inclusion, trimming, and proceduralism—all have the effect of bringing the major social groups of the city into the operation of the constitution in a meaningful way.

Third, we might think that Aristotle believes that the Spartan, Cretan, and Carthaginian constitutions "are rightly held in high esteem" (II.11 1273b25–26) precisely because they are real-world illustrations of how mixed government promotes stability. All three of these constitutions described in *Pol.* II.9–11 appear to have a similar, tripartite structure. In each, there is an office that appeals to people at large (overseers, the assembly, and the 104), an office of high honor filled by an elite group of preeminent citizens (the senate, the council, the senatorial board), and another office focused on generalship and religious functions that is limited to distinguished families (kings and order-keepers). In a similar vein, we might think that it is on this basis that Aristotle offers the following observation: "As for Solon, some think he was an excellent legislator because: he abolished an oligarchy which had become too unmixed; he put an end to the slavery of the common people; and he established the ancestral democracy, by mixing the constitution well" (II.12 1273b35–39). In all these cases, Aristotle seems to praise these constitutions for possessing qualities that later political theories would champion as exemplifying mixed government.

But this, I believe, is a misinterpretation. It is true that Aristotle thinks incorporating both poor democrats and rich oligarchs into civic institutions can promote stability. But the analysis I offered in chapter 3 makes it clear that, unlike later thinkers, Aristotle has no faith that *long-term* civic stability can be achieved by balancing problematic sociological groups against one another. In fact, we have seen that, far from thinking of mixed constitution as a solution to the challenge of mistrust in average cities, Aristotle considers mixing rich and poor to be little more than the initial description of a constitutional problem. Though a city might need to include both groups in the ruling class to increase stability, the respective psychological repertoires of democrats and oligarchs are so antagonistic and destabilizing that no ingenious scheme or grand mechanism of social physics could balance them against one another within a specific government. The *only* way to address the fundamental instability caused by mixing rich and poor is to introduce a third group into the constitution with an altogether different psychology; only by swamping the city with middlings of passable virtue can genuine polity be established.

Indeed, Aristotle's description of the Spartan, Cretan, Carthaginian, and Solonian constitutions is no celebration of mixed government, but it is rather a depressing portrait of how mixtures fail. The Spartan system, on Aristotle's telling, cannot withstand the slide toward tyrannical democracy because of the people's control of the *ephors* and the lack of upstanding characters in the senate.[21] The Cretan system morphs into dynastic oligarchy because the intensely elitist office of order-keepers inspires constant intriguing that pushes the city toward civil war. The Carthaginians, though they elect citizens to offices on the basis of merit, also believe people should be elected for their wealth—and this emphasis on wealth is sufficient to turn this constitution toward oligarchy and burden it with the problems of wealth-based constitutions. Even the reformed ancestral democracy created by Solon in Athens is portrayed as a long-term failure: allowing the people control of the law courts leads to the diminution of the Areopagus, and this undercuts any reliable opposition to the poor who transform Athens into "the democracy now in place" (II.12 1274a6–7). Not a single one of these constitutions is ultimately able to maintain a successful long-term balance among all the sociological elements included in the ruling class and avoid a transformation into one of the deviant forms of constitution.

It would, therefore, be a mistake to think of Aristotle as a theorist of mixed government in any modern sense. I believe he would probably doubt the wisdom of Polybius's theory of mixed government,[22] would balk at Machiavelli's advocacy of offsetting rich and poor in republics,[23] and maybe have doubts about the later English theories of balanced constitution wherein a kingly power, an aristocratic power, and a plebeian power were all included in government (albeit with demarcated functional roles).[24] All such constitutional theories anticipate that political conflict will take place among the major groups, but they also seem to take it for granted that the conflict among the groups will reliably take the form of a rational dispute, or perhaps even friendly competition, and so stay within recognized boundaries. Schemes of mixed government set out rules about which groups get positive powers to initiate specific governmental tasks (e.g., the power to wage war, the power to create new law) and which receive negative powers to block those tasks (e.g. the power to deny war funding, the power to veto a proposal) and then expect the groups to abide by these rules that contain and shape their struggles with one another.

We have seen that Aristotle is fully aware of the possibility of such mixes: Sparta, Crete, and Carthage illustrate such arrangements; he imagines different mixes created by inclusion, trimming, and proceduralism; and he carefully considers, in some detail, complicated institutional proposals (such as having separate boards of democratic and oligarchic preliminary councilors that might check one another during the process of setting an assembly's agenda, the power of which both boards could check). Yet, despite appreciating the possibilities for such blends, Aristotle ends up concluding that it is only by incorporating a large group of middlings that average cities will be able to manage mistrust effectively—a pessimistic solution that is dourer given that Aristotle believes large middle classes to be exceedingly rare (IV.7 1293a40–41, IV.11 1296a36–38).

In the end, Aristotle is too wedded to thinking of politics in terms of character to embrace, or develop, some version of constitutionalism that treats social groups as nondescript rational actors or as abstract "forces" that might be balanced according to transcendent natural laws in quasi-mechanical fashion.[25] What a constitution is remains a function of *who* a constitution is, and unless this character is good, Aristotle has no hope. Perhaps, if we are desperate to find a physical analogy that captures Aristotle's theory of how best to manage mistrust in cities that mix partisans, we could say that polity is the solution because it *ballasts* the mix with a third group instead of attempting any *balance* among major social blocks. But even this analogy is misleading. For Aristotle's faith in this third group rests not merely on the fact that it is large or that it disrupts a dangerous dynamic of bipolar power. Rather, Aristotle's view rests squarely on the distinctive middling psychology of the "ballast." It is a unique character repertoire that allows those in the sociological middle to be a source of civic stability.

Chapter 7

Conflict and Democratic Theory

In the last chapter, I argued that the role conflict plays in Aristotle's theory of politics is not that which it plays in constitutionalism. Constitutionalism recognizes the problems posed by imperfect people. In particular, it recognizes the possibility of civil war and also theorizes the condition of "managed mistrust" that must be handled properly if civil war is to be avoided, offering such tactics as the rule of law, limited government, and divided government as a way of keeping *stasis* at bay. However, while Aristotle recognizes principles that bear some similarity to these constitutional tactics, he never develops them in a way that suggests he has confidence in them as reliable and widely applicable tactics for preventing civil war. On the contrary, he portrays (his nascent version of) constitutionalism as always posterior to, and dependent upon, the prior sociological realities of those who inhabit the city. So it is that constitutionalism offers little protection against the characterological conflict that takes place between people who have been habituated to feel differently and who think differently about worth, justice, and happiness—the type of conflict I have called "partisanship." The deep conflict of partisanship cannot be counted on to stay within agreed-upon boundaries, as would intellectual debate or a collegial rivalry, and Aristotle nowhere entertains the even more abstract notion that partisan groups could be safely balanced against one another like so many opposing physical forces.

Moreover, we should note that constitutionalism, born primarily from worries about nonvirtuous people ascending into ruling positions, is essentially nothing but a tool for avoiding civil war. In and of itself, it has little to say about the structure of rational debates among citizens or the nature of competitions for honor and influence that would take place among the vicious and virtuous alike. So, of the five different kinds of conflict that I have argued we find in Aristotle's text, it seems constitutionalism per se really only addresses two: civil war and managed mistrust. Partisanship, disagreement, and competition are largely ignored as independent political phenomena.

In this chapter, I'd like to show that a wider range of conflict types is recognized in certain forms of contemporary democratic theory and that it is with respect to such theories that we can make the most plausible case for the continued relevance of Aristotle's views on communal struggle. Admittedly, given that Aristotle's own conception of democracy is rather contrived, this might seem like an inauspicious suggestion. Aristotelian democracy is little more than a regime in which poor partisans dominate civic decision making—a view that most would agree is of limited value when attempting to think about large, inclusive, democratic nation-states. There is no reason, however, for us to limit ourselves to this restricted conception. When raising the general question of whether Aristotle's understanding of conflict could be relevant to contemporary democratic thought, we should take into consideration how he portrays conflict in all aspects of his work, not just that part that deals with one specific constitution type.

In similar fashion, it would be a mistake to assume that "contemporary democratic theory" could refer only to one way of understanding democracy. Different thinkers have offered dissimilar explanations of what, exactly, makes a given political community democratic. Were we simply to assume one conception of democracy, and then ask whether Aristotle was relevant to it, we would severely constrain the ways in which his ancient views about conflict might still bear upon contemporary approaches.

So, in order to cast a wide net, this chapter explores whether Aristotle's views on conflict bear any similarity to the way this topic is handled by five leading accounts of contemporary democracy. While it is true that Aristotle embraces principles that bear some resemblance to what I will call the "self-government," "deliberative," "agonistic," and "interest-pluralism" models of democracy, all of these views tend to theorize conflict as a homogenous condition that can be treated univocally. It is only the so-called democratic theory of "plebiscitarianism," I will argue, that incorporates the variegated and multivocal approach to conflict that I have argued we find in Aristotle's political philosophy.

I. Democracy as Self-Government of the People

The conception of democracy that is most familiar is what we might call the "We the People" conception, or what I will call the "self-government" model of democracy. On this view, a community is democratic when all its citizens are treated equally and help rule the government to which they submit. All citizens are, in some sense, citizen-governors who can exercise political autonomy.

This model admits of many types, the most recognizable of which are expressed using two distinctions that (taken separately or taken together) demarcate substantially different versions of self-government. The first distinction is that between direct democracy and representational democracy—a distinction that tracks whether there are intermediary officials between citizens and the ultimate decisions of government. In direct democracy, citizens are citizen-governors that regularly (not occasionally) participate in the decision making that yields policy and government action. By contrast, the representational view of democracy features equal citizens who govern by meeting occasionally to choose intermediaries who will then go on to represent the citizens' decisions.

The second distinction that helps distinguish different versions of the self-government model concerns the question of what, exactly, is being registered or expressed in communities that govern themselves. On one view, citizen governors come together to aggregate their preferences, so self-government ends up expressing the preference of the majority. On another view, democracies are self-governing only when they express the single *united* will of *all* citizens (a "general" will), which may or may not be captured by merely counting votes and aggregating preferences.

It is not uncommon to make use of both distinctions when drawing a contrast between politics of the ancient and modern worlds. The small, face-to-face city-states of ancient societies might look like direct democracies in which the collective/general will of citizens prevailed, while democracy in modern nation-states seems to be a process of aggregating citizens' preferences to pick representatives who then do the people's bidding. But however stark these distinctions may be, and no matter how dissimilar city-states and nation-states may appear when described in such terms, all these differences take place within a general framework that understands democracy as self-government. Equal citizens may express themselves through a general or aggregated will, and they may rule directly or through intermediaries—but here all citizens are citizen-governors programming the operation of government.

Aristotle's views on conflict expose some interesting ways in which the self-government model does not resemble Aristotelian political theory. It is true that when Aristotle imagines the political life of the best sort of *polis*, he imagines a city wherein a relatively small group of citizens, living in close proximity, are involved in governance. But when contemporary democracy is understood in terms of self-governance, where is political conflict allowed to take place or even encouraged?

If we understand democracy as government expressing a united general will, it seems that conflict has *no* place in a self-governing community and that such a community would be completely incompatible with an Aristotelian *polis* in which debate and dispute are welcomed as essential techniques of leading a virtuous life. But even if we reject the notion of a general will, and instead maintain that a community is democratic because it is guided by a majority preference discovered via aggregation, it still appears we are describing a political system unlike that which Aristotle describes and recommends. For understanding conflict as a process of aggregating dissimilar preferences actually sheds very little light on the ways in which these citizens are at odds with one another. On the contrary, this process is little more than a mechanism by which citizens can agree to disagree: aggregating need not involve the sort of deliberative debate that I have argued Aristotle attributes to assemblies, nor need it refer to the competitions for social status, honor, and political influence that Aristotle believes take place in the best sort of political communities.

The aptness of the self-government model isn't improved by invoking the applicability of either direct or representative versions of democracy. Both of these versions are starkly opposed to Aristotle's ancient view as both actively *erase* the potential for conflict between rulers and ruled: rulers simply *are*, either directly or indirectly, the ruled acting autonomously. By contrast, the role of conflict in Aristotle's political philosophy shows that, in his mind, the distinction between rulers and ruled is a kind of first principle of political theory. We can see Aristotle's firm commitment to the fixity of this distinction in a number of ways.

First, as we have seen, he articulates a very well-developed theory of civil war and the mistrust that arises in typical cities. He surveys, conceptualizes, and theorizes all sorts of different motivations possessed by inhabits who come to feel that the constitution of their city is unjust, and he is keenly aware that this conflict usually takes places in cities where the ruled have become increasingly unhappy with those who rule. Remarkably, however, nowhere in this extensive diagnosis does Aristotle entertain the notion that *stasis* could be prevented, or mistrust controlled, by simply eliminating the distinction between rulers and ruled and conceiving of *all* inhabitants as citizen-rulers. On the contrary, the category of "being ruled" is treated as a fixed category throughout all of Aristotle's discussions, and he has no thought that civil war could be avoided by creating a constitution controlled by "The People" that would be different from the distrust-laden democratic regimes ruled by the poor.

Indeed, so committed is Aristotle to the notion that unity within a community requires a fixed distinction between a ruling group, on the one hand, and those who are ruled, on the other, that he even attributes this distinction to the politics *internal* to each of the main sociological groups of every city. For example, in an Aristotelian democracy, the poor rule; but this group never takes shape as a leaderless "People." Rather, Aristotle thinks poor partisans will always gravitate toward a structure ruled by a demagogue. Similarly, in an oligarchy, the rich who rule do not coalesce into a well-heeled, leaderless cell; on the contrary, oligarchy is exceedingly prone to civil war precisely because partisan oligarchs reliably tend toward ever more restricted forms of dynastic domination. Again, when the virtuous rule (as is passably the case in polity or in the best-case scenario of aristocracy), we have seen that Aristotle does not imagine the virtuous *politeuma* as a leaderless collective united as an elite "People." Rather, the virtuous take each other to be good and upstanding competitors for honor, office, and influence. In other words, the virtuous create a political whole by forming a hierarchy of rulers and ruled.

The fixity of this recurring distinction between rulers and ruled could perhaps be motivated by Aristotle's general metaphysical treatment of wholes and his belief that cities are wholes.[1] Unlike mere heaps, any genuine whole possesses dissimilar parts that together serve some common function; it is in this way that dissimilar parts achieve some type of unity. Now, cities are not wholes in the same way natural substances are. Natural substances have parts whose being consists *only* in serving the function of the whole; such parts are *mere* potentialities. Cities, by contrast, do not feature merely potential parts, but rather parts that are themselves actual substances (fully functioning human beings). Thus, it is impossible for cities to be either whole or unified in exactly the same way as are natural substances.[2] Nevertheless, though cities may not possess the *level* of unity featured in a living organism, it does not thereby follow that cities are mere heaps. On the contrary, somewhat like what we find in all animals, cities too can be said to possess a soul-like ruling part that is dissimilar to a bodylike part over which it rules. The fixed distinction between rulers and ruled is, in Aristotle's mind, not a contingent arrangement that happens to obtain in some cities but not others; rather, the hierarchy of rulers over ruled is constitutive of the very being of any city as a city.

In any case, this sharp and fixed distinction between rulers and the ruled highlights a radical dissimilarity between an Aristotelian political community and that featured by the "self-government" model of democracy; his theory bolsters the very distinction between rulers and ruled that this model elides. Nevertheless, we still might wonder whether Aristotle's portrayal of the fixed divide between rulers and ruled is really all that different from the beliefs of a staunch advocate of representational democracy who derides direct democracy as quixotic. If Aristotle were to conceive of good rulers as those who do their best to *represent* the ruled, then his belief in the permanence of the ruler/ruled distinction might not distinguish his view from the "self-government" model of democracy as much as it might have seemed.

I find no evidence, however, to support the notion that Aristotle conceived of good rulers as those with the ability to represent the views of the ruled. In fact, two aspects of Aristotle's political theory seem wholly incompatible with such a suggestion. First, during his discussion of the "political" rule that exists among those who are similar in birth and free, he claims that the virtue unique to rulers is practical wisdom, and he contrasts this wisdom with the "correct belief" that distinguishes those who are ruled in rather stark terms: "[T]hose ruled are like makers of flutes, whereas rulers are like the flute players who use them" (*Pol.* III.4 1277b29–30). This isn't to say that the ruled are completely without political agency, just as makers of flutes are not figures of complete inaction. The ruled exercise their rational souls to produce correct opinions, and Aristotle recognizes that in this capacity they can deliberate about the direction of the city and pass judgment on officials who control it (III.11 1281b31–38). Nevertheless, the activity of the ruled is here conceived of as being different *in kind* from that undertaken by rulers. Rulers are *distinctive* for their decision making, their initiation of political action, and their exercise of forward-looking practical wisdom (*NE* 1141b23–24, *Pol.* I.13 1260a17–20, IV.1 1289a5–13, V.8 1308a31–35); they no more do the "People's" bidding than flute players follow directions of flute makers.[3]

Second, the role that conflict plays in Aristotle's political theory is not that which we would expect if rulers had a truly representative function. For example, I have argued that Aristotle conceives of excellent public deliberation and the distribution of public power within the *politeuma* in competitive terms. But at no point does Aristotle suggest that the function of competition in assemblies is to discover a shared proposal with which all agree, or to uncover a policy that accommodates all citizens' preferences. Quite to the contrary, the goal of public competition is to weed out weaker proposals and politicians so that the best proposal and its best advocate can come to the fore. Articulating superior positions, not exposing collective or representative proposals, is the function of political struggle in the best of cities.

Moreover, at no point in Aristotle's extensive diagnosis of *stasis* do we find the failure to reflect beliefs of the ruled being offered as a cause of civil war. Despite the fact that *Politics* V is a systematic account of the origins of faction, Aristotle never registers unrepresentative behavior of rulers as a factor. Admittedly, some of the long-term causes appear, at first glance, to imply that the ruled become distrustful of rulers when their preferences are not being taken seriously by those who rule. For example, we might assume that when Aristotle says *stasis* can be caused by the ruled feeling "contempt" [*kataphronēsis*] for rulers, or that "superiority" [*huperochē*] and "arrogance" [*hubris*] can lead citizens to civil war, he is articulating different ways in which citizens come to distrust those rulers who no longer heed their views.

Aristotle's discussion of these causes, however, undercuts such first impressions. Contempt is what one feels after judging another person or group to be weak, incompetent, or disorganized.[4] If the ruled felt contempt for rulers, it would be the result of a judgment that the rulers were ineffective, not that the rulers had dismissed their preferences. The notion of superiority is even less relevant to the self-government model. Superiority acts as a cause of *stasis* when some group is not content to be treated in the same way as others, believing that it deserves a greater share of civic power because it possesses more of some good (e.g. wealth, virtue) than other inhabitants.[5] Fighting on behalf of superiority, then, is hardly conflict motivated by lack of representation. Superiority is an elite motivation for contemplating civil war, not a demand of the ruled to have their preferences better registered. Likewise, while citizens in the contemporary world might associate arrogance with politicians who fail to take views of the ruled seriously, Aristotle thinks of arrogance as that which motivates the rich and powerful to shame the poor, weak, and powerless for the mere pleasure it. Citizens treated arrogantly do not begin contemplating regime change because their voices are not being heard; rather, they distrust the constitution because they believe that they have been *belittled* by those in positions of power.[6]

Again, if Aristotle viewed representation of the ruled as a function of excellent rulers, we might expect the notion of representation to show up in his discussion of mixed government; for a mixed government, we would assume, will better represent the views of the poor and rich than would an unmixed group of rulers. But that, as we have seen, is not how Aristotle diagnoses the appeal of mixed regimes. He investigates this form of government in terms of power sharing—as an arrangement in which both rich and poor citizens have the honor of holding offices—not as an arrangement in which the poor and rich *who are ruled* are able to have their voices heard. Indeed, this is why, when Aristotle considers which forms of mixed government are viable (and not just conceivable in the abstract), he settles on a polity dominated by those in the middle. The possibility of mixed government depends on the sociology of rulers, not on whether rulers faithfully register views of the ruled.

Finally, and perhaps most dramatically, consider Aristotle's conception of voting. For contemporary readers who subscribe to the self-government model of democracy, voting is a mechanism by which people make their voice heard in government. But nowhere in this study of conflict is the struggle for winning elective office assigned this role. As we have seen, it is true that Aristotle believes that voting can, like auditing, be used to constrain officials and hold them to account for their actions. But *limiting* rulers is something quite distinct from picking *representative* rulers who allow voters to act as governors behind the organized power of government. Tellingly, Aristotle calls an arrangement wherein all inhabitants pick officials from a small group of candidates "aristocratic" (IV.15 1300b4–5), but he is only willing to call voting "democratic" when all inhabitants select from all (a31–34). If Aristotle had recognized a representative function of voting, then this change in title would make little sense for members of an elite group of candidates could excel at representing all inhabitants. But instead of thinking about the representational possibilities of voting, Aristotle considers only the sociological outcomes: if the voting will result in virtuous people ruling, then the voting is "aristocratic." If the voting will result in poor people ruling, then it is "democratic." But in neither case does Aristotle entertain the possibility of many poor inhabitants acting as autonomous rulers, serving as the governors behind the aristocratic government of virtuous rulers.

In conclusion, no matter which version of the self-government model of democracy we consider, Aristotle's conception of conflict shows that he understands political communities in very different terms. Aristotelian governments do not avoid civil war by successfully expressing a general will or an aggregate opinion. The sharp distinction Aristotle draws between the rulers and the ruled is completely at odds with theories of direct democracy, and the structured debates and competitions for rule are nowhere depicted as attempts to uncover the views held by the ruled.

II. Deliberative Democracy

Rather than turning to the familiar self-government model, some have suggested that key themes of Aristotelian political thought are better captured by a model of democracy called "deliberative democracy."[7]

Like advocates of the self-government model, deliberative democrats agree that equality requires citizens to be involved in the governmental decision making that affects them. However, deliberative democrats believe that there is profound flaw in the way in which self-government is usually conceived of: self-government sanctions registering and reflecting (in either the aggregate or in general) *whatever* preferences citizens happen to have, even if these preferences are uninformed, irrational, tainted with power imbalances, or even overtly manipulated.[8] Deliberative theorists not only worry that collecting such arbitrary preferences will rarely result in generating wise policy (the epistemological worry). In addition, they worry that registering whatever citizens prefer will not even allow them to rule in any genuine sense—for unreflective citizens endorse policies that *they themselves* would not endorse on reflection.[9]

From such considerations, deliberative theorists conclude that democratic political societies are those that embrace procedures and develop institutions that allow citizens to *cultivate* their beliefs in a reflective and informed manner before making political decisions. On this model, democratic legitimacy isn't achieved by simply reflecting people's views (whatever those happen to be), but rather by registering views that have emerged from civic dialogue guided by norms such as transparency, accountability, and reciprocity.

There are a number of reasons someone might plausibly think that Aristotle's political philosophy foreshadows deliberative democracy in several key respects. First, it is certainly true that deliberative democrats, like Aristotle, imagine a flourishing political community as one in which citizens are engaged in a great deal of dialogue and deliberation before decisions are made on behalf of the city. Aristotle's commitment to the importance of political discussion seems to be suggested by many of the most well-known elements in his political thought. There is his participatory conception of citizenship (*Pol.* III.1), his argument that the multitude of people who are ruled can contribute some kind of wisdom to political judgments (III.11), his repeated declarations that complex and difficult issues often require more minds than one (III.16), and his portrayal of the best city as a face-to-face community (VII.4) featuring venues like mess halls, leisure *agorai*, and gymnasiums (VII.12). All of these details help to paint a portrait of a community deeply engaged in the sort of conversations that deliberative democrats might applaud.

Second, like the deliberative democrats, Aristotle is quite skeptical that good communal decisions can be reached by simply tallying citizens' beliefs, regardless of how those beliefs were formed. When Aristotle claims that a multitude can aid group decision making only if it is in possession of a certain level of virtue (III.11 1281b15–21), he implies that everyone participating in the political process must be able to engage issues with *some* level of rational virtue. Just as deliberative democrats believe that it is impossible to attain democratic legitimacy in an environment where citizens uncritically aver positions without deliberation, so too Aristotle's multitude could in no way improve public deliberation "as a mixture of roughage and pure food" (b36–37) without some level of critical evaluation and reflection.

Moreover, a recent debate among deliberative democrats highlights a third way in which Aristotle seems relevant to this model of democracy. On one version of contemporary deliberative democracy (that espoused by Rawls and Habermas),[10] the genuine dialogue that legitimizes democratic decisions takes place only when properly informed citizens are able to offer impartial reasons in public discussion. On this view, citizens should engage in a deliberative process that does not privilege any particular interest or viewpoint, and agreement should be reached only by identifying positions with which any impartial person, in-so-far as he or she is rational, would agree.

But a different strain of deliberative democracy has emerged that claims it is a mistake to conceptualize deliberative dialogue as a trading of impartial reasons. The worry is that this portrayal of dialogue sets the barrier to entry into public discussion at too high a level to be considered democratic (this is the view of Gutmann and Thompson).[11] This alternative approach encourages citizens, rather than searching for wholly impartial reasons, to embrace instead an "economy of moral disagreement" and to search for reasonable accommodations with other citizens who, while not offering compelling reasons, nonetheless advance reasons with which others can negotiate. Participants thus need not keep all their controversial (and partial) beliefs out of the public sphere. Rather, when entering democratic dialogue, citizens should make an effort to conduct their deliberation under a norm of reciprocity.

If I am right about the role that conflict plays in Aristotle's thought, then the Gutmann/Thompson strain of democratic theory bears an important similarity to Aristotle's political philosophy. In chapter 4, I argued that Aristotle not only believes that virtuous citizens have divergent views before they enter into the realm of public deliberation but also that such differences can persist even *after* lengthy discussion. In other words, Aristotle does not depict virtuous citizens as always being able to discover impartial considerations that, all by themselves, garner universal assent by rational agents. Moreover, in chapter 5, I argued that Aristotelian group deliberation could itself be conceived of on a competitive model and that the best sort of citizens will not simply disagree with one another, but they will shepherd their proposals through a competitive process that not only ranks the proposals but also implicates the citizens' own standing among their peers. The theory of deliberative democracy articulated by Gutmann and Thompson has similar features: it recognizes that persistent political conflict is unavoidable even among outstanding citizens and offers rules and values that structure dialogue in a way that does not force participants to divorce their publicly held views from who they really are. This version of deliberative democracy is thus far closer to Aristotle's than that which conceives of dialogue in terms of universal impartiality.

Nevertheless, despite the attribution of a conversational culture to the best sort of *polis*, the implied skepticism about reaching acceptable public decisions by tallying opinions, and the depiction of public dialogue as laden with disagreement and competitive assessment, it still seems that deliberative democracy does not properly capture Aristotle's views of conflict and community.

First, like advocates for self-government, deliberative democrats adopt a theoretical framework that erases the distinction between rulers and ruled that, as I discussed earlier, Aristotle finds virtually axiomatic for communal life. Here again, deliberating citizens are conceived of as autonomous participants who create the rules by which they themselves will live. Though the norms according to which agreed-upon laws and policies are discovered may be different from those of democracy as self-government, deliberative citizens are still modeled as citizen-governors controlling government. As a result, deliberative democrats do not sharply distinguish ruling citizens from the ruled, and they do not attribute distinct and unique virtues to these two groups as does Aristotle.[12]

Indeed, Aristotle's valorization of the divide between rulers and ruled strikes me as being an even greater problem for deliberative democrats than for those advocating self-government. For at least according to a representational version of democratic self-government, the exact nature of the representative relationship is open to different interpretations. Some conceptions of representation could involve robust conversation and dialogue between representatives and those they serve, but we can imagine other conceptions of representation that would downplay any need for discussion. By contrast, it seems that every version of deliberative democracy requires a dialogic relationship among *all* citizens in *any* role.

Yet, time and again, we find Aristotle characterizing the relationship between rulers and ruled in starkly *nondialogic* terms. The most glaring example of this is, of course, his infamous suggestion that the best-run cities will deny slaves and women *any* voice in the political community (*Pol.* I.13). But even in the course of his extended *Pol.* IV.3–4 discussion of how "city-states are constituted not out of one but many parts, as we have often said" (1290b38–39), which deals with the ways in which Greek males typically enter into different social roles, Aristotle describes the civic relations in noticeably noncommunicative terms. For example, he compares the different parts of a political constitution to air currents in winds, different notes in harmonies, and distinctive parts in animals, and he suggests that different civic parts relate to one another in a way analogous of that of soul to body. None of these comparisons suggest the sort of dynamism commonly attributed to a genuine dialogue. Indeed, analogizing the relation of civic parts to that which holds between soul and body seems especially nondialogic. For even the communication of rational soul and desiderative soul amounts to little more than a one-way command wherein an irrational element in the soul may "obey and listen" (*EE* II.1 1219b30–31), listen to soul "as to a father" (*NE* I.13 1103a3), and merely be "persuaded in some way by reason" (1102b33). There is little here that suggests the back-and-forth or give-and-take that we would associate with meaningful discussion in group deliberation.[13]

Moreover, deliberative democrats conceive of the goal of dialogue in a much different way than does Aristotle. According to the deliberative model, citizens come together in conversation in order to reach *rational consensus*. Working together, they discover commonalities and locate issues where there are areas of overlapping belief. Now, as we have seen, not all deliberative democrats believe this goal can be perfectly realized, so they deny that detecting "impartial reasons" is the correct approach. But even these conflict-friendly democrats who lower the bar for what counts as a "public reason" still seem to think of consensus as a *regulative ideal* and embrace norms such as reciprocity in order to allow citizens to come together on terms acceptable to all.

By contrast, the role that conflict plays in his political theory shows that Aristotle nowhere adopts consensus as an ideal for political community. First, consider Aristotle's theory of *stasis* as analyzed in chapter 1. The psychology of those who are ready to factionalize is motivated by a desire for equality, not a desire to attack those who disagree with them. The triggers for civil war are money and honor, and the long-term causes of this type of conflict are profit, honor, arrogance, fear, superiority, contempt, and disproportional growth. Lacking agreement, or falling short of consensus, is nowhere cited as a cause of *stasis* (let alone offered as a root cause of *stasis*). Indeed, recall that Aristotle depicts oligarchs as citizens who actually *agree* on a theory of justice, *agree* on a theory of the highest good, *agree* with one another about the relationship of rulers to ruled and the qualifications for ruling . . . and yet are every bit as likely to engage in civil war with one another as with those with whom they disagree.

Second, Aristotle never turns to the notion of reaching consensus or finding areas of overlapping agreement as an ideal that cities might adopt for managing civic distrust. Aristotle, I have argued, portrays democratic and oligarchic partisans in such a way that simply erases the possibility for any productive dialogue between them. When Aristotle explores tactics for stabilizing mixed constitutions, he discusses different kinds of voting mechanisms for proposals and office-holders, techniques for pushing careless partisans out of the ruling class, and the proposal of simply swamping hostile groups with a large middle class. But nowhere does he propose bringing disputing groups together to engage in joint deliberation that fosters agreement; nowhere does he promote a tactic of encouraging dialogue under shared communicative norms that might yield consensus. The same is true of Aristotle's descriptions of how monocratic regimes are stabilized. Neither monarchs nor tyrants are advised to hunt for reasons that can be shared with the ruled; instead, Aristotle recommends acting moderately and limiting the areas over which these rulers exercise their power.

Third, even if we restrict our attention to the soul-like part of constitutions—the part that engages in deliberation and civic decision making—we see that Aristotle does not think of consensus among *all* citizens as some kind of political ideal. Aristotle has no hesitation in recommending that citizens be dropped from, rather than included in, civic deliberation as soon as that would lead to better civic outcomes. As I have already pointed out, Aristotle thinks that populations falling below a certain level of virtue should not be allowed to be involved in deliberating. Moreover, even those multitudes who manage to meet this virtue threshold are not thereby granted full-fledged participation: achieving the minimum level of rationality may only mean that a group is capable of serving as a negative bulwark to the active deliberators, not that group members will be able to engage in full-fledged participation themselves.[14] Again, Aristotle recognizes a need for occasional ostracism, even when it is a preeminently virtuous citizen who will suffer the ostracism (*Pol.* III.13 1284b3–17). And, finally, he proposes that when citizens reach a certain elderly age they be removed from the assembly and be given nondeliberative religious responsibilities (*Pol.* VII.9 1329a27–34). In all of these cases, Aristotle's approach is not to try to overcome differences in virtue among citizens via conversation and dialogue. Culling, rather than consensus, is Aristotle's preferred method for civic improvement in these situations.

Finally, I have offered a number of arguments for the claim that even active citizens within the soul-like part of the constitution do not deploy their virtue in service of consensus. In chapter 4, I argued that when *phronimoi* strive to articulate what they deem the best course of action for the city, such virtuous citizens often end up disagreeing with one another even after a great deal of conversation. Again, in chapter 5, I tried to show that Aristotle's upstanding citizens will be bent on competing with one another for political power since it is through such positions of influence that they can best orient the city and exercise virtue on a major scale. None of this, I argued, contradicts the fact that these citizens live with one another as political friends: for their collective *homonoia* is never defined by consensus or collaboration (for they disagree and compete) as much as by shared habits and background assumptions founded in a common education.

In conclusion, the role that conflict plays in Aristotle's political thought rules out the possibility that a deliberative model of democracy could best capture Aristotle's approach to politics. Though Aristotle and deliberative democrats do share an appreciation for deliberation in the pursuit of good decision making, the deliberative model conceives of the political community as a place where all the different constituencies affected by government decisions can come together to craft a rational consensus (or at least an economized disagreement) and exercise autonomy. By contrast, Aristotle thinks of political deliberation as an exclusive activity engaged in by a sociologically elite group of rulers who, quite separate from the ruled, hunt for the best proposals and struggle for the top honor of implementing them.

III. Democracy without Self-Government

Where, then, should we turn? It seems that Aristotle's way of understanding conflict will be in tension with any model of democracy that embraces the ideal of all citizens seeking consensus to exercise rule together. For Aristotle, consensus as such never serves as a regulative ideal, deliberative debates are best undertaken by virtuous elites, and rule itself is to be exercised by elite victors of political struggle. And Aristotle's causal theory of civil war rules out the possibility that these ruling victors cause distrust by failing to be representative. If we are to locate a contemporary model with which Aristotle's theory of conflict may be more compatible, we will need to consider theories of democracy that embrace conflict and that also cut the link between democracy and universal self-government.

This means considering models of democracy that are, admittedly, *profoundly* different from those that most readers would identify as properly democratic. Abandoning the notion that successful democracies feature rule by will of the people (whether that will is generalized, aggregated, refracted, or improved through deliberation) and jettisoning consensus as a regulative ideal will strike many as both dangerous and blatantly antidemocratic. Indeed, this is why the models of democracy that I will now take into account are often dismissed as accounts of democracy.

The goal of this chapter, however, is not to defend such controversial theories. Rather, the goal is to show that, with a proper appreciation of the role that conflict plays in Aristotle's political theory, we find that his ancient approach to politics bears a remarkable similarity to one of these alternative models of contemporary democracy: plebiscitarianism. In order to highlight this similarity fully, I will begin by discussing what I take to be two other models that embrace conflict and also conceptualize democracy as something quite different from a government of self-governing citizens. The theories I will refer to as "agonism" and then "interest pluralism" do feature some key Aristotelian commitments but then run afoul of many others. By contrast, so-called plebiscitarianism conceptualizes conflict in democracy in a way that I believe is profoundly Aristotelian.

IV. Democracy without Self-Government: Agonism

The core intuition animating agonistic conceptions of democracy is that in genuinely democratic communities, *all* values, *all* offices, and *all* political orders are subject to the possibility of challenge and renegotiation.[15] On this view, the people constituting the democratic community need not play a fixed role within a particular arrangement of a government; in fact, on this theory, it need not even be the case that government decision making tracks a collective (or aggregated) will of citizens. Rather, what makes an agonistic community democratic is that the political system is contingent upon the continued acceptance of the people who, if they doubt any aspect of the system, may challenge it.[16] So understood, democracy isn't one kind of government among many, but rather an ever-present "fugitive" potential for new modes; it is a protean, revolutionary power that always rests with the human beings outside current political arrangements.[17]

Not surprisingly, agonists contrast their view with those of political theorists who depict democracy in terms of a permanent framework or in terms of a settled hierarchy of values. Even if a political community explicitly includes an institution meant to allow political contestation, the agonist may not accept this as sufficient for democracy; for by placing conflict within a well-defined, institutionalized silo, such an arrangement might place certain structures beyond criticism. Large corporations, bureaucracies, and even constitutionalism itself can threaten agonistic democracy by establishing patterns that protect certain aspects of political organization from contestation.[18]

There are obviously profound differences between agonism and Aristotle's theory of politics. First, some doubt that ethics could ever guide political theory, and turn to agonism due to the belief that, without ethics to guide political decision-making, contestation is the only alternative. To the extent that agonism is so motivated, it locates conflict within political theory in a way that departs from Aristotle's view. Aristotle does not promote disagreement and competition in civic life because ethics provides no guidance. These sorts of conflict, which I believe Aristotle accepts, are completely compatible with his conviction that there are correct constitutions that aim at a common good, that this common good is the happiness of every citizen, and that one conception of happiness is objectively superior to others. In fact, the very structure of debate and competition I have attributed to Aristotle's political theory depends on there being extralegal standards by which debate is made productive and competitors are ranked.[19]

Again, nothing seems less agonistic than Aristotle's contention that nature itself recommends permanently blocking slaves and women from any kind of rule in political communities (I.13 1260a4–36) or Aristotle's recommendation that manual craftsmen [*banausoi*] be blocked from citizenship in the best sort of city due to their inferior habits (III.5 1278a8–21). Aristotle's aristocratic and elitist sensibilities directly oppose both the letter and the spirit of the agonistic models of democracy as entire cohorts of inhabitants are cast into permanently supportive roles for a system they should not, on Aristotle's view, distrust or debate.

Moreover, aside from these normative differences, it seems that Aristotle's way of conceptualizing the very warp and woof of political community stands in tension with the agonistic view. According to Aristotle, every city as a city features a constitutional form that organizes human beings into a specific type of political community (III.3 1276b1–4)—a form that also expresses itself as an organization of inhabitants (III.1 1274b38). Thus, whereas the agonistic ideal of democracy stresses the *aconstitutional* nature of democracy, Aristotle first and foremost emphasizes that all cities possess an organizing constitutional principle that provides them with a civic identity over time. And while agonism embraces democratic conflict for its anarchic, destabilizing potential,[20] Aristotle (on my interpretation) believes that destabilizing types of conflict like civil war, partisanship, and distrust should be avoided (or managed) to the extent that is possible, while debate and competition are actually features promoted by excellent constitutions.

Given all these divergences, it is unlikely that contemporary agonism offers a theory of conflict in politics that resembles how Aristotle understands it.[21] Yet, despite the differences, we should not overlook a key similarity: for both Aristotle and agonists, the conflict of politics is an *ineliminable* feature of all genuine political communities. While Aristotle uses notions of nature and habit to police the boundary between the political realm and the apolitical realm in well-organized *poleis*, these notions by themselves do not tip the balance toward any specific arrangement *within* the smaller community of naturally equal, mature, and well-habituated (ethical) citizens. Nature and habits do ensure that, within this political realm, citizens conduct themselves honorably and rationally. But we have seen that such generalities in no way entail civic unanimity (chapter 4), or anticompetitive, orchestrated coordination (chapter 5). Among *phronimoi* in the best sort of city, there is a pervasive *homonoia* and feeling of comradery; but such general feelings only ensure that citizens abide by the basic norms and rules that structure their virtuous contests and debates. Aristotle makes a sharp (and rigid) distinction between the political and apolitical realm, and then he also endorses another distinct hierarchy between the rulers and ruled within the political realm. But who, exactly, rules in which offices and leading positions and how decisions are made within groups will be matters of ongoing contestation and dispute.

V. Democracy without Self-Government: Interest Pluralism

What we need, then, is a democratic theory that does not conceptualize all citizens as autonomous governors programming government decisions and that accepts potential for conflict among citizens as an ideal (like agonism) but that is nevertheless compatible with political hierarchy and constitutional organization (unlike agonism).

At first glance, it might seem that the model of democracy depicted as an agglomeration of divergent interest groups (a position I will refer to as "interest pluralism") meets these conditions. This is the sort of view that was, for example, advocated by the twentieth-century political scientist Robert Dahl. Dahl argued that the very meaning of popular sovereignty could be understood only in terms of the empirical conditions that operationalized the concept of majority rule, and he saw little in these empirical accounts to support any version of the "self-government" conception of democracy.[22] Rather than democratic governments being those which are programmed by the will of the people, democracies are instead "polyarchies" wherein many smaller groups of organized interests compete to influence elected leaders whose power depends upon them:

> Elections and political competition do not make for government by majorities in any very significant way, but they vastly increase the size, number, and variety of minorities whose preferences must be taken into account by leaders in making policy choices. I am inclined to think that it is in this characteristic of elections—not minority rule but minorities rule—that we must look for some of the essential differences between dictatorships and democracies.[23]

It is no surprise that this model of democracy found wide appeal in the latter half of the twentieth century, in the world of contemporary nation-states featuring tens of millions or even hundreds of millions of citizens, any number of whom are organized into formal and informal associations, organizations, and constituencies.

This view has a number of interesting similarities to the conflict-compatible theory I have attributed to Aristotle. First, Aristotle does not conceive of rulers, even in the best of cities, as forming a monolithic, conflict-free collective. The pluralists emphatically agree: power in democratic societies, even the power possessed by those in the most prominent offices of contemporary government, is never consolidated into a singular voice that expresses the intention of a sovereign people; rule in pluralistic democracy is splintered among a wide variety of interest groups. In fact, not only is rule fragmented, but it is also always contested. Clashes and contests among interest groups, as well as clashes among politicians who are jockeying for influence with such groups, are understood by this theory to be fundamental to democracy. For the interest pluralists, as for the agonists and Aristotle, political conflict isn't conceived as an aberration from a fallen ideal, but as key to genuine political community.

Unlike agonistic theory, however, interest pluralism is also straightforwardly compatible with the sorts of hierarchical structures that Aristotle posits between rulers and the ruled. According to Dahl, democratic governments will always be run by elite officials who excel at vote-getting and responding to interest groups[24] (which themselves are nearly always arranged hierarchically).[25] In such a system, the ruled exercise "rule" only in the sense that they influence the informal conditions for successful politicking:

> [I]n this sense the majority (at least of the politically active) nearly always "rules" in a polyarchal system. For politicians subject to elections must operate within the limits set both by their own values, as indoctrinated members of the society, and by their expectations about what policies they can adopt and still be re-elected.[26]

By limiting the role of nonpoliticians to little more than setting conditions, Dahl is not recommending that politicians *ignore* those whom they rule—that is out of the question since successful rulers must be responsive to the electorate to stay in power. Rather, Dahl is pointing out that the ruled, as a group, are simply not in a position to speak with any sort of voice. Unlike politicians who actively engage in some sort of dialogue with one another, the people at large form a fundamentally passive landscape through which active politicians and interest groups must navigate. As is the case with Aristotle's political theory, Dahl's theory posits a fundamental distinction between virtues of rulers and ruled—even for well-functioning societies.

But this similarity with respect to political conflict also brings to light a profound difference between Aristotle and Dahl. While interest pluralism may be conflict-friendly, it theorizes conflict in exceedingly nondescript and abstract terms. Each interest group is treated as if it were an atom with a certain vector that may (or may not) align with other vectors in a political space; conflict is what happens when political atoms collide. By contrast, conflict in Aristotle's political theory isn't the mere by-product of social physics. According to the analysis I have offered, partisanship and civil war are different *kinds* of conflict, which in turn are different *in kind* from the social and political competitions of a well-ordered city. Aristotelian citizens do not conflict in some abstract sense—they *debate* about *the common good*; they *compete* with one another *for honor*. The political science of interest pluralism strips away character and virtue from conflict, saying only that all clashes of the city take place within a set of shared expectations; the struggle of the virtuous is no different from the disorder of the vicious.

This comparatively thin conception of conflict is closely related to another major difference between the interest pluralists and Aristotle: because the interest-pluralism model ignores character, it tends to transmute sociological differentiation into the model of clashing preferences. Indeed, on the pluralist view, there is a deep analogy between the way political power is fragmented in democracies and the way economic power is fragmented among multiple firms in competitive free markets. However, as I argued in the last chapter, Aristotle seems consistently wary of abstracting from sociology in such a way that renders politics as a "balance of forces," and he never countenances a theory depicting political community as a "market of preferences." Such talk downplays the way in which politics must ultimately be understood in terms of the sociologically distinct groups that different kinds of human beings form with one another. Indeed, the pluralist view seems to reduce politics to nothing but marketlike negotiating and alliance-making—a view that Aristotle explicitly rejects (III.9 1280a34–b12).

Third, and finally, while it is true that interest pluralism is compatible with political hierarchy (indeed, with the existence of many interest groups that are each arranged hierarchically), this model of democracy never features cities that must be theorized as being *formed* by a hierarchical constitution. The interest-pluralism model sees democratic structure in terms of temporary alliances and an ever-changing cast of leaders whose traits depend upon emergent collations of interests. By contrast, Aristotle pictures each and every city as an organized, compound whole, wherein a distinct controlling group possess the unique qualities of rulers, and another distinct group of people, who are ruled, feature a different set of traits.[27]

Thus, while the interest-pluralism model of democracy accommodates nonrepresentationalism and political hierarchy, the way it situates conflict in politics is different from the Aristotelian approach. For Aristotle, certain kinds of conflict threaten the formal order of a city, but other kinds of conflict play an important role in civic order; treating all conflict as a clashing of plural interests strips away such distinctions and ends up rendering political life as less stable and organized than Aristotle believes it should be. What is needed is a contemporary theory that incorporates notions of political organization as does Aristotle, that accepts the language of virtue and character in politics as does Aristotle, and that then offers a multivocal conception of conflict that is informed by organization and character and is richer than a theory of "clashing preferences." Such a theory, I believe, is found in the "plebiscitarian" model of democracy advocated by Max Weber.[28]

VI. Democracy without Self-Government: Plebiscitarianism

Max Weber made significant contributions to an astonishingly large number of different areas of social science. To attempt any kind of systematic comparison between the totality of Weber's thought and that of Aristotle would not only take me far beyond the subject of this book but would require a book-length treatment in itself dealing with ethics, rhetoric, history, economics, sociology, and political science. In the remainder of this chapter, I wish to focus only on the narrow topic of how Weber understands conflict in democratic societies and argue that this understanding of conflict is similar, in important ways, to Aristotle's view.

Weber accepts a role for conflict in struggling, average, and even successful communities: "Conflict cannot be excluded from social life . . . '[P]eace' is nothing more than a change in the character of conflict."[29] Indeed, as far as Weber is concerned, politics itself just *is* "the struggle to alter the distribution of power, whether within states or between them."[30] To imagine a community that had achieved total permanent unity would be to imagine a community that had altogether stopped being political. In this regard, Weber sounds very much like a democratic agonist or interest pluralist. However, what is striking is that he does not leave his analysis of conflict in democracy at the abstract level of clashing preferences or in terms of a protean antifoundationalism, but he imagines different kinds of conflict taking place among, and within, distinct social groups that are hierarchically related.[31]

VI.1. Weber and the Sociology of Democratic Struggle

First, consider Weber's sociological portrait of successful politicians in modern democracies. This group is comprised of people who live a distinctive kind of life oriented around politics. Part of such a life involves possessing enough financial security to allow politicians to be able to live *for* politics, in sharp contrast with others who must settle for living *off* politics in order to make a living. Though the latter may be intensely interested in political subjects, they can only remain, in an important sense, witnesses to what goes on in the political world. For not only do they lack the time and energy for politics, but because they earn a living from the current political order, they are naturally motivated to favor the status quo. By contrast, those who live *for* politics are able to devote all of their attention to politics, and they are in a position to fight for, or against, transformational change largely on the basis of what they take to be best.

In addition to this financial and social independence, democratic leaders possess a distinctive motivation for politics. These are people who genuinely believe that they have been *called* to join the fray and who are so committed to their calling that they take the end for which they strive to be a justification of their lives. Moreover, besides feeling inwardly called, democratic politicians have a special kind of charisma and talent for public rhetoric that allows them to generate a sense of legitimacy from large numbers of voters. In other words, successful politicians not only organize their own lives around ends for which they personally care deeply, but they possess the capacity to communicate their passion to others and to form connections with nonpoliticians on the basis of it.

Though they share these psychological and social traits, however, democratic politicians do not on that account form a unified and monolithic community. On the contrary, they will frequently disagree. On Weber's view, when someone believes she is called to the vocation of politics, what she takes herself to be doing is embracing some ultimate value on behalf of which she is ready to take a public stand, stake her credibility, and struggle. This attitude leads to dispute in many ways. In average communities of normal size, there will be many politicians who have decided to stake their claim on some ultimate value—and different politicians will find themselves fighting for different values that cannot be rationally reconciled. But Weber thinks that even when different politicians advocate the *same* ultimate value, they will often come to discover—through critical discussion and debate—that this one value can be understood in many different ways, so it offers plenty of room for additional dispute.[32] Again, even if a group of politicians happened to stand for the same value, and even if (amazingly) they found that they understood this value in the same manner, Weber believes that they would *still* often disagree with one another over how this value should be operationalized in the given situation of the political community.

These sorts of disputes are never dismissed as mere expressions of stupidity, prejudice, or self-interest. While such petty conflict is common,

Weber does not believe that it is the sort of thing that defines the disagreement endemic to a life of politics. The democratic politician is someone who feels inwardly motivated to strive for power that increases *responsibility* to voters: "The struggle for personal power and the individual responsibility which flows from this power—this is the life-blood of the politician."[33] The political struggle, qua *political* struggle, is not a dreary fight of self-interested politicians preening for attention. Rather, it takes place among those who want to help their community stand for something, who have the independence of mind to fight for such change, and who hope to be held accountable by their community for the progress made toward that goal.

In addition to such disagreements that take place even among successful politicians, Weber describes competition that takes place among those aspiring to be leaders in the first place. For better or worse, any association larger than an informal committee will be formed into a hierarchical organization so that it can regularly and predictably reach its goals. Weber calls such organization "administration," and it always features a small group of leaders being put in a position of domination over a larger group of followers. The formation of such hierarchical domination takes place in all kinds of institutions, interest groups, associations, and political communities themselves: "Everywhere the principle of the small number—that is, the superior political maneuverability of small *leading* groups—determines political activity."[34] Nation-states ruled democratically are no exception to this "principle of the small number." Weber believes that democratic governments, as well as the political parties vying to gain power over them, are subject to the same functional necessities of administration.

But who, exactly, gets the opportunity to be one of the "small number" of rulers in a democratic administration? Weber thinks that every society promotes those who have traits uniquely suited for victory in that society's sanctioned conflicts (Weber calls this general process "selection" [*Auslese*]).[35] Thus, different kinds of rulers will emerge from the competitions for leadership that take place in different kinds of societies: "Every type of social order, without exception, must, if one wishes to evaluate it, be assessed according to which type of man it gives the opportunity to rise to a position of superiority through the operation of the various objective and subjective selective factors."[36] Just as democracies are subject to the "principle of the small number," as are all other societies, so too are democratic governments sites of competitive selection, like all other governments: "The advent of democracy changed the rules of selection, but not the process of selection itself."[37] So, on Weber's view, it is not a lack of competition for leadership that distinguishes democracy from other forms of government, but it is rather the specific set of traits that are needed by those who will prevail in the democratic selection process.

The traits required of successful democratic politicians are quite different from those needed in other kinds of communities. In democracy, political hopefuls will not find victory by promising to uphold old traditions, by possessing vast wealth, by holding some administrative job, or by displaying technical or scientific knowledge. Rather, what is distinctive of the democratic selection process is that it favors those who can inspire voters with rhetoric, charisma, and a special sort of demagogic prudence revealed in the process of vying for votes: "Only those characters are fitted for political leadership who have been selected in the political struggle, since all politics is in its essence 'Kampf.' The much abused 'word of the demagogue' provides this training on average better than the administrator's office."[38] The democratic political process is a special sort of challenge that requires unique aptitudes and training. While the demagogic skill set may not be appropriate for aristocracies or oligarchies, it is the sort of repertoire that the struggles of the democratic selection process favor.

Weaving all these points together, we see that in Weber's model of contemporary democracy, rulers are described as forming a distinctive social group: these are financially independent demagogues who engage in competition in order to take control of a small number of positions at the top of an administrative hierarchy and who involve themselves in dispute over the highest ends and ideals to which they feel called.

But what about members of society who do *not* reach the pinnacles of power? How does Weber portray those who are *ruled* in democracies? The fundamental fact about the group of ruled citizens is that, because of its large size and deep diversity, it simply is not organized enough to exercise any kind of coordinated social action. Being subject to a wide variety of conflicting rational, irrational, and emotional influences, the ruled (as a large group) are inevitably passive and can never be thought of as exercising or expressing any kind of focused "will." Indeed, Weber explicitly abandons any such notion: "Ah! How much disillusion you still have to endure! Concepts such as 'the will of the people,' the true will of the people, have long since lost any meaning for me; they are fictions."[39] While the small number of leaders are able to exercise political will in the sense that they independently stand for and struggle toward, that which they believe best for the city, the ruled people (as a group) have no such freedom.

The stark contrast that Weber draws between the sociology of active rulers and the sociology of the passively ruled has ramifications for the way in which he understands the relationship that exists between these two groups. In particular, Weber abandons the idea that democratic leaders are taking directions or orders from the people in the manner that is often attributed to elected officials.

> The elected official will conduct himself entirely as the mandated representative of his master the electors, whereas the leader will see himself as carrying sole responsibility for what he does. This means that the latter, so long as he can successfully lay claim to their confidence, will act throughout according to his own convictions (leader democracy) and not, as the official, according to the expressed or supposed will of the electorate (imperative mandate).[40]

The notion of the elected "official" who dutifully follows the command of the electorate is far too passive to capture the lives of active democratic rulers. In Weber's model, "leader democracy" features rulers who are acting according to their own convictions rather than responding to imperatives issued by those over whom they rule. It is thus no accident that Weber referred to this as the "Caesaristic principle" of his democratic theory.[41]

Despite the imperial connotations of the word "Caesaristic," however, it is important to realize that Weber is not recommending that democratic leaders simply *ignore* the ruled, take them for granted, or treat them as fodder for their lofty ambitions. On the contrary, Weber's democratic leader is someone who seeks to carry the weight of a very special kind of *responsibility*—a responsibility to the people upon whom her own political fate depends: "In democracy the people elect a leader in whom they have confidence. Then the elected leader says: 'Now shut up and obey me.' People and parties may no longer meddle in what he does . . . Afterwards the people can sit in judgment. If the leader has made mistakes—to the gallows with him."[42] In other words, while the leader's actions are not in any sense programmed by the decisions of the people, the democratic politician continues to be disciplined by them. Though the leader is an active force, deploying rhetoric to sway the ruled, his political charisma is still being tested by the people—and, in a genuine democracy, this is a test that can be failed.

With the relationship between active rulers and passive citizens portrayed this way, it is certainly accurate to call Weber's model of democracy an "elitist" theory: Weberian democracy is rigidly hierarchical, it abandons any robust notion of popular sovereignty, and it theorizes a small group of political specialists who exercise uniquely active powers over a large and passive populace. Nevertheless, it should be clear from this short overview that his account is still a description of a *political* community that differs from that which operates by, say, Michels's "iron law of oligarchy." Weber's leading politicians are not the beneficiaries of any kind of automatic, lawlike process that lifts them to the height of power; they must engage in constant competition to reach positions of influence. Moreover, even those who are talented enough to win battles for political power must (unlike genuine oligarchs) be able to retain a *relationship* of responsibility and accountability to those who are ruled.

Indeed, Weber believed that preserving democracy in the modern world requires political rulers to take active steps to preserve this accountability relationship—for modern conditions make such a relationship exceedingly precarious. This is no simple matter of finding well-intentioned politicians who promise to keep the people in mind and who then occasionally communicate with voters in charismatic fashion. On the contrary, preserving the relationship of responsibility that makes for a democratic community requires that leaders actively combat the two great social forces that will incessantly favor less accountability to the ruled: elite economic interests and bureaucracies.

Because of the wide range of influences upon citizens and the diversity of their proclivities, the natural tendency of voters in a mass democracy will be to splinter into discrete groups, each of which seeks to secure, first and foremost, its own preservation and success. In other words, the normal condition of typical democracies is similar to that portrayed by the interest pluralists: the political realm is a space for aggregating interests and building coalitions. However common this condition may be, however, Weber thought that choosing it as a model for democracy was deeply misguided. For the political realm provides the *only* opportunity average citizens have to influence issues affecting the community as a whole; politics is the *only* occasion average citizens have to weigh in on a common good that is broader than their own immediate self-interest. If a democratic community is conceived of as nothing but an aggregation of narrow interests, then the political realm itself is transmuted into a "banausic" exchange of goods and services—and citizens end up being left with nothing but a choice among politicians promising to give them some personal benefit.[43] While citizens, of course, want to be personally benefited, democratic citizens also want the opportunity to support a politician who takes a distinctive stand on the whole; on an aggregation model, citizens lose this (already slender) opportunity. Indeed, when the political realm becomes nothing but a market of bartering interests, the more powerful interests will tend to dominate the weaker, and citizens will find it increasingly difficult to locate a politician who can even deliver on the promise to improve their own narrowly conceived interest.

Weber's complicated and apparently conflicted views about parliamentary democracy highlight these worries. Early on, Weber believed that parliament was the very best training ground for leaders who could preserve a genuinely political realm for citizens. Parliament would allow leaders to develop the kind of charisma and outreach that would not simply make voters excited but that would also give them an opportunity to affect national interests and common concerns. It seems that over time, however, Weber came to have a darker view: rather than acting as a training ground for democratic leaders, parliament functioned as little more than a bartering house for economic interests making trades to capture portions of state power.[44] In such an arrangement, rulers were only minimally responsive to the ruled: the richest and most powerful interests simply divided up the rent-seeking opportunities among themselves and shrunk to virtually nothing the citizens' (already meager) opportunity to influence anything of national import.[45] It appears that, in light of this, Weber came to think that genuine democracy—a relationship of genuine accountability of rulers to ruled for their stand on important issues of national concern—is possible only in states where the people elect their presidents directly, as opposed to having them chosen by parliament. Direct election is the "Magna Carta of democracy" and the "palladium of true democracy" precisely because the alternative tends to snuff out *any* possibility for democracy.[46]

Thus, when Weber's leaders feel called to live *for* politics and when they enter into the competitions for power and the disagreements over highest ends, they are not promoting democracy only by virtue of their ability to connect with voters. In addition, by struggling on behalf of common goods and highest values of national import and by fighting for power that will be accountable to such ends, democratic politicians counteract the tendency of communities to splinter into plural interests. Successful leaders are doing their part to resist the banausic politics that such fragmentation entails and keeping alive the democratic opportunity for voters to influence national issues.

Preventing the political realm from being carved up by elite economic powers, however, is only one of the great struggles that must be fought to preserve democratic responsibility between rulers and ruled. If democracy is to be supported in the modern world, leaders will also need to confront and control bureaucracy. As I mentioned earlier, Weber thinks that all communal organizations are hierarchies of domination—that is, they are administrative. That said, Weber distinguishes different kinds of administrative hierarchies, based on the sort of thing that legitimizes the structure. If, for example, a given order is accepted because it simply maintains the way things have always been ordered, then we have traditional administration, which gives those in power a kind of legitimacy based on the sanctity of precedent. If, by contrast, a group of people accepts being dominated by some individual due to the perception that she is talented and persuasive, the resulting hierarchy is a type of charismatic administration. On Weber's view, bureaucracy is a different kind of dominating structure whose hierarchies are not accepted on the basis of traditional loyalties or a feeling of awe in the face of talent but rather because they are run by technical experts who work in functionally defined offices governed by policies. Bureaucratic administration can thus be thought of as more "rational" than traditional or charismatic administration in the sense that its activities are rendered as procedures undertaken in accord with general rules that form (some sort of) coherent whole.

According to Weber, an important trait of modern society is that it favors bureaucracy over other types of administration in areas where it is believed that domination is appropriate. Bureaucracy is taken to be more stable, predictable, and efficient than the comparable alternatives. This, Weber points out, is why the trend to favor bureaucracy is not found only in modern government, but also in large associations, universities, powerful corporations, and even political parties. In the face of constant challenges, modern organizations have little faith that traditional structures can cope with change, and they deem it unrealistic to place trust in arrangements that mostly depend on the inspiration of leadership. Almost universally, administration in the modern world leads to the creation of a number of specialized and stable offices arranged bureaucratically.

However comprehensible this trend may be, however, Weber also believed that bureaucracy was deeply opposed to democracy in two important ways. First, a bureaucracy is an organization that functions by *compulsion*: a small group of active officials at the top of the bureaucratic organization issue policies and decisions *as commands* that the rest of the bureaucracy (and those subject to the bureaucracy) have no choice but to accept with complete passivity. As a result, bureaucratic administration tends to habituate people into being dominated in routine ways, distributes responsibility throughout the entire organization and so diminishes the accountability of any given individual within it, and even incentivizes secrecy: there are few rewards for officials admitting to anything aside from the fact that they are following commands, and the cost of admitting any mistake is to lose control to competing bureaucratic offices.

Nearly all the aspects of bureaucracy so conceived tend to undercut the sort of relationship between charismatic leaders and the voters that Weber believes is the hallmark of modern democracy. Excepting those at the very top of the structure, it is almost impossible for individual bureaucrats to be judged by the people, to have their activities disciplined by the people, or to be held accountable to the people. Rather than being related to the ruled as members of a common political community, the bureaucracy presents itself to the ruled as, in Weber's famous phrase, an "iron cage."

But bureaucracy does not oppose democracy only through the structure of its domination; it also tends to work against democracy by promoting the formation of a distinct group within society. In his political writings, Weber claims that it is an illusion to conceive of government bureaucracy as a frictionless machine that can be oriented this way or that at the behest of top political officials. In point of fact, bureaucratic positions tend to be filled by individuals from a specific social class. As a result, government bureaucracy forms a distinct "clique" within society that will, both purposively and inadvertently, steer the operation of government toward the interests of its own group. For example, Weber criticized those who conceived of German bureaucracy as a neutral system that would straightforwardly implement whatever policies were issued by rulers. Bureaucrats were hardly cogs—they were drawn from a distinct Junker class that systematically oriented the operation of government toward the narrow interests of the Junkers. While democracy depends on charismatic leaders who fight over issues of national concern and who strive to be held accountable to all the voters, bureaucracy tends to align itself furtively with the interests of one specific class.

On Weber's model, preserving democracy thus depends heavily on finding leaders who, in addition to their charismatic talents, possess a special sort of ethic for autonomous leadership. Surrounded by bureaucrats and powerful economic interests fostering unaccountable structures of power, democracy-preserving politicians will need to be able to resist the constant testing of their inner conviction that such powers will attempt. Moreover, they cannot engage in such resistance by simply pretending such forces do not exist: they will need to be skilled at organizing a following, and they will need to possess a talent for leading an apparatus that will make such resistance consequential. As Weber puts it, they have to be able to provide the active "soul" that will direct some sort of passive "soulless" political body that will aid in resistance: "[T]he leadership of the parties by the plebiscitary leader entails the 'soullessness' of his following, their intellectual proletarianisation, one might call it."[47]

How, exactly, does one lead such an organization? As we've seen, a politician needs a certain kind of inward calling and a certain talent for rhetoric, not to mention an ethic of autonomy strong enough to resist capture by wealthy elites and bureaucrats. But Weber also claims that leading an effective movement will require a special kind of insight into the *social realities* at play in any political argument—a trait Weber called "*Sachlichkeit*."[48] Efficacious democratic leaders appreciate that progress is not "simply a matter of designing appropriate institutions and policies, but also of identifying the constellation of social forces, in particular class forces, which supported the existing structure, and of assessing the chances for change in this social basis of support."[49] Successful politicians do more than appreciate how rational actors might mutually contract with one another in the face of different sorts of incentives—they also grasp the social identities and conflicting proclivities of the major groups in the political community.

VI.2. Weber and Aristotle

Viewed through the lens of more familiar models of democracy, Weber's portrayal looks terribly undemocratic: it features a rather low opinion of the capacities of average voters to organize, and it abandons the notion that a democratic government is one directed by the will of all citizens who equally serve as governors behind the government.[50] The goal of this chapter, however, is not to defend Weber's account or to argue that his theory is (or is not) a satisfactory account of democracy; rather, it aims only to point out that the role conflict plays in his understanding of political order is quite similar to that which I have argued we find in Aristotle's own understanding of politics. The account I have offered here suggests seven comparisons.

First, both Weber and Aristotle embrace the notion that the life of a successful politician is one that involves a competition for power. When Aristotle claims that "the actions of the politician also deny us leisure; apart from political activities themselves, those actions seek positions of power and honors" (*NE* X.7 1177b12–14) and Weber asserts that "all politics is in its essence 'Kampf,'" they both embrace a model of political life that sees competition for power as perfectly acceptable. Indeed, we have seen that both thinkers conceptualize the opportunity to win power as an occasion to exercise special virtues of political rhetoric that result in persuasion.

Second, neither thinker believes that those who win positions of honor and influence will thereby be initiated into an insular club devoid of disagreement. Even in the best possible ancient *poleis*, as well as in the most flourishing of modern democracies, outstanding politicians of great integrity will disagree. Though they will be similarly educated and will thus share the habits of like-minded citizens from the same nation or city, this in no way entails unanimity on the question of how to promote the common good in this or that situation. On the one hand, both thinkers recognize that average political communities will feature politicians who not only disagree over particulars but who also disagree on which ultimate goals should take priority in political decision-making. Aristotle has no faith that partisan democrats, partisan oligarchs, and virtuous citizens (middling or exemplary) will be able to reconcile their conflicting conceptions of the common good through rational deliberation; Weber too believes that typical politicians will strive for values that are not rationally reconcilable. On the other hand, neither thinker assumes that political disagreement is limited to average environments—neither assumes that dispute is always an expression of value pluralism, self-interest, or vice. Even excellent communities featuring political leaders who agree on ultimate ends will host debates over operationalization and issues of prudence.

Third, competition and dispute are given roles that support a distinctly hierarchical order; indeed, for both thinkers such conflict helps to define a group of rulers who are clearly distinct from the ruled.[51] For Aristotle, all genuine substances are wholes with a ruling part, and the city, though not a substance in a strict sense, is nevertheless some kind of a whole that must also feature some kind of ruling part. For Weber, observation of large organizations convinces him that all contemporary democratic nation-states must necessarily be structured in such a way that a small, active part rules over a larger group of passively ruled inhabitants. While Weber may never have been interested in grounding his "principle of the small number" in metaphysics, he, like Aristotle, embraces this elitist notion as a general principle that applies across communities. Strikingly, in the political imagination of both Aristotle and Weber, such ubiquitous hierarchical structure is not undermined by, or even in tension with, the conflict of competition and dispute. On the contrary, successful politicians who belong to the small group of rulers are included precisely because they are *uniquely* suited to compete for positions of power and *uniquely* qualified to stake out and articulate positions in debates affecting the community as a whole. As I have argued, what makes Aristotelian leaders exceptionally qualified isn't that they are skilled at rearticulating the view of the ruled, translating the voice of the people into a more eloquent package, or uncovering a consensus that exists among citizens. Rather, as is also the case for Weber, successful rulers are suited for leadership because they have the skill to emerge as victors in competition and winners in political debate; they are masters of political prudence and the rhetoric that inspires assent. In well-ordered political communities, rulers who lead like Pericles[52] constitute the active "soul" of the more passive "body" of the politically ruled, and the competition and disagreement in which rulers engage is not a threat to that status but rather a crucial component in its legitimization.

Fourth, neither thinker takes the hierarchical arrangement of rulers over the ruled to excuse self-absorption or to validate what I termed in chapter 2 "discriminatory elitism." On both the Weberian and Aristotelian views, leading politicians are not philosopher-kings whose legitimacy is based on grasping esoteric science, oligarchs whose legitimacy is based on wealth, or pure demagogues who simply have a clever knack for making unrealistic and irrational promises. On the contrary, though it is true that successful rulers must possess sufficient financial resources to be able to live a life that is uniquely free and *for* (rather than from) politics, these leaders have to retain a distinct kind of relationship to those over whom they rule. Weber's elite democratic politicians believe themselves to be called to engage in debates over the highest ideals of the community, and they strive on their own to exercise a prudence that is oriented toward national goals; but they must also be held to account for their actions through elections. Similarly, Aristotle's leaders exercise their own rational virtues in an independent way as free citizens and realize a happy life as they engage in political decision making; but these *phronimoi* are held to account for their actions both by their elite peers and through the institution of the audit [*euthuna*].

Fifth, Weber and Aristotle are aware of similar threats to the best sort of political community, and they are keen to rebuff comparable misinterpretations of politics that might downplay such dangers. For example, both thinkers are dissatisfied with attempts to conceive of the political realm only in terms of clashing and contracting economic interests. Aristotle's dissatisfaction with such a view is expressed in many different ways: he criticizes the suggestion that a city is simply a large market, explicitly contrasts the economically oriented ends of households with the virtue-oriented ends of political community, and separates the commercial *agora* from the virtue *agora* in the best possible city. Similarly, Weber too disputes the view that the political realm should be conceived of as (let alone be allowed to transform into) a space for nothing but bartering economic interests. Indeed, Weber explicitly derides this approach as "*banausic*"—which is startling given that Aristotle himself is overtly critical of the way in which oligarchies, in particular, often promote economically successful *banausoi* as citizens (*Pol.* III.5 1278a21–25).

Sixth, we have seen how both thinkers are wary of theorizing political order in terms of *abstract* interests, with the social character of major political groups edited out of the account. While Aristotle entertains notions that bear some similarity to constitutional notions such as "balance" or "separation" of abstract powers, he ultimately concludes that it is the sociology of cities with which politicians must come to terms if they are to preserve and stabilize them. Similarly, though Weber is clearly capable of making abstract claims about politics (e.g., his famous definition of a state as that which monopolizes legitimate use of violence), it is fundamentally the case, as Beetham puts it, that "Weber recognized that forms of government could not be considered in abstraction from their social basis of support, nor politics explained apart from the activities of class. His theory of politics rested on a theory of society."[53] Theorizing bureaucracy as a neutral mechanism, conceiving of political forces in the abstract, and conceptualizing democratic leaders as spokespersons of "interests" are all approaches that would overlook the key sociological dimension that preserves the democratic aspects of democracy. Weber resisted such approaches and argued that successful politics will need to avoid such views as well. As a result of this commitment to social theory, both Aristotle and Weber conceptualize conflict itself as multivocal, with both portraying the struggle for political honor as a much different kind of activity than, say, clashes of economic interests or partisan cliques.

Finally, we have found that both Aristotle and Weber believe that certain sociological forces will tend to threaten politics by promoting monopoly at the expense of political struggle for leadership. Aristotle may not be worried about the antidemocratic "iron cage" of monocratic bureaucracy as is Weber—but we have seen that Aristotle is very much worried about the tendency of democracies to coalesce around a dissent-crushing demagogue as well as the dynastic inclinations of ever-present oligarchs. In every average city, rich and poor partisans will be mutually distrustful, and whether the regime is monocratic, ruled exclusively by partisans, or even ruled in a "mixed" way, Aristotle's politicians will need to fight to keep the monopolizing tendency of partisans at bay.

Once the role of conflict in politics is properly understood, we see that Aristotle anticipates a number of the ideas that distinguish Weber's theory so sharply from other models of contemporary democracy. Of course, this is not to suggest that Weber was an Aristotelian, or that Aristotle was a Weberian. This brief analysis has tried to suggest only that the way both thinkers approach the subject of conflict plays intriguingly similar roles in their respective political philosophies.

Unlike the self-government and deliberative models, neither Aristotle's model nor Weber's depicts excellent rulers as those who articulate "a voice" or "a will" of all citizens and both understand politics in terms of competition and dispute rather than in terms of collaborative searches for a rational consensus. Again, though both see a role for such conflict in a theory of politics, neither thinker is an agonist who places conflict outside of settled political hierarchies or who interprets conflict as a persistent threat and challenge to constitutional order. However, unlike the interest pluralists, Weber and Aristotle do not incorporate conflict into democratic communities by thinking of the political realm in terms of clashing "interests." Weber's democratic rulers have entered the fray to fight for ultimate values and national goals; Aristotle's leading politicians are advocating for a highest and common good. For both, an important aspect of political theory is articulating the distinctive sociological characteristics of rulers and ruled and the ends that define them.

Conclusion

Among political philosophers working in the social contract tradition, consensus is the core requirement of political association. While there is a great deal of debate over the nature of this consensus and the qualifications of those who are party to it, it is the authority of agreement that plays the lead role in the formation of political society.

As Hume long ago pointed out in his essay, "Of the Original Contract," there is something peculiar about this notion. The oddity is not so much that agreement must be invented in theory rather than discovered in history (the social contract is, after all, a heuristic); the philosophical oddity is that this position seems to assume that all forms of political legitimacy must be traced back to a single primary source. Hume argues that this assumption is arbitrary, especially because it implies that most of what has been called political activity and political authority in the history of the world would need to be expurgated from political thought. Hume's point is not that consensus should be abandoned altogether, but rather that we should be ready to acknowledge other ways in which human beings attach themselves to each other and those who govern.

At no point in this work have I argued that Aristotle abandons social agreement. He believes that citizens who inhabit an optimal city will find consensus on many basic issues. One factor that keeps cities together is *homonoia*; another is agreement on the nature of justice; another is agreement about the quantity and quality of basic resources required for human beings to flourish. Civil war, partisanship, and rampant distrust are not compatible with optimal city life because, in part, these conflicts undermine key agreements upon which the success of any city depends.

But Aristotle, like Hume, believes that political rulers draw their support from a far broader array than universal assent. It is not only that Aristotle depicts citizens as being attached to one another by "thick" human goods such as honor, friendliness, and wit. Rather, as this book has argued, it is also because Aristotle opens up the possibility that citizens can be connected together *in and by their conflicts*. Cities are held together by politicians airing their disagreements, debating one another, and undermining unanimity with competition. Cities are held together by citizens sticking up for their friends and families in the face of peers doing the same. Cities are held together by virtue friendship built on an interpersonal architecture of out-doing, out-accomplishing, and struggling for limited opportunities for excellence. While contemporary politicians and political scientists seem to recognize these connections, the social contract tradition struggles to acknowledge them because they feature human beings at odds with one another.

Some readers may conclude that, if my interpretation of the role of conflict in Aristotelian political theory is correct, his vision should play no role in current discourse because it is too gloomy to serve contemporary ideals. But it seems to me that this interpretation of an ancient thinker is a cause for optimism. For surely it is dispiriting to believe that contemporary political bickering is a unique blight of our generation, or even our modern age, and to worry that our politicians are particularly contentious or somehow remarkably problematic because they keep fighting. If the thesis of this book is true, it should come as a relief—to be reminded that human beings have been at odds with one another for a very long time, and to discover that conflict has been understood to be part and parcel of politics from the beginning of Western political thought.

Indeed, it is particularly helpful for Aristotle to remind us that we should welcome certain kinds of conflict. If we travel through life believing that every conflict is incipient civil war, then it may never dawn on us that our heated discussions, our learned debates, and our passionate disputes are actually part of a successful life. Moreover, by not realizing that such conflicts are achievements of what is good for us, we inevitably trivialize the horrors of actual civil wars that have ruined the lives of so many in every era.

The world, thankfully, has made much progress since the days of ancient Greece. But Aristotle reminds us that this progress cannot, and should not, be measured in terms of ending political conflict.

Notes

Introduction

1. Held, *Models of Democracy*, p. 14.
2. Hampshire, *Justice Is Conflict*, p. 22.
3. MacIntyre, *After Virtue*, p. 157.
4. Throughout this work, I have relied upon the Oxford Classical Text editions of the Greek text for quotations from the *Eudemian Ethics, Nicomachean Ethics, Politics*, and *Rhetoric*; Walzer and Mingay, *Aristotelis Ethica Eudemia*; Bywater, *Aristotelis Ethica Nicomachea*; Ross, *Aristotelis Politica* and *Aristotelis Ars Rhetorica*. As a default, quotations from the *Eudemian Ethics* (hereafter cited as *EE*) are based on Inwood and Woolf's translation; *Nicomachean Ethics* (hereafter cited as *NE*) are based on Irwin's or Reeve's translation; quotations of the *Politics* (hereafter cited as *Pol.*) based on Reeve's translation; and quotations of the *Rhetoric* (hereafter cited as *Rhet.*) are based on Freese's translation. Slight modifications will not be noted; Greek terms have been added by me; major departures from these translations will be discussed in the notes.

Chapter 1

1. Finley, *Politics in the Ancient World*, p. 105.
2. I can find no textual support for Wheeler's suggestion that the distinction between *metabolē* and *stasis* should be understood as that between "completed act" and "situation." See "Aristotle's Analysis of the Nature of Political Struggle," p. 161. Mulgan claims that "because each can occur without the other, neither can be classed as a species or type of the other." *Aristotle's Political Theory*, p. 119. I disagree; while there are types of change that can take place without *stasis*, *stasis* always aims at some kind of political change.
3. Some contemporary writers have claimed that a necessary condition for political violence to count as a "civil war" is that the participants must be trying

to seize control or rule. See, for example, Keegan and Bull, "What Is a Civil War?" On my interpretation, Aristotle thinks of *stasis* along similar lines: the definition of *stasis* requires that force or fraud be used for the sake of attaining some sort of power with constitutional ramifications. There is no such thing as a-political *stasis* or *stasis* oriented around goals that have nothing to do with constitutional control.

4. There is an on-going discussion in the scholarly literature about how Aristotle's doctrine of four causes could be most successfully applied to the causal treatment of *stasis*. It seems to me that using the doctrine of the four causes as an interpretive heuristic (which, note, is all such an analysis can be since it posits an analogy between an individual natural substance and a *polis*) often leads to more confusion than clarification. Nevertheless, examples of this sort of approach can be found in Kalimtzis, *Aristotle on Political Enmity and Disease*, pp. 103–56; Polansky, "Aristotle on Political Change," pp. 324–32; Weed, *Aristotle on* Stasis, pp. 52–60; Keyt, "The Four Causes in Aristotle's Politics," pp. 101–07; Coby, "Aristotle's Three Cities and the Problem of Faction," p. 912. Like me, Hatzistavrou is skeptical of this approach. See "Faction," p. 298n15.

5. Wheeler claims that "Aristotle does not use the word *aitia*, but distinguishes three factors," "Aristotle's Analysis of the Nature of Political Struggle," p. 161. On the contrary, Aristotle uses the word at 1302a18 and a23.

6. Notice that Aristotle's factionalizers are thus not motivated by self-interest in any narrow sense; they are not "realists" trying to acquire power for its own sake. As Yack puts the point, "perceived injustice, rather than competing interests" is the general cause of *stasis*. *Problems of a Political Animal*, p. 224. Similarly, Mulgan writes, "Aristotle would disagree with those political analysts who argue that the appeal to moral principle is merely hypocrisy, a front to gain support." *Aristotle's Political Theory*, p. 121.

7. Hatzistavrou, in "Faction," pp. 277–79, 281–82, criticizes my reading of V.2 1302a22–29 and offers a competing interpretation. Whereas I believe Aristotle is attempting here to identify one common feature of all factionalizers, Hatzistavrou sees Aristotle here distinguishing two different psychologies animating two different types of "politically motivated" faction. On the one hand, there is political faction that is a reaction against unfair exclusion from power and motivated by a correct desire for equality. On the other, there is political faction that is a reaction against equal treatment and motivated by a greedy and hubristic incorrect desire for oligarchic superiority. I am not persuaded by Hatzistavrou for four reasons. First, since Aristotle thinks that democrats, oligarchs, and despots are all in some way unjust, it seems strange that only the characteristic faults of oligarchs would demarcate the "incorrect type" of faction. Second, Hatzistavrou's description of oligarchic faction is incorrect: as I will describe later in the chapter, Aristotle explicitly declares that it is "absurd" [*atopon*] (*Pol.* V.12 1316a39) to think that oligarchs engage in faction because of greed. Third, there are many cases that would not fall into either of Hatzistavrou's two categories: for example, how would Aristotle classify a revolt

of democratic *banausoi* against a genuine aristocracy? This *stasis* would be political and motivated by a desire for equality—but Aristotle would not consider such a democratic revolt to be either oligarchic or correct. Fourth, it seems to me that Hatzistavrou's typology is at odds with the way Aristotle describes the overall project of *Politics* V. Aristotle begins the book by announcing that he will investigate the sources of constitutional change, what destroys constitutions, how they usually change, and what preserves them. There is no suggestion that book V is an attempt to distinguish and classify good and bad factions, just and unjust factions, and acceptable and unacceptable factions.

8. In my opinion, analysis of this second cause has been an Achilles heel of the two book-length treatments of Aristotelian *stasis*. Both Weed, *Aristotle on* Stasis, and Kalimtzis, *Aristotle on Political Enmity and Disease*, claim that Aristotle's description of this cause entails that factionalizers are always people who have mistakenly adopted honor and wealth as the highest human good. The text does not support that reading: *Pol.* V.2 1302a31–34 only claims that each act of *stasis* needs to be explained as aiming at honor or wealth; it does not say that anyone who engages in *stasis* adopts profit or honor as the overarching human good, nor does it suggest that all constitutional changes attempted by factionalizers aim for nothing but getting more money or honor. Because Weed and Kalimtzis make this mistake, and also suggest that honor and wealth are fake or dubious goods (which I also believe to be incorrect), they are led to a misinterpretation whereby all factionalizers are inherently irrational. For similar reasons, I disagree with Wheeler's claim that factionalizers are always people who seek political privilege to reap profit from office. See "Aristotle's Analysis of the Nature of Political Struggle," p. 162.

9. Saxonhouse, "Aristotle on the Corruption of Regimes," proposes that Aristotle's theory of *stasis* is largely an exploration of the psychology of resentment. Saxonhouse is clearly right that Aristotle is attempting to offer a universal account, and I also agree that he portrays all factionalizers as being motivated by a belief that they are being treated unjustly. I worry, however, that conceptualizing the psychology of factionalizers as resentful makes *stasis* seem exclusively driven by self-concern. The second cause of *stasis* involves an event that bears upon either the actors themselves or their friends. Moreover, as the next section will make clear, the third cause of *stasis* consists of spectacles that may not involve potential factionalizers themselves but that strikes them as worrisome for the *polis*. As long as we acknowledge that it is possible to feel resentment on behalf of others, then I agree with Saxonhouse's summary.

10. Hatzistavrou, "Faction," p. 277n6, criticizes my interpretation for concentrating exclusively on faction caused by a perception of injustice; he thinks my reading ignores a "small-issue" type of *stasis* that constitutes an entirely separate apolitical branch of Aristotle's "typology of faction." To defend the claim that Aristotle recognizes such a distinct "small-issue" type of *stasis*, Hatzistavrou cites *Pol.* V.4 1303b17–04a17 and V.6 1306a31–b1, but it seems to me that these passages

only give examples of how the second and third causes of faction lead to *stasis*. In them Aristotle describes specific events involving money and/or honor that lead someone to think he has been treated unjustly in social (e.g. marriage) or legal (e.g. courts) institutions; in each case, a person witnesses some spectacle that makes him feel that he deserves better from the civic order. When Aristotle then summarizes the lesson readers should draw from such events—"Factions arise from small issues, then, but not over them; it is over important issues that people start faction" (1303b17–19)—he is not demarcating a new type of "small-issue" faction. On the contrary, he is announcing that it would be a mistake to confuse a minor personal affront that helped to cause *stasis* with full-blown *stasis* itself. Moreover, it is telling that Hatzistavrou himself admits that faction motivated by a perception of political injustice is the "paradigmatic type of faction" for Aristotle. It seems to me that this admission undercuts the claim that Aristotle wished to carve out a separate "small-issue" type of *stasis* as one branch in a typology of faction.

11. My interpretation should be contrasted with Weed's: he believes that causes of the third type are "occasioning causes" that "trigger or provoke" factional conflict. See *Aristotle on* Stasis, p. 118. Thus, whereas I place the third cause first in the temporal sequence, Weed puts the third cause last in the temporal sequence. My interpretation is also different from Balot's. Following Newman, Balot thinks the third cause of *stasis* is distinguished from the first two only by being more detailed. *Greed and Injustice in Classical Athens*, p. 47.

12. Hatzistavrou, "Faction," pp. 283–84, 298–99nn20–21, advances two criticisms of how I interpret the third cause of *stasis*. First, he thinks that I am wrong to claim that the third cause generates the relevant mental states of factionalizers (e.g. a desire for political power); Hatzistavrou suggests that the third cause may simply put a would-be factionalizer "in the grip" of an already existing desire. Second, he thinks that my interpretation "does not square with the level of entrenchment of the relevant mental states and aims of either the oligarchs or the democrats which motivate them to start faction." Both of these criticisms rest on the mistaken view that, on my interpretation, Aristotle's theory of *stasis* is offered as an account of the entire psychology of factionalizers. I actually agree with Hatzistavrou that oligarchs, for example, have a distinctive elitist psychology that predates any factionalizing they may do. Nevertheless, oligarchs qua oligarchs do not factionalize, so we need an explanation of what transforms an oligarch into an oligarch who wants to factionalize. The origins of this new, factionalizing element in the oligarch's psychology is what needs explaining, and on my interpretation, that is what Aristotle's third cause provides.

13. After describing these seven causal factors of *stasis*, Aristotle goes on in *Pol.* V.3 to list three causes of constitutional change in which *stasis* is not present (electioneering, carelessness, and small alterations) as well as one factor (dissimilarity) that sometimes causes *stasis* but sometimes does not since people can "learn to pull together" (1303a25–26). It is dissimilarity, I think, that explains why Aristotle

says that the causal factors of *stasis* are seven "or more" at 1302a37. For scholarly attempts to group and classify all eleven of these causes in different ways, see Mulgan, *Aristotle's Political Theory*, pp. 124–25; Wheeler, "Aristotle's Analysis of the Nature of Political Struggle," pp. 161–63.

14. Using the word "spectacle" to describe the factors of the third cause was suggested to me by R. Polansky, "Aristotle on Political Change," pp. 336–37. Hatzistavrou, "Faction," p. 293, criticizes my interpretation for being a "psychologically reductionist" account—an account that claims that only mental states can count as the cause of faction. But this criticism ignores the role that the third cause of faction plays in my interpretation. On my reading, worldly events, situations, arrangements, and so on are nonpsychological spectacles that do play a role in causing faction.

15. My interpretation of how profit and honor function as the third kind of cause is similar to Simpson's: "[P]rofit and honor appear again [in V.3], but this time as provocations and not as goals, when people are incited by seeing others getting more profit or honor, and whether justly or unjustly." *A Philosophical Commentary on the Politics of Aristotle*, p. 370. My only concern here is that the word "provocation" may suggest that honor/profit, when factors of the third cause, directly cause the activity of *stasis* to begin. On my interpretation, honor/profit, when factors of the third cause, do not provoke *stasis* itself, but rather a desire for equality (i.e. the first cause of *stasis*).

16. I disagree with Michael Davis, "Aristotle's Reflections on Revolution," who argues that the themes of sexuality and frustrated sexuality explain Aristotle's choice of anecdotes. While sexuality is involved in some of these examples, I believe Aristotle mentions the sexuality only to the extent that it involves issues of honor and dishonor.

17. See Kalimtzis, *Aristotle on Political Enmity and Disease*, pp. 3–9; Weed, *Aristotle on* Stasis, pp. 15–18; Loraux, *The Divided City*, pp. 24–25. Finley makes the point in dramatic fashion: "All levels of intensity were embraced by the splendid Greek portmanteau-word *stasis*. When employed in a social-political context, *stasis* had a broad range of meanings, from political grouping or rivalry through faction (in its pejorative sense) to open civil war. That correctly reflected the political realities. Ancient moralists and theorists, who were hostile to realities, understandably clung to the pejorative overtones of the word and identified *stasis* as the central malady of their society." *Politics in the Ancient World*, p. 105.

18. Nicole Loraux argues that not only was this way of conceptualizing *stasis* very common, but it was also an ideological construction. Referring to all conflict with a loaded term like *stasis* would trick people into thinking that all conflict was to be avoided and that the city was an organic unity. This, in turn, would make citizens feel it was inappropriate to question rulers or even to think carefully about the rough-and-tumble tactics being used by those with the power [*kratos*] to dictate civic policies. See her *Divided City* and "Reflections of the Greek City on Unity and Division."

19. Yack, *Problems of a Political Animal*, p. 219n31.

20. *Stasis* (twenty-nine occurrences): 1264b8, 1265b12, 1266a38, 1271a39, 1272b32, 1273b18, 1296a8, 1301b5, 1301b27, 1302a11, 1302a13, 1302a16, 1302a22, 1302b11, 1303a14, 1303b17, 1304a5, 1304a36, 1304a37, 1304b4, 1304b7, 1305b1, 1306a32, 1306a37, 1306b22, 1307b25, 1308a31, 1308b31, 1319b17; *diastasis* (six occurrences): 1296a8, 1300b37, 1303b14, 1303b15, 1321a15, 1321a19; *stasiastikōs* (two occurrences): 1306a38, 1284b22; *astasiastos* (five occurrences): 1273b21, 1286b2, 1296a7, 1296a9, 1302a9; *epanastaseōs* (one occurrence): 1302b33; *stasiōtikon* (one occurrence): 1303a25; *stasiazō* (twenty-one occurrences): 1266b38, 1267a38, 1267a41, 1272b12, 1286b1, 1301a39 (used twice), 1301b6, 1301b29, 1302a20, 1302a25, 1302a30, 1302a31, 1302a32, 1302a34, 1302b7, 1302b12, 1302b21, 1302b25, 1303b18, 1316b22; *katastasiazesthai* (one occurrence): 1306a33.

21. Mulgan points out that, at *Pol.* V.3 1303b1–2, Aristotle distinguishes *stasis* from "the milder 'rivalry' or competition for office between individuals and groups." *Aristotle's Political Theory*, p. 118. About this same passage in V.3, Simpson writes the following: "It is interesting that Aristotle regards vote getting as a cause of faction and change when we regard it nowadays as the very condition of free and democratic government. But that is perhaps because we have institutionalized faction as part of the political process." *A Philosophical Commentary on the Politics of Aristotle*, p. 370n10. I disagree with Simpson's interpretation. First, Aristotle is citing vote-getting as a non*stasis* cause of change. Second, Simpson is using "faction" as a portmanteau word in precisely the way I am arguing against. As I will argue in part III, while it is true that America has institutionalized some type of conflict, that type is not Aristotelian *stasis*.

22. Indeed, even the most violent of ancient athletic competitions required agreed-upon rules and norms. See Poliakoff, *Combat Sports in the Ancient World*, pp. 7–23.

23. Similarly, consider Aristotle's comments about ostracism in *Pol.* III.13: while ostracism can, in principle, be used justly for the benefit of a city, actual city-states have used ostracism factiously (1284b22). *Stasis* is here being contrasted with what would otherwise be appropriate and beneficial for a city.

24. The notion that oligarchic elites are just as dangerous as the poor is an important theme repeated throughout *Politics* IV–VI. By stressing the arrogance of the oligarchs, and by readily associating oligarchs with outbreaks of *stasis*, Aristotle is distancing himself from one kind of elitist tradition that simply defined *stasis* as "revolution" or demagogic mob revolt. See Kraut, *Aristotle: Political Philosophy*, pp. 449–51; Lintott, *Violence, Civil Strife and Revolution*, p. 242.

25. Note that in the *Republic* Plato does claim that every average city "consists of two cities at war with one another, that of the poor and that of the rich" (422e). This is another sign, as I will discuss in the next section, that Plato adopts a portmanteau conception of conflict and tends to treat all sorts of civic conflict

as being expressions of one and the same kind of internal war. Translations of the *Republic* will be those of Grube, as revised by Reeve.

26. Mulgan makes the same point: "Plato had said that constitutional change was always due to dissension within the ruling class whereas Aristotle believes that it may originate from any quarter of the community." *Aristotle's Political Theory*, p. 125.

27. The *Republic* is not the only Platonic work that traces all conflict to appetite. Socrates says in the *Phaedo*, "Only the body and its desires cause war, civil war, and battles, for all wars are due to the desires to acquire wealth, and it is the body and the care of it, to which we are enslaved, which compel us to acquire wealth, and all this makes us too busy to practice philosophy" (66c–d). Grube translation.

28. I thus disagree with those scholars who, in my opinion, Platonize Aristotle's conception of *stasis*, connecting it in some essential way to brutish appetite, greed, or uncontrolled passion. See Weed, *Aristotle on* Stasis, pp. 99–103; Kalimtzis, *Aristotle on Political Enmity and Disease*, pp. 118–23. Balot, *Greed and Injustice in Classical Athens*, explicitly calls Aristotle's analysis of greed Platonic (p. 39) and argues that greed plays a major part in Aristotle's account of revolution and civil strife in practical regimes (pp. 44–55).

29. Simpson puts the point well: "This account of political change makes human beings and their opinions and actions the fundamental cause or starting point . . . [W]hat will make them act is the desire to act, not merely the opportunity to act, and what will move the desire is the conviction that their action would be good and just." *A Philosophical Commentary on the Politics of Aristotle*, p. 365.

30. Aristotle's critique of Phaleas in *Pol.* II.7 1267a37–41 can be taken as making a similar (but not identical) point: the political scientist should avoid reductive explanations of factionalizers that interpret all their actions as nothing more than the expression of economic difference.

31. Though scholars agree that this text was written during Aristotle's lifetime, they disagree on authorship. Some think Aristotle himself was the author, others that a student or colleague wrote the work to be included in Aristotle's large-scale project of cataloging all Greek constitutions.

32. Quotations from the *Athenian Constitution* (hereafter cited *Ath.Pol.*) are Rackham's translation. In their note for this passage, Von Fritz and Kapp explain that "the last word of this quotation is not clearly legible in the papyrus and has been read in various ways by the editors." They suggest *klinomenēn*, and so offer the translation "I look upon the oldest land of the Ionian world as it totters." By contrast, Sandys thinks the best proposal is *kainomenēn*, so his translation has the Ionian world "being slain" (which is similar to Rackham's "being done to death"). In any case, all of these variations support my claim that the trouble *stasis* poses for the Ionian world is profound and cataclysmic.

33. The phrase "*mē thētai ta hopla*" itself supports the claim that *stasis* implies a violent, warlike type of conflict. For a helpful overview of the scholarship on this

Solonic fragment, see Leão and Rhodes, *The Laws of Solon*, pp. 59–66. It should be noted that there is doubt about the authenticity of this passage.

34. In chapter 3, I will refer to such periods as "constitutional mistrust" and explore Aristotle's theory of how such mistrust is managed so as to avoid *stasis*.

35. This is my translation of the Jones edition of the text.

36. This is my translation of the Paton edition of the text.

37. Admittedly, there are some differences between the causal accounts of Polybius and Aristotle. Polybius seems to think that there is always something dubious about a "pretext" [*prophasis*], and we might thus translate this word as "excuse" just as well as "pretext." By contrast, nothing in Aristotle's account suggests that the factionalizers' near-term goal of gaining honor or profit (or avoiding dishonor or loss) is mere pretense. Moreover, Polybius uses the word "beginning" [*archē*] to pick out the last step in the temporal sequence of events, and "cause" [*aitia*] the first step; by contrast, Aristotle uses "*aitiai*" and "*archai*" to refer to multiple stages of the temporal sequence.

38. Because the number of virtuous inhabitants of a typical *polis* will be so much smaller than the number of nonvirtuous, it will almost always be practically impossible for the virtuous to overcome the superior strength of the opposition (*Pol.* V.4 1304b4–5). Christoph Horn, "Law, Governance, and Political Obligation," argues that virtuous people will be restrained from factionalizing not only because they are in the minority, but also because they will be obligated to be strictly loyal to the community in which they live. This loyalty is ultimately grounded in the fact that some degree of loyalty among citizens is necessary for maintaining minimal stability in suboptimal political orders. Nevertheless, Horn admits that (rare) political conditions can be so bad that revolt is defensible.

39. It seems to me that passages like these pose insurmountable problems for Davis's thesis that, for Aristotle, the "nature of the polis is revolution." See "Aristotle's Reflections on Revolution," p. 58.

Chapter 2

1. I will elaborate on the contrived quality of Aristotle's portraits later in the chapter. Mulgan, following Newman, believes that Aristotle's portraits of oligarchies and democracies are not particularly well suited to capturing historical reality. See "Aristotle on Oligarchy and Democracy," pp. 313–21. For an examination of the inadequacy of Aristotle's specific diagnosis of Athens as an extreme democracy, see Strauss, "On Aristotle's Critique of Athenian Democracy," pp. 212–33.

2. Broadly speaking, Aristotle's political science is a science of human beings rather than an investigation into civic institutions and basic structures of society that can be evaluated independently of citizens' character. See Kraut, *Aristotle: Political Philosophy*, pp. 433–37.

3. Mulgan summarizes the apparent inconsistencies in the way Aristotle characterizes oligarchs and democrats in "Aristotle on Oligarchy and Democracy," pp. 316–17nn6–7.

4. In Athens, possessing the political prerogatives of citizenship by virtue of having been born of citizen parents was clearly an important status marker, especially for the poorest, landless citizens whose actual economic condition resembled that of slaves. See Ober, "Aristotle's Political Sociology," p. 124.

5. At first it appears that *Pol.* V.9 1309b38–10a2 poses a problem for my claim that beliefs about merit are more important traits of social identity than how much wealth is possessed: Aristotle claims that whenever the property of citizens is equalized in a democracy or oligarchy, the constitution is destroyed because it is impossible for these constitutions to exist without rich and poor. I do not think, however, that this V.9 passage is relevant to the definitions of democracy and oligarchy (in contrast to Ober, "Aristotle's Political Sociology," p. 120). Aristotle is here encouraging partisans to make laws that preserve [*sōzei*] rather than destroy [*phtheirei*] their respective regimes; his point is that if democrats liquidate the property of the rich they will make civil war likely and quickly destabilize their democracy. As I read it, this piece of advice actually supports my interpretation: the danger will result from oligarchs being deprived of the very thing—wealth—that they qua oligarchs believe makes a human being happy and meritorious.

6. Mulgan, *Aristotle's Political Theory*, pp. 64–65, accuses Aristotle of changing his mind from *Pol.* III.8 to IV.4. He repeats this charge in "Aristotle on Oligarchy and Democracy," pp. 316–17.

7. My translation should be contrasted with Reeve's: "[I]t is democracy when the free and the poor who are a majority [*hoi eleutheroi kai aporoi pleious ontes*] have the authority to rule, and an oligarchy when the rich and well born, who are few, [*hoi plousioi kai eugenesteroi oligoi ontes*] do." It seems to me that *kai . . . ontes* is here being used as a circumstantial concessive participle phrase. Reeve's translation of this sentence, taken out of context, is perfectly acceptable. But if my argument is correct, and Aristotle believes that it is the way freedom legitimates rule in a city that makes it a democracy, and the way wealth legitimates rule in a city that makes it an oligarchy, then my way of translating these phrases seems more accurate.

8. The lesson here is that Aristotle classifies constitutions primarily in terms of the principle that rulers believe justifies their rule. An upshot of this is that we should be wary of describing constitutions in terms of the worldly consequences that usually arise from these justifying principles. For example, I find the following somewhat misleading: "Aristotle's best polis . . . exemplifies (in a fashion at least) the aristocratic, oligarchic, and democratic conceptions of justice as well as the Aristotelian. The aristocratic conception, whose standard of worth is political virtue alone, is fully realized. The democratic conception is realized in the sense that every free man who does not die prematurely eventually becomes a full citizen. And the oligarchic conception is realized to the extent that those, and only those, who own

land are full citizens." Keyt, "Aristotle's Theory of Distributive Justice," p. 267. To his credit, Keyt does offer the caveat, "in a fashion at least." But it seems to me that the democratic and oligarchic conceptions of justice are only exemplified or "realized" in the ideal city in a completely coincidental manner.

9. Mulgan, *Aristotle's Political Theory*, p. 65. Similarly, see "Aristotle on Oligarchy and Democracy," pp. 316–17.

10. As Miller puts it, majoritarian rule is a "corollary" of freedom. Miller, *Nature Justice, and Rights in Aristotle's Politics*, pp. 124–25.

11. For additional analyses of how Aristotle's theory of constitutional change is not grounded in economics, see Yack, *The Problems of a Political Animal*, pp. 209–18; Ober, "Aristotle's Political Sociology," pp. 121–28; Balot, *Greek Political Thought*, pp. 138–39.

12. For two attempts to interpret Aristotle as endorsing this kind of pluralism, see Garver, *Aristotle's Politics*, chapter 3; and Yack, *The Problems of a Political Animal*, chapters 2 and 5.

13. This debate is described in Herodotus, *Histories*, III.80–83. Miller explicitly compares the conflict between democrats and oligarchs to the sort of conflict that takes place in court: "Politics, III, contains two important references to the discussions of distributive justice in the treatise on justice. The context in which these references occur is a dispute over the constitutions, concerning which inhabitants will hold offices, comprise the government, and possess authority over the *polis* (cf. III 6 1278b8–11, 7 1279a25–27). The verb *amphisbēteō*, "to dispute," is also used in connection with legal disputes, e.g. over the ownership of property or over an inheritance. The dispute over the constitution is thus modeled after a lawsuit in which individuals dispute over their rights." *Nature Justice, and Rights in Aristotle's Politics*, p. 123. Interestingly, Miller's thesis that there are "rights" in Aristotle depends on the idea that conflicts over distributive justice are analogous to types of legal dispute: to the objection that someone can deserve something without having a "right" to it, Miller counters that when two desert claims are opposed, each party is making a bid "to have one's claim legally enforced," p. 98.

14. Thus, while I disagree with Mulgan's interpretation of partisan identity as being based (in part) on economic status (see Aristotle's *Political Theory*, pp. 63–64), I agree with his claim that "Aristotle believes that political conflicts of his day are principally due to a clash between two economic groups," p. 64. The fighting between these two groups is a particularly prominent political phenomenon that demands its own, special explanation. Frank offers an excellent description of the intractable quality of this partisan conflict in *A Democracy of Distinction*, pp. 165–69.

15. I will explore the character of those in the middle in the next chapter.

16. The thesis that greed best explains partisan conflict is defended by R. Balot in *Greed and Injustice in Classical Athens*, pp. 34–57. Balot believes that the deviancy of all three incorrect constitutions is to be understood in terms of greed: "Almost every practical regime—which is to say, the 'deviant' regimes, oligarchy,

democracy, and tyranny—is unstable at its very core, but not because of a desire for freedom from constraint, much less from eros. These regimes are inherently unstable because they promote and reward greed and they encourage destructive, competitive ambition (philotimia)," p. 55. Balot argues that greed itself can be understood as the result of misconceptions of the good life (p. 38) but that this misconception is ultimately traced back to unrestrained desire: "Attempting to understand the psychology of greed, then, Aristotle pointed, like Plato before him, to the body's viselike grip on human desire and to its tendency to pervert the individual's conception of well-being," p. 39.

17. Additional passages in which it is suggested (or implied) that greed leads to conflict: *Pol.* V.8 1308b31–33; VI.3 1318b1–5.

18. Greed does not appear among the long-term causes of *stasis* listed in *Pol.* V.2: profit, honor, arrogance, fear, superiority, contempt, and disproportionate growth. Nor is it listed among the specific and immediate ends of *stasis*, which are "profit, honor, and the opposite of these" either for the agents or their friends (V.2 1302a31–33).

19. Yack, *Problems of a Political Animal*, pp. 224–31, takes democrats and oligarchs to differ first and foremost in their conceptions of justice. However, he believes that the particular animosity they have for one another can be attributed to the bitterness friends feel when their friendship (and the mutual expectations of that friendship) is betrayed. This passage and others, however, pose a problem for that reading: there is no textual evidence that oligarchs and democrats ever had a political friendship to betray.

20. Miller, *Nature Justice, and Rights in Aristotle's Politics*, p. 268, notes that Aristotle does not make people's emotional repertoire a simple function of their economic class; similarly, Ober argues in "Aristotle's Political Sociology" that Aristotelian political sociology always supplements economic class differentiation with status differentiation.

21. The citizens of the ideal city are financially well-off because they own private land (*Pol.* VII.9 1329a17–26) that is productive (VII.8 1328b5–6) and their land generates enough wealth so that citizens lead lives that are "both free and temperate" (VII.5 1326b31–32) and magnanimous (VII.7 1328a9–10, VIII.3 1338b2–4). The best sort of city will be as devoted to education as are Sparta and Crete (*NE* I.13 1102a10–12, X.9 1180a24–26, *Pol.* VIII.1 1337a31–32), and this education is "one and the same for all" young citizens (1337a22–23). Finally, military service is required of all ideal citizens when they are young adults (VII.9 1329a2–17).

22. I could have just as easily called this the "for whom" mistake, for in these same passages Aristotle explains that while democrats embrace "equality," and oligarchs "inequality," they both leave off the "for whom" (*Pol.* III.9 1280a13–14).

23. There is no important connection between the *haplōs* mistake and the subject matter of politics. Indeed, this is the same sort of mistaken inference that Plato portrays Protagoras protesting during one of the arguments about the unity of

virtue (*Protagoras*, 329d–31e). Socrates slips in an assumption that since two things are the same (or different) in one respect, they must be the same (or different) in all respects. Protagoras objects that it is unacceptable to call things "similar" just because they have some point of similarity, nor "dissimilar" if they have one dissimilarity.

24. My interpretation of partisans as cliquish rather than selfish should be contrasted with Balot's: "[H]uman beings, in Aristotle's view, tend to be self-aggrandizing and to make interpretations, either of others or of situations in which they find themselves, on the basis of self-interest." *Greed and Injustice in Classical Athens*, p. 49. Aristotle does say that most people are bad judges about their own affairs (*Pol.* III.9 1280a14–16, a20–21)—but this is a far cry from saying that they are acting from the motive of "self-interest." Like Bernard Yack, I do not believe that the notion of "competing interests" can adequately explain oligarchic and democratic friction. See *Problems of a Political Animal*, pp. 218–19.

25. Just because rich oligarchs and poor democrats tend to treat everyone outside their respective groups poorly, it does not follow that there is never conflict within their groups. On the contrary, Aristotle explicitly says that oligarchs, unlike democrats, have a tendency to fight with one another (*Pol.* V.1 1302a8–15).

26. Mulgan also sees that the despotic attitude Aristotle attributes to democrats is something quite different from a democratic conception of justice: "Arithmetic equality, after all, requires equal shares for all; though it implies the majority principle as a means of resolving disputes by counting every voice equally, it does not necessarily imply majority rule, in which the same people are always in the prevailing majority." "Aristotle on Oligarchy and Democracy," p. 317.

27. J. S. Mill claims in *Utilitarianism* that a large difference in degree can sometimes be taken as difference in kind, p. 53.

28. Other scholars who note that the conception of happiness possessed by partisans is an element in their psychology distinct from their belief about justice: Miller, *Nature Justice, and Rights in Aristotle's Politics*, pp. 157–59; Mulgan, *Aristotle's Political Theory*, p. 63; Kraut, *Aristotle: Political Philosophy*, pp. 12–15, 368.

29. This is the traditional way of numbering these books. There are scholars such as Carnes Lord and Peter Simpson who argue that this ordering and numbering are erroneous. For an overview of the debate, see Kraut, *Aristotle: Political Philosophy*, pp. 181–91.

30. On my interpretation, Aristotle's oligarchs and democrats could truly be said to suffer from some brand of political fanaticism.

31. Contra Balot, *Greed and Injustice in Classical Athens*, p. 54n82. I do not think Aristotle thinks of this advice to democracies as democratic. My interpretation is more in line with that of Mulgan: "This illustrates an important distinction: the principles which support and preserve a constitution are not necessarily the same as those on which the constitution is itself based and which determine the distribution of power and the values of the ruling class. Indeed the dominant principles of the constitution may work against its continued existence . . . To

make their subjects contented and loyal democrats must in certain respects become less democratic and oligarchs less oligarchic." *Aristotle's Political Theory*, pp. 131–32. Inasmuch as Aristotle understands democracy as that constitution which is run by (despotic) democrats, it no surprise that he refers to the most extreme democracy as "final" [*teleutaia*] democracy (for a helpful discussion of this claim, see Strauss, "On Aristotle's Critique of Athenian Democracy," pp. 213–16). Also note that, on my reading, there will be a difference between being a "good democrat" and a "good citizen" stuck in a democracy (for discussion, see Kraut, *Aristotle: Political Philosophy*, pp. 368–71; it could be that Aristotle believes his advice for democracies will be accepted only by the latter.

32. Herodotus describes Cylon's plot in *Histories*, V.71. In Thucydides's account (*History of the Peloponnesian War*, I.126), Cylon wins a victory but seizes the Acropolis only after making an inquiry at Delphi.

33. My colleague, J. Fenno, has reminded me that many writers before Aristotle complained about this inappropriate translation of athletic success into political prominence. See, for example, Xenophanes's complaint that it is "not right to honor strength above excellent wisdom," frag. 2, Robinson, *Sources for the History of Greek Athletics*, p. 91. More generally, Plato was also clearly aware of the need to distinguish bogus from relevant claims of political desert, as his analysis of whether women deserve to rule makes clear (*Republic* 451c–57c).

34. *Pol.* I opens with an explicit declaration that each community aims at a distinct good (1252a2–3). The entire first book of the *Politics*, as I read it, is a sustained argument for this thesis and the important corollary that communities differ in kind. Moreover, note that Aristotle feels so strongly about the distinction between business affairs and political affairs that he believes ideal cities will physically separate the business-related agora from the agora of leisure (*Pol.* VII.12 1331a30–b4).

35. For an account of the complexities of political life in Athens from the end of the Peloponnesian War to the end of the (surprising) Corinthian War, see Strauss, *Athens after the Peloponnesian War*. Strauss argues that Athenian political behavior cannot be reduced to class analysis but must be seen as a complex product of many different factors that often cut against simple political caricatures. Strauss also describes in "On Aristotle's Critique of Athenian Democracy" how actual rich Athenians and "working citizens" had a more or less productive and cooperative relationship with one another throughout the fourth century.

36. Another interesting example of Aristotle's simply setting aside a commonly recognized trait as politically irrelevant is when he confidently reduces "being well-born" into the components of old money and virtue (*Pol.* IV.8 1294a20–22). Even though actual "well-born" individuals frequently interpret themselves in terms of heritage and tradition (just as actual individuals frequently define themselves in terms of athletic victories), Aristotle seems to think that such notions do not, in fact, end up cultivating people's social identity in the way that being brought up rich does.

37. For a recent philosophical argument that much partisanship originates from rational commitments that must be made to sustain large political movements, complicated personal relationships, and cutting-edge scientific projects, see Morton, "Partisanship." Both Schütrumpf, "Little to Do with Justice," and Rosler, "Civic Virtue," argue convincingly that Aristotle's *Politics* is not a work devoted to moralizing or merely measuring how far away flawed cities are from achieving an aristocratic ideal. The *Politics* offers a great deal of realistic appraisal about how flawed groups and actions can contribute to civic stability.

Chapter 3

1. Coby, "Aristotle's Three Cities and the Problem of Faction," conceptualizes Aristotle's analysis of average cities in terms of two types. Unitary regimes hand over rule to one (relatively) unified element and permanently lock out from power all other inhabitants who are different from the rulers. In this group, Coby places tyranny, monarchy, democracy, oligarchy, and aristocracy. By contrast, mixed regimes incorporate different kinds of inhabitants: this is the type of regime best illustrated by polity. On Coby's view, Aristotle thinks the main cause of instability in unitary regimes comes from the population locked out of power, while the main cause of instability in mixed regimes is the inability of rich and poor to agree without the presence of a middle class. I agree with much of Coby's analysis, but it strikes me as too abstract: the problems afflicting partisan democracies and oligarchies are significantly different from those facing monarchies and tyrannies, and this explains why we find Aristotle offering very different kinds of palliatives. Because he groups together so many types of regimes, Coby ends up neglecting many of the tactics Aristotle develops to manage mistrust and decrease the likelihood of faction.

2. An anonymous reviewer points out—rightly I think—that depicting tyranny as uniformly despotic is somewhat anachronistic since there were Archaic tyrants who were thought of as successful rulers. Indeed, this reviewer notes, the author of the *Athenian Constitution* seems to depict the rule of Peisistratus in such positive terms. In my opinion, this is another sign of Aristotle's taxonomic ambitions in the *Politics*: just as Aristotle's portrait of democrats and oligarchs seems (suspiciously) driven by theoretical commitments, so too his account of tyranny in the *Politics* is probably being driven by the need to portray this type of rule as the (conveniently) incorrect mirror image of correct kingship.

3. Von Fritz, *The Theory of the Mixed Constitution in Antiquity*, pp. 314–18, makes a helpful distinction between tyranny, monarchy established through support of a party that is an integral part of the city, and Caesarism, monarchy established through support of some group that is alienated or even physically separated from the rest of the community. Aristotle's description of tyrants as betrayers suggests

that he, too, thinks of tyrants as arising through the internal dynamics of a political community.

4. Although he does not explicitly talk about cultivating public symbols, Aristotle may well believe that a monarch who is constantly associating himself with honor and beauty will be thought of as a kingly figure who embodies something greater than his own personal rule. Consider Von Fritz's description of the kingly monarch: "If and when the king is placed so high above every individual, and also every social or economic group within the country, that he does not ally himself with any group against any other, he may indeed appear not only as the protector of the law but also as its very incarnation, and may be readily obeyed, if not by every individual member, yet by the great majority within any group of the population. In other words, the interest which most, if not all, the members of the commonwealth have in the preservation of a rule of law and justice is, so to speak, transformed into personal loyalty to the monarch." *The Theory of the Mixed Constitution in Antiquity*, p. 314.

5. The poor plunder by means of confiscatory lawsuits (*Pol.* VI.5 1320a4–11); the rich plunder by taking money from the multitude but then not spending these funds on public works (III.10 1281a25–28, VI.7 1321a31–42).

6. In fact, given the argument I made in chapter 2, I doubt very much that Aristotle expects democrats and oligarchs to follow this advice of appeasing opposing partisans. Simpson believes Aristotle is only mildly hopeful and offers his advice conditionally: "[Taking Aristotle's advice] requires them to restrain, in a variety of ways, their passions for dominance and oppression. They will be reluctant, of course, to oppose their passions, as most of us are, but past examples about the fate of others who did not do so might be enough to shock some into accepting the advice. If not, then the legislator will be in the same position as any doctor before a recalcitrant patient. He can give the best advice he has, but if the patient refuses to listen, the doctor can only issue a last, friendly warning and leave him to his fate." *A Philosophical Commentary on the Politics of Aristotle*, p. 402.

7. John Locke also believes in the benefit of less frequent assemblies: "Constant frequent meetings of the legislative, and long continuations of their assemblies, without necessary occasion, could not but be burdensome to the people, and must necessarily in time produce more dangerous inconveniencies." *Second Treatise*, XIII.156.

8. "A remedy that prevents this [change into lawless democracy], or diminishes its effect, is to have the tribes nominate the officials rather than the people as a whole" (*Pol.* V.5 1305a32–34).

9. Aristotle consistently portrays oligarchs, who already have wealth, as wanting more of it. He points out that "the acquisitive behavior of the rich does more to destroy the constitution than that of the poor" (*Pol.* IV.12 1297a11–13), and he is just as worried about oligarchs abusing political offices to make money as he is the poor: "But the most important thing in every constitution is for it to have

the laws and the management of other matters organized in such a way that it is impossible to make a profit from holding office. One should pay particular heed to this in oligarchies" (V.8 1308b31–34). This constant desire for more wealth can be traced to oligarchs' conception of happiness, which was discussed in chapter 2.

10. This is not to say that, even in the incredibly auspicious conditions that are necessary for aristocracy, civil war could never take place: after all, Aristotle explores the possibility for *stasis* in aristocracies in *Pol.* V.7. However, note that when Aristotle investigates this topic, his main cases involve nonvirtuous people agitating; he says that "polities and aristocracies are principally overthrown, however, because of a deviation from justice within the constitution itself" (1307a5–7). In other words, it turns out that these "aristocracies" became problematic when they began transforming into something other than aristocracy.

11. "That is why democracy, despite all its talk of equality, is really inequality, for with respect to what the city properly is democracy is inequality, namely the dominance of one part of the city (the populace or mass of farmers, mechanics, laborers, and the like) over the other parts (the well-off and the virtuous)." Simpson, *A Philosophical Commentary on Aristotle's Politics*, p. 427.

12. Unlike Kraut, *Aristotle: Political Philosophy*, pp. 457–60, I do not believe Aristotle offers this system of weighted voting as a democratic device. It seems to me that Aristotle offers it as a plan that might satisfy both oligarchs and democrats. That is why he introduces the plan to readers like this: "What sort of equality there might be, then, that both would agree on is something we must investigate in light of the definitions of justice they both give" (VI.3 1318a27–29). My interpretation is closer to that of Simpson, *A Philosophical Commentary on Aristotle's Politics*, pp. 434–35.

13. Barker clearly recognizes that polities (which he identifies as the "mean constitution") constitute only a subset of the large class of conceivable mixed constitutions: "The mixed constitution is a wider thing than the mean constitution. The mean constitution is only a species: the mixed constitution is of the nature of a genus." *The Political Thought of Plato and Aristotle*, p. 478.

14. I agree with Frank, *A Democracy of Distinction*, pp. 163–78, that Aristotle is extremely pessimistic about the possibility of creating a stable rich/poor balance in any constitution. Our skepticism should be contrasted with Kraut's view that such a balance is possible. See *Aristotle: Political Philosophy*, pp. 447–48.

15. Aristotle was not alone in thinking that "mixed constitution" could only be successful by including people of the middling sort: "Thus the Solonian constitution in a way clearly represented a mixture of oligarchic and democratic elements, and therefore may be called a mixed constitution of a sort. But the slogan of Solon's time and of the following century was not 'the mixed constitution' but 'the middle of the road' (τὸ μέσον, ἡ μεσότης) and 'the middle-of-the-road party' (οἱ μέσοι)." Von Fritz, *The Theory of the Mixed Constitution in Antiquity*, p. 77. Coby, "Aristotle's Three Cities and the Problem of Faction," p. 908, claims that Aristotle favors

political education as the best tactic for mixing, but it seems to me that Aristotle is far more pessimistic than is Coby about the willingness of most people to "adopt the perspective" of other inhabitants.

16. All of this shows why it would be misleading to think of "those who are in the middle" as a middle class animated only by economic class interests. While it is true that wealth helps to pick them out, their level of wealth does not disclose everything, or even the most important things, about who they are as human beings and political agents. See Kraut, *Aristotle: Political Philosophy*, pp. 438–44.

17. Reeve, *Politics*, p. 59n139, claims that Aristotle identifies polity and aristocracy at 1273a4–6 and 1294b10–11. I disagree with this interpretation of these two passages. In the former, Aristotle says that the deviations of the Carthaginian constitution from the best resemble democratic or oligarchic deviations from the "principle of an aristocracy and [*kai*] a polity." But this seems to imply only that there are democratic or oligarchic deviations from the principle of an aristocracy, on the one hand, and democratic or oligarchic deviations from the principle of a polity, on the other. There is no claim that the principle defining aristocracy is the very same principle that defines polity. The latter passage is a bit more muddled and, admittedly, perhaps more compatible with Reeve's reading: "it is aristocratic, therefore, and characteristic of a polity to take one element from one and another from the other [*to ex hekateras hekateron labein*]." In my opinion, however, Aristotle is here saying only that the device of "making officials elected" (1294b12) on some basis other than property (b13) is a feature of polity and adding an aside that this device makes polity resemble an aristocracy more than it otherwise would have. From the fact that polities and aristocracies share this feature, however, it does not follow that they share all features and are one and the same constitution.

18. "In cases where the attack is motivated by love of honor, however, the explanation is of a different sort from those previously discussed. For some attack tyrants because they see great profit and high office in store for themselves, but this is not why someone whose attack is motivated by love of honor deliberately chooses to take the risk" (V.10 1312a21–25).

19. I thus think Garver is somewhat misleading when he claims, "There is no party of virtue, not in Book III or anywhere else in the *Politics*." *Aristotle's Politics*, p. 71. Those in the middle, though not genuinely virtuous, will behave together in a way that is passably virtuous.

20. Lockwood, in "Polity, Political Justice and Political Mixing," argues that this mixing, which is a distinct feature of polity, also entails that political justice (ruling in turns) is only found in polity. I think that is slightly too strong: I would say that this mixing ensures that there is a distinctive version of political justice that one finds only in polity. My interpretation is similar to Balot's, "The 'Mixed Regime' in Aristotle's Politics," who argues that the middlings who rule the stable mixed regime are animated by a distinctive "middling or *metrios* ideology." The middlings form a distinctive sociological group with its own distinctive behaviors and outlook.

21. Kraut claims that there will be friendship in cities dominated by middlings because other inhabitants will trust them. *Aristotle: Political Philosophy*, p. 442. I think this is too optimistic. While I do believe that those in the middle will trust one another, I see no evidence that the rich and poor will actively exercise any goodwill toward middlings. Rather, partisans would only be less wary of those in the middle than they would be of their ideological opponents. Partisans, after all, have epistemic defects that will lead them to misinterpret actions of both virtuous and passably virtuous citizens.

22. Reeve, *Politics*, p. 52n109, points out that Aristotle expresses this principle in two slightly different ways that "should probably be distinguished." In some passages Aristotle claims that the part of the city that wishes the constitution to continue must be stronger than the part that does not (a somewhat low bar). In other passages Aristotle claims that, if a constitution is to survive, all the parts must want it to exist (a far higher bar). Interestingly, as will be discussed, Aristotle seems to think that only farming democracy and polity will regularly meet even the low hurdle.

23. Aristotle's explanation for why extreme oligarchies tend to be weak relies overtly on the notion that strength is the product of size and something akin to organization (*Pol.* VI.6 1320b30–21a1). This conception of political strength is not unique to Aristotle. For example, Von Fritz explains the ability of a small number of Roman and Spartan citizens to maintain stable rule over vast subject populations this way: "[I]in relation to their noncitizen subjects, or 'allies,' the Spartans and the Romans constituted a highly organized minority as against unorganized majorities." *The Theory of the Mixed Constitution in Antiquity*, p. 346.

24. It should be kept in mind that, like other principles describing events in the world of practical action, these are generalizations. Aristotle is not claiming that every oligarchy and every tyranny must be short-lived; he was well aware of long-lasting regimes of both types. See Simpson, *A Philosophical Commentary on the Politics of Aristotle*, pp. 416–17.

Part II: Prelude

1. Parts of an animal exist only as potentialities [*dunameis*] (*Metaphysics* VII.16 1040b5–15) and could be nothing but "heaps" and "parts in name only" when separated from the animal (*Parts of Animals* 640b29–641a21, *De Anima* 412b18–24). Such parts could not be substances since genuine substances like living creatures cannot be composed of other substances (*Metaphysics* VII.13 1039a3–4). For elaboration, see Mayhew, *Aristotle's Criticism of Plato's Republic*, pp. 15–20.

2. By contrast, human beings whose maturation does not culminate in full development and who fully belong to someone else as a part belongs to a whole are natural slaves (*Pol.* I.4 1254a13–17).

3. Mayhew, for example, makes the following argument: "This gives the household a high degree of unity (for a community) because this one ruler has complete authority, and thereby gives the household one direction, without the tension that almost inevitably accompanies a number of people having to agree." *Aristotle's Criticism of Plato's Republic*, pp. 20–21. I agree whole-heartedly with Mayhew that Aristotle believes tension will break out in communities larger than families; what needs explaining is why Aristotle has this belief.

4. Aristotle's analysis of *phronēsis* involves a suite of five excellent aptitudes. First, it involves a proper understanding [*nous*] of *eudaimonia*. Second, good deliberation [*euboulia*] determines the means one should use to promote the end of action in a fine way. Third, this deliberation must be motivated by correct desire: the ethical agent begins with a rational wish [*boulēsis*] which itself is desiderative; desire motivates deliberation; and the agent must then desire to carry out the means ultimately recommended by thought. Fourth, *phronēsis* involves an ability to grasp specifics and particulars. And, fifth, it involves the ability to follow through on a decision (the correct deliberated desire), avoiding incontinence [*akrasia*]. For helpful summaries, see Reeve, *Practices of Reason*, pp. 94–98; Lear, *The Desire to Understand*, pp. 141–51.

5. For a good overview of "particularist" readings of Aristotle, see Irwin, "Ethics as an Inexact Science," pp. 100–04. Scholars of Aristotle's political theory have also emphasized the way *phronēsis* grasps specifics. For example, Frank describes *phronēsis* as a "discursive practice" that resembles "felicitous analogy," *A Democracy of Distinction*, p. 97. Salkever characterizes this virtue as an ability to employ a "metaphor of the mean" in problematic situations in a way that cannot be predicted ahead of time with any precise measurement or a priori rule; exercises of *phronēsis* are "like well-informed guesses, resting on complex perceptions of that balance of importance and urgency that is likely to be best for us." *Finding the Mean*, p. 138.

6. Nussbaum, *The Fragility of Goodness*, pp. 334–36, describes some deliberative conflicts as "Agamemnon-like" and "tragic" because she believes different virtues can offer conflicting motivations in given situations. Notice, however, that even if there were situations of divergent virtues, it would not follow that *phronimoi* would disagree about which virtue should be followed in them. The analysis of deliberative conflict offered by White in *Individual and Conflict in Greek Ethics*, pp. 213–89 is particularly helpful on this issue. On his reading, Aristotle's agents do indeed face ineradicable deliberative conflict when choosing between goods that have intrinsic worth. Such choices can be rationally made, but they are made by "adjudicating" among the goods, not by (re)conceptualizing goods in such a way that deliberative conflict is completely eradicated. For example, White believes that the choice between whether to lead a life devoted to ethical virtue or a life devoted to theoretical contemplation is such an adjudication. Even though there is deliberative conflict between these two lives, Aristotle believes that the theoretical life is happier.

7. Disagreement among excellent citizens is a neglected topic in the literature. Five scholars come close to discussing this issue, but I believe they do not tackle the problem directly in the way I am attempting to do in this chapter. Rosler, in *Political Authority and Obligation in Aristotle*, pp. 193–218, clearly endorses the view that nondivine virtuous agents will disagree, but he doesn't explain how Aristotle's analysis of *phronēsis* makes this possible. Kraut, *Aristotle: Political Philosophy*, p. 232, briefly acknowledges the possibility for interpersonal political disagreement among "people of good will and practical intelligence," but it isn't clear whether he thinks this is possible because some tricky situations don't allow for the exercise of *phronēsis*, or whether *phronimoi*, even when exercising *phronēsis*, can disagree. In either case, he offers no explanation of how, exactly, this intellectual virtue would allow for such dispute. Since Aristotle refuses to discount private bonds of friendship and family in the name of maximal civic unity, Nussbaum, *The Fragility of Goodness*, p. 353, argues that "the possibility of contingent conflict of values is preserved as a condition of the richness and vigor of civic life itself." The question of how, when, and why virtuous citizens would dispute when deliberating about the common good, however, is not developed, nor is there any explanation for how *phronēsis* would allow this to take place. Yack, in *The Problems of a Political Animal* and "Community and Conflict in Aristotle's Political Philosophy," argues that political community itself entails contestation over theories of justice and inspires deep distrust when expectations of virtue are thwarted by self-interest, but he never shows how the *phronēsis* of *phronimoi* could permit such conflicting views and such mistaken judgments. And Bickford, in "Beyond Friendship," argues that Aristotle's theory of deliberation and rhetoric allows legislators to hold cities together by exercising a kind of attention that tracks others' conflicting perspectives rather than through friendly mutual concern. Her analysis, however, is explicitly limited to the association of nonexcellent citizens (pp. 418–19). At one point, Bickford theorizes that conflict can take place among civic deliberators because (1) people have different conceptions of what counts as an end in a given situation, (2) uncertain questions have imprecise answers, (3) people have different opinions, and (4) deliberation concerns real-world results rather than mere academic exercises (pp. 399–403). But she never discusses whether or how intellectual excellence would suppress or eliminate these four sources of disagreement.

Chapter 4

1. I do not believe Aristotle's *phronimoi* will disagree over the nature of the ultimate, common good of the city: the happiness of each and every citizen. For a convincing defense of this interpretation of the common good, see Morrison, "The Common Good."

2. Aristotle also stresses the necessary universality of law in *Rhet.* I.1: "What is most important of all is that the judgment of the legislator does not apply to a particular case, but is universal and applies to the future" (1354b4–6).

3. I agree with Irwin that Aristotle does not believe all ethical principles are usually the case and inexact. For discussion, see Irwin, "Ethics as an Inexact Science," pp. 110–13.

4. It is worth noting that even if actions did deal with universals, this would still not entail that each *phronimos* is guaranteed epistemic success. Even in the realm of science, perfect success is often unattainable: "To study the truth is in one way difficult and in another way easy. A sign of this is the fact that no one [*mēdena*] is capable of reaching the truth adequately, but on the other hand not everyone completely fails to attain it" (*Metaphysics*, II.1 993a30–b1).

5. This is Burnyeat's helpful way of describing Aristotle's characterization: the phrase "*sullogismos tis*" should not be understood to mean "a sort of sullogism" but rather "a sullogism of a sort": the "*tis*" is an alienans qualification. See "Enthymeme: Aristotle on the Rationality of Rhetoric," pp. 94–105.

6. As Burnyeat explains, Aristotle's sign arguments feature *probabilitas consequentiae*—which is a kind of inference appropriate to an issue where there are things to be said on either side (if, by contrast, the likelihood being expressed in such arguments qualified the conclusion rather than the inference—*probabilitas consequentis*—one would be able to generate examples where true premises—"the sky is clouded over" and "the barometer is high"—necessitate both p "it is likely to rain" and not-p "it is not likely to rain"). Burnyeat also points out that Aristotle allows rhetoricians to use relaxed forms of induction: whereas strict *epagōgē* requires including all cases to develop some principle (*Prior Analytics* II.23 68b27–29), rhetorical example allows for a speaker to move from one particular (or a few) to another particular (*Rhet.* I.2 1357b27–29). "Enthymeme: Aristotle on the Rationality of Rhetoric," pp. 101–05.

7. When Aristotle says "the excellent person is far superior because he sees what is true in each case, being himself a sort of standard and measure" (*NE* III.4 1113a31–33) or "what is really so is what appears so to the excellent person" (X.5 1176a15–16), we should keep the context of these claims in mind. The point Aristotle is making in both cases is that the person who is excellent with respect to a given domain will also be best at registering items in that domain. So it is that the healthy will best register what is truly health, the well-sighted will best register what is truly seeable, those with a proper regard for bodily pleasure will best register the pleasures of the body, and so on.

8. In the *Gorgias*, Socrates seems to offer only two options by which public speakers can convince audiences: either they exercise a craft with knowledge, or they practice flattery with guesswork (cf. 461b–65d). A speaker can offer demonstrative proof or irrational trickery, and there are no other options.

9. *Topics* I.2 describes dialectic this way: "dialectic is a process of criticism wherein lies the path to the principles of all inquiries" (101b4–5). Although I disagree with his ultimate conclusion that Aristotle is quite content to let truth be sacrificed to victory, Wardy provides a helpful account of the agonistic nature of dialectic as described in the *Topics*. See Wardy, "Mighty Is the Truth and It Shall Prevail?"

10. Rosler, *Political Authority and Obligation in Aristotle*, pp. 182,193–218, also describes how Aristotle never explicitly siloes excellent citizens from his claims about typical disagreements.

11. That he would attribute majority rule to the best city is clear from *Pol.* IV.4 1290a30–33. In this passage, he rejects the idea that democracy is the only constitution that operates by majority rule and makes the sweeping claim that "in oligarchies and everywhere else the greater [*pleon*] part has authority" (a31–32). Given that democracy, oligarchy, and even aristocracy (*Pol.* IV.8 1294a11–14) work by majority rule, it seems best to attribute it to the city of *Pol.* VII–VIII as well. By "majority rule," I mean the majority of those who are active ruling citizens (which in an aristocracy might be very few people), not the democratic principle of majoritarianism that would give rule to the majority of inhabitants.

12. The citizens are owners of private plots of land (*Pol.* VII.9 1329a17–26), upon which sit citizen households capable of generating an amount of wealth sufficient to meet the needs of family, friends, and city (VII.8 1328b10–11, VII.10 1329b39–30a9).

13. By claiming that citizens engage in economic exchange, I do not mean to imply that the citizen owners themselves will always travel down into the commercial agora where such business is conducted (*Pol.* VII.12 1331b1–4). On the contrary, since Aristotle looks down upon merchants (VII.9 1328b39–40), it is more likely that a citizen would turn such transactions over to some sort of household manager [*epitropos*] (cf. I.7 1255b31–37). Regardless of who travels to the marketplace, the point remains that price setting allows for divergent assessments of value.

14. I agree with Irwin when he writes in his notes that "the discussion of disputes is a further defense of the claim of complete friendship to be complete. It avoids the conflicts and quarrels that make the others fall short of complete friendships." *Nicomachean Ethics*, p. 287, note for VIII.13 §2. Nevertheless, just because virtue friends avoid the quarrels of utility friendships, it does not follow that there is no conflict of any kind among them.

15. Economic exchange is a basic necessity for all cities (*Pol.* I.9 1257a28–30, *EE* VII.10 1242a6–9). *EE* VII.10 1242a6–9, b21–27, and b31–34 seem to depict political friendship itself as being a kind of utility friendship. Even if we resisted this interpretation, and insisted that Aristotle draws some sort of distinction between political and utility friendship, this wouldn't spare political friendship from conflict: *EE* VII.4 1239a13–21 claims that the kind of quarrels we find in utility exchange are emblematic of all types of friendship as friends become more and more equal to one another. Similarly, in *EE* VII.10 1243b14–38, Aristotle explains that the

same sort of difficulties that attend exchanging different kinds of utility goods also haunt the exchanges found within complicated friendships where different parties receive different kinds of goods from the relationship.

16. At *NE* V.4 1132b11–20, Aristotle describes buying and selling as voluntary exchanges, allowed by law, in which it is possible either to profit or suffer a loss. This is not a completely unregulated market: the best city needs market wardens (*Pol.* VII.12 1331b9–12)—officials who "ensured that commodities were pure and unadulterated, that merchants used fair weights and measures, and that foodstuffs were not unjustly priced." Miller, *Nature Justice, and Rights in Aristotle's Politics*, p. 330.

17. I think there are two interpretive strategies one might use to argue that *phronomoi* qua *phronimoi* would never appear in court. One strategy might be to argue that *phronimoi* would be involved in court cases or punishments only because of nonphronetic outbursts of appetite: "appetite is like a wild beast, and passion perverts rulers even when they are the best men" (*Pol.* III.16 1287a30–32). Kraut uses this sort of strategy to explain why citizens of the best city will need to dole out punishments: "It might be wondered why the citizens of the best city need to be threatened with punishment; these, after all, are the best citizens one can hope to have. But, Aristotle can reply, the legislator cannot entirely control the quality of the material he has at his disposal, and so some citizens may not have as great a natural capacity for virtue as one would like. He is reluctant to assume conditions that are extremely unlikely." *Aristotle: Politics Books VII and VIII*, p. 149. I agree with Kraut that Aristotle is reluctant to assume extremely unlikely conditions. However, it seems to me that it would be highly unlikely that the only reason courts are used is to punish vice. Another strategy one might use to show that *phronimoi* will never appear in court would be to cite passages like this: "For it is not natural for good people to bring suit and these people make contracts as good and trustworthy people" (*EE* VII.10 1243a10–11). But in this passage context matters: Aristotle's point is not that good people always avoid court; rather, the point is that when good people explicitly base a contract on trust instead of legal guarantees, they cannot then turn around and cite law to ground a complaint. Indeed, consider how the passage continues: if parties disagreeing over an exchange "did not make a stipulation that it was to be done on the basis of character then someone has to make a ruling and neither of them should cheat by pretending. The result is that each has to put up with his luck" (1243b6–9).

18. Aristotle also says that the law educates people to be officials (*Pol.* III.16 1287a25–27) so that they can deal with "the sort of things that the law seems unable to decide" (a23–24).

19. White, *Individual and Conflict in Greek Ethics*, pp. 264–74, has a particularly illuminating discussion of how not all virtuous people will necessarily be able to deploy their virtue in a given situation. In particular, I think he is correct to argue that "Aristotle treats opportunities for virtuous action as potentially scarce, as not always present in abundance, as moderns are usually disposed to think that they are," p. 269.

20. Here I am using the translation offered by White, *Individual and Conflict in Greek Ethics*, p. 269. He criticizes Irwin's translation for downplaying Aristotle's use of the word "*pleon*" in these passages, stripping them of the comparative claim Aristotle is making.

21. For more discussion about such cases, where some friends flourish and others flail, see Nussbaum, *The Fragility of Goodness*, p. 360.

22. My claim here is similar to Nussbaum's: "We find, then, in Aristotle's thought about the civilized city . . . the idea that the value of certain constituents of the good human life is inseparable from a risk of opposition, therefore of conflict." *The Fragility of Goodness*, p. 353. Garver highlights the way in which Aristotle's position here contrasts with modern political thought. Thinkers like Rousseau, Rawls, and Habermas "look for commonality in shared opinion" and so embrace "visions of politics [that] produce a divided self, an alienated self that keeps one side private and shows another face in public." By contrast, "Aristotle's strategy is more modest. Private ownership and common use avoid dividing the self into private comprehensive views or preferences and the common public reason of a neutral political framework. Civic participation never means casting aside and bracketing one's particularity." *Aristotle's Politics*, p. 57.

23. For a convincing explanation of why *dei* should not be translated "ought," see Kraut, "Doing without Morality."

24. This is Irwin's translation, which I believe best captures the meaning. It should be pointed out, however, that this phrase could mean a number of slightly different things. Reeve translates it as "out for the same things, in a word." Rackham offers: "as they always stand more or less on the same ground." Rowe translates it: "since generally speaking they have the same objectives." Since *epi* can have the causal sense of a person having charge over others (e.g. "*ho epi tōn hoplitōn*"—an example under definition A.III.1 of "*epi*" in Liddell and Scott's Greek-English Lexicon, 9th ed.), we might also translate this phrase as "since they take charge over themselves." See EE VII.5 1239b12–16 and VII.6 1240b11–30 for additional passages that contrast the stability of virtuous characters with the quarrelsomeness of base characters.

25. Kraut, *Aristotle: Political Philosophy*, p. 468. I am here following Kraut's description of Aristotle's own examples. Other scholars also recognize that *homonoia* is compatible with disagreement: Balot, *Greek Political Thought*, p. 247; Rosler, *Political Authority and Obligation in Aristotle*, pp. 209–14. *EE* VII.1 1234b22–25 offers more evidence that political friendship presupposes little more than avoiding injustice. In VII.7 1241a15–33, the notion of like-mindedness is used in a very broad way: it can refer to thoughts, desires, appetites, and decisions and is compatible with certain sorts of fights.

26. A glance at our own news media shows that governments often confront situations in which both of these dispute-producing features are present. One group of widely respected experts endorses option A, another group of widely respected

experts advocates option B, and both these options seem equally reasonable but fallible to intelligent voters [3ii], even though the predicted effects on different citizens' groups may be radically unequal [3iii].

27. Here, for example, is the rather expansive list of goods Aristotle offers in *Rhetoric* I.5: noble birth, numerous friends, good friends, wealth, good children, numerous children, a good old age, health, beauty, strength, stature, fitness for athletic contests, a good reputation, honor, good luck, virtue.

Chapter 5

1. The fact that when someone receives an honor and another person cannot receive that same honor does not imply that honor-seeking must always be excessively zero-sum in the way Gouldner, for example, depicts it: "[H]ere a loser does not leave the contest with as much fame as he entered." *Enter Plato*, p. 49. This strikes me as rather implausible. If two competitors engaged in an amazingly good rivalry with a mutual display of virtue, no element in Greek culture that I know of would require denying that both contestants had honored themselves. Even though the top honor for which competitors were struggling could only go to the winner, this would not mean that the loser must walk away with diminished honor.

2. For example, in ancient Athens, a very large number of people were given the honor of citizenship in the democracy. However, one of the reasons this was considered an honor was precisely because being born of citizen parents acted as a status marker, allowing the poorest, landless citizens to have some way to differentiate themselves from slaves and other noncitizens who shared their economic situation. For discussion, see Ober, "Aristotle's Political Sociology," p. 124.

3. The contests of aristocrats are described by Ober, *Mass and Elite in Democratic Athens*, pp. 10, 84–85, 250–51.

4. The centrality of competition in ancient democratic politics is described by Whitehead, "Competitive Outlay," pp. 55–56.

5. At first glance, the claim that honor is the greatest external good seems to contradict the claim that "having friends seems to be the greatest external good" (*NE* IX.9 1169b9–10). However, since Aristotle's defense of the latter involves the political nature of humans (b16–19), and the giving and taking of honors is itself an aspect of the political life, perhaps there is not as much tension as one might think: having friends in a political way may be the greatest good precisely because it involves the greatest of external goods, honor.

6. Aristotle claims in the *Rhetoric* that it is precisely the tie between honor and excellence that makes honor pleasant: "Honor and good repute are among the most pleasant things, because everyone imagines that he possesses the qualities of a worthy man [*spoudaios*], and still more when those whom he believes to be trustworthy say that he does" (1371a8–10).

7. More evidence that Aristotle distinguishes honor from mere fame or reputation can be found at *EE* I.2 1214b6–9, III.5 1232b14–25, and VII.10 1242b18–21. It is useful to contrast Aristotle's conception of honor, properly regarded, with Gouldner's rendition of honor seeking in ancient Greece: "The aim of participants is to achieve as much individual recognition as possible . . . What is being sought, then, is not a limited recognition among a small group of knowledgeable peers, or a small number of experts or specialists similar to oneself but, rather, a communal recognition and fame among all members of the public comprised by the citizen group." Gouldner, *Enter Plato*, p. 48.

8. All of this evidence, in my opinion, poses a major problem for interpreters who depict Aristotle's ideal citizens as actively avoiding honor. Frank, for example, says that Aristotle's *choregos* "defrays the cost of the chorus to display not himself but his work, in this case, the play. When used properly the 'great sums,' along with the *choregos* himself, disappear into their work." *Democracy of Distinction*, p. 63. It seems to me, however, that Frank relies more on Heidegger than Aristotle to support her claim. Because honor shows up in Aristotle's causal explanation of *stasis* in Book V, Kalimtzis, in *Aristotle on Political Enmity and Disease*, ends up dismissing honor altogether as a merely "apparent" good and "ultimately destructive," p. 108. This is not surprising given that Kalimtzis confuses honor and fame, turning honor into nothing but "public recognition or influence," pp. 170–71. Salkever asserts that, for Aristotle, "love of honor has approximately the same moral status as vulgar money grubbing," "Women, Soldiers, Citizens: Plato and Aristotle on the Politics of Virility," p. 171. He bases this claim on a reference to *Pol.* II.9 1269b23–4. But the cited passage, as far as I can tell, does not concern honor at all.

9. For descriptions of this transformation in the nature of aristocratic competition, see Whitehead, "Competitive Outlay," pp. 55–60.

10. "A qualifying phrase or clause is invariably added to the mention of the honorand's *philotimia* (which may be expressed by either noun or verb), to make absolutely clear the group which has reaped its benefits. Thus, for instance, Theaios in IG II^2 1176+ (deme of Peiraieus) *philotimeitai pros tous dēmotas* (line 26), and by the same token one finds mention made of *philotimia* towards the tribe, the genos, the *koinon*, the *hippeis*, and so forth." Whitehead, "Competitive Outlay," p. 63.

11. Aristotle makes it clear that the citizens of the best city are magnanimous at *Pol.* VII.7 1328a9–10 and VIII.3 1338b2–4.

12. Aristotle describes how cities depend on wealthy citizens in the following: *Pol.* III.12 1283a17–19, IV.4 1291a33–34, VII.8 1328b10–11, VII.9 1329a17–19.

13. Ideal citizens are well-off in multiple senses. First, they own private plots of land (*Pol.* VII.9 1329a17–26) that are equally vulnerable to attack (VII.10 1330a9–25) and profitable enough to meet needs of family, friends, and city (VII.8 1328b5–11, VII.10 1329b39–30a9). Second, they are well-off in the sense that they do not suffer from either the haughtiness of the elite rich or the envy of the poor; their wealth is great enough to allow them to pursue the higher things, but it does

not distract them from pursuing other goods. In short, they have enough wealth to lead a life "both free and temperate" (VII.5 1326b31–32).

14. Virtue is the result of harmonizing nature, habituation, and reason (*Pol.* VII.13 1332a38–b11). Aristotle (notoriously) thinks that he will have assured the proper nature of ideal citizens by making them Greek (VII.7 1327b29–38). With regard to developing proper habits and the use of reason, the ideal city will be as devoted to education as are Sparta and Crete (*NE* I.13 1102a7–12, X.9 1180a24–26, *Pol.* VIII.1 1337a29–32), and this education is "one and the same for all" young citizens (VIII.1 1337a22–23).

15. For a helpful discussion of how a wide range of reciprocation of gifts and benefits was embodied in the notion of *charis*, see Kalimtzis, *Aristotle on Political Enmity and Disease*, pp. 170–73. See Balot, *Greek Political Thought*, chapter 1, for a convincing defense of political thought as an inclusive category that includes drama, literature, speeches, and a host of other activities in addition to philosophical theory.

16. Miller provides a very lucid overview of Aristotle's differentiation of communities in "The Rule of Reason." He argues that the reason Aristotle begins the *Politics* by attacking Plato's notion that there is only one skill of ruling is that the counterproposal, that there are different kinds of rule appropriate to different kinds of communities, is central to the rest of the entire work.

17. For additional descriptions of rulers, see *Pol.* III.5 1278b3–5; III.18 1288a36–39; *NE* VI.8 1141b24–29.

18. Ruling and being ruled in turn is described at *Pol.* II.2 1261a29–b6 and III.16 1287a8–18.

19. Kraut uses the word "utopian" to describe Aristotle's best city. *Aristotle: Political Philosophy*, p. 193.

20. This is Kraut's interpretation: "It does not matter, then, that some offices are more powerful than others. All citizens have the same chance of being allotted high or low offices. They have not only equal power as members of the assembly, but also an equal chance to participate at all levels in the apparatus of government." *Aristotle: Political Philosophy*, p. 227.

21. "What is remarkable, then, about Aristotle's ideal city is that it is ruled by amateurs: people of ordinary ability who have learnt no abstruse science accessible only to those of rare intellectual talent." Kraut, *Aristotle: Political Philosophy*, p. 228.

22. Hansen describes how the "universal rotation" interpretation seems to attribute to Aristotle a meaning of "to rule and be ruled in turn" that Aristotle himself criticizes in his *Pol.* VI.2 account of democracy. For discussion, see Hansen, *Reflections on Aristotle's Politics*, pp. 79–90.

23. Recall that Aristotle says in *Pol.* VII.8 1328b7–10 that ideal citizens possess weapons not only for military purposes, but also for enacting punishments—a claim that seems to suggest ideal citizens have (at least slightly) different levels of virtue.

24. Miller, *Nature, Justice, and Rights in Aristotle's Politics*, p. 224, also reaches the conclusion that the best possible city will use elections to assign office.

25. "All men are naturally impelled toward things good, each claiming them in a special degree for himself; a fact especially manifest in the case of riches and office [*archēs*]. Now the good man is ready to yield these things to another; not that he lacks a preeminent claim to them, but if he perceives that another will be able to make better use of them than himself. Other men, on the contrary, will fail to do this, either through ignorance (for they do not believe that they would make bad use of these good things) or through the ambition to hold office [*dia philotimian tou archein*]." *Magna Moralia* II.13 1212a34–b2, Armstrong translation.

26. Cooper points out that for Aristotle—and even for citizens in contemporary liberal societies—what is distinctive about political communities is that citizens "care what kind of people their fellow-citizens are. They want them to be decent, fair-minded, respectable, moral people (anyhow, by their own lights)." "Political Animals and Civic Friendship," p. 72.

27. "The stress on the necessity of good character for good political action led quite naturally to the politician's life as a whole being open to public scrutiny. For the expert Athenian politician, politics was a full-time occupation." Ober, *Mass and Elite*, p. 127.

28. It thus seems that elective offices will depend on both what Waldron calls "backward" and "forward" looking considerations of merit. See Waldron, "The Wisdom of the Multitude," pp. 153–55.

29. For a more fully developed account of competition, see my "Categories of Competition" and "Revisiting Competitive Categories."

30. I agree with Christopher Bobonich, "Aristotle, Political Decision Making, and the Many," that none of the analogies Aristotle offers in *Pol.* III.11 explain how real-world multitudes, which Aristotle elsewhere portrays as having many vices, could end up participating in politics in a way that would allow them to render better judgments than the virtuous few.

31. Because Aristotle says so little, a number of scholars have suggested additional elements that would help flesh out the *Pol.* III.11 account. For example, Balot, *Greek Political Thought*, p. 65, emphasizes the way in which group deliberation would require a role for courage and frank speech. Nichols, *Citizens and Statesmen*, p. 66, stresses that the process would require someone to synthesize all the inputs. Waldron, "Wisdom of the Multitude," pp. 151–53, describes how a deliberative process would need to be dialectical and synthetic, resembling Aristotle's own endoxic method in the *Ethics*.

32. The connection between good deliberation and prudence is discussed at *NE* VI.9 1142b28–33. Aristotle describes the difference between mere cleverness and prudence at VI.12 1144a23–b1. Halliwell discusses the significance of these distinctions for political speech in "The Challenge of Rhetoric to Ethical Theory."

33. Waldron, "The Wisdom of the Multitude," p. 158.

34. A fully developed account of this distinction can be found in my "Categories of Competition" and "Revisiting Competitive Categories."

35. For these sorts of methods, see Yack, *Problems of a Political Animal*; Frank, *A Democracy of Distinction*; Waldron, "The Wisdom of the Multitude."

36. In particular, the reader should contrast my interpretation with Nietzsche's position in *Homer's Contest*. According to Nietzsche, political contest among the Greeks emerges from the following source: "Thus the Greeks, the most humane men of ancient times, have in themselves a trait of cruelty, of tiger-like pleasure in destruction," p. 51. His essay is an extended defense of this "fearful impulse," which can be shaped into productive competition. The tigerlike instinct for destruction is the explanans, contest the explanandum. On the interpretation I am advancing, the explanans will be what is fine and impressive in giving superior benefit to the city.

37. See Ober, *Democracy and Knowledge*, chapter 2, for a helpful overview of the dangerous and competitive environment *poleis* inhabited in ancient Greece.

38. "Following the model of Aphytis or Asea, the total citizen population [of Aristotle's 'ideal state'] is likely to have been in the range of 2000–2500 with about 500 households." Nagle, *The Household as the Foundation of Aristotle's Polis*, p. 75.

39. "Canvassing and lobbying were surely continuous and unremitting, of a kind that we are unfamiliar with precisely because it was directed ultimately to actual decision making rather than to the election of representatives who would have the power of decision." Finley, *Politics in the Ancient World*, p. 83.

40. This is not the only passage suggesting that political power is required for happiness: "[H]appiness evidently also needs external goods to be added, as we said, since we cannot, or cannot easily, do fine actions if we lack the resources. For, first of all, in many actions we use friends, wealth, and political power just as we use instruments" (*NE* I.8 1099a31–b2).

41. This passage poses a major problem for any anticompetitive interpretation of Aristotle's political theory. Note that Kraut, to sustain his "universal rotation" interpretation of the ideal city (according to which citizens do not have to pursue power but are rather placed in assigned offices by lot), is forced to set this passage aside: "At *EN* X.7 1177b4–15, [Aristotle] claims that political activity is in a certain way unleisurely, but we find no explicit statement of that thesis in the *Politics*." *Aristotle: Politics* VII and VIII, p. 141.

42. Finley, *Politics in the Ancient World*, p. 118. Famously, in *Pol.* III.13, Aristotle does say that ostracism can sometimes be considered just; however, he goes on to repudiate the use of ostracism as a tool for liquidating rivals—that is, as a tool of civil war (1284b20–22). At any rate, the suggestion that ideal citizens would be in the habit of ruthlessly factionalizing as part of typical civic life is clearly not acceptable since Aristotle opposes being "excellent in soul" with such factionalizing at III.15 1286b1–3. Cf. Miller, *Nature, Justice, and Rights in Aristotle's Politics*, p. 277.

43. "Constitutions, in the general sense of the Greek *politeia*, may be thus usefully compared to the rules of a game. While regulative rules such as 'no smoking' govern pre-existent activities, constitutive rules such as 'field players may touch the ball with their feet' or 'bowl down the wicket' make a practice possible for the

first time." Rosler, *Political Authority and Obligation in Aristotle*, p. 188. A rule-free melee makes any sort of game impossible, and it would destroy any constitutive rules of the competition I am describing in this chapter.

44. Aristotle says that *poleis* that are most concerned to turn their children into athletes "distort the shape and development of their bodies" (*Pol.* VIII.4 1338b10–11). Such preparation is not "useful from the point of view of health or procreation" (VII.16 1335b5–7), and it focuses athletes on "just one thing" (b9–10) that actually decreases their military efficacy. None of this, obviously, implies that children should not be trained in athletics at all. Indeed, Aristotle lists "fitness for athletic contests" [*dunamin agōnistikēn*] as a component of happiness at *Rhet.* I.5 1360b22, and his description of this fitness (1361b21–6) makes it clear that athletic conditioning can be very good for the body.

45. For examples of scholars who interpret political friendship as a version of utility friendship, see Mayhew, *Aristotle's Criticism of Plato's* Republic, pp. 59–94, and Yack, *Problems of a Political Animal*, pp. 109–27.

46. *EE* VII.8 1241a33–b9 explains why it is not merely justice that motivates the paying back of a gift: by giving, one possesses the great good of activity. It is also worth noting the similarity of this aspect of Aristotelian magnanimity to a specific kind of Athenian virtue described in Pericles's Funeral Oration: "We are quite different from most men with respect to virtue [*es aretēn*], for it isn't by receiving things well, but rather by conferring them well that we acquire friends. The one conferring the gift is the firmer friend, so that, insofar as he has given help through goodwill, the recipient is indebted. By contrast, the one indebted is more dulled, knowing that his return won't be given as a gift, but rather as a repayment of a debt owed for virtue." *History of the Peloponnesian War*, II.40.4.

47. Similarly: "Certainly there are some who do not simply choose such actions to get a good reputation [*doxēs*]—they act even if they are not going to win esteem. But the majority of politicians do not really deserve the name; they are not politicians in strict truth. The politician is one with the propensity to decide on fine actions for their own sake, but most people take to this kind of life because of money and greed" *EE* I.5 1216a21–27.

48. In *EE* VII.10 1242a1–6 Aristotle claims that the striving seen among brothers for elder privileges [*epilambanousi . . . presbeiōn*] resembles that found among political comrades.

49. When discussing *NE* IX.8 1169a6–11, Kraut describes the competition among the virtuous this way: "His claim is that when individuals compete with one another in the moral arena—each striving to be a better person than every other—then everyone benefits and no one loses." *Aristotle on the Human Good*, p. 116. I agree with Kraut that, considered as a participant in a "moral arena," no virtue competitor would emerge from a contest with less virtue than that with which she began. But, considered as an entrant into a political arena, she may win or lose an object of political struggle (votes, office, an honor, etc.).

Chapter 6

1. *Leviathan*, 13.8.
2. *Prince*, 7–8.
3. *Second Treatise*, VII.93.
4. *Leviathan*, 2.29.
5. Simpson, *A Philosophical Commentary on the Politics of Aristotle*, pp. 308–10, offers a very helpful account of how incorrect regimes fail to posit law.
6. Kraut, *Aristotle: Political Philosophy*, p. 437, also notes this potential for change in tyrants. It is interesting to compare and contrast Aristotle's recommendation to tyrants that they follow laws to the medieval constitutional notion that the King, who possessed absolute power within government (*gubernaculum*), needed to take an oath to exercise power outside of government in accordance with established community norms (*jurisdictio*). As far as conditioning the consequent behavior of an all-powerful monarch is concerned, Aristotle's approach bears some similarity to the medieval one. But, unlike Aristotle's recommendation, the medieval arrangement is motivated by the thought that the timeless, customary norms of the community are reflections of God's will and should be followed for this reason. For discussion, see McIlwain, *Constitutionalism: Ancient and Modern*, pp. 69–94.
7. There are additional passages showing that the function of law is to enable the virtue of citizens, not merely to secure agreement among them: *NE* V.1 1129b19–25; *Pol.* II.5 1263b36–64a1, III.9 1280b6–12.
8. Aristotle believes that all successful constitutions will, to some extent, resemble what he calls "natural justice" in *NE* V.7—the patterns found within a political community of free and naturally equal people who are jointly aiming for self-sufficiency in a way that would redound to their flourishing no matter the physical location. This notion of natural justice, however, should be distinguished from the natural law tradition developed by later philosophers. The latter tradition claims not only that there is an independent standard against which constitutions are deemed better or worse, but that constitutions can be deemed legitimate or illegitimate depending on whether the rulers' actions accord with transcendent imperatives. For elaboration, see McIlwain, *Constitutionalism: Ancient and Modern*, pp. 25–42; Schroeder, "Aristotle on Law"; Brunschwig, "Rule and Exception."
9. For example, Miller, *Nature, Justice, and Rights in Aristotle's Politics*, pp. 82–84, describes these statements as exceptions to Aristotle's otherwise consistent commitment to the rule of law.
10. "[T]he Greeks did not envisage the continuous or even frequent creation of new law which is implicit in the modern view of the legislative function." Vile, *Constitutionalism and the Separation of Powers*, p. 24.
11. "The idea of an autonomous 'legislative power' is dependent upon the emergence of the idea that law could be made by human agency, that there was a real power to make law, to legislate. In the early medieval period this idea of making

law by human agency was subordinated to the view that law was a fixed unchanging pattern of divinely-inspired custom, which could be applied and interpreted by man, but not changed by him. In so far as men were concerned with 'legislation' they were in fact declaring the law, clarifying what the law really was, not creating it." Vile, *Constitutionalism and the Separation of Powers*, pp. 26–27.

12. In my opinion, Aristotle here advocates the republican notion of freedom as nondomination rather than the more familiar conception of freedom as noninterference championed by some forms of liberalism. Note, however, that conceptualizing freedom as nondomination does not, by itself, make Aristotle a republican; republicanism also requires that such freedom be given some sort of default priority over other political values, and it is far from clear that Aristotle makes any such commitment. For a careful overview of all the different ways Aristotle uses the notion of freedom, see Hansen's *Reflections on Aristotle's Politics*, pp. 71–96. For a contemporary analysis and defense of the republican theory of freedom, see Pettit's *Republicanism*.

13. "But this division, or rather (in Aristotle's language) combination of powers is only incidentally mentioned . . . [F]or Aristotle there is no idea of a check exercised by one department (or even class) on another: the different departments will work harmoniously together, because each is permeated by the same spirit as the rest." Barker, *The Political Thought of Plato and Aristotle*, p. 485. See also Vile, *Constitutionalism and the Separation of Powers*, pp. 23–26.

14. "For a constitution is the organization of offices, and all constitutions distribute these either on the basis of the power of the participants, or on the basis of some sort of equality common to them (I mean, for example, of the poor or of the rich, or some equality common to both). Therefore, there must be as many constitutions as there are ways of organizing offices on the basis of the superiority and varieties of the parts" (*Pol.* IV.3 1290a7–13).

15. An overview of the emergence of a distinct judicial power can be found in Vile, *Constitutionalism and the Separation of Powers*, pp. 32–34.

16. For analysis of how Aristotle's three constitutional parts are not identical to modern notions of legislative, executive, and judicial power, see Miller, *Nature, Justice, and Rights in Aristotle's Politics*, p. 166; Simpson, *A Philosophical Commentary on the Politics of Aristotle*, pp. 341–42; Mulgan, *Aristotle's Political Theory*, pp. 57–60.

17. Both Vile, *Constitutionalism and the Separation of Powers*, pp. 23–26, and Barker, *The Political Thought of Plato and Aristotle*, pp. 471–86, claim that no separation of powers doctrine can be found in Aristotle's political philosophy.

18. I agree with Simpson's commentary on this 1322b12–15 passage; see *A Philosophical Commentary on the Politics of Aristotle*, p. 451. Though there is some ambiguity in the Greek, it seems clear from context that Aristotle believes that in democracy, unlike in oligarchy, there is a distinction between the body that convenes the assembly (the council) and the part that controls the regime (the multitude in the assembly).

19. My caveat bears some resemblance to the position adopted by Miller, *Nature, Justice, and Rights in Aristotle's Politics*, pp. 258–61, who readily attributes a doctrine of "checks and balances" to Aristotle. However, there are two main differences between our interpretations. First, Miller does not systematically distinguish modern theories of separation of powers from modern theories of balanced/mixed constitution, instead grouping these together as "checks and balances." As a result, many of his examples seem to illustrate mixed power rather than separated power, and it is sometimes difficult to tell which theory he takes his textual evidence to support. Second, Miller interprets Aristotle's descriptions of how mixtures can be formed in the deliberative, magisterial, and judicial parts of the constitutions as descriptions of how rights are to be portioned, and according to Miller, a partition of rights entails a partition of political authority, which in turn entails a system of checks. This, I think, is too quick. For example, just because a constitution gives all citizens the right to decide some specific set of issues, and gives some smaller elective body the right to decide upon a different set of issues, it does not follow that these two groups are checking one another rather than, say, dividing labor efficiently.

20. "The characteristic theory of Greece and Rome was that of mixed government, not the separation of powers." Vile, *Constitutionalism and the Separation of Powers*, pp. 25, 38–39; for similar declarations, see Von Fritz, *The Theory of the Mixed Constitution in Antiquity*, p. 344, and McClellen, *Liberty, Order, and Justice*, p. 17. Machiavelli attributes part of Rome's success to mixed government in *Discourses on Livy*, I.2, and declares in I.4 that "in every republic are two diverse humors, that of the people and that of the great." The *Prince* makes the point this way: "For in every city these two diverse humors are found, which arises from this: that the people desire neither to be commanded nor oppressed by the great, and the great desire to command and oppress the people," 9. Translations of Machiavelli are those of Mansfield.

21. This is why Aristotle is careful to indicate that praise for Sparta as a successful mixed constitution is coming from people other than himself: "Some people [*enioi*] believe, indeed, that the best constitution is a mixture of all constitutions, which is why they commend the Spartan constitution" (II.6 1265b33–35). "For many people attempt to speak of it [*polloi gar encheirousi legein*] as if it were a democracy because it has many democratic elements in its constitution . . . But other people call the Spartan constitution an oligarchy on account of its having many oligarchic elements" (IV.9 1294b19–32).

22. Aristotle's criticism of Polybius would, I believe, be similar to that offered by Von Fritz in *The Theory of the Mixed Constitution in Antiquity*. Because Polybius was enamored of the theory that a good balance among a kingly element, an aristocratic element, and a democratic element accounted for Rome's success, he did not realize that what he took to be a mixed constitution was actually a complex institutional arrangement being controlled by one and the same sociological block. The fifth-century consuls of the Republic had nearly all of the power of government

in their hands, but the consuls in turn were more or less instruments of the patrician class, and the plebeians had no real positive/initiating power that could meaningfully balance this patrician aristocracy (pp. 184–219). Moreover, Polybius's approach led him to assume that the plebeian tribunes represented "the people" since that is what his theory of a judicious mix demanded, so he "did not see that, in spite of these appearances, they had actually, as individuals, become members of the senatorial aristocracy and that this fact was at least as important, if not more important, than their official function and position," pp. 332–33.

23. Machiavelli famously declares, "I say that to me it appears that those who damn the tumults between the nobles and the plebs blame those things that were the first cause of keeping Rome free, and that they consider the noises and the cries that would arise in such tumults more than the good effects that they engendered. They do not consider that in every republic are two diverse humors, that of the people and that of the great, and that all the laws that are made in favor of freedom arise from their disunion, as can easily be seen to have occurred in Rome." *Discourses on Livy*, I.4. In *Discourses* I.6, Machiavelli goes on to argue that it is impossible to have a long-lasting republic that avoids such conflict between the nobles and plebs for the only way to do that would be by so diminishing the people that either the republic would not be able to expand when forced to do so by circumstances, or the republic would become idle and subject to external attack and inner division. In *Discourses* I.7, Machiavelli describes how successful republics institutionalize the conflict between nobles and plebs so that an official "outlet is given by which to vent," and in I.8 he contrasts such ordered venting with unofficial calumnies that destroy republics. However, Machiavelli may have become less optimistic later in his career about the ability of republics to institutionalize the conflict between plebs and nobles. For discussion, see Maynor, *Republicanism in the Modern World*, pp. 121–27.

24. The so-called English "balanced constitution" was actually a hybrid of mixed government and separation of powers. On the one hand, the constitution clearly demarcated a judicial function, an executive function, and a legislative function, and it embodied the principle that the judicial and executive functions should be carried out with independence from the operation of the legislative. On the other hand, traditional social agents were selectively assigned to these different functions: elite Lords exclusively held the judiciary, the king held the executive position, and commoners carried out the legislative function (albeit with advice from the lords and under threat of the king's veto). For discussion, see Vile, *Constitutionalism and the Separation of Powers*, pp. 58–82.

25. That Aristotle's political philosophy does not operate at a level of abstraction that erases the particular character traits of different social groups is a point stressed by both Kraut, *Aristotle: Political Philosophy*, pp. 433–37, and Yack, *Problems of a Political Animal*, pp. 231–39. Although I believe Barker, *The Political Thought of Plato and Aristotle*, makes too strong of a claim when he says that Aristotle has "no idea" of a balanced or separated constitution (p. 485), I nevertheless agree with

his core thesis that, according to Aristotle, the "social solidarity which springs from equity" of the middle class is the only viable solution to the problems facing most average cities (p. 484). Miller, after listing some of the safeguards Aristotle recommends for mixed governments and democracies, criticizes Barker for this view: "If Aristotle were as sanguine about the exercise of political power by the citizens of polity as Barker's interpretation suggests, these constitutional provisions would be unnecessary." *Nature, Justice, and Rights in Aristotle's Politics*, p. 261. It is true that Aristotle imagines some constitutional safeguards in polities. However, Miller's criticism ignores the possibility that these "constitutional provisions" are not meant to control the middlings as much as the partisans in their midst. Miller's best piece of evidence, *Pol.* IV.14 1298b38–99a1, seems to show only that, in Aristotle's opinion, real-world polities do not do enough to block the democratic multitude who will want to initiate decrees.

Chapter 7

1. For a helpful overview of this civic metaphysics see "The Unity of the City," chapter 2 in Mayhew, *Aristotle's Criticism of Plato's Republic*, and Deslauriers, "Political Unity and Inequality."

2. Deslauriers, in "Political Unity and Inequality," argues that there are two more ways in which the unity of a human community is distinguishable from that found in an organic whole: first, the degree of unity of the former is far less because the goal of a human community is to promote virtuous living by individual citizens rather than the mere biological continuation of a group; second, unlike the case with an organism, the parts of a human community must be unequal in terms of virtue if they are to be dissimilar enough to serve as different parts of the civic whole.

3. The way in which Aristotelian rulers are distinct from the ruled and never portrayed as following any sort of mandate of the ruled is the main theme stressed by Green, *The Eyes of the People*, pp. 34–42.

4. Here, for example, are situations in which Aristotle describes one group having contempt [*kataphronēsis*] for another. At IV.11 1295b21–23, rich oligarchs, acting like masters, have contempt for the poor. In V.3 1302b25–33, the stronger majority has contempt for the ruling oligarchs being so weak and few, and democratic rulers are portrayed as being held in contempt for their poor organization. In V.7 1307b6–13, impatient young men with ability are said to have contempt for current military generals. V.10 1311a25–28 describes how outstanding subjects are the ones most likely to attack monarchies because of contempt. In V.10 1311b40–12a20, a ruler earns contempt for carding wool with women, being drunk, and seeming weak and soft from luxury.

5. "Those who desire inequality (that is to say, superiority) do so when they believe that, though they are unequal, they are not getting more but the same or

less" (V.2 1302a26–28). "For either those who envy them for being honored start *stasis*, or they themselves, because of their superior achievement, are unwilling to remain as mere equals" (V.4 1304a36–38).

6. In the *Rhetoric* Aristotle describes arrogance as dishonoring others by shaming them for the mere pleasure of it (1378b23–29). Aristotle associates such gratuitous behavior exclusively with the rich (*Pol.* IV.11 1295b5–11; V.7 1307a17–20; V.8 1309a22–25) and the successful (VII.15 1334a25–28). Arrogance is described as being politically dangerous when it is directed at the poor, weak, and powerless (IV.13 1297b6–8; V.3 1302b5–10; V.11 1314b23–27, 15a14–16) who then become angry and long for revenge (V.10 1311a33–b6, 12b29–32).

7. Waldron, "The Wisdom of the Multitude," is a classic example of an interpretation that portrays Aristotle as a deliberative democrat. It was also recently pointed out to me that the Wikipedia page for "deliberative democracy" announces in the Overview section, "The roots of deliberative democracy can be traced back to Aristotle and his notion of politics."

8. Deliberative democracy has been motivated also by the worry that liberal constitutionalism leads too easily to forms of "epistocracy"—too many of the debates about rights, liberties, and opportunities in contemporary society end up being decided by an elite group of lawyers and judges, rather than by all citizens. For discussion of this threat, see Bohman, "The Coming of Age of Deliberative Democracy."

9. For a general overview of deliberative democracy, see Held, *Models of Democracy*, pp. 231–53. For a critical response to this entire theoretical approach to democracy, see *Deliberative Politics*, edited by Macedo.

10. In "Three Normative Models of Democracy," Habermas explains how his notion of deliberative democracy differs from both the "liberal" view and the "republican" view. Liberal democracy is largely an exercise of individuals having their private preferences aggregated in a way that is administratively registered. By contrast, republican democracy involves citizens coming together in dialogue to forge a common will that expresses the shared social identity of the preexisting ethical community. Habermas rejects mere aggregation, but he also rejects republicanism for being too communitarian and for failing to ascend beyond articulating the needs of the community to (Kantian-inspired) morality. Habermas instead recommends a model whereby citizens engage in dialogue to help orient administration without imagining some unified community; their dialogue merely embodies overlapping norms of far-ranging communicative networks instead of serving as the voice of a specific people in a particular society.

11. See Gutmann and Thompson, *Democracy and Disagreement*. For an overview of the debate between the "impartialists" and their critics, see Held, *Models of Democracy*, pp. 238–45.

12. See Garsten, "Deliberating and Acting Together." Garsten argues that for deliberative democrats, deliberation is a tool whereby individuals can shape laws that they themselves have partly authored. By contrast, in Aristotle's political theory,

deliberation is a tool for making a political society of free and equal people, divided into rulers and ruled, into a civic whole.

13. Jill Frank, "On Logos and Politics in Aristotle," argues Aristotle does not think of political rhetoric as a simple matter of rulers actively commanding and the ruled passively listening. Rather, the logos of rhetoric involves a persuasion that is "middle voice" and allows for a type of dialectic between speaker and listener. I agree with Frank that Aristotle's ruled citizens are not utterly passive. After all, they must be psychologically active enough to form and comprehend correct beliefs, there is a chance that they might rule in the future, and their involvement in elections, voting, and auditing presupposes some degree of activity. But I disagree with Frank to the extent that "middle voice" rhetoric implies that rulers and ruled engaged in the genuine, two-way dialog of joint deliberation.

14. See Lane, "Claims to Rule: The Case of the Multitude." Lane attacks "wisdom of the multitude" interpretations of *Pol.* III.11 that would read this chapter as a justification for full-scale democratic participation. She argues that the broader context of III.10–18 shows that participation of the multitude is treated as a hypothetical response to the claim that only a few rich or virtuous should rule; Aristotle only considers how the multitude could influence decision-making in specific offices—not wield complete authority. On her reading, Aristotle never celebrates how diversity or deliberation in a group might improve decision making. On the contrary, he only thinks there is power and safety in large numbers—traits suggesting, at most, that the multitude could "rule" by overseeing elections and inspections.

15. The agonistic view accepts "reasonable disagreement all the way down (in theory as well as practice), not only over different conceptions of the good within a framework of fundamental principles of justice, procedures of deliberation, or constitutional essentials but over any such framework as well. If this is true then 'dissent is inevitable' among citizens, representatives, lawyers and supreme court justices, as well as theorists. As a consequence, the orientation of practical philosophy should not be to reaching final agreements on universal principles or procedures, but to ensuring that constitutional democracies are always open to the democratic freedom of calling into question and presenting reasons for the renegotiation of the prevailing rules of law, principles of justice, and practices of deliberation." Tully, "Exclusion and Assimilation," p. 208. For an extended treatment of agonism, see Mouffe, *The Return of the Political*, which argues that democracy is best understood as an agreement to have unending contests for power.

16. Tully, "Exclusion and Assimilation," writes that democracy entails "that no rule of law, procedure, or agreement is permanently insulated from disputation in practice in a free and open society," p. 195.

17. This is the description of democracy offered by Wolin, "Norm and Form," pp. 57–58.

18. "After all is said and done, the democratic-constitutional citizen is not Lenin. She does not aim for the end of politics and the administration of things. She is more akin to the young Olympian athlete who greets the dawn's early light

with a smile, rises, dusts herself off, surveys her gains and losses of the previous days, thanks her gods for such a challenging game and such worthy opponents, and engages in the communicative-strategic agon anew." Tully, "Exclusion and Assimilation," p. 209.

19. For a competing account, see Yack, *The Problems of a Political Animal*. Yack argues that, for Aristotle, successful political life isn't a matter of implementing extralegal standards (as he believes most interpreters of Aristotle assume) but rather "the means by which we identify the changing and often conflicting standards," p. 132.

20. "Instead of a conception of democracy as indistinguishable from its constitution, I propose accepting the familiar charges that democracy is inherently unstable, inclined toward anarchy, and identified with revolution and using these traits as the basis for a different, aconstitutional conception of democracy . . . This democracy might be summed up as the idea and practice of rational disorganization." Wolin, "Norm and Form," p. 37. "Democracy needs to be reconceived as something other than a form of government: as a mode of being that is conditioned by bitter experience, doomed to succeed only temporarily, but is a recurrent possibility as long as the memory of the political survives. The experience of which democracy is the witness is the realization that the political mode of existence is such that it can be, and is, periodically lost." Wolin, "Fugitive Democracy," p. 43.

21. Wolin, "Norm and Form," explicitly and repeatedly identifies Aristotle as a writer who advocates for a position contrary to his own aconstitutional theory.

22. The eight empirical conditions described by Dahl are these: (1) some act (e.g. voting) is accepted as the expression of individual preference, (2) individuals' votes are treated equally, (3) among the options for which votes can be cast, the option with the greatest number of votes is declared winner, (4) all individuals can add new options for which votes can be cast, (5) individuals are equally informed about the options, (6) the winning option displaces those that do not win, (7) orders of elected officials are executed, and (8) elections in some sense bind decisions made between elections. The general sketch of "polyarchy" can be found in Dahl, *A Preface to Democratic Theory*, pp. 63–89. His argument that defining democracy in terms of the ideals of popular sovereignty and equality leads only to empty analytic claims that cannot be operationalized in the real world can be found at pp. 34–62.

23. Dahl, *A Preface to Democratic Theory*, p. 132.

24. Dahl, *Who Governs?* offers an empirical case study of the democratic politics in New Haven. He argues that decisions are controlled by leaders and their professional understudies, but that for such leadership to be successful, it must engage voters.

25. Dahl does not think that there is anything odd about the fact that advocacy groups in democracies are often themselves arranged nondemocratically. See Dahl, *After the Revolution?* pp. 44–79.

26. Dahl, *A Preface to Democratic Theory*, p. 132.

27. Although he doesn't mention Aristotle in his discussion of interest pluralism, Green draws this same contrast between interest pluralism and political theories that assign characteristic traits to ruling citizens and ruled citizens. See Green, *The Eyes of the People*, pp. 54–58.

28. In earlier versions of this chapter, I examined ways in which Aristotle's political theory resembled what I called "competitive democracy." I am indebted to those who recommended that I read Green's *The Eyes of the People*. Reading Green showed me that behind my notion of "competitive democracy," which was largely inspired by Schumpeter, was the towering work of Weber. Green argues explicitly (albeit briefly) that Aristotelian and Weberian political theory share some themes. See Green, *The Eyes of the People*, pp. 34–42.

29. Quoted in Beetham, *Max Weber and the Theory of Modern Politics*, p. 41.

30. Quoted in Beetham, *Max Weber and the Theory of Modern Politics*, p. 252.

31. The following summary of conflict in Weberian political theory is meant to stay squarely within the bounds of agreed-upon, standard interpretations of Weber, not to offer a novel interpretation. My portrait is drawn from Beetham, *Max Weber and the Theory of Modern Politics*; Breiner, *Max Weber and Democratic Politics*; Eliaeson, "Constitutional Caesarism: Weber's Politics in their German Context"; Green, *The Eyes of the People*; Held, *Models of Democracy*; and Lassman, "The Rule of Man over Man: Power, Politics, and Legitimation."

32. Weber seems to think that the full meaning of an ultimate value can be disclosed only after one has committed himself to it and then defended it in the face of dispute. See Beetham, *Max Weber and the Theory of Modern Politics*, p. 36.

33. Quoted in Beetham, *Max Weber and the Theory of Modern Politics*, p. 51.

34. Quoted in Beetham, *Max Weber and the Theory of Modern Politics*, pp. 105–06.

35. Beetham, *Max Weber and the Theory of Modern Politics*, p. 41.

36. Quoted in Beetham, *Max Weber and the Theory of Modern Politics*, p. 110.

37. Beetham, *Max Weber and the Theory of Modern Politics*, p. 103.

38. Quoted in Beetham, *Max Weber and the Theory of Modern Politics*, p. 110.

39. Quoted in Beetham, *Max Weber and the Theory of Modern Politics*, p. 111. Schumpeter, following Weber, memorably puts the point this way: "[D]emocracy does not mean and cannot mean that the people actually rule in any obvious sense of the terms 'people' and 'rule.' Democracy means only that the people have the opportunity of accepting or refusing the men who are to rule them . . . Now one aspect of this may be expressed by saying that democracy is the rule of the politician." *Capitalism, Socialism and Democracy*, p. 284.

40. Quoted in Beetham, *Max Weber and the Theory of Modern Politics*, p. 231.

41. Breiner, *Max Weber and Democratic Politics*, pp. 163–64.

42. Quoted in Beetham, *Max Weber and the Theory of Modern Politics*, p. 236.

43. "It will be this kind of people, for whom national politics is an anathema,

and even more, who in effect operate under an imperative mandate from economic interests, who will set the tone of Parliament. It will be a 'banausic' assembly, incapable in any sense of providing a selection ground for political leaders." Quoted in Beetham, *Max Weber and the Theory of Modern Politics*, p. 234.

44. There is considerable scholarly controversy about Weber's ultimate, settled views about the proper role of parliament. See Eliaeson, "Weber's Politics in Their German Context," pp. 144–48, for a helpful overview of the debate.

45. Following Green, *The Eyes of the People*, pp. 171–77, it seems we could understand Schumpeter's *Capitalism, Socialism, and Democracy* as an attempt to combine Weber's hierarchical model of democracy with the "interest pluralism" model. Schumpeter sees an almost perfect analogy between leadership competition in democracies and the competitive struggle businesses undertake in the marketplace. Notably, then, while Schumpeter does not completely forgo making sociological claims that differentiate the psychologies of leaders from ruled citizens (see, for example, *Capitalism, Socialism, and Democracy*, pp. 256–64), this difference is described only in terms of thoughtful versus thoughtless, composed versus flighty: there is no distinctive repertoire of character traits that marks a leader who leads a distinctive kind of idealized life. For more discussion, see Breiner, *Max Weber and Democratic Politics*, pp. 158–60, 166; Beetham, *Max Weber and the Theory of Modern Politics*, pp. 43–44.

46. Beetham, *Max Weber and the Theory of Modern Politics*, p. 267.

47. Quoted in Beetham, *Max Weber and the Theory of Modern Politics*, p. 266.

48. Beetham, *Max Weber and the Theory of Modern Politics*, p. 23.

49. Beetham, *Max Weber and the Theory of Modern Politics*, p. 151.

50. Beetham says that Weber's theory of democracy presents "under the title of democracy something which has very little to do with democracy at all." *Max Weber and the Theory of Modern Politics*, p. 266. Green points out that Weber's plebiscitarian theory is often dismissed out of hand as a "sham or simply bad democracy." Green, *The Eyes of the People*, p. 5.

51. Green, *The Eyes of the People*, pp. 34–42, explicitly draws this connection between Aristotle's political theory and the Weberian model of democracy. He argues that, according to both thinkers, citizenship is not a uniform condition, the citizen-being-ruled is a certain kind of distinct figure in democratic societies, and being ruled involves different virtues than ruling—even in the best sort of city.

52. "That is why Pericles and such people are the ones whom we regard as prudent, because they are able to study what is good for themselves and for human beings; we think that household managers and politicians are such people" (*NE* VI.5 1140b7–11). "Democracy is of interest to Weber depending on whether it permits the rise of individuals with leadership qualities. Even though Weber saw parliamentary democracy as the means for producing such leadership, there is nothing in this form of politics that expresses the values that Weber finds intrinsically desirable. It is not just Gladstone, the great parliamentary leader, that is Weber's

model here but also Pericles, who often without formal office led the ecclesia by sheer dint of his demagogy, his speech to the demos of Athens." Breiner, *Max Weber and Democratic Politics*, p. 164.

53. Beetham, *Max Weber and the Theory of Modern Politics*, p. 215.

Bibliography

Textual Editions and Translations Cited

Aristotle. *Aristotelis Ars Rhetorica*. Edited by W. D. Ross. Oxford: Clarendon, 1959.
———. *Aristotelis Ethica Eudemia*. Edited by R. Walzer and J. Mingay. Oxford: Clarendon, 1991.
———. *Aristotelis Ethica Nicomachea*. Edited by I. Bywater. Oxford: Clarendon, 1894.
———. *Aristotelis Politica*. Edited by W. D. Ross. Oxford: Clarendon, 1957.
Aristotle: *Art of Rhetoric*. Translated by J. H. Freese. Cambridge: Harvard University Press, 1926.
———. *Aristotle: Athenian Constitution*. Translated by H. Rackham. Cambridge: Harvard University Press, 1935.
———. *Aristotle: Eudemian Ethics*. Translated and edited by B. Inwood and R. Woolf. Cambridge: Cambridge University Press, 2013.
———. *Aristotle: Magna Moralia*. Translated by Cyril Armstrong. Cambridge: Harvard University Press, 1935.
———. *Aristotle: Nicomachean Ethics*. Translated by H. Rackham. Cambridge: Harvard University Press, 1934.
———. *Aristotle: Nicomachean Ethics*. Translation, introduction, and commentary by Sarah Brodie and Christopher Rowe. Oxford: Oxford University Press, 2002.
———. *Aristotle Nicomachean Ethics*. Translated with introduction and notes by C. D. C. Reeve. Indianapolis: Hackett, 2014.
———. *Aristotle Politics*. Translated, with introduction and notes, by C. D. C. Reeve. Indianapolis: Hackett, 1998.
———. *Aristotle Politics Books VII and VIII*. Translated with a commentary by Richard Kraut. Oxford: Clarendon, 1997.
———. *Aristotle's Constitution of Athens*. Revised text with an introduction, critical and explanatory notes, testimonia, and indices, by John Sandys. John New York: Arno, 1973.
———. *Aristotle's Constitution of Athens and Related Texts*. Translated with an introduction and notes by Ernst Kapp and Kurt Von Fritz. New York: Hafner, 1950.

———. *Aristotle's Politics*. Translated with an introduction, notes, and glossary, by Carnes Lord. Chicago: University of Chicago, 1984.
———. *Politics of Aristotle*. Translated, with introduction, analysis, and notes, by Peter Simpson. Chapel Hill: University of North Carolina Press, 1997.
Machiavelli, Niccolò. *Discourses on Livy*. Translated by Harvey Mansfield and Nathan Tarcov. Chicago: University of Chicago Press, 1996.
———. *Prince*. Translated by Harvey Mansfield. Chicago: University of Chicago Press, 1985.
Nietzsche, Friedrich. "Homer's Contest." Translated by M. Mügge. In *The Complete Works of Friedrich Nietzsche*, vol. 2 Oscar Levy. New York, Gordon, 1974.
Plato. *Phaedo*. Translated by G. M. A. Grube. In *Plato: Complete Works*, edited by Cooper. Indianapolis: Hackett, 1997.
———. *Protagoras*. Translated by Stanley Lombardo and Karen Bell. In *Plato: Complete Works*, edited by Cooper. Indianapolis: Hackett, 1997.
———. *Republic*. Translated by G. M. A. Grube with Reeve rev. In *Plato: Complete Works*, edited by Cooper. Indianapolis: Hackett, 1997.
Polybius. *The Histories*. Translated by W. R. Paton. Cambridge: Harvard University Press, 1922.
Solon. *The Laws of Solon*. A new edition with introduction, translation, and commentary by Delfim Leão and P. J. Rhodes. London: I. B. Tauris, 2015.
Thucydides. *Historiae*. Edited by Henricus Jones. Oxford: Clarendon, 1963.

Other Works Cited

Balot, Ryan. *Greed and Injustice in Classical Athens*. Princeton: Princeton University Press, 2001.
———. *Greek Political Thought*. Oxford: Blackwell, 2006.
———. "The 'Mixed Regime' in Aristotle's *Politics*." In *Aristotle's Politics: A Critical Guide*, edited by T. Lockwood and T. Samaras, 103–22. Cambridge: Cambridge University Press, 2015.
Barker, Ernst. *The Political Thought of Plato and Aristotle*. New York: Dover, 1959.
Bickford, Susan. "Beyond Friendship: Aristotle on Conflict, Deliberation, and Attention." *The Journal of Politics* 58 (1996): 398–421.
Bobonich, Christopher. "Aristotle, Political Decision Making, and the Many." In *Aristotle's Politics: A Critical Guide*, edited by T. Lockwood and T. Samaras, 142–62. Cambridge: Cambridge University Press, 2015.
Bohman, James. "The Coming of Age of Deliberative Democracy." *The Journal of Political Philosophy* 6 no. 4 (1998): 400–25.
Brunschwig, Jacques. "Rule and Exception: On the Aristotelian Theory of Equity." In *Rationality in Greek Thought*, edited by Michael Frede and Gisela Striker, 115–55. Oxford: Clarendon, 1996.

Burnyeat, Miles. "Enthymeme: Aristotle on the Rationality of Rhetoric." In *Essays on Aristotle's Rhetoric*, edited by A. O. Rorty, 88–115. Berkeley: University of California Press, 1996.
Coby, Patrick. "Aristotle's Three Cities and the Problem of Faction." *The Journal of Politics* 40 no. 4 (1988): 898–919.
Cooper, John. "Political Animals and Civic Friendship." In *Aristotle's Politics: Critical Essays*, edited by Kraut and Skultety, 65–90. Lanham: Rowman & Littlefield, 2005.
Dahl, Robert. *After the Revolution?* rev. ed. New Haven: Yale University Press, 1990.
———. *A Preface to Democratic Theory*, expanded ed. Chicago: University of Chicago Press, 2006.
———. *Who Governs?* 2nd ed. Yale University Press, 2005.
Davis, Michael. "Aristotle's Reflections on Revolution." *Graduate Faculty Philosophy Journal* 11 no. 2 (1986): 49–63.
Deslauriers, Marguerite. "Political Unity and Inequality." In *The Cambridge Companion to Aristotle's Politics*, edited by M. Deslauriers and P. Destrée, 117–43. Cambridge: Cambridge University Press, 2013.
Eliaeson, Sven. "Constitutional Caesarism: Weber's Politics in Their German Context." In *The Cambridge Companion to Weber*, edited by S. Turner, 131–50. Cambridge: Cambridge University Press, 2000.
Estlund, David. *Democratic Authority: A Philosophical Framework*. Princeton: Princeton University Press, 2008.
Finley, Moses. *Politics in the Ancient World*. Cambridge: Cambridge University Press, 1983.
Frank, Jill. *A Democracy of Distinction*. Chicago: University of Chicago Press, 2005.
———. "On Logos and Politics in Aristotle." In *Aristotle's Politics: A Critical Guide*, edited by T. Lockwood and T. Samaras, 9–26. Cambridge: Cambridge University Press, 2015.
Fritz, Kurt von. *The Theory of the Mixed Constitution in Antiquity*. New York: Arno, 1975. First published 1954 by Columbia University Press.
Garsten, Bryan. "Deliberating and Acting Together." In *The Cambridge Companion to Aristotle's Politics*, edited by M. Deslauriers and P. Destrée, 324–49. Cambridge: Cambridge University Press, 2013.
Garver, Eugene. *Aristotle's Politics: Living Well and Living Together*. Chicago: University of Chicago Press, 2011.
Green, Jeffrey. *The Eyes of the People: Democracy in an Age of Spectatorship*. Oxford: Oxford University Press, 2010.
Gouldner, Alvin. *Enter Plato: Classical Greece and the Origins of Social Theory*. New York: Routledge & Kegan Paul, 1965.
Gutman, Amy, and Dennis Thompson. *Democracy and Disagreement*. Cambridge: Harvard University Press, 1998.

Habermas, Jürgen. "Three Normative Models of Democracy." In *Democracy and Difference: Contesting the Boundaries of the Political*, edited by S. Benhabib, 21–30. Princeton: Princeton University Press, 1996.

Halliwell, Stephen. "The Challenge of Rhetoric to Ethical Theory." In *Essays on Aristotle's Rhetoric*, edited by A. O. Rorty. Berkeley: University of California Press, 1996.

Hampshire, Stuart. *Justice Is Conflict*. Princeton: Princeton University Press, 2001.

Hansen, Mogens Herman. *Reflections on Aristotle's Politics*. Copenhagen: Museum Tusculanum, 2013.

Hatzistavrou, Antony. "Faction." In *The Cambridge Companion to Aristotle's Politics*, edited by Deslauriers and Destrée, 275–300. Cambridge: Cambridge University Press, 2013.

Held, David. *Models of Democracy*, 3rd ed. Cambridge: Polity, 2006.

Horn, Christoph. "Law, Governance, and Political Obligation." In *The Cambridge Companion to Aristotle's Politics*, edited by M. Deslauriers and P. Destrée, 223–46. Cambridge: Cambridge University Press, 2013.

Irwin, Terence, "Ethics as an Inexact Science: Aristotle's Ambitions for Moral Theory." In *Moral Particularism*, edited by Hooker and Little, 100–29. Oxford: Oxford University Press, 2001.

Kalimtzis, Kostas. *Aristotle on Political Enmity and Disease*. Albany: State University of New York Press, 2000.

Keegan, John, and Bartie Bull. "What Is a Civil War?" *Prospect*. November 16, 2006. https://www.prospectmagazine.co.uk/magazine/whatisacivilwar.

Keyt, David. "Aristotle's Theory of Distributive Justice." In *A Companion to Aristotle's Politics*, edited by Keyt and Miller, 118–41. Oxford: Blackwell, 1991.

———. "The Four Causes in Aristotle's Politics." In *Aristotelian Political Philosophy*, vol. 1, edited by K. I. Bourdouris, 101–7. Athens: International Center for Greek Philosophy and Culture, 1995.

Kraut, Richard. "Are There Natural Rights in Aristotle?" *The Review of Metaphysics* 49 (1996): 755–74.

———. *Aristotle: Political Philosophy*. Oxford: Oxford University Press, 2002.

———. *Aristotle on the Human Good*. Princeton: Princeton University Press, 1991.

———. "Doing without Morality: Reflections on the Meaning of *Dein* in Aristotle's Nicomachean Ethics." *Oxford Studies in Ancient Philosophy* 29 (2005): 159–200.

Lane, Mellisa. "Claims to Rule: The Case of the Multitude." In *The Cambridge Companion to Aristotle's Politics*, edited by M. Deslauriers and P.Destrée, 247–74. Cambridge: Cambridge University Press, 2013.

Lassman, Peter. "The Rule of Man over Man: Power, Politics, and Legitimation." In *The Cambridge Companion to Weber*, edited by S. Turner, 83–98. Cambridge, Cambridge University Press, 2000.

Lear, Jonathan. *The Desire to Understand*. Cambridge: Cambridge University Press, 1988.

Lintott, Andrew. *Violence, Civil Strife and Revolution*. Baltimore: Johns Hopkins University Press, 1981.

Lockwood, Thornton. "Polity, Political Justice and Political Mixing." *History of Political Thought* 27 no. 2 (2006): 207–22.

Loraux, Nicole. *The Divided City: On Memory and Forgetting in Ancient Athens*. Translated by Corinne Pache with Jeff Fort. New York: Zone Books, 2002.

———. "Reflections of the Greek City on Unity and Division." In *City States in Classical Antiquity and Medieval Italy: Athens and Rome, Florence and Venice*, edited by Julia Emlen, Anthony Molho, and Kurt Raaflaub, 33–51. Stuttgart: Franz Steiner Verlag, 1991.

Macedo, Stephen, ed. *Deliberative Politics: Essays on Democracy and Disagreement*. Oxford: Oxford University Press, 1999.

MacIntyre, Alasdair. *After Virtue*, 3rd ed. Notre Dame: Notre Dame University Press, 2007.

Mayhew, Robert. *Aristotle's Criticism of Plato's Republic*. Lanham: Rowman & Littlefield, 1997.

McIlwain, Charles Howard. *Constitutionalism: Ancient and Modern*. Clark: Lawbook Exchange, 2006. First published 1940 by Cornell University Press.

Miller, Fred Jr., *Nature Justice, and Rights in Aristotle's Politics*. Oxford: Oxford University Press, 1995.

———. "The Rule of Reason." In *The Cambridge Companion to Aristotle's Politics*, edited by M. Deslauriers and P. Destrée, 38–66. Cambridge: Cambridge University Press, 2013.

Morrison, Donald. "The Common Good." In *The Cambridge Companion to Aristotle's Politics*, edited by M. Deslauriers and P. Destrée, 176–98. Cambridge: Cambridge University Press, 2013.

Morton, Adam. "Partisanship." In *Perspectives on Self-Deception*, edited by McLaughlin and Rorty, 170–82. Berkeley: University of California Press, 1988.

Mouffe, Chantal. *The Return of the Political*. London: Verso, 2005.

Mulgan, Richard. "Aristotle on Oligarchy and Democracy." In *A Companion to Aristotle's Politics*, edited by Keyt and Miller, 307–22. Oxford: Blackwell, 1991.

———. *Aristotle's Political Theory*. Oxford: Clarendon, 1977.

Nagle, D. Brendan. *The Household as the Foundation of Aristotle's Polis*. Cambridge: Cambridge University Press, 2006.

Nichols, Mary. *Citizens and Statesmen*. Lanham: Rowman & Littlefield, 1992.

Nussbaum, Martha. *The Fragility of Goodness*, rev. ed. Cambridge: Cambridge University Press, 2001.

Ober, Josiah. "Aristotle's Political Sociology: Class, Status, and Order in the *Politics*." In *Essays on the Foundations of Aristotelian Political Science*, edited by Lord and O'Connor, 112–35. Berkeley: University of California Press, 1991.

———. *Democracy and Knowledge: Innovation and Learning in Classical Athens*. Princeton: Princeton University Press, 2008.

———. *Mass and Elite in Democratic Athens*. Princeton: Princeton University Press, 1989.

———. *Political Dissent in Democratic Athens: Intellectual Critics of Popular Rule*. Princeton: Princeton University Press, 1998.

Pettit, Philip. *Republicanism: A Theory of Freedom and Government*. Oxford: Oxford University Press, 1997.

Polansky, Ronald. "Aristotle on Political Change." In *A Companion to Aristotle's Politics*, edited by Keyt and Miller, 324–32. Oxford: Blackwell, 1991.

Poliakoff, Michael. *Combat Sports in the Ancient World*. New Haven: Yale University Press, 1987.

Reeve, C. D. C. *Practices of Reason*. Oxford: Oxford University Press, 1992.

Robinson, Rachel Sargent. *Sources for the History of Greek Athletics*. Ann Arbor: Cushing-Malloy, 1955.

Rosler, Andrés. "Civic Virtue: Citizenship, Ostracism, and War." In *The Cambridge Companion to Aristotle's Politics*, edited by M. Deslauriers and P.Destrée, 144–75. Cambridge: Cambridge University Press, 2013.

———. *Political Authority and Obligation in Aristotle*. Oxford: Oxford University Press, 2005.

Salkever, Stephen. *Finding the Mean*. Princeton: Princeton University Press, 1990.

———. "Women, Soldiers, Citizens: Plato and Aristotle on the Politics of Virility." In *Essays on the Foundations of Aristotelian Political Science*, edited by Lord and O'Connor, 165–90. Berkeley: University of California Press, 1991.

Saxonhouse, Arlene. "Aristotle on the Corruption of Regimes: Resentment and Justice." In *Aristotle's Politics: A Critical Guide*, edited by T. Lockwood and T. Samaras, 184–203. Cambridge: Cambridge University Press, 2015.

Schroeder, Donald. "Aristotle on Law." *Polis* 4 (1981): 17–31.

Schumpeter, Joseph. *Capitalism, Socialism, and Democracy*. New York: HarperCollins, 2008.

Schütrumpf, Eckart. "Little to Do with Justice: Aristotle on Distributing Political Power." In *Aristotle's Politics: A Critical Guide*, edited by T. Lockwood and T. Samaras, 163–83. Cambridge: Cambridge University Press, 2015.

Simpson, Peter. *A Philosophical Commentary on the Politics of Aristotle*. Chapel Hill: University of North Carolina Press, 1998.

Skultety, Steven. "Categories of Competition." *Sports, Ethics & Philosophy* 5 no. 4 (2011): 433–46.

———. "Revisiting Competitive Categories: A Reply to Royce." *Sports, Ethics & Philosophy* 9 no. 1 (2015): 6–17.

Strauss, Barry. *Athens after the Peloponnesian War: Class, Faction and Policy 403–386 B.C.* Ithaca: Cornell University Press, 1986.

———. "On Aristotle's Critique of Athenian Democracy." In *Essays on the Foundations of Aristotelian Political Science*, edited by Lord and O'Connor, 212–33. Berkeley: University of California Press, 1991.

Tully, James. "Exclusion and Assimilation: Two Forms of Domination in Relation to Freedom." In *Political Exclusion and Domination, Nomos XLVI*, edited by Melissa Williams and Stephen Macedo, 191–229. New York: New York University Press, 2005.

Vile, M. J. C. *Constitutionalism and the Separation of Powers*, 2nd ed. Indianapolis: Liberty Fund, 1998. First published 1967 by Oxford University Press.

Waldron, Jeremy. "The Wisdom of the Multitude." Reprinted in *Aristotle's Politics: Critical Essays*, edited by Kraut and Skultety, 145–66. Lanham: Rowman & Littlefield, 2005.

Wardy, Robert. "Mighty Is the Truth and It Shall Prevail?" In *Essays on Aristotle's Rhetoric*, edited by Amélie Oksenberg Rorty, 56–87. Berkeley: University of California Press, 1996.

Weed, Ronald. *Aristotle on Stasis*. Berlin: Logos Verlag, 2007.

Wheeler, Marcus. "Aristotle's Analysis of the Nature of Political Struggle." In *Articles on Aristotle 2*, edited by Barnes, Schofield, Sorabji, 159–69. London: Duckworth, 1978.

White, Nicholas. *Individual and Conflict in Greek Ethics*. Oxford: Oxford University Press, 2002.

Whitehead, David. "Competitive Outlay and Community Profit: *Philotimia* in Democratic Athens." *Classica et Mediaevalia* 34 (1983): 55–56.

Wolin, Sheldon. "Fugitive Democracy." In *Democracy and Difference: Contesting the Boundaries*, edited by S. Benhabib, 31–45. Princeton: Princeton University Press, 1996.

———. "Norm and Form." In *Athenian Political Thought and the Reconstruction of American Democracy*, edited by Euden, Wallach, and Ober, 29–58. Ithaca: Cornell University Press, 1994.

Yack, Bernard. "Community: An Aristotelian Social Theory." In *Aristotle and Modern Politics: The Persistence of Political Philosophy*, edited by Aristide Tessitore, 19–46. Notre Dame: University of Notre Dame Press, 1997.

———. "Community and Conflict in Aristotle's Political Philosophy." In *Action and Contemplation*, edited by Bartlett and Collins, 273–92. Albany: State University of New York Press, 1999.

———. *The Problems of a Political Animal*. Berkeley: University of California, 1993.

Index Locorum

Aristotle
  Athenian Constitution
    5.2: 24
    8.5: 24
    9.2: 24
    13.1: 24
    13.2: 25
    13.4: 24
    14.1: 25
    14.1–2: 99
    14.3: 25
    15.1: 25
    20.4: 25
    29.1: 26
    33.1: 26
    34.3: 26
    41.2: 25

  De Anima
    412b18–24: 234n1

  Eudemian Ethics
    I.2 1214b6–9: 242n7
    I.4 1215b3–4: 145
    I.5 1216a21–27: 246n47
    II.1 1219b30–31: 192
    II.10 1226b6–8: 135
    III.5 1232b14–25: 242n7
    III.5 1232b21–23: 126
    VII.1 1234b22–25: 240n25
    VII.4 1239a13–21: 238n15
    VII.4 1239a21–27: 118
    VII.5 1239b12–16: 240n24
    VII.6 1240b11–30: 240n24
    VII.7 1241a15–33: 240n25
    VII.8 1241a33–b9: 246n46
    VII.10 1242a1–6: 246n48
    VII.10 1242a6–9: 238n15
    VII.10 1242b18–21: 242n7
    VII.10 1242b19–20: 120
    VII.10 1242b21–27: 238n15
    VII.10 1242b31–34: 238n15
    VII.10 1243a2–3: 104
    VII.10 1243a10–11: 239n17
    VII.10 1243b6–9: 239n17
    VII.10 1243b14–38: 238n15
    VIII.3 1248b27–28: 119
    VIII.3 1248b30: 119

  Magna Moralia
    II.13 1212a34–b2: 244n25

  Metaphysics
    II.1 993a30–b1: 237n4
    VII.13 1039a3–4: 234n1
    VII.16 1040b5–15: 234n1

  Nicomachean Ethics
    I.3 1094b11–95a2: 96
    I.3 1094b27–95a2: 99
    I.5 1095b23: 120
    I.5 1095b24: 119

Aristotle: *Nicomachean Ethics* (continued)
I.5 1095b26–29: 120
I.7 1097b2–5: 119
I.8 1099a31–b2: 245n40
I.13 1102a7–12: 243n14
I.13 1102a10–12: 227n21
I.13 1102b33: 192
I.13 1103a3: 192
II.3 1104b30–34: 111
II.6 1106b21–22: 111
II.6 1106b22: 111
II.6 1106b28–29: 111
II.6 1106b30–31: 111
III.1 1110b7–9: 97
III.3 1112a24–25: 97
III.3 1112b8–9: 97
III.3 1112b8–11: 100
III.3 1112b9: 134
III.4 1113a31–33: 111, 237n7
IV.2 1122b19–23: 121
IV.3 1123b20–21: 119
IV.3 1123b22–24: 120
IV.3 1123b30: 120
IV.3 1123b35–24a1: 120
IV.3 1124b9–12: 144
IV.3 1124b18–22: xv, 129
IV.3 1124b23–26: 129
IV.6 1126b12: 101
IV.6 1126b12–13: 101
IV.6 1126b15: 102
V.1 1129b19–25: 247n7
V.1 1129b30–30a2: 124
V.1 1130a1–2: 62
V.2 1130b2: 118
V.2 1130b31–32: 9
V.2 1130b32: 118
V.3 1131a25–26: 62
V.3 1131a25–29: 37, 139
V.4 1132a19–24: 105
V.4 1132b11–20: 239n16
V.5 1132b31–33b28: 123
V.6 1134a31–32: 15

V.10 1137b11–29: 171
V.10 1137b13–19: 95
V.10 1137b23–24: 96
VI.5 1140a28: 100
VI.5 1140a31–b4: 97
VI.5 1140b7–11: 256n52
VI.7 1141b14–23: 99
VI.7 1141b16: 96
VI.8 1141b23–24: 186
VI.8 1141b24–9: 243n17
VI.8 1141b24–28: 171
VI.8 1141b24–33: 95
VI.8 1141b32–33: 171
VI.8 1142a14–15: 99
VI.9 1142b2: 97
VI.9 1142b12: 97
VI.9 1142b22: 132
VI.9 1142b26–28: 141
VI.9 1142b28–33: 244n32
VI.10 1143a13–15: 132
VI.12 1144a13–22: 111
VI.12 1144a23–b1: 244n32
VI.12 1144a29–30: 99
VI.12 1144a29–b1: 94
VI.13 1144b30–32: 124
VII.6 1150a7–8: 153
VIII.1 1155a22–26: 30
VIII.1 1155a25–26: 18
VIII.1 1155a26: 112
VIII.8 1159a18–21: 120
VIII.8 1159a22: 120
VIII.13 1162b6–9: 145
VIII.13 1162b16–21: 104
VIII.13 1163a12–17: 104
IX.4 1166a10–29: 112
IX.6 1167b5–7: 112
IX.8 1169a6–11: 145, 246n49
IX.8 1169a32–b2: 107
IX.9 1169b9–10: 241n5
IX.9 1169b16–19: 241n5
IX.10 1171a6–8: 108
X.5 1176a15–16: 237n7

X.7 1177b4–15: 245n41
X.7 1177b12–14: 211
X.7 1177b12–15: 142
X.8 1178a9–10: 119
X.9 1180a18–b7: 45
X.9 1180a24–6: 227n21, 243n14

Parts of Animals
640b29–641a21: 234n1

Politics
  I.1 1252a2–3: 229n34
  I.1 1252a17–23: 35
  I.2 1252b1–5: 170
  I.2 1252b27–30: 114
  I.2 1253a1–29: 88
  I.2 1253a7–18: 141
  I.2 1253a29: 153
  I.2 1253a31–33: 153
  I.2 1253a38: 105
  I.2 1253a38–39: 105
  I.4 1254a13–17: 234n2
  I.5 1254b16–20: 48
  I.7 1255b31–37: 238n13
  I.9 1257a28–30: 238n15
  I.12 1259b7–8: 123
  I.13 1260a4–36: 196
  I.13 1260a17–18: 124
  I.13 1260a17–20: 186
  II.2 1261a13–22: 88
  II.2 1261a22–24: 122
  II.2 1261a23–24: 89
  II.2 1261a29–32: 125
  II.2 1261a29–b6: 243n18
  II.2 1261a32–33: 123
  II.2 1261a33–34: 126
  II.2 1261a39–b1: 122
  II.2 1261b5–6: 123
  II.2 1261b6: 126
  II.4 1262b8–9: 30
  II.5 1263b36–37: 114
  II.5 1263b36–64a1: 247n7

II.6 1265b28–29: 78
II.6 1265b33–35: 249n21
II.7 1267a37–41: 223n30
II.7 1267b1: 43
II.8 1268b4–22: 170–71
II.8 1268b31–69a12: 158
II.8 1269a12–28: 158
II.8 1269a20–22: 158
II.9 1269b23–24: 242n8
II.9 1271a1–8: 162
II.9 1271a9–18: 129
II.9 1271a16–18: 119
II.10 1272a35–39: 162
II.10 1272b11–15: 31
II.11 1273a4–6: 233n17
II.11 1273b9–15: 170
II.11 1273b25–26: 177
II.12 1273b35–39: 177
II.12 1274a6–7: 178
II.12 1274a12–15: 67
III.1 1274b38: 197
III.1 1275b18–19: 123
III.1 1275b20–21: 123
III.3 1276b1–4: 197
III.4 1276b27–29: 122
III.4 1276b28–29: 110
III.4 1277a5: 122
III.4 1277a5–12: 89
III.4 1277a14–16: 124
III.4 1277a20–25: 123
III.4 1277b7–9: 89, 122
III.4 1277b7–16: 62
III.4 1277b13–16: 126
III.4 1277b25–26: 62
III.4 1277b25–30: 124
III.4 1277b29–30: 186
III.5 1278a8–21: 196
III.5 1278a21–25: 213
III.5 1278a24–25: 45
III.5 1278b3–5: 243n17
III.6 1278b8–10: 35, 168
III.6 1278b8–11: 226n13

Aristotle: *Politics* (continued)
   III.6 1278b11: 35
   III.7 1279a25–7: 226n13
   III.7 1279a37–38: 78
   III.7 1279a37–39: 74
   III.7 1279b1–2: 78
   III.7 1279b2: 78
   III.7 1279b3: 78
   III.7 1279b4: 78
   III.8 1279b34–80a6: 36
   III.8 1280a1–6: 37–38
   III.9 1280a7–25: 46
   III.9 1280a13–14: 227n22
   III.9 1280a14–16: 228n24
   III.9 1280a15–16: 46
   III.9 1280a20–21: 228n24
   III.9 1280a23: 46
   III.9 1280a24: 46
   III.9 1280a34–b12: 200
   III.9 1280b6–12: 247n7
   III.9 1280b34–35: 114
   III.9 1280b40–81a1: 122
   III.9 1281a2–8: 108, 139
   III.9 1281a9: 33
   III.10 1281a25–28: 231n5
   III.10 1281a31: 125
   III.10 1281a31–32: 118
   III.11 1281a40–1: 131
   III.11 1281a41: 131
   III.11 1281a42: 55, 131
   III.11 1281b4–5: 99
   III.11 1281b12–13: 100
   III.11 1281b15–21: 132, 163, 190
   III.11 1281b25–30: 131
   III.11 1281b31: 125
   III.11 1281b31–38: 186
   III.11 1281b36–37: 190
   III.11 1282a12–14: 106
   III.11 1282a25–26: 162
   III.11 1282a26–27: 125
   III.11 1282a34–37: 169
   III.11 1282a38: 125
   III.12 1282b27–30: 54
   III.12 1283a9–14: 54
   III.12 1283a14–17: 54
   III.12 1283a17–18: 55
   III.12 1283a17–19: 242n12
   III.13 1283a26–29: 46
   III.13 1283a40–42: 67
   III.13 1283b1–3: 57
   III.13 1283b3: 57
   III.13 1284a13–14: 157
   III.13 1284b3–17: 194
   III.13 1284b20–22: 245n42
   III.13 1284b22: 222n23
   III.15 1286a31–32: 63
   III.15 1286b1–3: 245n42
   III.15 1286b8–22: 54, 65, 82
   III.15 1286b11–13: 63
   III.15 1286b27: 64
   III.15 1286b31–33: 63
   III.15 1286b35–37: 64
   III.16 1287a8–18: 243n18
   III.16 1287a23–25: 96
   III.16 1287a23–4: 239n18
   III.16 1287a25–7: 239n18
   III.16 1287a30: 63
   III.16 1287a30–2: 239n17
   III.16 1287b8–9: 63, 168
   III.16 1287b8–15: 101
   III.16 1287b8–35: 171
   III.16 1287b14–15: 131
   III.16 1287b26–30: 101
   III.17 1288a19–24: 37
   III.18 1288a36–39: 243n17
   IV.1 1288b22–24: 114
   IV.1 1289a5–13: 186
   IV.1 1289a6–10: 70
   IV.1 1289a11–13: 159
   IV.1 1289a13–15: 157
   IV.1 1289a15–16: 35, 168
   IV.1 1289a18–20: 159
   IV.2 1289b5–11: 51
   IV.3 1289b28–31: 17

IV.3 1290a7–13: 248n14
IV.4 1290a30–32: 141
IV.4 1290a30–33: 238n11
IV.4 1290a31–32: 141, 238n11
IV.4 1290b7–14: 39
IV.4 1290b8: 40
IV.4 1290b14–15: 39
IV.4 1290b17–20: 39
IV.4 1290b23–1291a10: 123
IV.4 1290b23–24: 122
IV.4 1290b38–39: 192
IV.4 1290b38–91b2: 34
IV.4 1290b39–91b2: 166
IV.4 1291a22–28: 123
IV.4 1291a24–28: 166
IV.4 1291a27: 105
IV.4 1291a27–28: 172
IV.4 1291a33–34: 55, 242n12
IV.4 1291b2–6: 172
IV.4 1291b7: 38
IV.4 1291b30–92a4: 51
IV.4 1291b32: 43
IV.4 1292a4–30: 50
IV.4 1292a6–7: 175
IV.4 1292a11: 53
IV.4 1292a11–18: 174
IV.4 1292a17–18: 53
IV.4 1292a19: 53
IV.4 1292a25–30: 175
IV.4 1292a31: 51
IV.4 1292a32: 156
IV.4 1292a32–34: 106, 158
IV.5 1292b4–7: 51
IV.5 1292b4–10: 174
IV.5 1292b10: 51
IV.6 1293a7–8: 68
IV.6 1293a16–17: 155
IV.6 1293a18–19: 68
IV.6 1293a26: 174
IV.6 1293a28: 174
IV.6 1293a33: 69
IV.7 1293a40–41: 179

IV.8 1293b29: 59
IV.8 1293b33–34: 74, 77
IV.8 1294a3–4: 155
IV.8 1294a11–14: 141, 238n11
IV.8 1294a20–22: 229n36
IV.8 1294a22–24: 75
IV.9 1294a36–b2: 75
IV.9 1294b2–6: 76
IV.9 1294b6–13: 76
IV.9 1294b10–11: 233n17
IV.9 1294b12: 233n17
IV.9 1294b13: 233n17
IV.9 1294b13–16: 75
IV.9 1294b14–17: 77
IV.9 1294b19–32: 249n21
IV.10 1295a14–17: 156
IV.10 1295a19–23: 160
IV.11 1295a31–34: 74, 82
IV.11 1295a35–b1: 83
IV.11 1295a40–b1: 35
IV.11 1295b1–3: 176
IV.11 1295b3: 78
IV.11 1295b5–9: 78
IV.11 1295b5–11: 252n6
IV.11 1295b10: 44
IV.11 1295b11: 44
IV.11 1295b12: 79
IV.11 1295b16–18: 44
IV.11 1295b19–23: 79
IV.11 1295b21–23: 251n4
IV.11 1295b21–24: xv
IV.11 1295b21–25: 44–45
IV.11 1295b22–23: 44
IV.11 1295b37–38: 79
IV.11 1295b38–39: 80
IV.11 1296a7: 30
IV.11 1296a7–9: 17
IV.11 1296a8–9: 79
IV.11 1296a8–21: 81
IV.11 1296a22–32: 17
IV.11 1296a26: 41
IV.11 1296a29–31: 41

Aristotle: *Politics* (continued)
    IV.11 1296a36–38: 41, 179
    IV.12 1296b13: 157
    IV.12 1296b14–16: 81
    IV.12 1296b17–18: 82
    IV.12 1296b34–38: 81
    IV.12 1296b38–97a7: 42
    IV.12 1296b40–a3: 79
    IV.12 1297a2: 17
    IV.12 1297a6–7: 78
    IV.12 1297a11–13: 231n9
    IV.13 1297a35–38: 69
    IV.13 1297a38–b1: 75
    IV.13 1297b6–8: 252n6
    IV.14 1297b37–98a3: 166–67
    IV.14 1298a3–7: 158–59, 172
    IV.14 1298a24–28: 127
    IV.14 1298a29–33: 174
    IV.14 1298a37–38: 155
    IV.14 1298a39–40: 76
    IV.14 1298b5–11: 76
    IV.14 1298b11–26: 75
    IV.14 1298b26–30: 175
    IV.14 1298b26–32: 76
    IV.14 1298b32–99a1: 76
    IV.14 1298b38–99a1: 251n25
    IV.15 1299a14–24: 168
    IV.15 1299a25–28: 168
    IV.15 1299a38–b1: 170
    IV.15 1299b1–10: 172
    IV.15 1299b30–38: 76
    IV.15 1299b38–1300a1: 175
    IV.15 1300a31–34: 188
    IV.15 1300a34–38: 76
    IV.15 1300b4–5: 188
    IV.16 1300b19–20: 175
    IV.16 1300b20–21: 176
    IV.16 1300b34–35: 171
    IV.16 1300b35–38: 16
    IV.16 1301a13–15: 76
    V.1 1301a28–33: 46
    V.1 1301a37–39: 17, 33
    V.1 1301a38–40: 30, 23, 57
    V.1 1301b6–10: 6
    V.1 1301b10–26: 6
    V.1 1301b26–29: 7, 43
    V.1 1301b35–02a2: 37
    V.1 1301b40–02a1: 73
    V.1 1302a1–2: 74
    V.1 1302a8–9: 17
    V.1 1302a8–15: 228n25
    V.2 1302a18: 218n5
    V.2 1302a20–22: 7
    V.2 1302a22: 10
    V.2 1302a22–29: 8, 218n7
    V.2 1302a23: 218n5
    V.2 1302a26–28: 251–52n5
    V.2 1302a28–9: 23
    V.2 1302a31–33: 227n18
    V.2 1302a31–34: 9, 219n8
    V.2 1302a34–37: 10
    V.2 1302a37: 221n13
    V.2 1302a37–38: 12
    V.3 1302b5–14: 12
    V.3 1302b21–24: 68
    V.3 1302b25–27: 67
    V.3 1302b25–33: 251n4
    V.3 1302b28–29: 67
    V.3 1303a1: 6
    V.3 1303a14: 6
    V.3 1303a16: 6
    V.3 1303a25–26: 220n13
    V.3 1303b1–2: 222n21
    V.3 1303b15: 23
    V.4 1303b17–04a17: 13, 219n10
    V.4 1303b17–19: 12, 220n10
    V.4 1303b19–20: 14
    V.4 1303b27–28: 14
    V.4 1303b31–32: 14
    V.4 1304a4–5: 14
    V.4 1304a36–38: 252n5
    V.4 1304a38–b2: 79
    V.4 1304b4–5: 224n38
    V.4 1304b8: 6

Index Locorum 273

V.5 1305a32–34: 231n8
V.6 1306a31–b1: 219n10
V.6 1306a31–b2: 16
V.7 1307a5–7: 232n10
V.7 1307a7–9: 77
V.7 1307a17–20: 252n6
V.7 1307b6–13: 251n4
V.8 1307b31–33: 155
V.8 1308a31–35: 186
V.8 1308b31–33: 227n17
V.8 1308b31–34: 232n9
V.8 1309a22–25: 252n6
V.9 1309b16: 81
V.9 1309b16–18: 162
V.9 1309b22: 51
V.9 1309b38–10a2: 225n5
V.9 1310a4–6: 70
V.9 1310a6–8: 70
V.9 1310a9–10: 41
V.9 1310a12–17: 157
V.9 1310a12–18: 45
V.9 1310a21–22: 51
V.9 1310a33: 49
V.10 1310b14–16: 60
V.10 1311a9–11: 49
V.10 1311a13–14: 41
V.10 1311a15–18: 41
V.10 1311a25–28: 251n4
V.10 1311a33–b6: 252n6
V.10 1311b40–12a20: 251n4
V.10 1312a21–25: 233n18
V.10 1312b29–32: 252n6
V.10 1312b34–37: 69
V.10 1313a5–10: 64
V.10 1313a10–14: 64
V.11 1313a22–23: 66
V.11 1313b32–39: 53
V.11 1314b23–27: 252n6
V.11 1315a3–40: 65
V.11 1315a14–16: 252n6
V.11 1315a41–b2: 66
V.11 1315b4–7: 65

V.11 1315b8–10: 157
V.12 1315b11–12: 60, 82
V.12 1316a39: 218n7
V.12 1316a39–b3: 22, 38
VI.1 1316b31–34: 167
VI.1 1317a4–10: 169
VI.2 1317b16–17: 49
VI.2 1317b28–35: 175
VI.2 1317b35–38: 167
VI.2 1317b38–41: 176
VI.3 1318a14–17: 76
VI.3 1318a27–29: 232n12
VI.3 1318a32–b1: 75
VI.3 1318b1–5: 161, 227n17
VI.4 1318b14–22: 125
VI.4 1318b21–22: 162
VI.4 1318b27–19a4: 125, 161–62
VI.4 1318b27–33: 71
VI.4 1318b40–19a1: 109
VI.4 1319a14: 159
VI.4 1319b25–27: 75
VI.5 1319b33–20a4: 51
VI.5 1319b37–20a2: 159
VI.5 1320a2–4: 51
VI.5 1320a4–11: 231n5
VI.5 1320a6–9: 159
VI.5 1320b11–16: 76
VI.6 1320b19–20: 69
VI.6 1320b22–29: 72
VI.6 1320b30–21a1: 234n23
VI.7 1321a5–11: 82
VI.7 1321a13–14: 67
VI.7 1321a26–31: 76
VI.7 1321a31–42: 231n5
VI.7 1321a35–39: 70
VI.7 1321a41–b1: 68
VI.8 1321b4–12: 168
VI.8 1321b10–12: 168
VI.8 1321b12–16: 127
VI.8 1321b39: 127
VI.8 1322a5–8: 105
VI.8 1322a10–19: 168–69

Aristotle: *Politics* (continued)
  VI.8 1322a30: 126
  VI.8 1322a31–32: 106
  VI.8 1322a31–33: 126
  VI.8 1322a33–b1: 127
  VI.8 1322b12–15: 173, 248n18
  VI.8 1322b29–30: 105
  VI.8 1322b29–37: 169
  VI.8 1322b34: 105
  VI.8 1322b37–39: 175
  VII.2 1324a29–31: 120
  VII.3 1325b10–14: 173
  VII.4 1326b11–20: 129
  VII.4 1326b14–19: 127
  VII.5 1326b31–32: 243n13, 227n21
  VII.6 1327a40–b15: 55
  VII.7 1327b29–38: 243n14
  VII.7 1328a9–10: 227n21, 242n11
  VII.8 1328b5–6: 227n21
  VII.8 1328b5–11: 242n13
  VII.8 1328b7–10: 243n23
  VII.8 1328b9: 105
  VII.8 1328b10–11: 55, 238n12, 242n12
  VII.8 1328b13–15: 167
  VII.8 1328b20–27: 167
  VII.9 1328b39–40: 238n13
  VII.9 1329a2–17: 227n21
  VII.9 1329a8–9: 123
  VII.9 1329a17–19: 55, 242n12
  VII.9 1329a17–26: 227n21, 238n12, 242n13
  VII.9 1329a27–34: 194
  VII.10 1329b39–30a9: 238n12, 242n13
  VII.10 1330a9–25: 242n13
  VII.10 1330a16–25: 109
  VII.10 1330a25–28: 123
  VII.12 1331a30–b4: 229n34
  VII.12 1331b1–4: 238n13
  VII.12 1331b9–12: 239n16
  VII.13 1332a15–16: 145
  VII.13 1332a32–b8: 95
  VII.13 1332a38–b11: 243n14
  VII.14 1332b35–36: 127
  VII.14 1332b39: 124
  VII.14 1333a35–36: 3
  VII.14 1333b32–33: 142
  VII.15 1334a25–28: 252n6
  VII.16 1335b5–7: 246n44
  VII.16 1335b9–10: 246n44
  VIII.1 1337a14–17: 35
  VIII.1 1337a21–32: 114
  VIII.1 1337a22–23: 227n21, 243n14
  VIII.1 1337a29–32: 243n14
  VIII.1 1337a31–32: 227n21
  VIII.3 1338b2–4: 227n21, 242n11
  VIII.4 1338b10–11: 246n44
  VIII.6 1341b8–12: 143–44

Prior Analytics
  II.23 68b27–29: 237n6

Rhetoric
  I.1 1354a1: 103
  I.1 1354a11–18: 102
  I.1 1354b4–6: 237n2
  I.1 1355a8: 97
  I.1 1355a29–30: 102
  I.1 1355a32: 102
  I.2 1356a2: 129
  I.2 1356b35–57a1: 103
  I.2 1357a2: 102
  I.2 1357b27–29: 237n6
  I.5 1360b22: 119, 246n44
  I.5 1360b28: 119
  I.5 1361a28: 120
  I.5 1361b21–6: 246n44
  I.6 1362b29–30: 136
  I.9 1366a28: 129
  I.11 1370b32–71a8: 145–46
  I.11 1371a8–10: 241n6
  II.2 1378b23–29: 252n6

II.12 1389a11–13: 118
II.23 1397b14–17: 98
II.25 1402a32–34: 102

Topics
I.2 101b4–5: 238n9
I.5 102a18–31: 37

Herodotus

Histories
V.71: 229n32

Plato

Gorgias
461b–465d: 237n8

Phaedo
66c–d: 223n27

Protagoras
329d–331e: 228n23

Republic
369b–372d: 71
373e: 21
415d–417b: 110
422e: 222n25
451c–57c: 229n33
461e–462e: 110
461e–465d: 20
462a–e: 88
469b–471: 21
500c: 20
501d: 20
520c–521a: 20
545c–d: 19
545c–575d: 18
547b: 21
550d–551a: 21
555b: 21
563d–e: 22
592b: 136

Statesman
294b–c: 155
294d–297e: 155
301d: 155

Polybius
Histories
III.6.6: 28
III.6.7: 28–29

Thucydides
History of the Peloponnesian War
I.23.5–6: 27–28
I.126: 229n32
III.69–85: 26
III.70: 27

General Index

action
   See decision
   See deliberation
   See wish
agonism, xiv, xviii, 182, 195–199, 201, 214
agora, 129, 142, 189, 213
Alcmaeonids, 25
aretē. See virtue
aristocracy, 8, 18, 21, 70, 74, 82, 128, 141, 169, 185, 188, 204
arrogance (including hubris), 11, 20, 44–45, 47, 53, 56–58, 60, 63–67, 69, 73, 77–78, 80, 83, 187, 193
assembly [*ekklēsia*], 17, 60, 71–72, 76, 80, 96, 98–99, 102–103, 106, 110–111, 125, 128–142, 168, 170, 174–175, 177, 179, 184, 186, 194
Athens, 23–28, 52, 54, 178
audit. *See* inspection

Balot, R., 220n11, 223n28, 226n11, 226–227n16, 228n24, 228n31, 233n20, 240n25, 243n15, 244n31
banausoi. See laborers
barbarians, 34
Barker, E., 232n13, 248n13, 248n17, 250n25

best constitution (city of prayers, ideal city), xi, xiii, xvi–xvii, 19, 30, 34, 45, 50, 55–57, 60, 87–88, 103, 105, 108–110, 113–114, 118, 121–122, 125–132, 138–143, 157, 170, 183–184, 187, 189, 191–192, 196–198, 213, 215
Bickford, S., 236n7
Bobonich, C., 244n30
Bohman, J., 252n8
Brunschwig, J., 247n8
Bull, B., 218n3
Burnyeat, M., 237n5–6

Carthage, 28, 177–179
classes (status groups, major parts of cities)
   See deliberation (deliberators)
   See democrats (the poor)
   See dynasties
   See farmers
   See judges (judiciary)
   See laborers (includes craftsmen and traders)
   See lawgiving (lawgivers)
   See middle (middling group)
   See oligarchs (the rich)
   See rulers (including officeholders)
   See virtue (virtuous people)
   See warriors (all military types)

citizenship, 88–89, 103, 107–111, 115, 122–130, 138–146, 157–159, 168, 170, 189, 191, 196
city. See *polis*
civil war (faction) [*stasis*], x, xiii, xv–xviii, 4–33, 41, 43, 55–58, 60, 87–88, 112–115, 117, 143, 149, 153–156, 161, 178, 181, 184–185, 187–188, 193, 195, 197, 199, 215–216
civil war, specific causes of
  See arrogance (including hubris)
  See contempt
  See disproportional growth
  See dissimilarity
  See fear
  See honor
  See justice
  See profit (and penalty)
  See superiority
Cleisthenes, 25
Coby, P., 218n4, 230n1, 232n15
commerce (exchange, trade), 103–105, 122–123, 144, 166, 206–207
common good (common benefit), x, xiv, 78, 94, 112, 121, 139–140, 142, 145, 174, 196, 200, 206–207, 211, 214
common meals. *See* public messes
communitarianism, xiv, 150
competition (contest, rivalry, jockeying), xi–xiii, xv–xvii, 15, 18, 20, 24–25, 31, 87–88, 117–146, 149, 179, 181–182, 184–185, 186, 188, 191, 194–200, 202–204, 206–207, 210–214, 216
concord (like-mindedness) [*homonoia*], 109, 112, 144, 194, 197, 211, 215
conflict in general (being at odds in any way), xiii, 5, 13, 30, 87–88, 149–151, 153–154, 182, 213, 216
conflict, specific types
  See civil war [*stasis*]
  See competition (contest, rivalry, jockeying)
  See disagreement (dispute, debate)
  See distrust of government
  See partisanship
consensus (unanimity), 102–116, 130, 144, 146, 186, 192–195, 197, 201, 211–212, 214–216
constitutions in general, 35, 83, 154, 162, 166–168, 196–197
constitutions, specific types
  See aristocracy
  See best constitution (city of prayers)
  See democracy
  See mixed constitution (balanced government)
  See monarchy (includes kingship and tyranny)
  See oligarchy
  See polity (middle constitution)
constitutionalism, xviii, 151, 154–160, 179, 181, 196, 213
  See also limited government
  See also mixed constitution (balanced government)
  See also rule of law
  See also separation of powers
contempt [*kataphronēsis*], 11, 27–28, 56, 57–58, 60, 62–64, 67–69, 72–73, 77, 80, 83, 187, 193
Cooper, J., 244n26
Corinth, 27
Corcyra, 26–28
council [*boulē*], 76, 130, 169, 174, 177
courts (includes trials, lawsuits), 15–16, 21, 27, 31, 50, 72, 76,

80, 105, 143, 170–171, 175–176, 178
See also judges (judiciary)
See also judicial function of government
See also juror
craftsmen. *See* laborers
Crete (Cretan), 162, 177–178

Dahl, R., 198–199, 254n22–26
Damasias, 25
Davis, M., 221n16, 224n39
decision (and decision-makers), 6, 9, 90, 93–94, 96, 111, 130–133, 137, 139, 140–141, 189–190, 195, 212
decrees, 51, 121, 156, 173, 175
deliberation (and deliberators)
  deliberation within a group, xvii, 44, 50, 75, 90–91, 93, 95–96, 100–103, 106, 109, 117, 123, 127–128, 130–143, 156, 158–159, 166–176, 186, 189–194, 211
  deliberation within an individual, 90, 96–100, 106, 117
deliberative democracy, xviii, 151, 182, 189–194
demagogues, 51, 72, 185, 204, 212–213
democracy (Aristotle's conception), xiv, xviii, 17–18, 21–22, 25–27, 34–43, 47–48, 50–51, 53, 56, 59, 66–77, 81–84, 87, 125, 128, 141, 151, 156, 158, 161–166, 173–178, 182, 185
democrats (the poor), xvi, 4, 8, 16–18, 20, 23–24, 31, 33–55, 58, 61, 65–80, 83, 155–156, 164–166, 176–178, 182, 185, 187–188, 211, 213

democratic theory (contemporary views), xv–xvi, xviii, 151, 181–214
  See agonism
  See deliberative democracy
  See direct democracy
  See plebiscitarianism (leadership democracy)
  See pluralism (interest pluralism)
  See representational democracy
  See self-government
Deslauriers, M., 251n1–2
despotism. *See* monarchy
direct democracy, 183–184, 186, 188
disagreement (dispute, debate), x–xiii, xvii, 13, 15–18, 24, 31, 34, 41–43, 45, 49, 52–55, 57, 87–117, 128–130, 133, 137–138, 144, 149, 166, 178, 181–182, 184, 188, 190–191, 193–197, 200, 202–204, 207, 211–212, 214, 216
disproportional growth, 11, 193
dissimilarity, 27–28
distrust of government, x, xiii, xvii–xviii, 4, 27, 57–87, 149, 154–156, 160–165, 176–179, 181, 184, 187, 193, 195–197, 215
dynasties, 51, 71, 73, 80, 174, 178, 185, 213

education (including upbringing, habituation), 11, 36, 44–45, 49, 54, 57, 73, 82, 99–100, 111, 115, 122, 128, 140–141, 143–144, 157, 170, 176, 181, 194, 197, 209, 211
egalitarianism, xiv, 126–128, 150
elections (including voting), 71, 76, 112, 125–130, 133, 162–164, 188, 193, 207, 212

Eliaeson, S., 255n31, 256n44
elitism, 52–55, 79, 117, 162, 196, 211–212
enthymemes, 97–98, 102
envy, 44–45, 48, 53, 78, 83
Ephialtes, 25
equality. *See* justice
equity (and the decent person) [*epieikeia*], 95, 162, 170
eudaimonia. *See* happiness
executive function of government, 164, 167–168, 173

farmers, 34, 36, 71–72, 83, 122, 139, 166
fear, 11, 27–28, 56–58, 60, 63–64, 66–69, 72, 77, 80, 155, 193
Federalists, 140
fine (beautiful, noble), 3, 61, 65, 70, 111, 136, 145–146, 149
Finley, M., 217n1, 221n17, 245n39, 245n42
force, 4, 6, 15, 25, 27–29, 31, 33, 57, 64, 81–82, 87, 179, 181, 200
Frank, J., xii–xiii, 226n14, 232n14, 235n5, 242n8, 245n35, 253n13
fraud (deceit), 4, 6, 15, 27, 29, 31, 33, 57, 60, 87
freedom, 37–40, 46, 48–55, 79–82, 109, 123, 125, 139, 150, 160, 186, 204
friendship, ix, xii–xiii, 12–13, 30, 43, 104, 107–108, 112, 117–118, 136, 138, 140, 144, 149, 194, 216
Fritz, K., 223n32, 230–231n3–4, 232n15, 234n23, 249n20, 249n22

Garsten, B., 252n12
Garver, E., xii, 226n12, 233n19, 240n22
greed, 43–44, 52, 55, 115, 140, 142

Green, J., 251n3, 255n27–28, 31, 256n45, n50–51
Gouldner, A., 241n1, 242n7
Gutmann, A., 190–91, 252n11

Habermas, J., 190, 240n22, 252n10
habits (habituation). *See* education
Halliwell, S., 244n32
Hampshire, S., 217n2
Hansen, M., 243n22, 248n12
happiness (flourishing) [*eudaimonia*], xvii, 11, 30, 48–58, 83, 89, 96, 112, 119, 121, 136, 181, 196, 212, 215
Hatzistavrou, A., 218n4, 218–219n7, 219–220n10, 220n12, 221n14
Held, D., 217n1, 252n9, n11, 255n31
Hobbes, ix, 115, 153–154
homonoia. *See* concord
honor, 9–13, 20, 29, 49, 56–57, 62, 65, 68, 71–72, 77, 79–80, 91, 118–122, 125–130, 136, 138–139, 141–143, 145, 156, 162, 177, 181, 184–185, 188, 193–194, 200, 211, 213, 216
Horn, C., 224n38
households (including estates), 34, 71, 88–89, 103–105, 108–109, 112, 115, 122, 141, 213
Hume, D., 215

inspection (audit) [*euthuna*], 106, 125, 161–164, 188, 212
Irwin, T., 217n4, 235n5, 237n3, 238n14, 240n20, n24

judges (the judiciary), 34, 76–77, 89, 105, 123, 166, 169–173, 175
judicial function of government, 158–159, 164, 167, 169–171
juror (and jury), 41, 71–72, 76, 166, 168–171

justice (including equality), xii–xiv, xvi, 7–13, 15–17, 20, 22–23, 29, 33, 37–40, 43, 45–53, 55–56, 58, 60, 62–64, 67, 74, 77, 87, 89, 105, 108, 112, 118–119, 122–130, 136, 138–139, 141, 149–150, 170, 178, 181, 184, 189, 193, 215

Kalimtzis, K., xiii, 218n4, 219n8, 221n17, 223n28, 242n8, 243n15
Kant, I., 140
Keegan, J., 218n3
Keyt, D., 218n4, 226n8
kingship. *See* monarchy
Kraut, R., vii, xiv, 222n24, 224n2, 228n28–29, 229n31, 232n12, n14, 233n16, 234n21, 236n7, 239n17, 240n23, n25, 243n19–n21, 245n41, 246n49n, 247n6, 250n25

laborers (including craftsmen and traders) [*banausoi*], 34, 36, 45, 71, 122–123, 166, 196, 213
Lane, M., 253n14
Lassman, P., 255n31
law (enacted, customary, and natural), 19, 24, 50–51, 56, 63, 66, 69, 95–96, 98, 150, 155–159, 162–164, 170–171, 173, 175, 179, 191, 206
See also rule of law
lawgiving (lawgivers, legislative science), 95–96, 158–159, 171
lawsuits. *See* courts
Lear, J., 235n4
legislative function of government, 158, 164, 167, 173
leisure, 3, 49, 69, 142, 189
liberalism, xiv, 150

limited government, xviii, 154, 160–163, 181
Lintott, A., 222n24
liturgy (public service, public outlay) [*leitourgia*], xvii, 15, 34, 121–122, 139
Locke, J., 154, 165, 231n7
Lockwood, T., 233n20
Loraux, N., 221n17–18
Lycurgus, 25
Lysander, 26

Macedo, S., 252n9
Machiavelli, N., ix, 153, 176, 178, 249n20, 250n23
MacIntyre, A., 217n3
magnanimity (greatness of soul), 58, 103, 119–121, 128–129, 140, 143
Mandeville, B., 140
masters. *See* slavery
Mayhew, R., xi, 234n1, 235n3, 246n45, 251n1
McIlwain, C., 247n6, 247n8
mean, 50, 52, 75, 83
Megacles, 25
middle constitution. *See* polity
middle (middling group) [*hoi mesoi*], 17, 41–42, 44, 77–81, 156, 163, 177–179, 188, 193
military (*See* warriors)
Miller, F., xiv, 226n10, n13, 227n20, 228n28, 239n16, 243n16, n24, 245n42, 247n9, 248n16, 249n19, 251n25
mixed constitution (balanced government), xviii, 41–42, 59, 73–81, 154–156, 164–165, 175–179, 187, 193, 213–214
monarchy (includes kingship and tyranny), 8, 11, 19, 41, 43, 46–48, 52, 54, 59–67, 81–83, 87,

monarchy *(continued)*
  96, 101, 156, 160, 162–163, 171, 173–174, 177, 193
Morrison, D., 236n1
Morton, A., 230n37
Mouffe, C., 253n15
Mulgan, R., xiv, 217n2, 218n6, 221n13, 222n21, 223n26, 224n1, 225n3, n6, 226n9, n14, 228n26, n28, n31, 248n16
multitude. *See* democrats (the poor)

Nagle, D., 245n38
nature (and natural conditions), xii–xiii, 89, 97, 111, 114–115, 122–123, 125, 127, 138–139, 149, 153–154, 159, 163, 179, 185, 196–197
Nichols, M., 244n31
Nietzsche, F., 140, 245n36
noble. *See* fine
Nussbaum, M., 235n6, 236n7, 240n21, n22

Ober, J., vii, 225n4, n5, 226n11, 227n20, 241n2, n3, 244n27, 245n37
offices, xvii, 24–25, 35, 40, 42, 49–50, 58, 64, 71–72, 75–77, 80, 91, 106, 112, 122–131, 140, 143, 145, 162, 167–177, 185, 188, 195, 197–198, 208–209
  See also assembly
  See also council
  See also executive function of government
  See also rulers (officeholders)
oligarchs (the rich), xvi, 4, 8, 11, 16–18, 20, 23–24, 27, 31, 33–56, 58, 61, 65–73, 74–80, 83, 123, 155–156, 164–166, 176–178, 185, 187–188, 193, 206, 210–211, 212–213

oligarchy (Aristotle's conception of), 17–19, 21–22, 25–26, 34–42, 47–48, 51, 56, 59, 66–74, 76–77, 81–83, 87, 128, 141, 156, 165, 166, 169, 173–176, 178, 185, 204, 213
ostracism, 143, 194

particularism, 90
partisanship, x, xiii, xv–xvii, 4, 16–18, 20, 24, 33–56, 58, 66–81, 87, 117, 149, 154, 160, 181, 197, 199, 213, 215
Peisistratus, 25
Peithias, 27
Pericles, 212, 246n46, 256n52
Pettit, P., 248n12
philotimia, 118–121, 129–130, 139, 227n16, 242n10, 244n25
Plato, x–xi, 5, 13, 18–23, 30, 43, 52, 70–71, 88, 109–110, 155, 166
plebiscitarianism (leadership democracy), xiv, xviii, 151, 182, 195, 201–214
pluralism (interest pluralism), xviii, 40–43, 52, 182, 195, 197–201, 206, 211, 214
Polansky, R., 218n4, 221n14
Poliakoff, M., 222n22
polis (city, city-state), ix, 31, 83, 88–89, 104, 107–110, 113, 115, 122–126, 141–143, 155, 163, 166–167, 169–170, 185, 197, 200, 213, 216
political community, 34, 46–47, 62, 122, 126, 186, 192–200, 206, 209, 212–213
polity (middle constitution), 17, 30, 33, 41–42, 44, 74–84, 178–179, 185, 188
Polybius, 28–29, 176, 178
practical wisdom (prudence) [*phonēsis*], 30, 57, 62, 89–116, 120–121,

123, 128, 130, 132–134, 137–140, 142, 159, 171, 186, 204, 212
profit (and penalty), 9–13, 15, 22, 27, 29, 56–57, 60, 105, 156, 193
property. *See* wealth
public messes (common meals), 189
public service. *See* liturgy

Rawls, J., 190, 240n22
Reeve, C.D.C., 217n4, 223n25, 225n7, 233n17, 234n22, 235n4, 240n24
regimes. *See* constitutions
religion, 177, 194
representational democracy, 182–188, 191–192
republicanism, xiv, 150
rhetoric, 102–103, 132, 137, 202, 204–205, 210–212
Robinson, R., 229n33
Rome, 28
Rosler, A., 230n37, 236n7, 238n10, 240n25, 245–246n43
rule of law, xviii, 66, 154–160, 162–163, 181
rulers (including officeholders), 34, 61–62, 89, 112, 123–124, 159, 166, 170–171, 185–188, 193, 197, 203–205, 208, 214
  relation of rulers to ruled, 61–62, 89, 117, 122–125, 155, 161–164, 184–188, 191–194, 197–200, 205–208, 211–212
  rotational rule (by turn), 83, 125–128
  See also offices

Salkever, S., 235n5, 242n8
Saxonhouse, A., 219n9
Schroeder, D., 247n8
Schumpeter, J., 255n28, 255n39, 256n45
Schütrumpf, E., 230n37

self-government, xviii, 151, 182–189, 191
self-sufficiency, 79, 123
separation of powers, xviii, 154, 164–176, 213
Simpson, P., vii, xiv, 221n15, 222n21, 223n29, 228n29, 231n6, 232n11, n12, 234n24, 247n5, 248n16, n18
slavery (and masters), 20–21, 34, 46, 48, 55, 79–80, 89, 122–123, 139, 192, 196
social contract, 115, 215–216
Solon, 24–25, 99, 177–178
soul, 123, 166–167, 174, 176, 185, 192–193, 210, 212
Sparta, 27–28, 50, 136, 162, 177–179
stasis. *See* civil-war
Strauss, B., 224n1, 229n31, n35
superiority, 11, 28, 53, 56–57, 62, 64, 67, 69, 73, 77, 80, 83, 187, 193

teleology, xii–xiii, 21, 49–50, 53
Theramenes, 25
Thompson, D., 190–191, 252n11
Thucydides, 26–29
tryanny (despotism). *See* monarchy
Tully, J., 253n15, n16, 253–254n18

vice (and vicious people), 4, 8, 19, 22–23, 44, 59, 61, 87, 103, 105, 109, 139, 143, 181, 200, 211
Vile, M.J.C., 247n10, 247–248n11, 248n13, n15, n17, 249n20, 250n24
virtue (and virtuous people) [*aretē*], 4, 8, 11, 19, 23, 30, 50, 52, 56–57, 59–62, 75, 77–81, 83, 87–91, 94, 96, 99, 101, 105–133, 136–140, 142–146, 149, 157–158, 163–164, 181, 184–185, 188, 190–191, 194–195, 200–201, 211–212, 216

Waldron, J., 244n28, n31, n33, 245n35, 252n7
war, 3, 13, 21, 25–29, 50, 115, 153–154, 179
Wardy, R., 238n9
warriors (all military types), 34, 45, 55, 61, 65, 67, 71, 78, 123, 127, 166
wealth (property, money), xi, 36–41, 45–53, 55, 65, 67–73, 75–77, 79–80, 82–83, 118, 121, 136, 139, 176–178, 204, 212
Weber, M., 151, 201–214
Weed, R., xiii, 218n4, 219n8, 220n11, 221n17, 223n28

Wheeler, M., 217n2, 218n5, 219n8, 221n13
White, N., xi, 235n6, 239n19, 240n20
Whitehead, D., 241n4, 242n9, n10
wisdom of the multitude, 100, 106, 125, 130–132, 189
wish, 6–7, 9, 30, 96, 111–112
Wolin, S., 253n17, 254n20, n21
women, 34, 89, 122, 192, 196

Yack, B., xii, 218n6, 222n19, 226n11, n12, 227n19, 228n24, 236n7, 245n35, 246n45, 250n25, 254n19

www.ingramcontent.com/pod-product-compliance
Lightning Source LLC
Chambersburg PA
CBHW030130240426
43672CB00005B/84